PHOENIX

SHIMON PERES AND THE SECRET HISTORY OF ISRAEL

The Phoenix is a mythological bird, born in the desert. The ancient Egyptians and Greeks considered the Phoenix as a symbol of excellence and longevity. At the end of its long life the Phoenix is burnt to death, then reborn out of its ashes and lives again.

In the Jewish tradition its existence is hinted in the book of Job (29:18) "I shall die with my nest, and I shall multiply my days as the Phoenix." And the greatest Bible scholar of the antiquity, Rashi, explains: "A bird named Phoenix, and death does not affect it... and after a thousand years is renewed and returns to its youth."

In the Talmud and the Jewish tradition the Phoenix is a symbol of the one who refuses to despair, doesn't lose hope, and has the capacity to withstand all the vicissitudes.

In the Middle ages, Dante wrote about the Phoenix:

Even thus by the great sages `tis confessed
The Phoenix dies and then is born again,
When it approaches its five hundredth year.
(Dante, Inferno, Canto XXIV)

ALSO BY MICHAEL BAR-ZOHAR

NONFICTION

Suez, Top Secret (French and Hebrew)
Ben-Gurion, the Armed Prophet
The Hunt for German Scientists
The Avengers
The Paratroopers' Book (Hebrew' with Eitan Haber)
Spies in the Promised Land: Isser Harel and the Israeli Secret
Service
Arrows of the Almighty: The Jewish Spy of Hitler
Ben-Gurion: A Biography (3 volumes, Hebrew)
Ben-Gurion: A Biography
The Quest for the Red Prince (With Eitan Haber)
Facing a Cruel Mirror: Israel's Moment of Truth
Lionhearts: Heroes of Israel (editor)
Bitter Scent: The Case of L'Oréal, Nazis, and the Arab Boycott
The Book of Valor (editor, Hebrew)
Beyond Hitler's Grasp: The Heroic Rescue of Bulgaria's Jews
To Be a Free People: The Saga of Israel (editor)
Yaacov Herzog: A Biography
Mossad: The Greatest Missions of the Israeli Secret Service
(with Nissim Mishal)
No Mission is impossible; The Death-Defying Missions of the
Israeli Special Forces (with Nissim Mishal)

FICTION

The Third Truth
The Man who Died Twice
The Secret List
Enigma
The Deadly Document

Phoenix

Shimon Peres and the Secret History of Israel

Michael Bar-Zohar

FOR INES—WHO NEVER GAVE UP

CONTENTS

AUTHOR'S NOTE

I MET SHIMON PERES when I was twenty-three. I was working on my Ph.D. thesis on "The Relations Between France and Israel" at the Fondation Nationale des Sciences Politiques in Paris. Peres was deputy defense minister. I went to his Tel Aviv office and he put at my disposal several documents. My thesis was later published as a book, *Suez Top Secret;* it was followed by Ben-Gurion's biography and other books. In some of my books, I praised Peres's vision and achievement; in others I criticized his political methods.

We took part in Israel's political life and were both active in the Mapai, Rafi, and Labor parties; I served beside him in the Knesset and in other political forums. At times we acted in harmony; at times we confronted each other on major issues. In 1977 I headed his campaign staff for the Labor primaries, but in 1981 I resigned from the chairmanship of Labor's electoral campaign, because I disagreed with his strategy. I supported Peres's quest for peace, yet I opposed his policy in 1986 and 1990; in 1992 I supported Yitzhak Rabin when he ran against Peres in the Labor Party primaries. My decision, as did that of other close friends, deeply hurt Shimon Peres.

Nevertheless, in spite of all the disputes and the clashes, our close ties remained solid, in good times and in bad times.

The issue of writing Peres's biography emerged in one of our conversations in 2001. He reminded me that he was of the same age as Ben-Gurion when I started writing his biography—seventy-eight. "I hope that Ben-Gurion's biographer would be my biographer as well," he said.

The subject fascinated me. There was no other person in Israel who had done so much, in so many fields and by such original methods, to strengthen her security, to bring her peace, and to improve her world stature. There was no other statesman in Israel who was so controversial, basking in boundless admiration on the one hand and stirring criticism on the other. Peres was an utterly intriguing figure, unique in Israel's political life. But his achievements, his personality, and his stubborn quest for peace carried him far beyond Israel's borders; he is considered today the last of the world's great statesmen of his generation.

"I'll write your biography on two conditions," I said to Peres. "One—I expect your full assistance and cooperation. Two—you will not see the manuscript before its publication."

"It goes without saying," he said.

Assisted by a gifted team, I spent about five years researching and writing this biography. I completed its updated version after Peres's death. During my work, I often recalled what Peres had said when I published my biography of Ben-Gurion: "At every page Michael Bar-Zohar is torn between the desire to describe Ben-Gurion as a man with problems and flaws, mistakes and sins—and the truth about a unique man, a man who has made our lives unique."

I hope that the same desire and the same truth have once again been my companions.

PROLOGUE

November 4, 1995

ON NOVEMBER 4, 1995, shortly after 11 P.M., a group of about ten people walked along the underground hallways of Ichilov Hospital in Tel Aviv. At the head of the silent group walked the hospital director, Professor Gabriel Barabash, and in his footsteps followed Leah Rabin; Health Minister Efraim Sneh; the director of the prime minister's office, Shimon Sheves; two relatives of the Rabin family; the author of this book and Foreign Minister Shimon Peres.

Nobody spoke. The hallway was deserted. The walls, painted in blue and green stripes, returned a hollow, metallic echo of the small group's footsteps. The hallway led to a large room bathed in dim light. Its walls were lined with green porcelain tiles. Behind a green screen stood a single bed, covered with a crumpled sheet, green as well. Professor Barabash lifted the edge of the sheet, revealing the lifeless face of Yitzhak Rabin.

A painful gasp escaped from the small group, as if only now did they learn the terrible truth. For a moment they faced the corpse, paralyzed by shock. Leah Rabin finally lurched forward and threw herself upon her dead husband, covering his still face with kisses. *"Abbaleh! Abbaleh!"*—"Daddy! Daddy!"—she shouted over and over, her voice breaking in sobs. Shimon Sheves and Efraim Sneh cried bitterly and hugged each other. Shimon Peres, grim and drawn, bent over the body and kissed Rabin's forehead. One after another, the rest followed suit.[1]

The small group returned to a narrow waiting room, crowded with government ministers and members of the Knesset, the Israeli parliament. Word of Rabin's death spread throughout the hospital. A bewildered nurse brought to one of the dignitaries a transparent plastic bag containing a copy of the "Song of Peace," which she had found in Rabin's pocket. The typed stanzas, speaking of peace and love and friendship, were stained with blood.

Peres stood alone, tense and pale. A short while before, he had sent Rabin's chief of staff, Eitan Haber, out to the reporters waiting on Weizman Street. Haber read a short statement, bitter and angry: "The Government of Israel announces in shock, in pain, and in deep grief the death of Yitzhak Rabin, who was murdered by an assassin this evening in Tel Aviv. Blessed be his memory." The crowd gathered at the hospital's entrance reacted with shouts of rage and despair.

Inside, one of the ministers approached Peres. "We must prepare immediately Rabin's funeral," he said urgently. "We must bury him tomorrow. It is forbidden to delay the dead." According to Jewish tradition, a deceased person should be buried with the shortest possible delay.

Peres's face was sealed. "Find the chief rabbi," he said quietly. Within minutes, Rabbi Israel Lau was at his side. Peres spoke with Lau briefly. Family members and VIP guests would be arriving from overseas, Peres said. Would it be possible to delay the funeral? Rabbi Lau answered that because of the extraordinary circumstances, a delay would be tolerated.

A few cabinet ministers stood next to Peres in silence. One of them gathered his courage. "What do we do now, Shimon? A meeting?"

"We must convene the cabinet," Peres said. He turned to one of his aides and instructed him to call an immediate cabinet meeting at the Kirya, the government complex. The president, Ezer Weizman, approached him.

"Shimon, I want to participate in the meeting," he said.

Peres didn't answer. "Get me Libai," he requested. He took

aside the justice minister, David Libai, and asked him if it was customary for the president to participate in cabinet meetings. Libai answered that such a thing had occurred only once before, during the term of Israel's first president. Peres went back to Ezer Weizman. "Ezer, take your car and go home. If we need you, we'll call you." The president left, insult painted all over his face.

And thus, minute by minute, people approached Peres with questions, suggestions, and remarks. Erect and tense, he gave short answers and concise instructions.[2] For a moment, he conferred with Giora Eini, a thin young man with long unkempt hair, who had served as a secret mediator between Peres and Rabin during their stinging confrontations.

What was he thinking at that moment? One of his rivals, watching him from across the hall, bitterly whispered to his neighbor, "He dreamed of this moment. Now he'll be prime minister again."

But that was not what Peres was dreaming about. Flashes of the momentous event that had taken place only a few hours before raced through his mind. It was a peace rally that was supposed to turn into an unforgettable memory, full of hope. He recalled the view of the vast expanse of Kings of Israel Square, one of the largest in Tel Aviv, the scores of thousands of enthusiastic supporters of the peace process, the hundreds of placards, the blue shirts of the youth organizations, the slogans, the songs, the excited youngsters jumping into the pool facing the podium.[3] He had been so proud of the rally's success. "I was in favor of the rally from the very beginning," he said later. "Others told Yitzhak that it would be hard to organize, and he was pessimistic. He was slipping in the polls; he thought the support for the peace process was dwindling. When he arrived at the square he was amazed. His eyes shone. He was beside himself. He hugged me. That was the happiest day in Rabin's life. We became friends that day. He suddenly showed me true comradeship. I had never before heard him sing—suddenly he broke into song. I had never before seen him hug someone—suddenly he hugged me. For me, it was the day when we became closer than ever."[4]

The rally had been intended to strengthen Yitzhak Rabin and Shimon Peres in their struggle for peace with the Palestinians, in spite of the difficulties that had arisen. The huge number of participants and the upbeat atmosphere had surprised even the organizers. A succession of cabinet ministers, Knesset members, artists, and rock stars appeared on the elevated platform, made speeches, and sang songs for peace. The crowd roared with approval when Peres and Rabin, the eternal adversaries, embraced each other for a brief moment.

The rally ended on a note of euphoria. The original plan was for Peres and Rabin to arrive and depart from the platform together, but the General Security Service (the Shabak) warned them that there were reports about a possible terrorist attack; therefore they should come down separately. The early warnings referred to a possible action by Arab terrorists; nobody could even think of an assassination attempt by a Jew. Peres was the first to come down. His car was waiting. Rabin's car was parked in front of his, and Peres asked his driver, Menachem Damti, "Where is Yitzhak?"

"Here he comes." The driver pointed at the prime minister, who was descending the stairs.

"It turned out that the assassin, Yigal Amir, was standing beside me and thought that he could take both of us," Peres said later. As soon as he entered his car and the door was closed behind him, three shots rang out. Peres's bodyguards ordered the driver to rush at full speed to a Shabak base. On arrival, they learned that Yitzhak Rabin had been shot and taken to Ichilov Hospital. Peres insisted that they drive there right away.

"You cannot go there," his bodyguards said.

"If you don't take me, I'll get out of here and go on foot," he said.

Having no choice, they acquiesced.

At the hospital, Peres met Leah Rabin and a few others. Rabin, they said, was still in surgery. But then the hospital director, Professor Barabash, took them aside. "We lost him," he said.[5]

BARABASH'S WORDS WERE "like the stab of a sword" for Peres. He was overwhelmed by a terrible feeling of disaster. And yet, he said, "I knew that we couldn't leave the country like this. We had to regain control immediately because hysteria was spreading all over."

After midnight, the convoy of ministers' cars left the hospital en route to the government complex, and the cabinet meeting began. Peres asked for Rabin's chair to be draped in black. He didn't want to sit in that chair. David Libai moved that Shimon Peres be chosen to replace Rabin until the Knesset approved his cabinet by a confidence vote. Peres decided then and there that he would keep Rabin's staff and not replace anybody. "I wanted to prevent any further shocks. I saw the people crying, the tears, the candles. Hysteria was sweeping the nation." He added, "This murder affected me much more than I showed."[6]

Two days later, at the Mount Herzl National Cemetery in Jerusalem, the world bade farewell to Yitzhak Rabin.

"My older brother," Peres called him in a farewell speech to an audience of world leaders who had come to Israel. His words sounded sincere, coming from the bottom of his heart. Yet the nation knew that right up to that last day at Kings of Israel Square, there had been no warmth or friendship between Peres and Rabin. On the contrary, their relationship had been one of bitter rivalry, confrontations, disputes, and mutual resentment that for Rabin had turned to open hatred.[7] Friends of the two men had tried to play down the level of mutual hostility between them, but up until the last moment, the chasm between them hadn't been bridged. Nevertheless, there was one aspect of their relationship that had changed significantly over the years: they learned to work together, to depend on and complement each other. Together they decided to offer a hand to Yasser Arafat, together they initiated the Oslo process, together they won the

Nobel Peace Prize and also together they became the target for fiery criticism and threats of assassination from Israeli radicals.

Now Peres was left alone at the helm. For the second time in his life, he was prime minister. For the second time, he was defense minister. In the course of his life he had been a kibbutz farmer, a senior official, a Knesset member, a deputy defense minister, and the minister of transportation, communications, immigrant absorption, information, foreign affairs, and the treasury. He had had a longer political life than any other Israeli leader. His associates, comrades, and political opponents came and went, entered the arena and left it, retired and died—and he remained, preparing for the next battle, watching for the next opportunity on the horizon. Throughout his life he had been surrounded by sworn admirers, but also by bitter adversaries. Ironically, the death of his staunchest rival had bound the two of them together. Rabin's death had left Peres completely alone, without a partner, without a wise companion with whom he could share his plans and his doubts. It wasn't like in the past, when he had worked alongside Ben-Gurion and Sharett, Eshkol and Meir, Dayan and Allon. His long and tortuous path was strewn with many stops and fateful crossroads that had determined the course of his life and, more than once, the fate of the nation as well.

To many, Shimon Peres was an enigma and remains one still. He was different from all the others who worked at his side. A son of Israel whose roots were in a faraway land; a master of the Hebrew language, yet with a foreign accent; the ultimate defense expert of Israel, who had never worn a uniform; a mediocre politician, yet a statesman of splendid vision; a kibbutznik without a formal education, yet abounding in culture; reserved and self-controlled, yet burning with an inner fire; romantic and ambitious, confident but shy, suspicious yet longing for love. A complex man of many faces and many contradictions.

There is no single solution to this riddle, and no single key will unlock the sealed compartments of Shimon Peres's world;

but many keys are scattered all along the road he has taken, with its challenges and perils, its scorching defeats and intoxicating achievements.

That road begins in a forgotten village on the Byelorussian-Polish border called Vishneva.

PART 1.

BLUE SHIRT AND KHAKI PANTS

CHAPTER 1.

A VOYAGE IN A SUBWAY

THE MOST MEMORABLE experience of his early childhood was listening to the Kol Nidre prayer in the synagogue on Yom Kippur, the Day of Atonement. The adults would cover his head with a prayer shawl, and he would feel "the awe of the Almighty."[1] The boy was tense, fearful, and imagined that he was leaving the earthly world and ascending to heaven; in his mind he saw the angels, but the devil, too. He would pray with deep conviction to God "to forgive our sins," but he wouldn't forgive himself for his own.[2] He was a religious boy, wearing a skullcap and observing every rule of the Jewish religion. He ate only kosher food and observed the Sabbath. His secular father turned on their new radio on a Sabbath, and Shimon, shocked by the sacrilege, smashed the radio to pieces. "When I was a boy," Shimon wrote years later, "I was a great believer. I was convinced of God's existence, I feared his wrath, I felt his overwhelming and invisible presence. I prayed for Him and for all of us, with restless enthusiasm. The first books I read were not books—but the Scriptures. Sanctity, and not children's stories, filled my young heart. I did not practice sports, I wasn't aware of the beauty of nature; I was not drawn to children's jubilation."[3]

The man whom he admired, and who "really educated him," also carried a religious aura. His grandfather on his mother's side, Zvi Meltzer, was a graduate of the famous Volozhin Yeshiva.

The father of two sons and six daughters, Meltzer had a clear forehead, black bushy eyebrows, a white beard, and a piercing look emerging from deep eye sockets. The Vishneva Jews described him as "a wise Jew, proud and strong-minded," the treasurer of the synagogue and a fine singer.[4] "He had a wonderful voice," Shimon recalled. A shudder would run through Shimon's body on Yom Kippur when his grandfather would sing Kol Nidre with "a tenor voice full of utmost tenderness .... His singing rings in my heart till this very day, and every Yom Kippur I feel this shudder deep in my bones."[5]

His grandparents owned a small workshop that produced felt boots. Shimon was Zvi Meltzer's favorite grandson. The boy's parents agreed that he was exceptionally gifted, as he knew by heart prayers and chapters from the Bible. They regarded his high forehead as a sign of great intelligence.[6] In his childhood he embraced his grandfather's teaching that the most important asset a man has is his wisdom; when Shimon heard that somebody was a genius, he regarded him as "a world champion in every field of endeavor."[7]

Every day, Zvi Meltzer would teach Shimon a few lines of the Talmud, but the old man was at home with universal culture as well. He played the violin, and read Dostoyevsky, Gogol, Tolstoy, and other Russian writers. Shimon emulated him—besides the Jewish writers Mapu, Peretz, Shalom Aleichem, and Mendele-Mokher Sefarim, he also read the Russian classics. Tolstoy was still difficult for him; his world was for Shimon "a Gentile, distant world." On the other hand, since the age of nine he had eagerly swallowed Dostoyevsky's books. Dostoyevsky haunted him; through his books the boy became acquainted with death. "Death appeared to me in Dostoevsky's books eternal and terrible like God himself. I passed nights of anxiety, immersed deep in his pages."[8] *Crime and Punishment* populated Shimon's nights with fearful nightmares.

He shared his love for books with his mother, Sarah, a short, black-haired woman who was a volunteer at Vishneva's public library. Like her sisters and her husband, she was secular. All the Meltzer daughters liked reading and singing. "They tried to be artistic with the encouragement of our grandfather," recalled Shimon's younger brother, Gershon Peres, known as Gigi.[9] But Sarah Meltzer Persky became an utterly avid reader. She would bring books to Shimon, discuss them with him, advise him what to read; she instilled in him a thirst for reading that would never be quenched. Her friends used to say that actually "she was the head of the family, a wise, warmhearted woman. She loved Shimon madly."[10]

These were the figures that shaped the world of young Shimon—his grandfather and his mother. In his memoirs he only fleetingly mentions his father, "a well-to-do merchant of wood, and forest lots"; there was no strong bond between the two. Shimon insisted that he loved his father, but he wasn't home most of the time. Getzel (Yitzhak) Persky was also a descendant of a dynasty of scholars. Shimon's paternal grandfather, Zalman Persky, was an offspring of the Volozhin Yeshiva's founder, Rabbi Chaim Volozhiner. But Shimon's father drifted away from his family heritage. He was a handsome, elegant man, full of joie de vivre, gifted with an adventurous streak.

Getzel started his business by trading in wood, and later supplied wheat to the Polish Army. He built warehouses by the Bogdanov train station and supplied goods to the neighboring villages, including sugar, flour, salt, beer, and herring. He built mills and got involved in real estate. "My business flourished and my fortune grew," he wrote in a history of the town.[11]

But the flourishing business made Getzel travel a lot, and Shimon didn't see him often. As an adult he couldn't recall any important conversation with his father, any advice that Getzel Persky gave him. He did recall, though, that his parents never punished him; they preferred the way of conversation and persuasion. Shimon inherited that talent for persuasion from his parents, and in the future he would develop it into a unique art form.

In the Persky family a clear division took place: Shimon was his mother's son, while the father's son was Gigi, a stronger, tougher child, who liked to carve wooden knives, enjoyed the outdoor life, and was eager to fight other kids.

"For my mother, my birth was something of a miracle," Shimon wrote. "I weighed more than five kilograms—more than eleven pounds—and she almost died at childbirth."[12] He was born on August 15, 1923 (the twentieth of the Jewish month of Av), and was named after his paternal grandmother, Shaine. In his childhood, he never felt need. The family was well-off, there was plenty of food, and those distant years settled in his memory as flashes of pleasant recollections—lots of bookshelves, a wooden floor covered with red varnish, a nearby well from which they drew cold and limpid water. The family lived in a spacious wooden house on Vilnius Street. The Olshansky River ran by Vishneva, which was surrounded by a dense forest. In summertime the children used to bathe in the Olshansky, and on Friday afternoon it seemed that the entire population was immersed to their chins in its cool waters.

Shimon loved the Byelorussian winters, when the village was covered with snow and ice. He would don warm winter clothes: thick pants, woolen socks, a heavy coat, and a hat with earmuffs. Besides reading, his favorite hobby was skiing in the pristine snow. He would return home, his cheeks red, and wolf thick slices of buttered bread.

One day, a Jew from the Land of Israel—at the time called Palestine, or Eretz-Israel in Hebrew—visited Vishneva. Shimon and his family were in the crowd that gathered that night at the home of the visitor's relatives, to hear his stories from the distant land. The stranger inspired them with pride by his descriptions of the Jewish pioneers' heroic feats; he then delved into his rucksack and produced "a small, round parcel." He peeled off several layers of paper, "and there was, held in his hand, a golden orange." The man held the fruit high and showed it to the crowd, like a crafty magician performing in front of a spellbound audience. "I'll never forget," Shimon recalled, "our town Jews gaping with feverish eyes at the small orange that symbolized for them their most precious hopes and dreams. And for the first time in my life I felt, almost physically, what was Eretz-Israel!"[13]

Another taste of Eretz-Israel was the Hebrew language, which Shimon learned at the Tarbut Jewish school, along with Yiddish. The school's spirit was overtly Zionist; Shimon's teacher was Yeoshua Rabinowitz, a future mayor of Tel Aviv and later a minister of finance in Yitzhak Rabin's cabinet.

Contemporary photographs show Shimon as a pale child, neatly combed and buttoned, looking at the camera with a grave, wistful expression. In his own words, he was a "rather lonely" boy. In his childhood, he suffered from "terrible stress," which intensive reading helped dispel. Shimon played in the mandolin band of his school, but without much success. "I don't have a musical ear," he admitted. "Sadly, the family's musical genes seemed to have stopped at my mother."[14]

On the other hand, he wrote poems—but didn't show most of them to a living soul. "When I discovered poetry," he wrote, "I thought that I had found my destiny." He dreamed of becoming a poet and filled notebooks with his verses.

Shimon was spoiled at home because of his talents; but those apparently caused a different reaction among his schoolmates. Gigi, who was two and a half years younger, said that Shimon's schoolmates harassed him, and often beat him up. He knew too much for their taste, and they resented his ambition to assert his superiority. Shimon, Gigi says, was an outstanding student, with an eloquent tongue and a quick mind. "The teacher would ask, 'Who killed Cain?' All the kids would raise their hands, and then Shimon would rise and say, 'The one who was killed was Abel, not Cain.' "

Shimon rarely played with the other kids. He would rather stay home and read. "The teachers," Gigi said, "were enthralled by Shimon. He was a sort of genius, he asked Talmudic questions, he argued brilliantly. That infuriated his classmates. They regarded his behavior as haughty and conceited, which children hate. In class some would say that he deserved a beating. He was a strong, healthy child, but he avoided any confrontation."[15] When the other children beat him up he came home devastated, sometimes crying. Gigi would ask him, "Why don't you hit back?" and Shimon always replied, "What do they want of me? I didn't do anything to them." He didn't know how to hit back, and this would remain his characteristic trait for the rest of his life. Gigi claimed that he often beat up other kids who had attacked his older brother. "When I would hear that the children hurt Shimon, I would run out to the street and thrash them." Once he even went to the home of one of the children, pulled him out of bed, and beat him up in front of his parents.[16]

Shimon, indeed, knew how to endure—he never said die. Once he went with a classmate to his grandfather's house. The two kids started a mock fight, each of them trying to bring the other down. Shimon's pal was a big, sturdy kid, and he threw Shimon to the floor over and over again. Each time Shimon would get up and ask for "one more time." Finally, Shimon's grandmother intervened. "Shimon, enough. Don't you see he is stronger?"

Shimon looked at her. "Perhaps next time I'll make it."

A relative commented: "This is Shimon. They'll knock him down over and over again, but he'll get up and keep trying—perhaps next time he'll make it."[17]

SHIMON PERSKY'S CHILDHOOD was isolated from the outside world by a sort of Jewish bubble. "We children," he wrote, "felt as though we lived in a Jewish island, surrounded by a sea of thick and threatening forests. We knew that there were great cities beyond the forest, full of excitement and novelty, but our horizons stopped at the tops of the graceful, swaying birches."[18]

Vishneva was an overwhelmingly Jewish town; Shimon's childhood passed with almost no contact with Gentiles; the town's Jewish population numbered about fifteen hundred people. Vishneva consisted of a few unpaved streets, a marketplace, and several public buildings—two synagogues, a bathhouse, and a Torah school. Shimon saw Gentiles once a week—on market day, when peasants from the neighboring villages came to sell their produce. To him they looked "odd"—strong, tough people, different from the Jews, people from another world.

Later, Shimon would often quote the French-Jewish philosopher Vladimir Jankelevitch: "Jewish life in the Diaspora was similar to a voyage in a subway—you travel underground, you don't see the scenery, and nobody sees you in the train."[19]

One day in 1933, Shimon suddenly emerged from the underground to face the real, mean world. That day, he learned that two Vishneva Jews had been murdered by Gentile peasants in the neighboring forest. Those were Abraham Leib, a butcher, and his brother-in-law.[20] Shimon was profoundly shocked on seeing the picture of the slain Jews in the Yiddish paper *Der Moment.*

The murder in the forest strengthened Shimon's conviction that life in Vishneva was only temporary. Shimon had never assumed that he would stay in the Diaspora. Vishneva was a vibrant Zionist community, with thriving Zionist organizations, parties, and youth movements, from the leftist groups Hashomer Hatzair (the Young Guardian) and Hehalutz (the Pioneer) to the right-wing Betar (its name came from the initials for Brit Trumpeldor, named after a Jewish hero in Eretz-Israel).

The dream of immigrating to the storied Land of Israel fired up the youth's imagination. Shimon himself wasn't a practicing religious boy anymore. His religious fervor had faded away and he embraced Zionism with all his heart. He followed his aunt Itka, who was among the leaders of Hashomer Hatzair,[21] while his beloved uncle Joseph was a leader of Betar. Shimon became very active in the youth movement, and was charged with instructing younger children.

He now had one dream—to set sail for the Land of Israel. The first to go were three of Shimon's aunts with their families. In 1932, when Shimon was nine years old, his father had immigrated to Palestine by himself. Getzel Persky was a sworn Zionist, but he had delayed his aliya—immigration to Israel—as long as his business was flourishing. Not the longing for Zion but Persky's economic situation was the main reason for his departure. He emigrated after the Polish administration hit him with heavy taxes and restrictions because of his Jewish origins. "I drew my conclusions," he wrote, "and I made Aliya."[22]

Getzel—Yitzhak—left for Palestine to prepare the ground for his family's aliya. In a few months, he promised, he would bring over his wife and sons. The months turned into three long years. In a photograph he sent his family from the Holy Land, Getzel looked handsome and elegant in his light summer suit and tie, standing on the seashore, looking at the frothing surf. Only in 1935 did Persky's family receive their immigration certificates, issued by the British authorities in Palestine.[23]

On the day of their departure, Shimon and Gigi dressed in long pants and woolen jackets, heavy shoes and visored caps. The Persky family boarded the train at Bogdanov station. On the station platform the boy faced his grandfather Zvi Meltzer. The old man cast a deep look at his grandson's face, and his voice trembled with emotion when he uttered his commandment to the boy: "Be a Jew, forever!"[24]

These were the last words Shimon ever heard his grandfather say. Zvi Meltzer, and with him all the members of the Persky and Meltzer families who remained in Vishneva, were massacred by the Nazis during World War II. The bearded face of his grandfather became for him the symbol of Judaism; whenever he saw a bearded rabbi, he would remember his beloved grandfather. One day, when prime minister, negotiating with Israel's religious leaders, he would see his grandfather looking at him from the faces of the twelve rabbis who sat at his table.[25]

The train brought the Persky family to Istanbul, where they boarded a Polish ship, the *Kosciusko*. The trip was short. Barely a few days had passed when young Shimon saw from the ship's deck the exotic mosques and domed roofs of Jaffa. From afar he watched the colorful crowd, the loose robes, red fezzes, checkered headdresses. From the old port a myriad of boats emerged, carrying Arabs in traditional dress, who offered the passengers their wares—from fresh dates in handmade baskets to green lemonade in jars filled with crushed ice.

And in one of the boats stood Getzel Persky, tanned and handsome, impatient to welcome his family.

It was a sunny day and the sky was painted in deep blue. The eastern wind carried toward the boy guttural shouts and strange voices in a multitude of tongues from the new world he was about to enter.

CHAPTER 2.

THE TALL SYCAMORES

THE ENCOUNTER WITH the Land of Israel was astounding. Shimon loved what he saw—the blue sky, the sun, the short pants, the open-collared shirts; all these things instilled in him an intoxicating sensation of freedom. "I was pale, introverted, speaking fluent Hebrew but with an Ashkenazi accent."[1] It was late spring and he delighted in the scents wafting from the orange groves. In Tel Aviv's modern houses he saw a symbol of the Jewish people's revival. "We had not merely come to a new place," he wrote, "but had become new and different people. Grandfather Zvi's stern authority had suddenly vanished from my life. Synagogue on Sunday mornings was no longer part of my weekly schedule, as dialogue with the distant Deity was now replaced by the intimate touch of the warm sand and sea."[2] He discarded the remains of his past: the heavy woolen clothes, the visor cap and the coat, the archaic Hebrew language he spoke back home.[3] He didn't succeed, however, in getting rid of his Polish accent; it stayed with him for the rest of his life.

Getzel Persky had rented a modest flat for his family in Tel Aviv, but his economic situation was far from brilliant. He had tried his hand in the wood trade, without much success. He started a grocery business, then opened a small restaurant. When the family arrived it wasn't easy to feed everybody; Getzel and Sarah decided to send Shimon and Gigi to Sarah's sister Brinka, who lived in Rehovot with her husband, Mendel Israeli. Rehovot was a small town; Israeli's house was surrounded by citrus orchards. The trees were in blossom, and every morning Shimon felt as if he were waking up in a perfume factory.

The two children spent the summer reconnoitering their new homeland. For the first time they saw a kibbutz and a moshav—a cooperative village—and met some pioneers, those legendary characters who populated the Zionist mythology. In the fall they came back to Tel Aviv and were enthralled by the city. In Tel Aviv there were cinemas, theaters, youth movements, a golden beach, soccer games, open-air cafés, tanned and elegant people, ice cream and watermelon and falafel, a local delicacy made of ground and fried chickpeas. Shimon believed that Tel Aviv was finer than Paris itself. Paris was in his eyes "a wrinkled old woman," while Tel Aviv, born only twenty-five years before, "was the lovely, spring-like maiden of Jewish renaissance."[4]

Twelve-year-old Shimon was admitted to the sixth grade of the Balfour School, but the following year his teachers dispatched the gifted boy right to the eighth grade.

The school principal, Yehudit Hararit, was an extraordinary woman who left her impact on Shimon. She was a history teacher and a devoted admirer of French culture, especially of the writer and philosopher Jean-Jacques Rousseau. "I developed a special bond to Rousseau, this great writer that Yehudit would often describe as a bearer of real humane values, a man who taught the love of nature and of humanity."[5]

In class, Shimon excelled in literature and history. Math and science, however, were not his forte. He was not great in sports, either. The kids at school were addicted to basketball, and they called Shimon "Two Left Feet."[6] He was great in discussing sports, but his performances were poor. According to a friend, when the kids went to the beach, "He always was white, never had a tan."[7]

Step by step, with endearing timidity, he integrated into the daily life of his class. He used to speak slowly, and his classmates agreed that he was "a very intelligent boy and in some ways older than us, even though he was our age. When he spoke everybody listened. He had a sound logic and used deductions to make his point."[8] In the sixth grade he was elected to the board of the class paper, *Our Newspaper*, and wrote essays and funny stories for it. The following year, he became a major contributor to *Our World*, the eighth-grade newspaper. But in secret he kept writing poems, which exposed a sad, lonely streak in his young soul.

Alone and lonely am I, and misunderstood
My life is shattered by fierce waves
My heart and my soul became my enemies
What I want I don't know and don't understand . . .
Do I seek my death, when my spirit collapses? No![9]

IN PALESTINE, SHIMON quickly became an independent teenager. His mother's influence declined, as she worked long hours in her husband's restaurant. She was not Shimon's guru in the world of books anymore; certainly, she knew Hebrew and kept a Hebrew book on her bedside, but under the bed she hid books in Russian that she would hungrily devour when by herself. Still, Shimon remained faithful to the love of literature that Sarah Persky had instilled in him. His literature teacher, who read his essays, told him that his style was "poetic."[10]

He also fell in love for the first time in his life, with his pretty, blue-eyed classmate Hannah Feigin. But being a very shy boy, he didn't even think of revealing his feelings to his beloved. He would longingly look at Hannah, and then confide in his bosom friend Rafael Vardi, who already strutted in the school hallways with his steady girlfriend. Another girl stirred Shimon's heart: the Yemenite Hephzibah Levy. Shimon would drag his friends to eat falafel in her neighborhood, the Yemenite Vineyard, hoping to chance upon the dark beauty. Hephzibah didn't even notice "that he had the hots for me."[11] He later fell in love with a girl named Carmella Franco, but revealed his feelings to her only twenty years later. "Why didn't you tell me?" Carmella lamented.[12]

His shyness played a role even in his choice of a youth movement. Most teenagers in the Jewish community were members of an ideological youth movement. Most of his classmates belonged to the Boy Scouts. Shimon, though, was reluctant to join a movement in which boys and girls danced together. "I would peek through the windows of their clubhouse," he wrote, "with all the bashfulness of a gauche and introverted young teenager, as the boys and girls within, perhaps insufficiently ideological, but certainly having a good time, would twirl and whirl in intricate polkas. I would watch with rapt but disguised attention as each boy boldly placed one hand on a girl's waist, grabbed her free hand, and flung them both into the tempo without, I marveled, tripping over his feet or kicking hers."[13]

Actually, in other youth movements the teenagers danced as well; but Shimon was a serious young man and didn't appreciate the insipid ideology of the Boy Scouts, which didn't carry a promise for the future. He was deeply opposed, though, to the fervent ideology of the right-wing movement Betar. (In Israel, "left" and "right" are terms that have to do, mostly, with foreign and defense issues.) He qualified it as "dark and dangerous." The members of Betar wore brown shirts and peaked caps, and to Shimon they seemed "bewitched by a totally alien value-system."[14]

Those were stormy days in Palestine, and the kids at school engaged in endless debates about current matters. Nineteen thirty-six marked the beginning of "the Arab Revolt," an armed uprising of Palestinian Arabs against the Jews who were pouring into the country, and against British rule. In those years, Great Britain was assisting the Jewish settling effort; in the year 1935 alone, sixty-five thousand Jews immigrated to Palestine.

The troubles broke out on April 15, when an Arab gang murdered two Jews; the Haganah, the Jewish self-defense organization, retaliated by murdering two Arabs. A few days later, a throng of Arabs massacred sixteen Jews in the streets of Jaffa; a "Supreme Arab Committee" was created in Nablus and assumed control over the revolt. The Jewish community, which numbered about 450,000 people, was attacked by Arab bands that ambushed the main roads. A trip from Tel Aviv to Lod or even to Jaffa turned into a risky venture. Yet the bloody clashes didn't prevent the Jews from founding the Tel Aviv Symphony; for the first time, Shimon heard the name of Arturo Toscanini, the great Italian conductor, who flew to Tel Aviv to conduct the gala opening concert.

The internal Jewish scene was in turmoil, too, as the Labor movement, led by David Ben-Gurion, and the right-wing Revisionist movement, led by Ze'ev Jabotinsky, fought for the leadership of the World Zionist Movement. Ben-Gurion won the 1934 elections and Jabotinsky split the Zionist movement, creating his own world organization.

Shimon wholeheartedly supported Labor and the Histadrut, the mammoth trade-union organization created by the workers' parties in Palestine. He joined Hanoar Haoved ("Working Youth"), the socialist youth movement affiliated with the Histadrut. The members of Hanoar Haoved, who wore khaki shorts and a blue shirt tied at the neck with a red cord, came from all strata of society—poor Yemenite kids, tough moshav youngsters, Ashkenazi teenagers from the better Tel Aviv neighborhoods. They met in ramshackle clubhouses to discuss their Zionist ideology of building a nation by their own hands, leaving the cities and erecting new kibbutzim in the wilderness. Shimon was impressed by many of the teenagers, who worked hard in factories and stores all day long but at the end of the day still came to the clubhouse to study and engage in ideological activity. "Everyone was imbued with the sense that together we were building a new homeland and a new workers' society."[15] For Shimon, the immigrant kid from Poland, Working Youth was the way of striking roots in the Land of Israel.

He also loved the Working Youth summer camps, the feeling of togetherness, the long evenings of songs and stories around the fire. "We would set out for our summer camp, and raise our tents by the Muslim cemetery north of Tel-Aviv. I thought there couldn't be anything better."[16] He became known for his night pranks, and admitted that smearing the faces of his sleeping friends with black shoe polish was a delightful experience.

In Working Youth, Shimon met three people who were to have a strong impact on his life. The first was the founding father of the youth movement, David Cohen. A tall, charismatic man, Cohen charmed his disciples with his fascinating stories, which he told in a husky, whispering voice. The stories described episodes of Hassidic life—but always led to a socialist conclusion. Shimon loved visiting Cohen's home by the sea, where he would stare at the laden bookshelves that covered entire walls, and listen, enraptured, to his stories.

In David Cohen's house Shimon met Cohen's son, Mulla, who became both a close friend and a tough rival.[17] They completed each other: Mulla was a strong, athletic youngster, Shimon was serious and an avid reader. They soon became the core of social life in the Dov Hoz Street club of Working Youth.

The third man Shimon met at Working Youth was his group leader, Elhanan Yishai—a handsome young man, muscular and blue-eyed. For a while, Elhanan was Shimon's idol and hero—but as years passed, they would trade roles, Shimon becoming the leader and Elhanan his faithful lieutenant.

When Shimon reached the age of thirteen, he didn't have a bar-mitzvah party. The Persky family couldn't afford one in those days of hardship.[18] What they could afford was a birthday gift for Shimon—a bicycle. He would ride his bicycle through the streets of Tel Aviv and make sure that the tall sycamores, Tel Aviv's pride, were still standing. "I tried to figure if they had grown during the night. Once in a while I would count the houses in the street—to find out if any new houses had been built. I used to measure the achievements of Zionism by the number of new buildings."[19] Shimon went on a few hikes in the neighboring fields with some boys and girls from his class; he came back laden with flowers and memories. Once he swore his friend Rafi to secrecy and took him home. Shimon's parents were not there, and he made Rafi drink his first glass of wine. Shimon even taught his enchanted friend a song in Yiddish:

Ein mol ein mol ein mol yash
A filu a gantze flash!
(A drink and two and three
Even the whole bottle!)

For Rafi, though, the most memorable episode of their friendship was not drinking a secret glass of wine, but something his friend told him that revealed the real concerns of a boy who wasn't fourteen yet. The year was 1936, and Nazi Germany had recently reoccupied the Rhineland. The news spread while the two friends strolled in Tel Aviv's streets; it was late afternoon, and at the elegant San-Remo Café it was "tea-dance" time. Men and women, fashionably dressed, danced on the floor to the mellow music of a big band. Shimon looked at them and blurted, "Here they dance and there, perhaps, the cannons are thundering already."[20]

IN THE FALL OF 1937, Shimon got a scholarship to the Geula Commerce High School. This was a school for the sons and daughters of well-to-do families. Shimon was different from his classmates. He didn't think of pursuing a business career. "I dreamed of my future as a brawny, sunburned kibbutz-farmer, ploughing the fields of the fertile Jezreel Valley by day, singing lustily at the common dining-room at supper-time, guarding the perimeter fearlessly by night, on a fleet-footed horse."[21] He was also the only member of Working Youth in his class; most of his schoolmates came from right-wing or moderate middle-class families, and belonged to the Boy Scouts or Betar. "Thus, in every ideological debate at school, I found myself in splendid isolation, hotly defending positions which left most of the pupils stone-cold."[22]

Nevertheless, Shimon was regarded by his schoolmates as a born leader with a great future. "He wasn't the best student," said his friend Moshe Shalit, who sat in front of him in class. "I can't say that he didn't copy my exam papers, peeking over my shoulder." When Shalit got an excellent grade on one of his tests and Shimon barely passed, their classmates joked that Shimon had copied the wrong answer.[23]

"He actually was quite mischievous," Shalit added. "He used to skip classes and run away to the beach. But in the class's social life—he was a meteor!"

Shimon was elected to the class council; in the class newspaper, *Nativ*, he demanded of the teachers that they discuss important world events with the students. "We should discuss the rearmament fever in Europe, and the condition of the Jews," he wrote.[24] He organized a public debate in class about Joseph Stalin, and attacked him "virulently." The Stalin debate stirred the teenagers' passions and "we all were captivated by Shimon. He emerged as the leader of our class," Shalit said.[25]

"He was mentally more mature than the other students," said another classmate.[26] Shimon was at his best at the public debates that took place at the students' club.[27] Shimon would arrive dressed in his Working Youth blue shirt, and engage in a debate with one of the students, with all the rest watching, enthralled.

Yet Shimon wasn't happy with his way of life. He studied at a school whose character he disliked; his dreams carried him to other horizons. That was why the surprising offer of Elhanan Yishai's landed on him like manna from heaven.

Yishai told him about the youth village Ben-Shemen, an agricultural boarding school. At that time, Ben-Shemen had absorbed a wave of young immigrants; the school staff wanted to have the newcomers live alongside some Palestinian youngsters, who would help them adapt to their new life. Elhanan suggested to the school that Shimon and Mulla be given scholarships, and the school agreed.

Shimon was thrilled. He didn't ask his parents for permission, but only told them about his decision. He packed his things and boarded a bus whose windows were covered by iron mesh, to protect the passengers from Arab stone-throwers. "I bought my ticket and embarked on what was to be one of the happiest periods of my life."[28]

CHAPTER 3.

A GREEN BOWL IN AN OCEAN OF HATRED

"MY GOAL IN LIFE is to serve my people," the fifteen-year-old Shimon wrote with fervor, on arriving at Ben-Shemen.[1] "The most important service to the people of Israel is building the country [by] working the land; without it there would be no connection to our soil. . . ."

"Life of peddling, money-lending, commerce, is an empty life. It is like a balloon that any gust of wind can blow away, away. . . ."

"People of Israel! For two thousand years you traded, you became rich, you enriched nations and peoples, but where is your happiness? Where, German-assimilated Jews, where is your wealth, where are your high positions?"

"Ah! You are like a balloon that one can prick with a tiny needle, and it collapses and falls."

"People of Israel! Redeem the land! Hold to it! The land will heal your maimed and broken soul; it will heal your bent back that carries the heavy burden of exile for two thousand years."

"We have enough doctors and professors and people with education. Hebrew Youth! We need simple workers of the land. . . . My place is not in the city, but in the village, behind the plough! In the field!"

"When I came to Ben-Shemen I saw my goal in its entire splendor . . . . When I saw the simplicity, the sincerity, the developed social life, the robust boys and girls, healthy in their body and soul, my spirit soared . . . ."

"Greetings from a son of the suffering people, who aspires to work the land of his fathers—Shimon Persky."

THUS WROTE SHIMON in September 1938, in an essay entitled: "Why I Aspire to Study and Live in Ben-Shemen." Shimon indeed fell in love with Ben-Shemen from the moment the bus came to a stop in the dusty inner court of the youth village. In his eyes it was "an island of greenery and flowers surrounded by enemies."[2] He felt that on this very day he "parted from his childhood, parted from his family, parted from his way of life and sailed like Columbus to a new world, mysterious and fascinating."[3]

In Ben-Shemen, Shimon found his place and his real home in the Land of Israel. Years later, when he wrote his memoirs, he wanted to start the book from the age of fifteen, "as if he was never born anywhere and had no past in the Diaspora at all."[4]

When he arrived in Ben-Shemen he looked like a child from Eastern Europe, mostly because of the way he was dressed. When he left, in two and a half years, he was a kibbutznik, active in Working Youth, a worker of the land, and deeply rooted in the Labor movement.

In Ben-Shemen, Shimon Persky became an Israeli.

ON HIS ARRIVAL, Shimon didn't know that the small village was connected with the man who had made the first step toward achieving the Zionist dream. Fifty-six years before, on July 6, 1882, thirteen young men and a young woman had landed in the port of Jaffa. They were the first members of the Zionist movement BILU, whose dream was to establish a Jewish state in the Land of Israel.

The leader of that group, Israel Belkind, founded a boarding school for Jewish orphans on the coastal plain, about two and a half miles east of Lod. The boarding school failed, and the place was used for different purposes: an oil factory, an experimental farm, even a village of Yemenite jewelers. But in 1927, Henrietta

Szold, the founder of the Zionist movement Hadassah, brought the school back to life. Now it was established as a youth village, whose new name, Ben-Shemen, was inspired by a verse from Isaiah.

Shimon had never seen a place like this. To him, the lush, flowering oasis was "a youths' republic."[5] Four hundred boys and girls lived in oblong wooden buildings, three or four in a room. They were supervised and taught by 120 teachers and instructors. The students spent half of their time studying and the other half working in one of the many agricultural sectors. Shimon, Mulla, and their friend Moshe Gerber were assigned a room in a cabin nicknamed, for some mysterious reason, "the Arab doghouse."[6]

In the summer their house was hot and stuffy; in the winter the floor would be so soiled with mud from the boys' rubber boots that they would wash it with water hoses. They deposited the clothes they brought from home in Ben-Shemen's warehouse, and every week would receive clean khaki clothes from the communal laundry.

The Israeli writer Amos Oz, who would later become Shimon's close friend, believed that Shimon desperately tried to win his schoolmates' affection and become a Sabra (an Israeli-born youth) like many of them. "He fell from the moon in the midst of the handsome Sabras, and tried to conceal the fact that he had come from another planet," Oz said. "He tried to be like them and emulate them. He didn't succeed in getting rid of his accent, even though he tried very hard." Oz noticed that Shimon's main weakness dating from his Ben-Shemen days was "his boundless craving for love, from all over."[7] His overwhelming desire to become a typical Israeli, loved and accepted by his friends, and to prove that he had immigrated to Israel while still a child made him advance the date of his aliya. Although Shimon insisted that he had immigrated to Israel in 1934, at the age of eleven, he actually arrived in 1935. Yet some claimed that he didn't get rid of his "Polish" character even in Ben-Shemen. One friend said, "He used to read books and write poems, and this was not exactly what the Sabras did those days."[8]

If Shimon was looking for a melting pot that would transform him into a son of Israel, he found it in Ben-Shemen. The school principal was the German-born Dr. Siegfried Lehmann, a teacher and an intellectual. He attracted to the village many men of letters and famous writers, either as teachers or as guest speakers. This connoisseur of culture and the arts enlarged the horizons of the students far beyond the Lod Valley. He introduced studies of Hebrew and world literature, poetry and prose, art and music. In his home Shimon saw, for the first time in his life, subtle Japanese and Chinese paintings, while the inner court of the village echoed every Friday afternoon with the sweet sounds of Mozart's *Eine Kleine Nachtmusik.* The classical piece was performed by the flutes and mandolins of the youth orchestra, which also played Haydn's *Toy* Symphony and accompanied the dance group of the village.

Lehmann was a friend of Albert Einstein, who had presented the village with an iron model of the solar system that served for the study of astronomy basics. Like Einstein and some other Jewish intellectuals, Lehmann adopted an endearingly nave attitude toward the Arabs, hoping that the Jews could buy peace with them by making far-reaching concessions. On the other hand, the grim reality forced him to be active in the armed defense of Ben-Shemen. The neighboring villagers kept shooting at Ben-Shemen and often assaulted its perimeter fence. Till peace came, the good Dr. Lehmann had to organize the defense of his village and arm its Jewish guards.

For Shimon, Ben-Shemen was "a green bowl in an ocean of Arab hatred." He was sworn into the Haganah in a secret ceremony: in the dark of night he had to sneak into a bare room illuminated by a single candle, and recite his oath while placing his hand on the Bible and on a pistol. Shimon and his friends spent many a night manning the guard posts surrounding the village. On January 16, 1939, some Arabs ambushed the village guards, killed two of them—Ze'ev Friedman and Zalman Rosenbaum—and wounded a third. The murders stunned the community.

Shimon was deeply affected by the death of his friends. In an early article he described harvesting the fields while Arab peasants worked in their lots nearby. "A few steps from me an Arab spreads a small carpet on the ground, kneels down and murmurs a prayer. He finishes praying, slowly rises, gets hold of his plough and prods his oxen. Who knows what he is hiding under his loose clothes? I grasp the scythe with both my hands."[9]

In spite of the tensions, Shimon, Mulla, and some friends started visiting the nearby Arab villages. "Those very Arabs who fired at us at night, welcomed us during the day, and we enjoyed a wonderful hospitality. It was like time-travel, like visiting another age, in ancient times. I had a feeling of strangeness, as if we were not of the same generation, the same world. We knew a little Arabic, they knew a little Hebrew. The visits were intended to create some mutual understanding. I remember the smells, the calls of the muezzin, the conversations. We refrained from speaking about politics and preferred to discuss agriculture, cattle, work in the fields."

"I knew that they could easily become fierce enemies. But beside the suspicions and the fear—there was something so romantic in these visits! I remember the food they used to eat with their hands, the delicacies, the shish kebab and the pita bread, the keffiyehs veiling those glinting eyes that both scared us and fascinated us."[10]

Shimon loved life on the farm. He would get up at four-thirty in the morning to milk the cows; that was how he acquired the habit of getting up early. "In the village, for the first time, I had a close look at a cow. It was so different from the cows that figured on the chocolate wrappings. It was a hungry, tired creature, plaintively mooing, often covered with mud."[11] He learned to harness a mule, "which was utterly indifferent to its surroundings." He delighted in the smells of the freshly cut grass, but most of all he loved the scent of the young cucumbers, which to him was "like bottles of perfume that arrived straight from Paris."

At night, Shimon avidly read all kinds of books—the classics, Hebrew literature, poetry, political essays. His writing was multifaceted, too—romantic poems, dramatic descriptions, skits, plays, or tiresome ideological articles. He sent a short article to *Bamaaleh*, the Working Youth biweekly magazine, and was deeply moved to see his name and his words in print.[12] In that first article, called "Harvest," he showed a sense of humor and amused self-criticism. "A dew-soaked morning," he wrote. "I pick up my scythe and go to the field. 'If you keep holding the scythe that way,' chuckles one of the guys, 'you'll harvest heads and not clover.' I correct my mistake. My friend sharpens his scythe like a veteran farmer, while I cut my hands. Only after a long while does the scythe in my hands become razor-sharp. It only touches the clover—and a lot of stalks fall down. Another stroke and another—and the cut clover already rises in a big heap. Slowly I get used to the motions. The scythe slashes as if by itself . . . . It's time to rest, and we lie on a huge heap and chew stalks of clover; they are juicy and tasteful."

Shimon described, with undisguised pride, his meeting with the members of a Working Youth club in Tel Aviv. "You're tanned, tall and broad-shouldered," said one of the youngsters. "We are like wimps compared to you! What is the secret that makes you so hardy?"

Shimon answered on the pages of *Bamaaleh:* "Come here, city boy! Here, in the fields, you'll find the secret. Once you feel the delight of harvest in green fields—I bet you'll never want to go back to the city."[13]

The independence he enjoyed in the "youth republic" of Ben-Shemen was a godsend for Shimon.[14] He was less enthusiastic about the school routine. He enjoyed studying literature and the Bible but used to sneak away from chemistry and physics lessons[15] and head to the orchard, where he would gorge himself with sweet, juicy figs. But for nothing in the world would he skip the daily debates at the youth assembly. In the youth's newspaper he attacked his teachers, "who don't teach us the real Bible," but only selected passages that didn't require an effort on their part. Dr. Lehmann, alarmed, turned to Professor Martin Buber for help, to refute the boy's heresy. With typical teenager's cheek, Shimon argued with Buber heatedly.[16] "I regret until this very day," he wrote years later, "that my *chutzpah* was bigger than his persuasive ability."[17]

Ben-Shemen, like many public institutions in Palestine, was a hothouse for political movements. Several left-wing youth movements were active in the village. The most leftist was Hashomer Hatzair, which advocated a binational, Jewish-Arab state in Palestine. Working Youth was more moderate, although its ideological leaders developed a theory about a Greater Israel that was strangely intertwined with the Soviet ideology of peoples' brotherhood. The odd infatuation of the left-wing leaders with the Soviet Union inspired the youngsters, who used to sing Russian songs by the campfire and compare the kibbutz to the Communist collective farm, the kolkhoz.

Shimon didn't share his friends' commitment to the Soviet Union, and strongly disliked Stalin. Still, he considered Working Youth to be his ideological home. In Ben-Shemen he soon became the ideological leader of the younger class. He also founded a literary circle for the children and taught them literature with inexorable zeal, painting before his wide-eyed audience a sweeping view of the world of books, starting with the Eastern European writer Zalman Shneur and reaching far into the verses of Heinrich Heine. He delighted in the works of the Jewish writers he now intimately knew—Heine, D'Israeli, Lasalle, as well as political thinkers like Trotsky, Blum, and Marx. "They're all Jewish," he wrote; "they all changed the world order. They apparently reached the conclusion that if the Jews can't change—they should change the world." Heine charmed him in particular. "In him I found something I was missing all along—irony. Irony so powerful that it was like poetry to me."[18]

Political activity being officially forbidden in Ben-Shemen, Shimon used to assemble the Working Youth disciples late at night, in the mules' stable, in conspiratorial secrecy. These nightly ventures in the stable exposed the complex mind of Shimon, where two different worlds already existed side by side: the world of the Israeli youngster, striking roots in the land, and the man of universal culture, flying on the wings of his imagination to the endless expanses of literature and history. This duality gave him an edge over his classmates, and won him their respect; but it also triggered a growing alienation between him and the others, instigating in them a sense of caution, even incredulity, toward this kid—who was, after all, one of them—who blabbered about Heinrich Heine, Benjamin Disraeli, and the faraway lands across the sea.

When a new boy arrived from Germany, wearing riding britches and tall boots, he was sent to the "Arab doghouse," where Mulla Cohen, Moshe Gerber, and Shimon lived. Shimon taught his new friend Hebrew, and the newcomer taught him a little German; he also translated for Shimon the book he had brought with him from Germany: *The Klapper-Zahnen Wonderful.* It was the story of the eleven kids of Mr. Klapper-Zahnen (the teeth-rattler), who founded a soccer team and traveled the world. "With the Klapper-Zahnen family," Shimon wrote, "I traveled across the entire globe, and I delighted in landscapes, people and legends I had never heard about in my life." He was especially beguiled by the fascinating descriptions of three places: "The island of Zanzibar, with its tall palms and the shark skins hung to dry; the Kamchatka peninsula, between Russia and Japan, where people walk covered in furs, in a never ending winter; and the Falklands, where the ranchers raise huge herds of sheep, and plough the waves of the Pacific with their sleek speedboats."[19] Shimon swore to travel, one day, to all those wondrous places. (He would make it only to Zanzibar.)

And on a parallel track, when Avraham Greidinger, a new boy from Czechoslovakia, arrived in Ben-Shemen and asked a

Sabra for an explanation of political life in Palestine, the youngster told him, "I don't know about these matters, but Shimon will brief you. He understands political issues." That's how Greidinger learned "that there is somebody named Shimon, who is the political leader of the group."[20] At the Working Youth convention, Shimon dared to rise to his feet and make a speech. To his surprise, he was elected to the national bureau of the movement. He believed that he owed his election, at least partly, to "the impressively low bass voice that I had been blessed with, even at this tender age."[21]

BEN-SHEMEN FLOURISHED—but the outside world was on fire. Shimon had just started his second year in Ben-Shemen when Hitler invaded Poland and World War II began.

The war had a direct impact on the Persky family. Getzel closed his foundering business and, in spite of his age—he was over forty—volunteered for the British Army. He was enrolled in the Palestinian sappers' battalion—and vanished from home. Shimon's mother got an exhausting job in a British Army spare-parts factory. Shimon went home only very rarely. He was entirely absorbed by Ben-Shemen and his activities there.

The world events and the persecutions of the Jews left their impact in the youngster's notebooks as well. In an essay he wrote in early 1939, he quoted the Arab newspapers published in Nablus that rejoiced in the Jews' sorry fate: "From one country they kick them out like dogs and another country locks her gates before them like before devils."

"Dear God—are we like dogs? Are we leeches on the nations' flesh?" But already, at this early age, Shimon formulated the answer that would guide him throughout his adult life: "Perhaps it is so because we are weak .... If we only had guns and airplanes, then ..."[22]

IN HIS SECOND summer in Ben-Shemen, Shimon and Avraham Greidinger attended an ideological seminar, organized by the Labor movement. Among the speakers were Yitzhak Tabenkin, the leader of "Faction B," the activist, pro-Soviet wing of Ben-Gurion's Mapai Party, and Ben-Gurion's friend Berl Katzenelson, the major ideologue of the Labor movement.

The subject was "Socialism in a Time of Crisis." Katzenelson stood in front of his young audience, short, stout, and curly, expounding his philosophy. His moderate view on socialism was based on the moral values of the Bible and Judaism. Katzenelson mercilessly bashed Stalin and the Marxist-Leninist teachings. Shimon was elated; he decided that this was the best lecture on this subject that he had ever heard. He pledged, then and there, to fight Marxism, communism, and the Stalinist dictatorship with all his force.[23] He was deeply impressed by Katzenelson, who didn't hesitate to admit that he didn't know all the answers; he was ready to question and examine again all notions, even the most sacred ones. A short time after their first contact at the seminar, Katzenelson read one of Shimon's articles in *Bamaaleh* and invited him to his home.[24]

That summer held in store another surprise for Shimon. He had to travel to the northern port of Haifa to take care of some Working Youth business, and his instructors arranged for him to get a ride in David Ben-Gurion's car.

When the moment came, he got into the car, thrilled by the prospect of passing two hours in the company of the mythic leader. But Ben-Gurion sat in silence, collected in his thoughts, and apparently ignoring the presence of his young guest. The silence lasted for more than an hour. Suddenly, Ben-Gurion turned toward Shimon and said, "Listen! Trotsky wasn't a statesman! At Brest Litovsk"—where the peace talks between Soviet Russia and Imperial Germany were held during World War I—"he said, 'Neither war nor peace.' This is not right. He should have said, 'War, with all its risks, or peace,' even if that meant territorial concessions. Lenin said, 'Peace.' Trotsky wasn't Russian—he was Jewish. He wasn't a statesman, he didn't understand Soviet Russia."[25]

Ben-Gurion was referring to the famous formula of Leon Trotsky, one of the leaders of Russia's Bolshevik Revolution, during the peace negotiations. While Lenin was ready to accept painful territorial losses in order to devote himself to building the Soviet Union, Trotsky gained support with his witty formula. At the end, though, the Soviet leaders rallied to Lenin's views.

Even when Shimon grew up and got to know David Ben-Gurion well, he remembered those few words of Ben-Gurion's, regarding them as the key to his character. They highlighted two basic traits in Ben-Gurion's personality: first, his unconventional approach, the willingness to reject widely supported concepts; and second, his belief in clear and bold decisions, despite the risks they might imply.

These meetings with Katzenelson and Ben-Gurion had a deep impact on Shimon's mind. From Katzenelson he learned that there was nothing wrong in hesitating, doubting, and testing oneself over and over again before making a decision. From Ben-Gurion he learned that a clearly defined decision was always better than a clever, ornate phrase.

But did he learn to implement those lessons himself?

THE HAGANAH COMMANDERS of Ben-Shemen appointed Shimon Persky deputy guard-post commander. One night he had to man the defense position by the house of the carpentry teacher, Yaakov Gelman. Shimon mounted guard all night long. At first light, in the hesitant grayness of the early dawn, he saw a girl coming out of the house. She was barefoot, in shorts, a heavy braid falling on her shoulder; as she turned, he saw her breathtaking profile, like one of those ancient Greek statues he had seen in his schoolbooks.

He looked at her for a very long moment, and fell in love.

CHAPTER 4.

A MAN IN LOVE

"ALL MY LIFE I was a man in love," Shimon wrote years later. "The girl I loved at every stage of my life—and I never loved but one girl—was in my eyes perfection itself. And the inevitable conclusion was that I wasn't worthy of her. Therefore I refrained from declaring my love, and I would torment myself in secret. Only once, with utmost difficulty, did I succeed to overcome this inhibition, and she became my great and everlasting love. The girl I loved became my ally for my whole life."[1]

His great and everlasting love, Sonia Gelman, won his heart by her beauty and by the irresistible mélange of simplicity, warmth, and honesty that she radiated. Sonia had immigrated to Israel at the age of three with her family. They had settled in Ben-Shemen; her mother was the village matron. Shimon had visited her house with a bunch of kids, where she served them each a piece of pie and a glass of orange juice.

Shimon was an incurable romantic. After tossing and turning in his bed for several nights, he decided to act. With great effort he managed to overcome his shyness and engaged the girl in conversation. She came to visit him at his guard post, and he tried to impress her by reading chosen pieces of literature to her by moonlight. That might have worked, if he hadn't chosen to read chapters from Karl Marx's *Das Kapital.* Sonia didn't care much about Marx, but the following night Shimon recited some of his own poems—that worked.[2] Soon, the two were a couple; their deep, passionate love left a lasting impression on Ben-Shemen's students. Hannah, the future wife of Elhanan Yishai, felt that "this was a love so intense that I don't have words to describe it."[3]

Once in a while, Shimon and Sonia traveled to Tel Aviv and went to the movies or a play; he would sport an open shirt and khaki pants, she an embroidered blouse and smiling eyes under arched eyebrows. The outings always ended at a soda fountain, where Shimon would swallow huge portions of ice cream, his favorite dessert.

While courting Sonia, Shimon was busy organizing a group of teenagers, "the Circle," who dreamed of building their own kibbutz. They intended to join a group preparing to settle at Alumot, a breathtaking spot on the hills overlooking Lake Tiberias. The idea came from Elhanan Yishai, and Shimon embraced it with enthusiasm. Shimon's roommates Moshe Gerber and Mulla Cohen also were in the Alumot Circle.

In mid-1941, thirty members of the Circle left Ben-Shemen for a training camp at Kibbutz Geva. There they had to work, together with the kibbutz members, and prepare for kibbutz life on their own.

While Shimon was immersed in the welding of the Alumot team, fateful events were taking place. In 1939, Great Britain had turned her back on Zionism and published an official statement, a "White Paper," severely limiting Jewish immigration and settlement in Palestine. The White Paper was a death sentence on the Zionist dream, and the Jewish community decided to fight it by every possible means. But then World War II broke out, and Ben-Gurion coined his wartime slogan: "We must help the British in their war against Hitler as though there were no White Paper, and we must resist the White Paper as though there were no war!"[4]

War against Hitler! Ben-Gurion's call fired up a tremendous response in the Palestinian Jewish youth. Thousands joined the British Army. Many others—mostly sympathizers of Tabenkin and his left-leaning "Faction B"—preferred to join the Haganah and its legendary fighting force, the Palmach.

Shimon's father had joined the British Army and sailed overseas. His younger brother, Gigi, joined the Palmach. Mulla Cohen joined the Palmach as well. In a long conversation that went into the night, Shimon tried to talk his friend out of joining the Palmach, but failed. Mulla Cohen left Geva and would become one of the most valiant Palmach commanders.[5] Another three members of the Alumot Circle joined the Jewish Brigade in the British Army.

Shimon's beloved Sonia volunteered as well, and spent the war years as a British Army nurse and driver. Sonia was an idealist; she considered army service as the most important contribution to the war effort and had dreamed of becoming a nurse in British uniform. She expected Shimon to enlist as well, and told him so. Shimon, though, showed a strange reluctance to serving in the army. "The army and the war didn't interest me," he said years later, sharply criticizing the character of career army officers.[6] He wrote a letter of appreciation to Sonia for her decision to join but stressed that he had to stay in Palestine, "to accomplish the undertaking for which you're fighting." He and his friends, Shimon added, were building a settlement for the survivors of the Nazi murders. "You're fighting for them too," he wrote to Sonia. "The front is different, and the role of each of us is different. But we know: we're fighting the same war."[7]

Indeed, even at the height of the war, the leaders of the Labor movement attached great importance to settling the land and building new kibbutzim. The term "to enlist" had a double meaning—either joining the army or volunteering for settling the land. Shimon was one of those who considered the building of a new settlement as important an endeavor as fighting the enemy. And yet it was odd that this young man—who had experienced the conflict between Jews and Arabs, and whose relatives in Poland were threatened with extermination by the Nazis—refrained from taking up arms and fighting. Only recently he had written a passionate call to arms, urging his friends to enlist in the Haganah and fight.[8]

Shimon wrote his call to arms but didn't implement it himself. His best friends, his father and his brother, the woman he loved, his bosom buddy—they all enlisted, and only he did not.

LEAVING BEN-SHEMEN opened a chapter of loneliness in Shimon's life. Many of his friends went in different directions. Apparently what hurt him most was the separation from the woman he loved. The issue of joining the army had hurt their relationship and made them separate.

When Sonia decided to go her own way, she cut her heavy braid and left Shimon. She gave him back his freedom, and they parted, knowing that henceforth each of them would start a new life. Sonia disappeared from Shimon's horizon, and traveled far, to Egypt and the Western Desert. Shimon remained all alone, haunted by a terrible feeling that "it's all over." He was tormented by the thought that he was only "a fleeting episode in a person's [Sonia's] life, and if something had happened [between them] it was only a part of a distant and forgotten past."[9] He met a few girls, but none won his heart, and his solitude deepened. Perhaps that was the reason he intensified his activities in the Circle and in Working Youth.

Kibbutz Geva, a thriving settlement in the Valley of Jezreel, had warmly welcomed the members of the Circle who arrived from Ben-Shemen. The "Ben-Shemniks" were sent to work in the orchards and the cornfields, the huge henhouses and the cowsheds. At night, they slept in tents; in the scorching afternoon hours they were admitted to the rooms of the kibbutz members, to rest on the cool floors.

In Geva Shimon saw the legendary General Charles de Gaulle, leader of the Free French. The Free French soldiers had a camp not far from Geva, and de Gaulle came to visit them in 1941. The entire population of Geva rushed to the French camp to see the brave leader. Shimon couldn't imagine that twenty years later he would remind President de Gaulle of that episode while lunching at the Elysée Palace in Paris, together with Prime Minister Ben-Gurion.[10]

Geva was different from Ben-Shemen, and Shimon didn't like his new home there. "This was no children's paradise," he wrote. "It was an adult world, stern and puritanical. Smiles were few and far between. Mistakes were seldom glossed over with a wink and a nod. Here each person was under constant collective scrutiny and was required to measure up to rigidly demanding criteria. Woe betide anyone leaving for work in the fields after the sun had risen, and woe betide him if he returned before it had set."[11] And yet Geva was a flourishing kibbutz, its fields fertile, its orchards laden with oranges and grapefruit, its cows producing the highest milk yields in Palestine.

Shimon kept working at the cowshed, but spent all of his free time campaigning for Working Youth among the teenagers of the Valley of Jezreel. He was also very active at the Working Youth national bureau and spent a lot of time traveling. The bureau put at his disposal an old Triumph motorcycle and he crisscrossed the Valley of Jezreel, carrying pamphlets and circulars. Geva's secretary reluctantly agreed to let him spend two days a week out of the kibbutz. Shimon stayed at his parents' home in Tel Aviv, as he had no expense account. "As you can imagine," he wrote to his friends in Geva, "the state of my finances and my clothes isn't brilliant. Could you send me a little of these two products?"[12]

Some Geva members criticized Shimon for his public activities and complained that he didn't work as hard as his friends. Very few knew that no matter what time Shimon returned from his travels, he would be at the cowshed before dawn, milking the cows and doing his chores.[13]

Shimon also attracted the fury of the kibbutzniks because he dared admit that he would like to hold public office. The unwritten moral code of the kibbutz movement stipulated that one should never express such a desire, and one should accept a public function only if the movement and the leadership forced him to do so. Shimon rejected those hypocritical rules, and said so openly. "Ambition is not a dirty word," he declared. "I appreciate ambitious people who don't conceal their aspirations."[14]

Shimon often lectured the teenagers of Kibbutz Geva about world affairs. Once again, his lectures displayed the duality in his character. Besides analyzing the issues of kibbutz life and the Labor movement, he would set sail for faraway worlds, speak of literature, history, and political events that nobody else ever described to the younger generation. His friend Nachman Raz, who was a year younger, admired his eloquence "and his knowledge, which was enormous compared to what we knew. Shimon would speak about European leaders, he would quote literary texts and describe events we had no idea about. He spoke about these subjects with such self-assurance that I always had doubts if he really knew those things or if it was a sort of trickery and pretense. One had the feeling that Shimon was exposed to the outside world, that he was familiar with the latest developments in philosophy and politics and literature; when he spoke to us we felt as if he were right now in London and had met Churchill an hour before."[15]

That manner of speaking contributed to create a stigma that stuck to Shimon for the rest of his life: a lack of credibility. One of the major reasons for this was Shimon's creative ideas, which made many of the kibbutzniks recoil in horror. He suggested to the Geva comrades that they establish a high-tech industry in the kibbutz, side by side with the agricultural work; the comrades reacted with mockery and contempt. Years later, on a visit to the Metro in Paris, Shimon learned that the passengers were using magnetic tickets made in a high-tech factory in Geva.[16] Indeed, today there is no kibbutz that does not have a highly successful high-tech industry.

Young Shimon Persky also suggested that Geva open a café, where the kibbutzniks could relax after a long day of work.[17] The leaders were stunned. A café in the kibbutz! Such a suggestion, in the very bastions of hard-toiling socialist Palestine, was at least heresy, if not high treason. Today, sixty years later, there is no kibbutz without "a members' club," and many have pubs; once again, young Persky had been ahead of his time.

Because of such ideas, many saw in the young man only a builder of castles in the sky, suffering from delusions and pipe dreams.[18] Others claimed that he didn't speak the truth. Some Geva members used to call him "Shimal'e the bluffer." Shimon himself was aware of the insulting nickname, and even tried to refute it in a semihumorous article he wrote at that time under the title "Autobluffography, a True Confession of a Bluffer."[19]

"Lately," Shimon wrote, "I heard many people talking about bluffers and bluff .... And as I am often identified with this group, I want to put forward some words of explanation and my true personal opinion on this matter." Shimon brought forth some amusing examples, to prove his theory that different people see different things. "There are people who see only certain colors and there are others who see also invisible colors; the latter are called bluffers." He mentioned some reactions to his speaking in public, like "Come on, we know your bluffs" or "What a sham." He sealed his article with some "friendly advice": "When you hear a story and think it is a bluff, you should know it is the truth, and when you hear a bluff and think it is the truth, you should know that it is a bluff."

The article was rather heavy-handed, but it betrayed the distress that Shimon felt in view of his friends' accusations.

IN JANUARY 1942, Working Youth organized an illegal expedition to Masada. Masada, the last fortress of the Jews who rebelled against Rome in A.D. 72-73, had become a symbol for the youth movements; it proved the right of the Jewish people to the Land of Israel.[20] But Masada was almost unattainable. To reach the legendary cliff, the travelers had to undertake a hard and dangerous trip through the desert; the British authorities prohibited the presence of Jews in that area, and the paths climbing to the top of the fortress had been destroyed. The famous "Serpent Path" and the "Back Path" had been barred by huge rocks during a 1927 earthquake.

A famous archeologist, Shmaria Gutman, planned the journey to Masada with the purpose of blazing trails to the top of the cliff; that way, the Jewish youth could return to the scene of the rebels' last stand.[21] He assembled a group of forty-seven young men and women, most of them members of Working Youth, and some members of the Palmach. The journey in the desert was to last ten days.

The expedition was organized in the utmost secrecy. The candidates received handwritten notes about a "5 days seminar" and a ten-day excursion, "whose location is still kept secret."[22] They assembled at Kibbutz Na'an, and loaded a truck with digging instruments, hammers and chisels, pegs, bags of cement and plaster, climbing ropes, first-aid kits, food, and even books about Masada. In a hiding place in the truck were concealed some dynamite charges.

The nineteen-year-old Shimon was among the chosen who set out on the trip on January 24, 1942. The old truck brought them to the city of Hebron. Shimon and his friends trod into the Judean desert behind three camels they had rented in an Arab village; after the camels turned back the teenagers kept walking, carrying huge loads on their backs. And on the second day, as the sun set in the west, they set up their tents in the purple shadow of the formidable Masada cliff.[23]

The following morning, the young men assailed the flank of Masada. They dug holes in the rock and stuck pegs in concrete that they mixed themselves. They hung rope ladders over the rock blocking the Back Path and fortified the access route to the plateau. That day they reached the fortress and watched, in awe, the biblical landscape that spread at their feet—the desert outcrops, the Dead Sea, the remains of the Roman camps built during the siege, two thousand years before. They were to spend five days on top of Masada, then descend with ropes to Herod's Palace and bury in the rocky soil a parchment scroll with the oath: "Masada will never fall again!"[24]

Three days later, the group descended to tour Masada's surroundings. When they assembled for lunch, Shimon pointed at a portion of the Serpent Path that could be seen clearly from below. "Shmaria," he said to Gutman, "from here there is no problem climbing. Let me climb, I'll be there in a minute!"[25]

"Go ahead!"

Shimon ran up the mountain slope as fast as he could. But quite soon the slope became very steep. "I shouldn't turn my head back," he thought. "Not because of the danger of turning into a pillar of salt, but because of the dizziness at the edge of the abyss." Only five yards separated him from the chiseled stones that marked the path's edge. He was breathing heavily, and he lay down to rest. All of a sudden an avalanche of sand and stones started around him. Shimon lost hold and was carried to the edge of the rock. "The sand and the gravel started cascading downhill, and I moved with them." The avalanche pulled Shimon down to the edge of the deep, rocky abyss. "I suddenly realized that I would fall into the chasm, and that would be my end."

Feverishly he started digging with his bare hands in the sand, to get a hold, but the sand kept moving, and he kept sliding downward. Exhausted, he crawled toward a large stone and grabbed it—but the stone moved and started slipping, too. "My last hope evaporated," he wrote later. "All my energy was gone."

What should he do? He was spread-eagled on the moving sands, desperately trying to grab a stone and hold on to it. He felt "a sweet fatigue spreading in all my body and an urge to let myself fall asleep." Shimon felt ashamed for getting into that situation and wouldn't call for help, even though he knew that a wrong movement, or no movement at all, could result in his death.

All that time he could hear the merry group chattering at the foot of the rock; he heard Batya, the chief cook, serve lunch. But at that moment his luck turned. Shmaria Gutman hadn't forgotten that he had allowed the boy to climb the rock. As time passed, and he didn't hear from Shimon, Gutman started scrutinizing the slope with binoculars. He called three of the boys, and they climbed the mountain, searching for their comrade.

"Up on the mountain, time stood still," Shimon recalled. "Every minute lasted a year. I dug one hole after the other, and they were filled right away. Perhaps I should call for help? After all I really can die. But the shame stops me. What am I, a woman or a baby, and start screaming?"

Suddenly he heard, quite close, Gutman's voice. "Where can he be?" he asked.

Shimon couldn't keep quiet anymore. "Shmaria!" he tried to shout. His mouth was full of sand. He hollered again. "Shmaria!"

This time they heard him and swiftly moved toward him. In the words of one of them, the place was "very dangerous."[26] Shmaria and one of the boys clasped each other's hands, forming a "live ladder." They cautiously hung over the moving sands, grabbed Shimon, and pulled him up to safety. He was in a "most tragic state."[27] His saviors stared in amazement at the holes Shimon had tried to dig in the sand, and realized how desperate he was. But he was safe now. They carefully descended and joined their comrades. Shimon's friends assailed him with questions about his feelings "on the threshold of death."

Later, when the entire group had ascended again to the top of Masada by a different path, Shimon's terrible stress overcame him. His friends served him a generous drink of brandy and he lay down to rest. But the moment he shut his eyes, he sank into a nightmare. "The eyes are closing, and I see many black and red dots, swirling around. One big black dot is rolling and rolling. This is the moving stone." For the following two nights he lay down, tense, in a fetal position. He finally recovered but did not overcome a lasting fear of heights.[28]

Back in Geva, he narrated his harrowing adventure to the fascinated teenagers.[29] He also described his experience in an article for *Bamaaleb*, seasoning the critical moments with some amusing remarks, as was the custom of brave and strong men.

That was how Shimon, for the first time, was confronted with death.

CHAPTER 5.

FIERCE WINDS

A BREATHTAKING VIEW welcomed the Alumot settlers at the peak of Mount Poriya, and with it fierce winds, driving rains, and poverty.

The members of the Circle reached their destination in mid-1942. More than a hundred people, the founders of the Alumot group, lived in Poriya already. From the mountaintop the young settlers contemplated the splendid panorama at their feet. "Look at every direction," Shimon wrote. "Start at the west, where tall mountains are rising in the fog; this is Upper Galilee .... Steal a look at the mountains of Lower Galilee, gray and furrowed, and you'll see the village of Yavniel with its rows of houses, surrounded by silver-green olive groves; turn to the south—and you'll discover the Jordan Valley, a sea of greenery and clusters of white houses." He described the Jordan River as "silver bands, running and snaking around each other." He was awed by "the blue lake Kinneret, a crater amidst purple mountains, whose rich colors reflect in its calm depths." And finally, "In the north rises Mount Hermon, a giant among giants, cheerful yet enigmatic, a view that bestows on you a poetic spirit."[1]

The poetic spirit indeed descended upon Shimon, and he wrote several poems to the blue lake, Kinneret. (Lake Tiberias is the modern name of the biblical Sea of Galilee; in Hebrew it is called Kinneret, which means violin.) He called the lake "a gift from God, a chunk of crystal / antique and glowing / from your violin shaped waters a voice rises / an ancient tune, a psalm in blue . . ."[2]

The view from the mountain peaks was magnificent, but life in Poriya was hard and poor. Poriya was a temporary settlement until the Zionist institutions allotted the Alumot pioneers a permanent site for their kibbutz. The Alumot members were lodged in a cluster of black ruins. These were the "Goldman houses," a settlement built by American Jews who had tried to set down roots at Poriya twenty years before. Beside the ruins the pioneers set up a few tents and cabins. The black ruins were the source of dark forebodings. "All around us destruction reigns," Shimon wrote to Sonia. "Only a score of years ago some good Jews, full of enthusiasm, tried to build their homes here, dug foundations, erected strong and beautiful stone buildings; and in a mere twenty years some destructive hand succeeded in erasing even the shapes of human dwellings, smothering every plant and tree . . . . We walk between those living tombstones, and the unbridled fear gnaws at our hearts: Even a strong and glorious enterprise can fail."

The conclusion, though, was typical of Shimon, the little boy from Vishneva who got up again and again to continue the fight. "But we'll never yield to despair. Destruction stimulates, devastation encourages."[3]

The pioneers had to carry water to Poriya from a well at Yavniel, five miles away. There was one shower in all of Poriya, and the kibbutzniks would stand in line for a quick wash in a cubicle enclosed by rags instead of walls. After the shower the water would be used for laundry and other needs. In the winter the settlers would huddle by the kitchen, to benefit from the warmth of the stove, and perhaps get a cup of tea from a compassionate cook. The food was poor and the menu never changed: canned fish and powdered eggs.

For a long time there was no sanitary equipment at Poriya, and the settlers relieved themselves in the fields. Finally, the Jewish

Agency magnanimously sent the kibbutzniks a check for twenty pounds (equivalent to twenty British pounds) to build a real toilet!

On their arrival in Poriya, the "comrades" had to deposit their clothes in the communal warehouse; every Friday they would get a clean change of clothes that had to last a week. The living facilities were inadequate, and the married couples often had to share their room with another young man or woman, nicknamed a "primus." Poriya was whipped by powerful winds, "winds raising dust, winds tearing apart roofs, winds hundreds of horsepower strong."[4] During the first winter a terrible storm broke out that blew many roofs down the slopes and tossed them into the raging waters of the Kinneret. In summertime, hot and dry winds rose from the Jordan Valley and parched the young people, body and soul.

Work was also hard to find. Some of the men worked in nearby kibbutzim; the women ran rest homes in Safed and Tiberias. The Poriya children were known as the poorest in all the area, and the number of patches on their clothes broke all the records. Some said that "there was a curse hanging over Alumot."

Shimon worked in Kibbutz Ashdot Yaacov as well as in Poriya's cowshed and in the fields; he herded cows and sheep to pasture. The long days with the livestock in the scorching heat were hard, but gave him unlimited time to conceive essays and articles for the newspapers. He published book reviews, sent letters to editors, sparred with right-wing reporters, wrote columns under various pseudonyms. His ideological articles mostly focused on a theme very dear to his heart: the unification of the various Labor movements into one party.

Shimon was a major contributor to the Alumot newspaper *Bahar* ("On the Mountain"). He actually wrote almost the entire paper by himself; in order to fill its pages he even invented a female identity and wrote a column for kibbutz women, signing it "Kibbutz Girl."[5] The *Davar* newspaper discovered the talented kibbutz girl, and decided that finally a female writer had emerged who could express the feelings of the kibbutz women. *Davar* proudly reproduced some of Shimon's columns.

Shimon was elected secretary, then treasurer of the kibbutz, and was at the center of Alumot's social life. When Elhanan and Hannah got married, Shimon was the featured speaker at the wedding, and even wrote some verses urging the young couple to bring children into the world. Bringing many children into the Land of Israel was considered a valiant Zionist act and Ben-Gurion publicly encouraged it. Shimon preached to the newly-weds "to show courage and pioneering spirit" and raise "a new generation" on Poriya's heights. He turned to Elhanan: "Ben-Gurion's urgent call / defines the nation's goal / There is no time to waste / Run, hurry, sprint and haste!"[6]

Shimon also wrote skits and stage comedies and conceived some hoaxes and pranks; at least one of them cost him dearly. When an Alumot member, Micha Talmon, started losing his hair, Shimon revealed to him, in secret, that he had obtained some "miracle powder" that grew hair on arid scalps. Shimon and his friends brought the miracle powder to Micha with detailed instructions: how to spread the powder over the bald spot, how to pour water over it, how to knead the moist mixture. But the "miracle powder" was nothing but flour, and when Micha poured water over it, his head was covered with a gluey dough, rather hard to remove.

The kibbutz had a good laugh, and Shimon committed his feat to eternity in a comedy he produced on the kibbutz stage. "The Miracle Powder; or, The Latin Medicine" was the play's title. It opened with Micha—in the play Micha von Michmoch—complaining about his misfortune, and his difficulty in finding a girl because of his baldness. Another character, Joel von Munchausen—actually our friend Shimon—tempted Micha to buy the miracle powder. Von Michmoch yielded to temptation and massaged his head with the miracle substance; but when he discovered (in the sixth act) that his friends had made fun of him, he collapsed on stage. *Curtain.*

Perhaps that was funny, but Micha Talmon decided to avenge his humiliated pate. He found out that Shimon was attracted to a young woman named Rachel.[7] Micha and his cronies wrote a torrid love letter, signed it "Rachel," and dropped it in Shimon's mailbox. They watched in secret as Shimon found the letter, blushed, and hurried to write a passionate reply. They fished Shimon's letter from Rachel's mailbox before it reached her. The fiery correspondence continued for a while, and Micha's clique delighted in Shimon's romantic epistles. They finally revealed the truth to their quarry, and the embarrassed Shimon vanished from Alumot for quite a while. "They made me Alumot's laughingstock," sadly admitted the inventor of the miracle powder.[8]

SHIMON'S ACTIVITIES DIDN'T DISPEL the feeling of loneliness that pervaded him. He missed Sonia, who had started her army service as a "practical nurse" in a British field hospital but soon got into trouble. After a bloody battle in the desert, hundreds of wounded soldiers were brought to the field hospital. The certified nurses couldn't cope with the influx of patients, and asked the practical nurses to help them and give the wounded treatments that they had not been trained to proffer. Sonia was taking care of a wounded soldier when into the ward walked the matron, the head nurse. The Englishwoman saw Sonia by the soldier's bed, and exploded in fury. "What are you doing, you bloody native!" she yelled in English. On hearing the words "bloody native," Sonia lost her cool. She slapped the matron forcefully, throwing her against a nearby wall. The two women were court-martialed. The matron was transferred to another hospital while Sonia Gelman was made a truck driver. She spent the rest of the war driving military trucks on the Egypt-Lebanon route. The girl—all her acquaintances concurred—had character.

Shimon was very excited whenever he found a letter from Sonia in his mailbox. "To the strange Sonia," he once wrote to her, "your letter was a total surprise to me—perhaps because I so much hoped to receive one. For me it came at a moment of crisis—I had given up completely on getting a letter from you."[9] In another letter he admitted that "the hand writing this is trembling. Maybe you don't agree with this distribution of roles [Sonia in the army and Shimon at the kibbutz] but what can we do? There are things that drive people apart and there are things that can't be helped." He once sent her a small present. "Sister," he wrote, "please accept this small gift. Let the feelings of a friend walking behind the plough go along with you. You should know—our fields are your fields, and our home belongs to you and to those you're fighting for."[10] He promised her that Alumot would be her home after her discharge from the army.[11]

He was now one of Working Youth's national leaders and a member of the organization's steering committee. The appointments were political; Shimon was one of the three Mapai members on the committee. They were in the minority, most of their colleagues belonging to Faction B, whose split from the party seemed imminent. Because of his functions, Shimon spent many days away from home. As in Geva before, some Alumot members criticized his frequent absences.

This time, though, their criticism was justified. Shimon had outgrown the kibbutz boundaries. True, he still considered himself a shepherd, a kibbutznik plowing the land and building a new settlement. But now he dedicated most of his energy to political activity in Working Youth and in Mapai's Young Guard. He was a rising young leader, and Alumot had become too small for him.

He was strangely attracted by the Negev, the desert in the south of the country that was in many ways terra incognita. In January 1945, Shimon organized a daring Working Youth expedition to the south, all the way down to biblical Eilat. With Shmaria Gutman, the Masada explorer, and Dr. Mendelson, a renowned zoologist, he led a group of fourteen young men from Working Youth and the Palmach. David Ben-Gurion and the Palmach commander, Yitzhak Sadeh, provided the budget for the expedition—three hundred pounds. For Ben-Gurion, who secretly dreamed of the Negev's conquest, the expedition's main goal was drawing a map of the desert and getting familiar with its paths and roads. Shimon had three goals: to penetrate into an unknown region, as big as half of Palestine; to check out the possibility of smuggling Jewish immigrants into Palestine via Sinai and the Negev; and, as he boyishly admitted, "to ride camels, the only animals that the desert still treats fondly."[12]

Riding on twelve camels, the group spent twenty-two days in the desert. They passed through the former Nabatean provinces and were amazed by the remains of an ancient agriculture based on the exploitation of every raindrop; they went along dry wadis; descended into steep canyons; toured the Ramon Crater; discovered hidden waterfalls inside rock clusters; rested in the shade of wild oaks, acacias, and palms; met desert animals; and even saw mirages. The days were scorching, but at night Shimon shivered in his sleeping bag. From a Bedouin he met on the road he learned a proverb: "The desert is like a bad wife—hot during the day and cold at night."[13]

Shimon described, with intense emotion, the magnificent landscapes the group saw on its way: "Bluish-red mountains, tall and steep and lofty on both sides of the wadi. The wadi itself is carpeted with pristine light-colored sand; from its depths emerge mountains as big as Mount Tabor. Now try to visualize all these colors: all around bluish-red mountains; beneath—a light, dry river-bed; and above it—mountains as black as tar."[14]

But beside the excitement from the beauty of the desert, Shimon didn't stop calculating how much land could be settled and cultivated, how much water could be stored in the dam system, and how to develop a flourishing agriculture in the area. He was convinced that the Jews who had once made the Negev green could do it again. Even at the end of the trip, when they reached Aqaba, on the Red Sea, Shimon visualized what would happen in the future. "The Arabs assured us, over and over again, that Aqaba is a huge city. Finally it turned out that it is a wretched village with mud houses and a desolate beach. On the beach we can build a big port, develop agriculture, industry etc. In a very short period, one or two years, we can erect on this beach a big city, much larger than Aqaba."[15] His prophecy would come true with the building of Eilat.

While riding his camel in the Negev wastelands, Shimon couldn't refrain from criticizing the Arabs. "They say that the Arabs are the sons of the desert. This is not true. The Arabs are the fathers of the desert. For all that region was once a fertile and developed agricultural country." He also spoke with contempt of the Bedouin they met on their way: "A great disappointment in our voyage was to meet 'the noble race'—the Bedouin. We actually saw in front of us very degenerate, very lazy, very dirty people, great cheats. Our disappointment had no limits. It is very painful to describe the Bedouin laziness. At summertime they die of dryness and thirst. The [British] government therefore dug eight wells for them, but four of them are blocked with sand already. In a half-day's work they can be cleaned, but 'the noble race' is lazy. This is not for them."[16]

During the trip the camels suddenly stopped in front of a rock on which perched a huge bird; its wingspan reached almost eight feet. This was a *peres*, a bearded vulture. The *peres* was even more dangerous than the eagle, Dr. Mendelson explained, for it often attacked children. The description was not pleasant, but Shimon liked the big bird's name. He dutifully noted the details, not knowing that at this very moment the desert had presented him with his Hebrew name.

The journey was interrupted shortly before its conclusion. Barely a few miles north of Eilat the group ran into a patrol of the British authorities—four Arabs under the orders of a British officer. They arrested the group, because it had entered a region "out of bounds for Jews." The squad took its prisoners to Eilat. The youngsters were deeply offended. "Here we are, four Arabs and fourteen Jews," Shimon grumbled, "and all the Arabs are legal."[17]

The team was brought back to Beersheba and interrogated. Shimon, the journey's organizer, and Dr. Mendelson, the zoologist, were the main suspects. "Why did you go to Aqaba?" a detective asked Shimon.

"We haven't been there for two thousand years," Shimon replied, "and we wanted to find out what was new."[18]

After nightfall he bribed his Arab guards, slipped out of jail, and traveled to Tel Aviv, where he met with Ben-Gurion and briefed him about the trip and the arrests.[19] He then returned to Beersheba and the following day was put on trial with his friends. Most of the young men got off with small fines, but Dr. Mendelson was sentenced to a fine of twelve Palestine pounds[20] and Shimon was sentenced to a fine and two weeks in jail. Afterward, back in Tel Aviv, he handed Ben-Gurion an album of photographs, a set of maps, and a detailed account of the expedition.

Davar proudly reported: "This is the first time that a group of young Jews, some of them members of Working Youth, toured the far regions of the Negev."[21]

IN THE SPRING OF 1945, Sonia Gelman was discharged from the British Army and joined Kibbutz Alumot. She and Shimon revived their relationship and their deep love became the talk of the kibbutz. Shimon wasn't alone anymore, and Sonia's return made him happy. On May 1, 1945, they were married. The wedding party was held at Ben-Shemen. Shimon's father, Getzel Persky, hadn't returned to Palestine yet. Rumor had it that he had been captured by the Germans but had survived the war; allegedly he was in England after being released from a prisoner-of-war camp.

For the wedding Shimon wanted to wear formal clothes for the first time in his life. His old khaki pants didn't fit the occasion, so the kibbutz storekeeper lent him the only pair of "formal pants" that the men of the kibbutz would wear, each in his turn, for important occasions. This was a pair of flannels that were a few sizes shorter than the groom's legs. Shimon didn't have a decent jacket, either, and spent most of the night before the wedding dying his khaki battle dress with black shoe polish. Finally the young man stood beside his radiant bride in pants that barely reached his ankles and a jacket whose black color dried up and peeled as the ceremony approached.[22] Sonia was wearing a white dress, and flowers were woven into her hair. The intoxicating scent of oranges in flower rose from the orchards as a cool spring evening settled on the Lod Valley. The wedding canopy was erected by the swimming pool, the rabbi spoke his words, and Shimon and Sonia became husband and wife.

CHAPTER 6.

HERBS AND LIZARDS

WHILE THE WILD WINDS chased Shimon and his comrades at Poriya's heights, other winds raged across the sea, in Greece's lofty mountains. The sun setting over Mount Olympus illuminated two figures trudging on a goat path. The first was a Greek priest, in black cassock and pipe hat. Behind him limped an emaciated, black-haired man, wearing frayed clothes and leaning on a stick. The two men reached a decrepit hut nestled in the shadow of an abandoned church. The priest handed his companion a bag full of bread and corncobs. "Stay here," he said. "Don't go away. I'll be in touch." He disappeared down the mountain slope.

The black-haired man gratefully hugged the food bag. He hadn't tasted bread for a long time. Since his escape from the Germans, he had eaten mostly herbs and lizards, and was lucky enough to taste real food only when pitied by priests or peasants. Finally, he had managed to join a resistance unit that fought the German occupiers. The Greek freedom fighters took good care of him. They knew that if the Germans captured him, they would shoot him like a dog. They passed the escaped soldier from one region to another. Now they had handed him over to the priest, who was to lead him to another group of British soldiers, which the resistance intended to smuggle into neutral Turkey.

At nightfall, the black-haired man entered the hut and fell

asleep on the floor. But strange noises woke him up. He opened his eyes and burst into terrified screams; he was surrounded by hundreds of rats, which assailed him from all over. Their red eyes shone eerily in the dark. Seized by panic, he threw away the bag of food and tried to escape. In the absolute darkness he couldn't find his way out. For a long while—it seemed to him an eternity—he ran around, bumping into the walls, as the swarms of rats attacked him relentlessly. He felt that if he stumbled and fell, they would overwhelm him and devour him alive. He finally managed to get out of the house, and collapsed. He had never experienced such horror. That night, he slept no more.

In the morning, the priest arrived, but when he saw him, he fell on his knees and crossed himself.

"What happened?" the fugitive asked.

"You walked in black, you came out white," the priest stuttered, then whispered something about "God's hand."

Only when he looked in a mirror, several days later, did the fugitive realize what had happened to him on Mount Olympus.

The coal-black hair of Getzel Persky had become white overnight.[1]

AFTER ENLISTING IN the sappers, Persky was sent to the Western Desert, then to Greece, where he was taken prisoner. Persky jumped off the train that was carrying him, along with other prisoners of war, to Germany. There followed months of wandering throughout Greece and hiding with the freedom fighters. After the night of the rats, the priest passed him to another resistance unit, and finally he joined a group of British and Australian fugitives. At night, the little group sailed on a fishing boat to Turkey.

At first light, however, the boat was spotted by German aircraft that dived toward it, mercilessly strafing the soldiers on board. An Australian boy sitting next to Persky was killed right away. German motorboats surrounded the fugitives' vessel; there was no escape. An Australian military chaplain rolled the body of the slain soldier into the sea and handed his dog tags to Persky. He apparently knew what fate awaited the Palestinian soldier if the Germans found out he was Jewish.

Persky was captured again by the Germans and put aboard another train heading to Germany. Persky didn't wait long; with a New Zealander he again jumped from the train. The two were captured immediately and the train commander ordered a firing squad to shoot them in front of the other captives. Persky stared into the rifle barrels trained on him and realized that his end had come. But at the last moment a chaplain stepped forth. He was Australian as well. An execution without proper procedure, he said to the German officer, was contrary to the Geneva Convention on the rights of POWs. The fugitives should stand trial, according to the convention. If the officer didn't comply with the rules, the chaplain threatened, he would stand between the two fugitives and the firing squad. "You'll have to kill me, too," he concluded.

The officer was furious but, having no choice, he dismissed the firing squad. Persky's life was saved. When the train arrived at its destination, the Lamsdorf camp, he was court-martialed and sentenced to a long term in solitary.

Lamsdorf—Stalag XVIII-B—was a huge POW camp, populated with thousands of inmates. The most impressive character Persky met there was a British prisoner, Sergeant Charlie Coward.

Coward was a man of unusual courage and resources. He was absolutely devoted to his goals: sabotaging the German war effort and organizing escapes from the camp. He escaped himself a few times and was captured, but kept organizing subsequent escapes with unfaltering enthusiasm. Coward and Persky dug tunnels, forged ID papers, sewed civilian clothes out of rags, and several times escaped together. Every time they assumed a different identity: once they were Bulgarian workers on leave, another time they were French or even German. They were caught over and over again and brought back to the camp where they had to face humiliations, beatings, and heavy punishments. Their escapes often failed because of the heavy Cockney accent of

Charlie Coward. Persky tried, in vain, to convince him not to open his mouth at the SS checkpoints. Persky suggested that Charlie play dumb; he knew German and could answer for both of them. But once, when they were close to the Swiss border, Charlie opened his mouth. They were immediately arrested, beaten, and sent back to their camp.

The Lamsdorf Stalag commander, exasperated by Coward's activities, decided to execute the troublemaker. Persky requested a meeting with the commander. We know you're a corrupt man, the Palestinian said. We know that the prisoners are bribing you with cigarettes, chocolate, and delicacies they receive in the Red Cross packages. We have written a detailed report of the favors you're trading for bribes. If you ever hurt Charlie Coward, we'll send the report to your superiors.

Persky was walking a tightrope, and could have paid with his life. But the German officer recoiled before the threat, and Coward's life was saved.

Shortly after, Coward conceived an idea that would bring him immortal glory. One of the temporary camps where the Lamsdorf prisoners were sent to work was close to the Auschwitz concentration camp. Coward, Persky, and their comrades had heard about the horrors taking place in the camp and had witnessed the marches of living skeletons near Birkenau. Coward had a crazy idea. He had seen Jewish prisoners marching to work from Birkenau; at night, on their return, some of them would collapse out of exhaustion; the German rearguard soldiers shot them dead where they lay.

Coward and his friends offered to buy the dead bodies from the Germans in exchange for cigarettes and chocolate from the Red Cross packages. The Germans thought they were crazy, but agreed. Coward then contacted the leaders of the Jewish inmates whose forced-labor squads often worked close to the POWs; they agreed that every night, on their way back to the camp, three or four men would fall by the road, feigning exhaustion, and Coward and his friends would put in their place the dead bodies they had "bought" during the day, allowing the Jewish prisoners to escape. In a few months, Coward's team succeeded in saving about four hundred Jewish prisoners. In Auschwitz a legend spread about a noble man who was saving lives. The Jews called Charlie Coward the "Count of Auschwitz."

Persky kept escaping till the war ended. When the American Army approached the camp, he jumped on the horse cart of a local peasant, broke through the German lines, and galloped toward General Patton's position, shouting, "I am a British soldier!" The Americans opened fire on the horse cart, but Persky was unharmed. He was interrogated for a long time by several American officers. They finally sent him to England, where he was interrogated again and then decorated. A telegram informed his family that he was alive. He returned to Palestine a few months later, having just missed Shimon's wedding. Getzel didn't tell anybody about his adventures. To his sons he only described his escape in Greece, in order to explain why his hair had turned white.

In the meantime, a new book came out in England—*The Password Is Courage*, written by John Castle. It described the adventures of Charlie Coward. The book became a bestseller and inspired a movie; Dirk Bogarde played the role of Charlie Coward. In the book, Coward and Castle changed the names of Charlie's comrades—and the Palestinian Persky became the "Pole Pilski."

In 1958, Charlie Coward was invited to Israel as a gesture of appreciation for his valiant actions in Auschwitz-Birkenau. Shimon, then director general of the defense ministry, got a phone call from the officials charged with Coward's visit. Their guest, the officials said, claimed to know somebody named Persky. Perhaps he knew who that person might be? Shimon called Gigi, who phoned their father.

Getzel Persky was stunned. "Charlie Coward is in Israel?" He brought Coward to his home. Their meeting was very emotional. They spent a night in Persky's apartment eating, drinking, and arguing about their failed escapes. In the early morning, Gigi went to visit his father. In front of the house he saw hundreds of people. "What happened?" Gigi asked one of them.

"Don't you know? The Count of Auschwitz is here, in the house across the street!"

Thus, thanks to the "Count of Auschwitz," Gigi and Shimon heard about their father's courageous deeds.

Getzel Persky told Shimon that his friend Charlie was in a bad financial position. He had sold all the rights to the book for 250 British pounds, and the rights to the film for another fifty. "My dear wife helped me dispose of that quickly enough," Charlie chuckled.[2]

Charlie worked now as a night watchman in England, and barely survived on a low army pension. Shimon immediately called a British friend, Chaim Morrison, who gave Charlie a job in one of his companies.

When Shimon learned the story of his father's heroic acts in Greece and Germany, he felt very proud. He wrote several articles about his father, as well as chapters in some of his books.[3]

THAT DAY IN 1945, the telegram about Getzel Persky's return reached his family barely a few hours before his arrival. Shimon and Sonia jumped on the old Triumph and rushed to the Lod railway station. Shimon watched, deeply moved, as the tall and handsome soldier came off the train. He hadn't seen him for almost five years, and a feeling of strangeness permeated his soul. "I feel as if I have a new father," he said to Sonia.[4]

The couple had just returned from their improvised honeymoon. "Our 'honeymoon' was enchantingly beautiful," Shimon wrote. "We spent it on the bank of the Jordan River, at Bitaniya. Our kibbutz comrades rigged up a shaded bower between two towering eucalyptuses, and this became our love nest for a week. Each morning, we awoke to the birds' singing .... We would climb down to bathe in the limpid river, and then tear off on my faithful old Triumph to some beautiful spot in Upper Galilee or down the Jordan Valley."[5]

At the kibbutz, Sonia and Shimon finally moved into their own room, and as a married couple they also received their "primus"—a girl named Shulamit. Years later, known as Shulamit Aloni, she became a cabinet minister and the leader of the Meretz Party.[6]

Sonia's new job was at night, taking care of the kibbutz children, who slept in several children's homes. The children's homes were far apart from from one another; at night the place was deserted, and Sonia was afraid of making the rounds by herself. Shimon came to the rescue. At night he would spread a blanket beside his wife's bed in one of the children's homes and sleep beside her. Every half hour throughout the night Sonia would wake him up and they would do the rounds together. This marital devotion stirred both jealousy and wonder among the Alumot women.[7]

Sonia's relationship with Alumot, however, started out on the wrong foot. She saw that Shimon had a bed and a cupboard. "Why don't I have a bed and a cupboard, too?" she asked the kibbutz secretary.

"Where did you sleep till now?"

"In my bed, at home."

"So bring your bed from home."

Sonia didn't like the answer. "I'll go to work in the city," she said. "I'll buy myself a bed and a cupboard and whatever else I need, and I'll bring them to the kibbutz."

Sonia and Shimon moved for a while to the town of Givataim, a suburb of Tel Aviv. He kept working at Working Youth and she became a secretary at the Mapai offices. She stuck to her decision: only a year later, when she was already pregnant, did she come back to Alumot; she brought her own bed and cupboard.

CHAPTER 7.

THE FIFTH CONGRESS

THE FIFTH CONGRESS of Working Youth opened in Tel Aviv on September 28, 1945. Two hundred and fifty-one teenagers from ninety-six branches of the organization as well as youth groups, kibbutzim, training camps, and twenty-one factories occupied the Mugrabi Theater's seats. A sign posted over the stage extolled "Zionist Socialism." The hall trembled at the sound of enthusiastic singing and cheering; scores of flag bearers ascended to the stage, carrying blue-and-white flags, Working Youth standards, and red banners.

The pompous slogans and the festive ambiance, however, couldn't dispel the feeling of gloom hovering over the convention. The Mapai Party, the patron of Working Youth, had split the previous year and Faction B, led by Yitzhak Tabenkin, had seceded. In their youth, Ben-Gurion and Tabenkin had held similar views. Both were Zionists and socialists, and both dreamed of a Greater Israel. But as time went by, Ben-Gurion abandoned his extreme positions and moved toward the center, while Tabenkin fanatically stuck to his original views. Ben-Gurion and Berl Katzenelson harshly criticized Tabenkin's exalted worship of Stalin and the Soviet Union. Ben-Gurion, now the chairman of the Jewish Agency, also learned the art of compromise. He understood that there would be no Jewish state without the partition of Palestine, while Tabenkin rejected any territorial compromise with the Arabs. As World War II broke out, both Ben-Gurion and Tabenkin urged their supporters to enlist; Ben-Gurion, though, believed that the Palestinian Jews should join the Jewish Brigade of the British Army, while Tabenkin's people preferred to join the Palmach, which operated inside Palestine.

During the war, Ben-Gurion reached the conclusion that the Zionist movement should define its goals. In May 1942, at a conference held at the Biltmore Hotel in New York, Ben-Gurion presented his program, declaring that "Palestine shall be established as a Jewish Commonwealth integrated in the structure of the new democratic world." The goal was stated—the creation of a Jewish state.

The Biltmore Program was adopted by the great majority of those in the Zionist movement. But Tabenkin and his Faction B abstained at the crucial vote. Tabenkin rejected Ben-Gurion's idea of a Jewish state, fearing it would lead to the partition of Palestine. "Settling the land is more important than a state," he proclaimed. Tabenkin clung to a vague, rather ludicrous idea about establishing an international mandate in Palestine that would encourage Jewish immigration and settlement. Tabenkin's overwhelming support of pro-Soviet socialism, oddly blended with visions of a Greater Israel, resulted in a befuddled and contradictory political concept.

Faction B left Mapai and turned into a new party called Ahdut Ha'avoda ("Unity of Labor"). That was a heavy blow to Ben-Gurion and Katzenelson. When he left Mapai, Tabenkin took with him the activist wing of the kibbutz movement, many of the party supporters in the cities, and the best Haganah members, organized in the Palmach.

Berl Katzenelson died suddenly in August 1944. Shimon was deeply shaken by Katzenelson's death. True, he admired Ben-Gurion, but it was Katzenelson's teaching that had shaped his ideas.

The split in Mapai triggered a crisis in Working Youth, too, as most of its leaders and instructors belonged to Faction B.[1] The

1945 Working Youth convention was the first since the Mapai split, and it soon turned into a battlefield between the two warring parties. The Labor movement feared that the split in Mapai would be followed by a split in Working Youth as well. Ahdut Ha'avoda was determined to preserve its predominant influence in the youth movement, which numbered thirteen thousand youngsters. Ahdut Ha'avoda's leaders considered it the main reserve of their party. Mapai's leaders, on the other hand, felt that they had neglected Working Youth, and that the important movement had slipped away from their control.

But nobody expected the dramatic confrontation that exploded at the convention's opening.

The first item on the agenda for Saturday, September 29, was the election of the steering committee. Binyamin Hachlili, Working Youth's secretary general, and an Ahdut Ha'avoda supporter, read a list of nine names. As usual, the list was to be approved by a unanimous vote.

Suddenly Shimon got on his feet. He, too, he announced, had prepared a list of nine names, and he asked to have it put to the vote as well.

Shimon's initiative had the effect of a thunderbolt. The movement leaders stared with amazement at the young man in khaki pants and blue shirt, his round face crowned with a shock of unruly hair. Never before had anybody strayed from the well-planned ritual. How did this insolent young man dare challenge the movement's leadership?

A stormy debate ensued, with some of Ahdut Ha'avoda's leaders furiously criticizing Shimon's move. Others tried to convince him to withdraw his motion. But he stood his ground. "We are a democratic movement," he said. "It is my right to put my own list to the vote."[2]

Finally it was decided to put both lists to the vote, one against the other.

Shimon murmured to his friend Nachman Raz, "I think we've got a chance."[3]

He had been secretly planning that move for a long time.

SINCE THE SPLIT in Mapai, Shimon had had the feeling that Working Youth was not a democratic movement any longer, but was becoming a tool in the hands of Ahdut Ha'avoda. The two other Mapai supporters in the Working Youth bureau, Amos Degani and Nachman Raz, also felt isolated and unwanted. In many meetings Amos heard the Ahdut Ha'avoda supporters speak of "father Stalin," "the world of tomorrow," and "the legacy of the Soviet Revolution." He regarded that pro-Soviet propaganda as a terrible danger to the Jewish youth. He admired Shimon, who fought against that policy in meetings, debates, and press articles. "Shimon didn't speak like a party activist," Amos said, "but like a man who carries a great idea in his heart. I was proud, with my friend Nachman, to hold Shimon's mantle. He had a great ambition: to turn Working Youth around. Why should Ahdut Ha'avoda, which, after all, was a minority in the Labor movement, control Working Youth?"[4]

Mapai's officials had the same ambition, but they had thrown in the towel and accepted defeat. And into that void stepped Shimon Persky. As the congress approached, he went on the offensive. He rode his Triumph from one kibbutz to another and visited faraway villages and factories that employed young people. Everywhere he went, he tried to convince the local Working Youth members to elect his candidates as delegates to the convention. He met with scores of elected delegates and spent nights debating with Working Youth activists.[5]

At the congress's opening night, Shimon's people stood close to the registration desk, preparing detailed lists of the delegates and which way they intended to vote. Shimon's assistants spoke to each of their supporters and instructed them how to vote. Shimon himself filled his notebooks with lists of delegates that he arranged in neat columns—Yes, No, Undecided.

And on that Saturday, September 29, when the tumult settled down, the delegates were asked to choose between the two lists:

"Binyamin's list," where the Ahdut Ha'avoda supporters had a majority, and "Shimon's list."

The votes were counted—and Shimon's won, by seven votes.

In the steering committee, Shimon's supporters were in the majority. "That was a dramatic battle—and we won!" rejoiced Saul Bauman, a delegate.[6] "We were stupefied," admitted Amnon Magen, an Ahdut Ha'avoda supporter.[7]

The vote had the effect of an earthquake. For the first time, a member of the youth organization had confronted the establishment—and had won.

In the subsequent votes Shimon's majority held. At the end of the congress, it was agreed that Working Youth would henceforth be governed by two general secretaries—Binyamin and Shimon. Shortly afterward, because of Shimon's relentless efforts, Mapai's influence in Working Youth became predominant, and the youth organization came under its full control.

Shimon was the great winner at the Fifth Congress. Ahdut Ha'avoda's leaders reacted with a surge of anger and deep hatred toward Shimon Persky, "who stole Working Youth from them."[8] There was hardly an insult they didn't hurl at him, hardly an accusation of cheating and deceiving that they didn't throw in his face. "Ahdut Ha'avoda never forgot it nor forgave it," Shimon sadly wrote. "Its members attributed to me powers I never had, and regarded everything I did or said with suspicion."[9] The loathing toward the young man who took Working Youth away passed from generation to generation of Ahdut Ha'avoda leaders and activists, and sixty years later it still stirs the fury of many party veterans.

"At the convention I saw Shimon Peres with his relentless intrigues," said an Ahdut Ha'avoda member who was sixteen years old during the convention.[10] Yitzhak Nishri, a leader of Working Youth, expressed the opposite view: "The Mapai members of Working Youth saved the movement from moving to the extreme left."[11]

FOR MAPAI, SHIMON was the hero of the day. His talents of

leadership and meticulous planning impressed the party leaders. They asked Kibbutz Alumot to release Shimon from his duties at home, so that he could dedicate himself to his functions as secretary general of Working Youth.[12] The members of Alumot agreed, though grudgingly.

In December 1946, Shimon boarded a passenger ship in Haifa and traveled abroad for the first time in his life. He was sent by Ben-Gurion as observer to the twenty-second Zionist Congress in Basel. Aboard the ship, Shimon had long talks with another young man who was on his way to the congress—Moshe Dayan, who was to play an important role in his life. At thirty-one, Dayan was eight years older than Shimon. In Basel they laid the foundations of a political alliance bound to last for more than thirty years.

The ship docked in Genoa, and Shimon took a train to Basel. He carried a press card as a correspondent for Mapai's newspapers. He signed some of his articles "Young Father," a pseudonym he had assumed that summer, when his daughter Zvia (Tziki) was born in Tiberias's Scottish Hospital.

For Shimon, Basel was both intriguing and inspiring. Forty-nine years before, in that serene Swiss city, Theodor Herzl had convened the First Zionist Congress. The casino building, the Rhine River, the Three Kings Hotel, the narrow, tortuous streets of the Old City—all these fired up Shimon's imagination. Here, in 1897, Herzl had shared with the congress his dream of creating a Jewish state in the Land of Israel. Today, the twenty-second congress had to decide how to make this dream a reality.

During the day, Shimon followed the congress debates. At night, he would visit the cafés and cabarets in the Old City. He was deeply impressed by the Swiss democracy and order—and by the beauty and the voice of a young singer at the Dove Coop nightclub.[13]

The opening session of the congress was lavish and elegant. Shimon disliked the fashionable suits and tails of some delegates, and was upset by the expensive jewelry and the glittering diamonds of the women at the visitors' balcony.[14] But in the back rows of the gallery he discovered the real diamonds—freedom fighters from Poland's forests; Palestinian men and women who had parachuted into occupied Europe to fight the Nazis; aliya activists, secretive organizers of illegal immigration to Palestine. He was full of admiration for these young people. "These are your real delegates, Israel!" he wrote in awe.[15]

He followed the fiery confrontation between the militant David Ben-Gurion and the moderate president of the Zionist movement, Dr. Chaim Weizmann, who wanted to put an end to the struggle against the British. Ben-Gurion held the opposite view: this was the moment, he believed, to intensify the struggle and speed the process leading to Jewish independence.

Ben-Gurion finally won, and Shimon triumphantly described his victory in his articles. He also wrote an enthusiastic profile of Golda Meir, Ben-Gurion's devout supporter, whom he sent to brief the world press. Shimon described her appearance before the media. "The foreign reporters remarked that for the first time a woman served as 'foreign minister,' and what a minister! Nobody had any doubt that Golda really deserved this position. Her integrity, her arguments and her simple and convincing way of explaining the most complicated political matters stirred emotion and admiration in everybody. Still there was one person who doubted that she was the right person for that job—Golda herself. I witnessed her hesitations and her serious approach to her functions. And I was gratified in my heart for the good qualities of our comrades fulfilling responsible functions. Not hollow careerism—but a real concern for our cause; not lofty vanity—but poised modesty. This is leadership that has emerged from the people."[16]

But soon after this ode to Golda, Shimon learned that she could be harsh and cruel. In one of his articles Shimon criticized a brilliant Zionist leader, Dr. Moshe Sneh, and accused him of inconsistency and of changing his ideas. Golda angrily attacked Shimon. "Golda cornered me and demanded how I dared to write such things . . . . This was the first time—though hardly the last—that Golda directed her ire at me. Her harsh words left a bitter taste in my mouth."[17]

As it turned out, Shimon was right in his views of Sneh, who kept sliding from one position to another, finally landing in the Communist Party and losing the respect of his peers.

AFTER THE CONGRESS was over, Shimon spent a few days in Paris. He visited the Louvre Museum and was enthralled by the vestiges of the ancient Egyptian, Greek, and Roman cultures. "I must admit," he wrote, "that when I stand in front of the Louvre, when I walk its hallways and see the glorious remains of many nations, the huge statues, the majestic buildings and the heroic feats engraved in their stones—I am overwhelmed by a feeling of double jealousy, the jealousy of the past and the jealousy of the present. What Jewish monumental building do we have in Palestine? Not an opera like the Parisian opera, not a Pantheon, not a Louvre, not even one room of the Louvre. Where are the remains of our history? In foreign lands, in alien tombs."

But his feelings changed completely when he saw the Roman eagle in the Louvre's Roman section. "At an elevated stand one can see, spread-winged and open-mouthed, the Roman eagle that symbolizes the past of Great Rome, and it is still stalking its prey. But those who see it are no more awed by its alertness, nor by its open beak." Shimon mused about the fall of the Roman Empire, symbolized by the broken statues surrounding the formidable eagle. "Here I understood the greatness of the Jewish room that *is not* in the Louvre. A room that encompasses the entire world, because it's alive and vibrant, it is the only national memory which still belongs to the present and not only to History—the Bible!"[18]

At the end of January 1947, Shimon returned to Palestine. A short time later, Kibbutz Alumot moved to its permanent site on a neighboring hill. After the building of the members' homes, the dining room, the children's home, and, of course, the showers, a merry celebration took place. The kibbutzniks arrived at their new home and the feast was memorable—songs, dances, and endless speeches by the movement's dignitaries. Shimon, in khaki pants and a white shirt, stood proudly on the running board of a truck carrying the kibbutz children to their new home.

Shimon was not to enjoy his new home at Alumot for long. In early May 1947, Joseph Izraeli, the deputy commander of the Haganah, came to Alumot. He asked the kibbutz to release Shimon for a new assignment at the Haganah headquarters in Tel Aviv.

Israel's War of Independence was about to begin.

CHAPTER 8.

A NEW WORLD

WHEN THE TWENTY-FOUR-YEAR-OLD Shimon entered the Haganah headquarters in Tel Aviv, he couldn't have imagined that the following months would revolutionize his life.

So far he had been a party activist and a leader of Working Youth. He used to hurry from one meeting to another, carrying a case brimming with papers, and took part in the tedious deliberations of the Mapai Central Committee. In the kibbutz he was rarely seen. His path seem paved: he was going to become another politician like those around him.

All of a sudden, he was catapulted into the world of security affairs. With his friend Elhanan Yishai and a few other promising young men, he joined the staff of Haganah headquarters, in a red-painted house on HaYarkon Street in Tel Aviv. David Ben-Gurion's office was also located in the "Red House." Shimon's direct superior was Levi Eshkol, a close aide to Ben-Gurion.

At first, Shimon dealt with manpower and the secret arms industry. Not for long, though. In the desultory atmosphere prevailing at Haganah headquarters, and later in the IDF (Israel Defense Forces) General Staff, Shimon was increasingly charged with random assignments as they arose.

Soon after his arrival, the head of the Haganah acquisitions delegation in the United States, Teddy Kollek, came for a visit. Kollek bitterly complained about the disorder at headquarters and demanded that a reliable man be put in charge of arms purchases in America.

Eshkol summoned Shimon Persky.

"Jungermann"—"young man" in Yiddish—"what are you handling here?"

"Manpower," Shimon replied.

"Do you know English?"

"No."

"Have you been to America?"

"No."

"You're the man I need," Eshkol announced with undisguised satisfaction.

"What are you doing?" Teddy Kollek was flabbergasted. "This guy has no experience whatsoever!"

"Don't worry," Eshkol reassured him, "he'll do the job better than anyone."[1]

In the Red House, Shimon was to find the love of his life: building Israel's military might.

Shimon was already burning the midnight oil in November 1947, when the United Nations voted to divide Palestine into two states, Jewish and Arab. The State of Israel was created on May 14, 1948, when the British Army left Palestine. But the Arabs of Palestine and the neighboring Arab states rejected the U.N. resolution and attacked the newborn country.

Shimon's activity was funneled into one main endeavor: buying weapons for the Israeli Army all over the world. Because of the embargo that many nations imposed on the Jewish state, the Israeli envoys had to use unorthodox methods, ruses, and elaborate ploys. Using false identities and forged passports in the names of unsuspecting South American or African states, Ben-Gurion's young men bought huge quantities of weapons, mostly from World War II surplus supplies. Czechoslovakia became one of the few countries that agreed to sell arms to Israel. The weapons were shipped in unregistered ships or unmarked aircraft.[2]

"I entered a new world," Shimon wrote, "a world of mysterious missions and anonymous agents, a world peopled by superb professionals and also by a sprinkle of mavericks and dreamers who would file dramatic reports that reflected their fantasies rather than the complex realities."[3]

Shimon threw himself into arms acquisition with boundless energy. He discovered that he had the power to work inexhaustibly day and night, especially with the people in the field who gradually came to trust him.[4] Another talent was his capacity to focus on an issue and study it in depth until he became all but an expert. The young man who until a few weeks before was dealing with Working Youth branches and summer camps, or listening to the Mapai elders in endless party meetings, was now dashing off coded letters and cables to Europe and America, dealing with buying rifles and mortars, aircraft and warships, guns and ammunition. From these beginnings Shimon Persky, more than any other figure in the State of Israel, would grow into the man known as "Mr. Security." Appropriately, perhaps, it was also at this time that he formally changed his name, and henceforth all his identity papers carried the name "Shimon Peres."

He was very proud of working with Ben-Gurion. For a while his tiny office was separated from Ben-Gurion's by only a thin plywood partition. Under the sheet of glass covering his desk, he had slipped a note in Ben-Gurion's handwriting: "Shimon, don't forget to turn off the lights!"[5]

Ben-Gurion hadn't forgotten Peres's journey to the wild Negev, three years before. He charged him and his friends Elhanan and Arthur Ben-Nathan with planning an operation to capture Eilat. Peres drew up a detailed plan for blazing a trail through the Negev and holding the road for a month, till the operation was completed. He didn't deal, of course, with the military operation, which Ben-Gurion assigned to Yitzhak Sadeh.[6]

Peres crafted the plan despite the refusal of the IDF General Staff to cooperate with the three civilians.[7] He filled Kibbutz Alumot notepads with the names of outposts, forward and main bases, sketches of lookout towers, numbers of soldiers, lists of armored cars, lanterns, gasoline, boats—even the cost of cigarettes and toothpaste for the troops. The design was detailed down to the last man, tent, and cent. After he completed it, on January 27, 1948, he submitted it to Ben-Gurion.[8] The "Old Man" pronounced Peres an expert on the problems of the Negev and continued seeking his advice on preparing for the conquest of Eilat.

SHIMON PERES REACHED the highest of his wartime assignments when he was appointed assistant defense secretary for navy affairs. This promotion came to him as a surprise.

It turned out that the navy commander, Paul Shulman, and the former assistant secretary, Gershon Zak, had made quite a few mistakes and Ben-Gurion decided to replace them. Peres was appointed in Gershon Zak's place and his close friend Colonel Munia Mardor became the navy commander.[9] Peres received Zak's big American car with its stylish navy pennant, and a driver would take him to Navy headquarters on Stella Maris hill in Haifa, or to the defense ministry in Tel Aviv. "So there I was," Peres wrote, "a twenty-six-year-old kibbutznik from Alumot, running complex defense programs and then, on top of everything, becoming the acting Secretary of the Navy. My naval experience consisted of a moderate proficiency at breast-stroke and one childhood attempt to build a raft and launch it off the coast of Tel Aviv."[10]

Peres and Mardor soon put the navy back on track. They bought frigates and torpedo boats and stocked the navy warehouses with fine equipment. They reorganized the Navy General Staff, and even obtained silver-plated rank insignia for its officers, an achievement that made them quite proud.

Shimon Peres had ascended to a high position, and he interacted daily with the nation's leaders. Perhaps because of his being so close to the levers of power, and his feeling that he was dealing with matters of vital importance for Israel's existence, he made one of the worst mistakes in his life.

He didn't fight in the War of Independence.

A clever young man like him should have understood that in those fateful days, when the nascent state was fighting for its life, every able citizen should don a uniform and fight. One of the most eminent Israeli poets, Nathan Alterman, volunteered for service in an artillery unit, and carried heavy shells on his back. Uri Avnery, a staunch leader of the radical opposition to Israel's establishment, served in the "Samson's Foxes" commando unit that fought in the Negev. "I instinctively realized that I must join the army. If you don't enlist, how can you raise your head after such a war? Shimon Peres had a very tempting job indeed. He was with Eshkol and Ben-Gurion. But he didn't understand that it would haunt him all his life . . . . He didn't share either the feelings or the memories of the guys of this generation, who were frontline soldiers. None of them could ever forgive him. All those who fought in the War of Independence regarded it as the definitive event of their lives."[11]

"Shimon didn't take part in the war," his friend Tzvi Tzur remarked, "and that was a mortal blow to his being an Israeli."[12] Another friend, Yossef Nahmias, believed that "the real Israeli elite with the establishment of the state and after, was Palmach, Haganah, army, uniforms. Shimon didn't belong to the elite."[13]

As time went by, many criticized and taunted Peres for not fighting. General Yigal Allon snapped, "In the trenches where I was, I never saw Shimon Peres."[14] A famous poet quipped that Peres belonged to those "who heard gunfire only on the telephone." Rabin's animosity toward Peres also came, partly, from the war. "In Rabin's world there was nothing more important than the War of Independence," said the ghostwriter of his autobiography, Dov Goldstein. "He never forgave Peres that in those terrible times he didn't serve in the army."[15] Some of Peres's friends maintain that all his life "Shimon apologized about his military service."[16]

Years later, Peres tried to explain why he didn't serve in uniform in 1948. "I didn't want to be an officer," he said, "because anybody who had a higher rank could give me orders. I therefore chose to be a private."[17]

But he was not a private; he was a civilian, and in his personal file he was designated as "clerk."[18] He maintained that the IDF chief of staff, Yaakov Dori, offered him the rank of colonel, but he refused, believing "that the rank would hamper him."[19] He also stressed that "even without the rank, I had the highest rank. There was nobody above me. I could move around and do whatever I wanted."[20]

This statement, of course, was exaggerated. There were others above Peres, and he certainly didn't do whatever he wanted. When friends asked him why didn't he serve in the army, he would repeat his criticism against high-ranking officers, and would declare that the army didn't interest him.

There was no doubt that Peres's activities at Ben-Gurion's side were equivalent to the contribution of hundreds of soldiers to the war effort. Yet, while the soldiers risked their lives, or at least served in the IDF, Shimon Peres was a civilian.

Actually Peres *was* drafted, together with other civilian employees in army headquarters, on August 15, 1948, and was even given an army ID number, 45446.[21] But nine days later, the conscription was annulled. The reason given was that Peres was only "attached" to headquarters, and didn't serve in any military unit.[22] Peres formally enlisted only four years later, on his return from a long stay abroad. He then asked that his service at the Ministry of Defense be recognized as military service. He took his oath to the army in August 1952, and received ID number 678444.[23]

After the War of Independence, the young generation of Israel's leaders emerged from the IDF. Among them were Yigael Yadin, Yigal Allon, Moshe Dayan, Yitzhak Rabin, Chaim Herzog, Ezer Weizman, Ariel Sharon, and others. Shimon Peres didn't belong to that group; his error became an obstacle to his political aspirations.

It took Peres many years to finally admit his mistake.[24]

AS THE WAR APPROACHED its end, Peres became concerned about his insufficient education. He was twenty-six years old, didn't know a word of English, and didn't even have a high-school diploma. "I felt, after the war, that I knew nothing."[25] He wanted to go back to school, and Ben-Gurion appointed him deputy director of the Ministry of Defense mission in New York, so that he could work during the day and study in the evenings. On June 14, 1949, he set out for New York with Sonia and little Tziki.

Once again, it was an overwhelming change in Peres's life. The kibbutznik who had been at the core of Israel's struggle for survival was suddenly cast into an alien world across the sea, in a huge country whose language he couldn't speak. America had a deep impact on him. He was deeply moved by its idealism, by its attachment to moral and humane values, by the role of the Bible in American society, by the diligence and the optimism of its people. The American Constitution, in his view, created "a fine balance between the rights of the individual and his duty to society, between religious tolerance and ethnic identity, between generosity and originality." He concluded that America "is not so much a continent as a constitution."[26]

Peres assumed his functions at the Ministry of Defense mission in New York; he was later appointed head of the mission. His small family lived in a seven-room apartment on the corner of 95th Street and Riverside Drive. They called their apartment "the kibbutz," as it was also home to quite a few young men, most of them bachelors, who were locally employed by the Israeli government. On Sunday Sonia would cook breakfast for the entire gang, and they would share *The New York Times* before setting off on trips out of town or heading for Radio City to watch the Rockettes. They also liked visiting nightspots and clubs in the city. Each of the "kibbutz" members had to babysit for Tziki in his turn.

The New York years were a great experience for Sonia and Shimon. Shimon threw himself with tremendous zeal into his night studies at the New School for Social Research. Among his professors were several eminent personalities such as Reinhold Niebuhr, Max Lerner, and Supreme Court justice Felix Frankfurter. Peres's main subjects were economics, history, and English. On his first night at the school, he listened to a lecture on "The Psychology of Economics." He heard the word "psychology," but didn't realize that in English one doesn't pronounce the first letter of that word. He was sure that it started with a "c" or an "s," and spent hours in fruitless search for "sychology" or "cychology" in the dictionary. Only the following morning did he learn the truth from his American secretary. He decided to take his English studies more seriously, hired a tutor, and assailed the secretaries at the office with questions. In a few months his English improved dramatically, and his marks soared.

In his fat notebooks Peres summarized the lectures he attended—ancient history, contemporary history, political science, economic geography, American economy, social and economic theories. In the margins he added remarks in English and Hebrew, or doodled Chinese faces, clowns' grimaces, and Ben-Gurion's head. He submitted to his teachers several essays, most of them dealing with the Land of Israel, the Negev, the kibbutz, Israel's society, and its political structures. For his semester paper he chose to analyze *The New Yorker* magazine. In another paper he reviewed two new movies, *All About Eve* and *All the King's Men*. He qualified them as expressions of self-criticism in American society. In an essay on language he quoted the poems of Zalman Shneur and borrowed the title from Tolstoy: "A Language Is Like a Red-Cheeked Apple."[27]

After completing several courses, Peres was admitted to a four-month course for advanced management at Harvard University. The other students in this program were businessmen, executives, trade-union officials, and army officers. At Harvard, Peres learned how to dress in a suit and tie; he also discovered the cocktail parties that took place twice a week. His own professor taught him how to drink two glasses of whiskey at a party. But he was absolutely devoted to his studies.

He was also devoted to his work for the defense ministry. His job involved taking risks or embarking upon strange adventures. Washington still applied harsh restrictions on arms sales to Israel. The mission, therefore, used illegal methods to buy weapons. In the United States Peres and his team bought torpedo boats; surplus Mustang, Mosquito, and Harvard aircraft; tanks; communication equipment; and spare parts. They dispatched the material to Israel with the help of friends. These deals were illegal and the Israelis often had to seek the paid assistance of dubious characters from the American underworld, as in the days before the establishment of the State of Israel. Peres met with many shady intermediaries, suspicious lawyers, and dealers. He had to establish relations of trust and cooperation with the teamsters. That's how he met the teamsters' leader Jimmy Hoffa. A few years after their friendly meeting in New York, Hoffa disappeared, presumably murdered by the Mafia.

Many of the planes Peres and his team bought came in parts, and their assembly was carried out at a small plant in Burbank, California, managed by a fiery young man named Al Schwimmer. Schwimmer was a flight engineer, and during the Second World War had crossed the Atlantic Ocean more than two hundred times in four years. During the War of Independence he joined the Israeli Air Force with a group of American pilots.[28] They formed a unique group—daring, boisterous, rowdy—and very soon clashed with their officers, with Al playing the lead role. Ben-Gurion had to intervene, and with the help of Peres succeeded in calming down the wild bunch. Since those stormy days Peres and Schwimmer had become close friends.

Peres flew to the West Coast to meet Schwimmer and his friends, who had stuck to their wild way of life. In a shed in a remote corner of the Burbank airfield, they assembled Mustang and Mosquito aircraft and overhauled the first two Constellation airplanes of El Al, the Israeli airline, which had started up in 1948.

Schwimmer and his gang of eleven fliers lived in a beautiful mansion rented from the Hollywood actress Jeanette MacDonald. "They had an impeccable black butler," Peres recalled, "and a swimming pool with 'blond water.' All the Hollywood girls used to hang out there. I used to come there often."[29]

The Mosquito aircraft assembled in Burbank were flown to Israel via the North Pole. In May 1951, a Mosquito flown by one of the best pilots, Roy Kurtz, vanished over the snowbound wastes of Newfoundland. Peres decided to send a rescue team on a search for Kurtz and the plane. The only aircraft suitable for the search was one of the two Constellations owned by El Al. The national airline agreed to lease it to the Ministry of Defense on condition that Shimon Peres would be put in charge of the rescue.

The entire team, including Roy Kurtz's wife, flew to Goose Bay, a remote Canadian town in Labrador. They settled in a small hotel adjacent to a Canadian Air Force base. Every morning they took off and spent long hours flying over endless snow plains, jagged mountains, and glaciers. The search was based on the testimony of some Eskimos who claimed to have seen the Mosquito diving toward the white desert, but the missing plane was never found. The search was stopped after seven days.

The grim mission had another result, though. During the long nights that the members of the rescue team spent in Goose Bay, they engaged in long conversations. Peres described his dream, which the other members of the team defined as a delusion. A day would come, he said, when Israel would no longer depend on the old, ramshackle airplanes that it bought in other countries—but on its own modern aircraft, which it would build itself.

All the pilots present looked at him "with pity."[30] All of them—except for Al Schwimmer. He took Shimon's dream very seriously and assured him it could be done. "At Goose Bay," Peres said later, "the Israeli aircraft industry was founded."[31]

On his return to New York, Peres heard that Ben-Gurion, who was on a visit to the United States, had just arrived in California. He followed the Old Man there, and took him to Schwimmer's shed in Burbank. Ben-Gurion was enthusiastic: "With so little equipment you're able to repair planes? Why don't you come to Israel right away?"

"For me," Peres noted, "this was the green light."[32]

On returning to Israel a year later, Peres brought Al Schwimmer with him. Here they were confronted with a choir of adversaries. The air force chief, General Dan Tolkovsky, declared that he didn't need an aircraft industry. El Al, which was later to become a partner in the venture, hastily shrugged off the idea. The minister of transportation refused to cooperate. The heads of the military industry feared that the creation of an aircraft industry would draw on their budgets. Pinhas Sapir, one of the heads of the Treasury, angrily declared that he wouldn't help achieve "this fantasy of Shimon Peres," and demanded that the budget be cut by half. Finally, Peres undertook the project himself, raised some money, set aside some funds from the defense ministry budgets, and started building the Israeli aircraft industry.

Peres invited Schwimmer to Kibbutz Alumot. In the evening they sat on Elhanan Yishai's porch and drank cold lemonade.

"You know," Shimon said to Elhanan, "this American guy says that he will build a jet."

"What jet?" Yishai asked. "How will he build a jet?"

"I'll build a jet," Schwimmer confirmed.

"You don't know this guy," Peres said to Elhanan. "If he says that he will build a jet, he'll build a jet."

"You know what," Elhanan said, "let's get down to the lake and take a swim. That way we'll remember the promise that he'll build a jet."

The three of them drove to the Kinneret, and dived into its dark waters.[33]

Peres remembered that night swim during all the vicissitudes that befell the aircraft-industry project. He remembered it when the first hangars were built near Ben-Gurion Airport; when Schwimmer bought an entire plant for overhauling aircraft in Miami; when he breathed new life into defunct carcasses of aircraft from all over the world—Dakotas, Norsemans, Spitfires, Mustangs, Mosquitoes, Harvards, Stearmans, and Consuls. From 1955 to 1956 the aircraft industry moved up another notch, when it started overhauling jet engines for the air force. Peres remembered the night swim on the day when the aircraft industry presented to the air force the first Fouga Magister, a French jet assembled in Israel. Peres named it Swallow.

That swallow indeed augured the arrival of several generations of Israeli-made aircraft: the Arava, the Jet Commander, the Nesher, the Kfir, the Lavi, sophisticated missiles, space satellites, the Arrow—an antimissile missile—and other superb products of Israeli technology.

Al Schwimmer kept his word. He had built a jet.

BUT ALL THIS was still a dream in the early fifties, when Peres and his team at the defense ministry mission in New York kept concocting wily plans to obtain more weapons and transport them to Israel. Peres learned that Colombia had purchased two destroyers in Britain, but didn't need them anymore. He and his assistants flew to Key West for a secret meeting with General G., a top Colombian Air Force commander. They persuaded him to mediate in the budding deal for the purchase of the destroyers. A few weeks later, Peres and his friends flew to Bogotá, the capital of Colombia, to meet with the president and the finance minister and conclude the deal. But before the final signing they had to see the ships. They flew in an aging Dakota aircraft to the port of Cartagena. While over the Colombian jungle, a sudden fire engulfed one of the engines. "You have to decide what to do," General G. told Peres. They could crash-land in the jungle—but that meant they would spend many weeks, perhaps months, getting back to civilization. The second possibility was to keep flying with a burning engine at the risk that the plane would explode in midair.

"Let's keep flying," Peres said.

The plane landed at Cartagena with its engine in flames. But the adventure had a happy ending. The destroyers were in good condition and the deal was successfully concluded.

Not all the operations ended in success. One day, a deal was negotiated with Mexico for the purchase of forty-six tanks. A special Mexican envoy arrived in New York and solemnly delivered to Peres the forty-six ignition keys of the tanks. Only later did the Israelis discover that besides the keys they were not going to receive anything else, and the tanks vanished in thin air over the Mexican border.

On the other hand, efforts to recruit the corrupt Cuban regime to help Israel bore fruit. Peres established contact with one of the heads of the Cuban secret services, Efraimo A. Peres and his assistant Nat Cohen flew to Havana, and at the prearranged time, twelve o'clock, entered police headquarters, which was also the headquarters of the secret services. When they informed the receptionists that they had come to meet Senor Efraimo A., the Cubans burst out laughing. "At what time is your meeting?"

"Twelve o'clock," the guests answered.

The merry receptionists kept laughing. "Senor [Efraimo A.] meant midnight, not noon. He never meets people during the day."

At midnight, Peres and Cohen went back to police headquarters. Efraimo was waiting for them with nine other friends. The Cubans took their guests to the Tropicana Nightclub. Efraimo was received with honors and flattery. Some breathtaking beauties danced on stage, and harried waiters served drinks. "The Cubans were ten, and we were two," Peres recalled. "All of a sudden, twelve ladies appeared by our table, and sat on our laps."

The ladies were supposed to show the guests a good time. "I came from Alumot. My face flushed like a tomato. I was terribly embarrassed. I said to Efraimo, 'Listen, at the place where I come from we used to sit men apart and women apart.' "

"Efraimo was okay; the ladies were sent away. Then we started to talk business."[34]

Peres and his friend spent two days in Cuba. They took walks in Havana, visited Hemingway's house, and on the second night were back at the Tropicana with their hosts. Out of these night meetings a promising deal was reached, and Cuba bought large quantities of weapons for Israel. "What could we do?" Peres sighed. "We had to conclude many of our deals with dark figures, even with gangsters. We had no other way."

DURING THE WINTER of 1951, Peres received an urgent request for cannons for the IDF. He found out that the Canadian Army was selling twenty-five-pounder cannons from their Second World War surplus. The Canadian authorities confirmed that Israel could buy these weapons. How much would that cost, Peres asked, and was told that he could get thirty cannons for $2 million. But soon after he sent his report to Israel, he got a negative answer. The director general of the Treasury, Pinhas Sapir, sent a special messenger to New York to inform Peres: You won't get a penny!

Peres decided to raise the money himself. He traveled to Montreal and went to the office of Sam Bronfman, a Jewish businessman who owned one of the biggest liquor companies in the world.

At the entrance, Peres and his assistant Yaacov (Shapik) Shapira were stopped by two heavyweight guards. "I represent the Israeli Defense Ministry," Peres said, "and I want to meet with Mr. Bronfman."

A few minutes later, Peres was admitted to Bronfman's office. He told the magnate about the possibility of buying cannons in Canada.

"How much do they want?" Bronfman asked.

"Two million dollars."

Bronfman didn't conceal his anger. "That's too much," he said. "Who is selling you the weapons?"

"The minister of munitions and supply, Mr. Howe."

"I'll talk to him," Bronfman announced. "I'll tell him this is too much." He invited the two Israelis to travel with him to Ottawa. The following day, his Cadillac stopped by their hotel, a uniformed driver ushered them in, and they set off for the Canadian capital. The roads were covered with snow, and the journey wasn't easy. But Bronfman feared flying, and preferred to travel by car, even if it was a long and complicated trip.

Complicated it was, but rather pleasant, as Bronfman offered his guests plenty of excellent whiskey at the bars on their route. The car also carried a large supply of liquor.[35]

In Ottawa they headed straight for the supply minister's office. Bronfman assailed the minister: "How dare you take two million dollars from poor and famished Israel?"

The Canadian minister hastily retreated and agreed to cut the price by half. He would sell the cannons to Israel for one million dollars, he said. Peres and Shapik were in seventh heaven.

They set off on their way back to Montreal. At one of the "whiskey stops," Bronfman said to Peres: "I got you one million off the price. Who will give you the other million?"

"You," Peres said quietly.

Bronfman was stunned. When he recovered, he called his wife. "Will you please invite fifty guests to dinner tonight?" he asked, and dictated over the phone the entire guest list.

Then he examined Peres closely. Peres was dressed in a blue suit and white socks. "You can't come to a dinner with such socks," Bronfman said. He ordered the driver to stop at the nearest store and bought Peres blue socks that matched his suit.

At dinner, Bronfman and Peres told the guests what the purpose of their meeting had been. Bronfman's guests responded warmly and raised close to a million dollars for the purchase of the cannons.[36] Peres later obtained the rest of the money as a long-term loan from Jewish businessmen in New York.[37]

At that time, Shimon Peres's uncle Avraham Dickenstein was managing a joint American-Israeli company in New York. He knew Bronfman well. When Shimon left for Canada, Dickenstein told him, "If you get one penny from Bronfman, I'll send you a case of whiskey." When Shimon came back, Dickenstein sent him two cases.

Peres sent a present to Sam Bronfman—a Bible in a silver cover, made by a Yemenite craftsman. "The ship carrying a thousand tons of the powerful equipment sails to Israel tomorrow," he wrote to Bronfman. "I believe this will bring real satisfaction to the people who contributed in order to make this equipment available to us."38

Peres summed up the Canadian venture: "I wrote Sapir that we had the money, we had the paperwork, everything . . . [but] he still was angry. Yet I brought him thirty cannons."39

In January 1952, Peres returned to Israel with his family. He had been very successful in his mission in America. Some Mapai leaders wanted to put him in charge of the party's young generation. Ben-Gurion offered him a job as his personal assistant, but Peres refused. Finally, Ben-Gurion reached a decision and on February 1, he dispatched a letter to Alumot.

"Dear comrades," Ben-Gurion wrote. "I appointed comrade Shimon Peres Deputy Director of the Defense Ministry, and I ask you to allow him to undertake this function."40

The General Assembly of Alumot approved Ben-Gurion's request, and twenty-nine-year-old Shimon Peres was promoted to his new job.

THE PERES FAMILY rented a tiny one-room apartment in Tel Aviv. They hung a curtain in the middle of the room, and Tziki slept behind the curtain. Sonia was carrying another child, and soon after their return a boy was born. They called him Yonathan (Yoni). He slept in a small bed beside his parents. He wasn't a healthy child, and Sonia took care of him with the utmost devotion.

And then, suddenly, Getzel Persky appeared in their apartment with a mysterious expression on his face. He took them to a cluster of new buildings at Derech Hashalom ("Peace Road") in Tel Aviv. He took a key out of his pocket and opened the door of a new apartment. This is yours, Persky said to the astounded family.

Getzel had saved money in secret—while his wife accused him of spending too much—and bought an apartment for his son. To a friend he said, "I've got two sons. One is a businessman, and he is doing well, the other is a government employee; he hardly makes it, but he's got a good wife."[41]

The "good wife" was devoted to her husband and her family. She went with Peres everywhere and the deep bond between them impressed all their friends. She spent a lot of time with Yoni, who went through a bad bout of polio. Many nights Shimon and Sonia would sit awake by the baby's bed, taking care of him. The suffering of his little son brought tears to Shimon's eyes.[42]

Sonia fought for the child, taking him to the best doctors and hospitals, and Yoni finally recovered. Sonia was a model mother and wife, but in her heart she carried a deep disappointment for having left Alumot. She loved kibbutz life, and during her years in New York dreamed of returning to her house on the hill. When Shimon was appointed to his new job, she realized that Alumot wouldn't be her home anymore. She missed it for the rest of her life.[43]

Peres's first steps at the defense ministry were not easy. The chief of staff, Yigael Yadin, didn't like him, and protested angrily when Peres appeared at the weekly meetings of the defense minister's staff. The meetings took place every Friday in Ben-Gurion's small office at the Kirya compound in Tel Aviv. This was the sanctum sanctorum of the defense establishment; beside Ben-Gurion, the meetings were attended by the chief of staff; Ben-Gurion's military secretary; the chief of intelligence and his deputy; and the director of the defense ministry and his deputy. Yadin argued that such a young man as Peres shouldn't be invited to meetings of that importance—even though Yadin himself was barely thirty-four. As for Peres, he went to the first meeting of the staff utterly excited, expecting to participate in a discussion about Israel's survival. But the item on the agenda was the bad health of President Weizmann and the preparations for a state funeral.[44]

Soon after Peres's arrival, the director general of the defense ministry, Ziev Shind, resigned and Peres became the acting director. In the following months the conflict between Peres and Yadin reached new heights. Actually, it was an almost natural by-product of the defense-community structure, where the IDF General Staff represented military power and the Ministry of Defense civilian power. The struggle between those two became an integral part of Israel's history.

Yet Yadin had another reason to oppose the acting director. Israel's financial situation was disastrous, and Ben-Gurion decided to cut the defense budget and lay off six thousand army officers and civilian employees. Peres was in full agreement with Ben-Gurion. The army should focus on purely military activities, he said; all the functions that were not directly connected with fighting—such as arms purchase, arms production, supplies, and services—should be transferred to the defense ministry.

The proposed changes infuriated Yadin, and he resigned. Ben-Gurion admired Yadin, a bold officer and a superb archeologist, and didn't want to let him go. He even offered to resign from the position of defense minister and appoint Yadin in his place. But his offer was rejected.

Ben-Gurion appointed as chief of staff Yadin's deputy, General Mordechai Makleff. But Makleff didn't like the chief of operations, the young Moshe Dayan, and wanted to replace him with Yitzhak Rabin.

Makleff confronted Peres as well, and demanded that most of the defense ministry functions be transferred to the army. Ben-Gurion tried to appease Makleff, but mostly sided with Peres and Dayan.[45] A year after becoming chief of staff, Makleff resigned.

Ben-Gurion immediately announced that the next chief of staff would be Moshe Dayan. In December 1953, Dayan was officially appointed the IDF chief of staff, and Peres was named director general of the Ministry of Defense.

Ben-Gurion resigned as well, but for a different reason. He was exhausted after leading the nation through a bloody war, a diplomatic struggle, and a huge effort to absorb hundreds of thousands of immigrants, and from building new cities and towns and laying the foundations of a modern state. He decided to quit politics and join Kibbutz Sde Boker, which had recently been founded in the very heart of the Negev.

Ben-Gurion first chose Levi Eshkol as his successor as prime minister. But Mapai preferred Moshe Sharett, the dovish foreign minister, whose views were at odds with Ben-Gurion's activist policy. Ben-Gurion appointed Pinhas Lavon, a hawkish politician, as defense minister, hoping that he would neutralize Sharett's dovish tendencies.

The trio he left behind—Pinhas Lavon, Moshe Dayan, and Shimon Peres—was meant to be the dream team that would defend Israel from her enemies.

CHAPTER 9.

DEATH ON THE NILE

SHIMON PERES WAS fascinated by Moshe Dayan.

Peres had never met anybody like him. He thought of Dayan as "original, handsome, the wisest of men."[1] Since their journey to Basel, he felt close to the balding, rugged young man who already carried a hero's aura about him. Dayan's voice was confident, resolute, a Sabra's voice; his face seemed chiseled by a master craftsman, and his black eye patch bestowed on it a pirate's bold, rebellious look. Peres was soon to discover that the dramatic appearance concealed a brilliant mind; the rough countenance shrouded a secret sensitivity, a love of poetry, and a romantic devotion to the Land of Israel. The two had a lot in common. They both admired David Ben-Gurion; they both loved books and poetry, especially the epic verses of Israel's national poet, Nathan Alterman; both of them regarded military might as the ultimate guarantee for Israel's existence; both of them grew up in the Labor movement, Peres at Ben-Shemen, Alumot, and in Working Youth, Dayan at Kibbutz Degania, Moshav Nahalal, and in Mapai's Young Guard. Both were men of action; Mapai's elders criticized them for not being "men of values" and labeled them "doers." The same character traits of Dayan that scared the Mapai leaders enthralled Peres. "Dayan is a partisan and an adventurer," Moshe Sharett wrote in consternation. "He is not a military leader, he has no clue and no idea how to manage the military."[2] Levi Eshkol didn't lag behind and nicknamed Dayan "Abu Jilda" after a wily and cruel Arab gang leader.

Dayan and Peres formed an alliance at the very beginning of their common ascent in the world of defense. They agreed that Peres would support Dayan in military matters, and Dayan would stand by Peres on subjects concerning the defense ministry.

It was an alliance, indeed, but not a beautiful friendship. The admiration between the two was rather one-sided. Dayan had a lot of esteem for Peres, but he didn't return his feelings of devotion and deep friendship; he often treated him with open disdain. To a large extent this attitude stemmed from Dayan's character—he was essentially a loner, a man with no friends. Peres would alert Ben-Gurion whenever Dayan felt hurt by him, or when he shared with Peres ideas that he was reluctant to present to Ben-Gurion personally.[3] Dayan never did the same for Peres.

"Moshe was allergic to Shimon's manner of speaking," recalled General Meir Amit, a friend of both men. "He couldn't stand Shimon's plays upon words and his diplomatic contortions. Moshe spoke Hebrew as if he were carving granite. Yet his aversion to Shimon was one of style and not of essence. They absolutely agreed on many things and acted in harmony. Perhaps there was no friendship between them, but there certainly was mutual trust."[4] Dayan's reserve toward Peres resulted, too, from their different backgrounds; from the gap between the tough peasant, war hero, and soldier deeply rooted in the Land of Israel, and the cosmopolitan politician whose heart was in Israel, his roots in Eastern Europe, and his head in the West.

Some used to say that Ben-Gurion had divided his legacy between the two. He gave the leadership to Dayan and the vision to Peres.[5] Ben-Gurion trusted Shimon Peres and listened to his ideas in spite of his young age, but he loved Moshe Dayan and felt he was "cast from Biblical material."[6] Peres himself defined the difference between him and Dayan: "I know how to *build* force," he said, "and Moshe knows how to use it."[7] Peres was a self-restrained man, in full control of himself, keen on keeping his public appearance in check, while Dayan acted more than once like a rascal—blunt, outspoken, offensive, and yet utterly charismatic, radiating charm and determined leadership, making people follow him with enthusiasm.

Peres's admiration for Dayan was deep and sincere. "Moshe incited jealousy," he wrote. "Many wanted to emulate him, but Moshe couldn't be emulated. He conquered the young people's hearts and fired up the world's imagination, not because he followed certain rules, but because he discarded them with surprising ability and tremendous personal charm." Peres loved the limpid Hebrew language of Dayan, his gift for the right expression, his original point of view. Peres was very conscious of the way he dressed, and later, when he became the minister of foreign affairs and then prime minister, he impressed his colleagues in the cabinet with his elegant clothes; yet he admired Dayan's casual way of dressing. He was thrilled by "his beige, sun-bleached jacket, his pants that fashion had never seen," and regarded them as "an explicit statement of his refusal to yield to conventions." He described Dayan's hands as "powerful hands, whose nails still carried the remains of his archeological digs." The picture was completed by Dayan's one eye, which "glimmered constantly."[8]

Peres was an optimist, charming and funny in private meetings, but stern and somewhat gloomy in public. Dayan was somber and pessimistic in private, but his public image was of a man full of humor, charm, and captivating vitality. Peres was a dreamer and a visionary, but many of his dreams were unrealistic. Dayan was down to earth, a skeptic, and a cynic. Peres cared a lot about his public image and always feared "what people would say" about him. Dayan happily ignored his image. He didn't conceal his womanizing, and all of Israel knew about his amorous conquests. Peres projected the image of a family man, and the gossip about his private life was minimal. Peres nurtured an intense ambition to climb to the very top of the country's leadership; Dayan wanted it and yet recoiled from it, aspired for leadership but drew back from the responsibility that national leadership implied. He wasn't ready to give up the earthly pleasures he enjoyed.[9] "Moshe," Peres said, "was a sailor who feared the coast."[10]

The political alliance and the mutual loyalty between Dayan and Peres were assiduously respected by both of them; that alliance lasted more than twenty-five years, mostly because Peres always accepted Dayan's authority and aligned himself with Dayan's positions. Peres had resigned himself to being number two in the team they had formed.

During Dayan's life, and long after his death, Peres spoke of him with deep admiration. Perhaps that admiration resulted from a basic truth: Dayan, like some mythological hero—a man without fear, wise and handsome, indifferent to what people thought of him, a charismatic speaker, a winner of many battles, a great lover who didn't conceal his amorous adventures—was all that Peres wanted to be but couldn't.[11]

And yet there were qualities that Peres had and Dayan didn't. Dayan didn't possess the dogged determination and the stubborn ambition of Peres. "He was constantly shifting his political positions," Peres wrote in a rare expression of criticism toward his friend. "It wasn't that his views lacked backbone; rather, they lacked permanence . . . . Perhaps it was a certain inconstancy in his character that caused him to seek stormy seas, even when he could have anchored securely in safe havens."[12]

Dayan himself recognized his shortcomings. "I am with you wherever you go," he said to Peres when they set off on their common venture, "but remember one thing—I am unreliable!"[13]

Their alliance's baptism of fire was the notorious Lavon affair.

BERL KATZENELSON, THE GURU of the Labor movement, called Pinhas Lavon "a brilliant mind in a muddy soul."[14] Others called him "an enigma," and some used harsher words—"wicked" or even "devious."[15] Many Mapai leaders had serious reservations about him. Lavon had been secretary general of the Histadrut labor union and a minister in Ben-Gurion's cabinets. He was a handsome man, slim and tanned, sporting a silver forelock over a clear forehead; a brilliant speaker, a gifted organizer and economist. However, something in his character was deeply flawed. He was arrogant and vain; he disliked teamwork and often displayed open disdain for his colleagues.

When Ben-Gurion chose Lavon to be defense minister, many feared that he was being groomed for prime minister. "He is the wrong choice," said Labor Minister Golda Meir to the Old Man. "He lacks the experience and the judgment." Golda deeply distrusted the new minister. "Lavon," she wrote later, "was one of the most gifted Mapai leaders, but also one of the most unstable among them, a handsome and complex intellectual, who used to be a great dove, but metamorphosed into a wild hawk."[16] The departing chief of staff of the army, General Makleff, also warned Ben-Gurion that Lavon was "a dangerous man . . . who had tried to stir up trouble between the Americans and the Jordanians by sabotage operations in Amman."[17] But Ben-Gurion failed to see the bad omens, and insisted on appointing Lavon.

Lavon's lightning ascent pumped his confidence. While still the acting defense minister, he started undermining Moshe Sharett; he disregarded his position as prime minister, didn't ask his advice, and didn't report to him. He didn't want Moshe Dayan as chief of staff and had reservations about Shimon Peres. Yet Peres and Dayan had supported Lavon in the preliminary discussions with Ben-Gurion. "I admired his analytical powers," Peres wrote, "his rhetorical skills and his ability to stand up for his opinions. I felt that the army could benefit from Lavon's leadership."[18] The main motive for Dayan's and Peres's support for Lavon was his militant standpoint on security issues. Lavon adopted fiery positions that embarrassed the prime minister. But he also drove Sharett to despair by an endless string of insults and mockery that rained down even in government and party meetings.

Sharett wasn't Lavon's only victim. Very soon, his relations with Peres and Dayan soured, and they were the first to call on

Ben-Gurion. On February 6, 1954, barely two months after the Old Man had settled in Sde Boker, Dayan and Peres drove to the Negev and complained to their leader about Lavon. Dayan accused Lavon of "harmful activism."[19] These words, coming from an activist like Moshe Dayan, should have alarmed Ben-Gurion, but once again he didn't react.

In June, Dayan was back at Sde Boker and bitterly attacked Lavon for planning to replace him with General Haim Laskov. Shimon Peres, too, clashed with the defense minister, who was trying to curtail the activities of the ministry. "It quickly became clear to me," Peres wrote, "that we had made a ghastly mistake."[20] Ben-Gurion's former military secretary, Colonel Nehemia Argov, wrote desperate pages in his diary about Lavon's vain and dangerous actions. "Your great deeds, Ben-Gurion, are sinking in the ocean," he wrote in distress, "and you are in Sde Boker!"[21]

The open confrontation between Lavon and the Peres-Dayan duo erupted at the end of May 1954. It was triggered by Peres's success in purchasing AMX-13 light tanks in France. Peres and Dayan regarded France's agreement to sell tanks to Israel as a major breakthrough. But Lavon didn't approve the deal, claiming that some officers had come to see him secretly to express their objection to the AMX tanks.[22] Dayan was furious.[23] A few days later, Dayan learned that Lavon was working on another project, again without Dayan's knowledge. Dayan dispatched two letters of resignation to Lavon.

At that stage, Ben-Gurion decided to intervene. The Old Man was still the most influential political figure in Israel; many expected him to return to the helm one day. Ben-Gurion summoned Lavon, who accused Dayan of misconduct and attacked Peres. "Apparently he's got a grudge against Shimon," Ben-Gurion told Nehemia Argov. "Lavon says that Shimon doesn't speak the truth."[24] However, Lavon promised Ben-Gurion to mend his relations with Dayan. He invited Dayan to lunch and tried to appease him. Dayan summed up the crisis in his diary:

"Lavon accused Shimon—who happens to be abroad—of causing all the misunderstandings."[25]

The chasm between Peres and Dayan, on the one hand, and Lavon, on the other, widened rapidly. Simultaneously, Lavon's unbridled attacks on Sharett, his mockery and insults aimed at the prime minister, reached new peaks. At the end of July, many Mapai leaders traveled to Sde Boker. They bitterly complained about Lavon's conduct toward Sharett. After the meeting, Eshkol went to see Lavon. "Ben-Gurion says that you are not going to be prime minister," Eshkol said. "Ben-Gurion doesn't support you anymore."[26]

Against that empoisoned background, reminiscent of a Greek tragedy, exploded the Lavon affair.

IN THE SPRING of 1954, the young Colonel Gamal Abdel Nasser seized power in Egypt. His first goal was to drive out of his country the eighty thousand British soldiers stationed in military bases and airfields. Great Britain decided to withdraw from its bases in Egypt and signed an agreement with the Egyptian government to that effect. Israel was extremely worried by this decision, as many bases, airfields, and stocks of matériel and equipment were going to fall into the hands of President Nasser. Some Israeli leaders desperately sought ways to prevent the departure of the British.

A strange and stupid plan emerged from secret talks between Lavon and the chief of Military Intelligence, Colonel Binyamin Gibly. They conceived the idea of carrying out acts of sabotage against British and American libraries, cultural centers, and other Western targets in Egypt's major cities. The operations would be executed by Israeli agents—but Great Britain would be led to believe the culprits were the fundamentalist Muslim Brotherhood or even factions close to the Egyptian government. This would prove that the Egyptian regime was incapable of maintaining order and shouldn't be relied upon. England, therefore, would be forced to reconsider the evacuation plan and perhaps cancel it.

The plan was astonishingly naïve and dangerous. Even if the operation were successful, only morons could believe that Great Britain would reverse its policy because of a couple of explosions in some libraries. Moshe Dayan opposed the plan, but Lavon and Gibly bypassed him and worked in direct contact with each other. They agreed to use for the operation a group of young Jews from Cairo and Alexandria who were members of secret Zionist cells. The agent in charge of the network was Avri El'ad, an Israeli acting under the assumed identity of a German businessman.

The operation started on July 2. Several rudimentary bombs exploded in Cairo and Alexandria, causing small fires that were rapidly extinguished. On July 23, El'ad sent his men on a simultaneous attack on five targets—two cinemas in Cairo, two cinemas in Alexandria, and a Cairo warehouse. That evening, a fateful hitch occurred. A small incendiary device went off prematurely in the pocket of Philip Nathanson, a member of the Alexandria cell, just as he was about to enter one of the cinemas. He was arrested by Egyptian police officers who saw him writhing in pain, smoke pouring out of his pocket. The police investigation spread to Nathanson's friends, and in a couple of days the entire network was behind bars. Avri El'ad, the head of the spy ring, wasn't connected with the attacks and left Egypt.

Moshe Sharett learned about the arrests from Egyptian press reports announcing the capture of "Zionist spies." Ben-Gurion heard about the operation from Moshe Dayan, who had recently returned from a trip to the United States and was not in Israel when the network had been activated. "Moshe told me about a strange order of P.L. while he was away, for an operation in Egypt that failed (they had to know it would fail)—[this is] criminal recklessness!"27 A few days later, Shimon Peres told Golda Meir that the senior officials at the defense ministry were fed up with Pinhas Lavon, who had planned dangerous operations in the Middle East and deceived the prime minister. Even Ben-

Gurion, Peres said, realized that he had made a grave mistake by appointing Lavon as defense minister.[28]

On December 11, the trial of the "Zionist spies" opened in Cairo. Now that the lives of the young Jews were in danger, Lavon and Gibly started hurling accusations at each other. Lavon claimed that he had never given Gibly the order to launch the operation; Gibly claimed that he had acted on Lavon's explicit order. Apparently they were both lying.

From Cairo, terrible news kept coming about the police beating and torturing the accused. On the trial's eve, an Egyptian Jew, Karmona, committed suicide. A Mossad agent, Max Bennett, killed himself in a Cairo prison. The only woman arrested, Victorine (Marcelle) Ninio, twice tried to commit suicide because she couldn't stand the dreadful torture.

Under his colleagues' pressure, Moshe Sharett decided to investigate the "Affair." In the deepest secrecy he ordered an inquiry by a board of two: former IDF chief of staff Yaakov Dori and Supreme Court justice Yitzhak Olshan. The board started its hearings, summoning Lavon, Gibly, and other witnesses, including Moshe Dayan and Shimon Peres.

The Olshan-Dori board stumbled upon a shocking imbroglio of lies, intrigues, and poisoned relations in the defense establishment. Sharett, a rather weak and irresolute man, was utterly distressed.

On January 27, 1955, an Egyptian tribunal sentenced six of the Jewish prisoners to long jail terms—between seven years and life. Two of the accused, Shmuel Azar and Dr. Moshe Marzouk, were sentenced to death. On January 31, they were hanged in the court of a Cairo prison. Israeli public opinion was badly shaken. The few people who were in the know felt that the two young Jews had died for nothing and their friends would spend years in terrible Egyptian jails for nothing, all because of a monumental folly. The poet Nathan Alterman published in the *Davar* newspaper a poignant poem, hinting that the people responsible for "the amazingly flawed tangle" and for "the heroes' death" should be punished.[29] He couldn't be more explicit because of the rigid rules of military censorship.

The Olshan-Dori board kept interviewing witnesses. As soon as Shimon Peres was called to testify, a rumor spread that he had harshly criticized Lavon.[30] Lavon, furious, stopped speaking to Peres and the contact between them was maintained by the exchange of scribbled notes. Lavon didn't forgive Peres for agreeing to testify before the board and for refusing to divulge the contents of his testimony.[31] Lavon accused his director general of systematically undermining his position.[32]

The truth was different. Peres later wrote that on January 5, *1955*, when he was called to testify before the board, Justice Olshan warned him "that everything that transpired there must remain secret—even the very fact that I had testified. Replying to the board's specific and detailed questions, I told them everything I knew, describing the proceedings at the Minister's Staff Meetings which I had attended."[33]

Years later, Justice Olshan removed the veil of secrecy from Peres's testimony. "We felt that Peres wasn't eager to provide detailed answers," Olshan wrote in his memoirs, "especially when he thought that our questions implied a critical attitude toward Lavon. Our impression was that Peres tried to evade the questions whenever he feared that his answers might be interpreted as hostile to Lavon. [By his answers] he didn't impress us as a friend or an enemy of Lavon. Perhaps he felt uneasy to testify before us, as he was Director General of the Defense Ministry." Olshan added that five years later Lavon would accuse Peres of being "his great enemy, who fabricated false accusations against him in his testimony."[34]

Lavon's criticism of Peres was unfounded, Olshan wrote. "I wasn't at peace with my conscience. I very much wanted to comment on the slanderous attacks raining on Peres, but . . . I decided to put a gag on my mouth."[35] Perhaps because of these pangs of conscience, Olshan wrote a personal letter to Shimon Peres. "You didn't testify before us from your own initiative; you were invited by the board to clarify some facts about a meeting that Gibly mentioned.... As far as I remember, we wrote in our report that you only answered the questions about that particular meeting and nothing else."[36]

In the tense, fateful days of January 1955, Lavon was furious at Peres for not giving him an account of his testimony. What made Lavon even more furious was the fact that Moshe Dayan disregarded the board's instructions and told Lavon everything he had said to the board.[37] At that stage, Lavon decided to get rid of Peres. He was confident that the board would clear him of any responsibility and started to speak openly of his upcoming revenge. At the same time, he told Sharett that if he were found guilty, he would "draw a much worse conclusion" than resigning his position. Sharett took that as a hint that Lavon would commit suicide. But if he were cleared, Lavon said, he would reorganize the defense ministry and the IDF General Staff. Peres and Gibly must go, Lavon said. He agreed to let Moshe Dayan stay, but his authority would be significantly curtailed; a "general inspector" of the armed forces would be appointed, and he would be under the direct orders of the defense minister.[38]

The Olshan-Dori board submitted its conclusions to Moshe Sharett on January 13, 1955. They were indecisive. "All we can say is that we were not convinced beyond any reasonable doubt that the Chief of Military Intelligence"—Gibly—"did not receive orders from the Defense Minister. Yet, we are not sure that the Defense Minister did give the orders attributed to him."

Lavon was beside himself with rage. At meetings with his colleagues he launched personal attacks against Olshan and Dori, uttered warnings and threats, demanded the establishment of a parliamentary board of inquiry. The poor Sharett, a meek and hesitant man, was at his wits' end; he vacillated, and summoned his comrades to endless discussions on which road to take.

On February 1, the day after the hangings in Cairo, Moshe Sharett headed a delegation that secretly traveled to Sde Boker to seek Ben-Gurion's advice. Besides Sharett, the small group included Levi Eshkol and Golda Meir. The main question debated was whether Lavon should be asked to resign. Ben-Gurion described the discussion to his devoted Nehemia Argov. "Our comrades didn't reach a decision," Ben-Gurion reported. "I told them what I thought. Lavon must go!"[39]

On learning of the leaders' trip to Sde Boker, Lavon rushed a letter to Sharett, hinting that he might reveal the state secrets that had triggered the crisis.[40] The letter had the desired effect. Sharett and his colleagues were terrified at the idea that Lavon might reveal the details about the fiasco in Egypt. Only a few days before, they had thought of forcing Lavon out of the cabinet; now they asked him to take back his letter of resignation.

Sharett's confidants kept producing new plans to satisfy Lavon. One of them, Zalman Aran, suggested that Peres take a plane ticket and leave the country on a world tour for six months.[41] Peres refused; he well knew that such a step would be regarded as a dismissal. Mapai's elders wanted to have their cake and eat it, too; in their fervor to satisfy Lavon they seemed to have forgotten what the entire crisis was about. The news reached Ben-Gurion, who dispatched to Peres an urgent message: "Don't resign!"

Ben-Gurion was to say later that if Lavon had come to him and presented him with a choice—Lavon or Peres—he would have said to Lavon, "You are the one who should go, because Shimon did more for Israel's security."[42]

Peres bitterly wrote to a friend, "Lavon's resignation was not accepted [by Mapai's leaders]. But they accepted his demand that Binyamin should leave and that I should leave. Actually I wanted to resign even without the demand, but I got a message from Sde Boker to stay put."[43]

This was one of the worst periods in Peres's life. He knew that the Mapai establishment had chosen him as a scapegoat.[44]

Moshe Sharett sank in despair again. "Once more I feel I am suffocating, with no way out," he wrote. He finally agreed to the solution offered by Eshkol—the removal of Gibly and Peres—but he warned his friends: "The root of the evil is leaving Lavon at his position."[45]

Sharett summoned Gibly and Peres to his office to inform them of his decision to dismiss both of them. On hearing Sharett's words, Gibly demanded that the prime minister meet first with the chief of staff. He wouldn't resign of his own will, Gibly said. Sharett summoned Moshe Dayan, who rushed to the office.

Dayan taught Sharett a lesson in statesmanship. When he heard of the prime minister's decision to fire Gibly, he asked him if that was the recommendation of the Olshan-Dori board. No, Sharett said, the board didn't recommend anything. So how can you remove him? Dayan asked. "Gibly would ask if that was the board's conclusion. If this is not the board's conclusion—why is he fingered as the culprit? And if that's the way he is treated even though the investigators didn't ask for it—why was he investigated in the first place? . . . The same is true about Peres. He is being punished. For what? If the Defense Minister can't work with this Director General—why did he wait until now? But if he removes him now, that would be considered as a direct result of the inquiry. This is, without doubt, the revenge of the Defense Minister for the testimony of the Director General before the two members of the board of inquiry. How can one draw conclusions that the investigators themselves didn't draw? Shimon won't keep quiet, but would fight to restore his honor, with all the implications."[46]

The clear and logical words of Dayan made Sharett, all of a sudden, see the light. "The Chief of Staff's analysis," he wrote in admiration, "was trenchant, but clear and poised, amazingly calm. At once the solution appeared, as if the heavy fog dispersed and one could see the entire landscape."[47] Sharett canceled the meeting with Peres and informed Lavon of his change of heart: nobody leaves, nobody resigns.

"At the last moment," Peres wrote, "they realized that my

removal meant casting suspicion on somebody who wasn't involved at all in the [Egyptian] affair."[48]

Lavon was left without a choice. On February 17, he submitted his final resignation to Moshe Sharett.

That day, an endless flow of delegations made its way to Ben-Gurion's hut at Sde Boker. They all had one purpose: to persuade Ben-Gurion to return and assume the functions of defense minister. "In the early evening, all of a sudden, Golda and Mordechai Namir arrived," the Old Man noted in his diary. "Our security is in jeopardy. Lavon is leaving and there is nobody to replace him. They suggest that I come back. I was deeply moved. I decided to accept their demand and return to the Defense Ministry."[49]

"Ben-Gurion changed his mind," Peres mused, "because of the fear that our great asset, the IDF, might be harmed. At the comrades' meeting in Sde Boker, the Old Man said that 'if he had to choose between all the ideals minus Security on one hand—and Security minus all the ideals on the other'—he had no doubt that he would choose Security."[50]

PART 2.

OUR FRIEND AND OUR ALLY

CHAPTER 10.

THE MAN IN THE BLUE SUIT

ON JANUARY 18, 1957, *Davar's* reporter in Paris, Elkana Gali, published an article titled "A Song of Praise for a Young Man." Gali heaped compliments on "the young man in a blue suit" who was the relentless architect of Israel's relations with France.[1] The article didn't mention the name of the young man. "Let him stay unknown," Gali wrote, "to the benefit of the cause he is serving." Gali described his hero. "He is of above average height, his hair is short, his face is round, his posture is athletic, he walks slowly .... His voice is calm but confident, he speaks softly although he deals with matters as hard as steel, his style is Israeli—simple and straight to the point."

The body politic understood that Gali wrote about Shimon Peres. Many considered the praise to be exaggerated. Only a few knew that the truth was much more amazing: Peres had succeeded, almost by himself, in achieving a rapprochement between France and Israel and finding the point where the interests and the values of the two nations met.

WHEN TAKING HIS FIRST STEPS toward France, Peres acted in almost total isolation. Israel's leaders regarded France with a mixture of misconception, suspicion, and alienation. None of them knew French, and it was only natural that they would be drawn to the Anglo-Saxon powers. After all, Great Britain had ruled over Palestine for years; its political customs, bureaucratic procedures, and cultural heritage were a model that Israel's leaders tried to emulate.

Others were drawn to the United States. It was the major power in the Western world and the home of six million Jews, many of whom had a deep commitment to the Jewish state. For the Israeli politicians, it was clear that the future of Israel was tied to the United States. "Our foreign policy was strongly oriented toward the Anglo-Saxon nations," Shimon Peres said. "France looked pleasant—but distant."[2]

Pleasant France wasn't a friend of Israel. It was a Muslim power. Tunisia and Morocco had been French protectorates until recently; Algeria was regarded as an organic part of France. France nourished the illusion that it had an important influence in some Arab countries, and saw a vital interest in the "radiation" of French culture in Lebanon and Egypt.

France also called itself "the elder daughter of the Catholic church." It believed it had a historic role to play as the protector of the Christians and the holy places in Palestine. Its close connections with the Arab world, on one hand, and with the Vatican, on the other, had a strong impact on its foreign policy. And yet, France had left warm memories in the hearts of many Israelis who had been active in illegal immigration or in smuggling weapons for the future IDF. They had discovered a strange duality in the French attitude toward their struggle. In spite of the government's cold and distant policy, which treated Israel with reserve and even hostility, many French people were eager to help in establishing a Jewish state. Israel found support in important sections of the army and the right wing, which regarded Great Britain as France's traditional rival and identified with Israel's struggle against the British mandate. In addition Socialist Party leaders considered Mapai a sister party, and former Resistance fighters and political figures who had suffered from Nazi atrocities felt a deep identification with the Jewish people.

The struggle of Israel, a small and enlightened nation, against the fanatic jihad of millions of Muslims determined to eradicate it fired up the imagination of many Frenchmen. But the war was over now, and the State of Israel had been created. In the corridors of France's Ministry of Foreign Affairs, located on the Quai d'Orsay by the Seine River, cold winds were blowing at the Israeli representatives. Together with Great Britain and the United States, France participated in the Near East Armament Coordination Committee (NEACC), whose task was to preserve the balance of power between the Middle Eastern nations. Israel was discriminated against from the very beginning by the NEACC, and France had no intention whatsoever of opposing the committee's policy.

SINCE PERES'S APPOINTMENT as director general of the Ministry of Defense, he had made arms acquisition his first priority. He realized that Israel, even though a sovereign state, was still operating as a clandestine organization. Israel had to use tortuous and sometimes illegal methods because nobody would sell her weapons openly. "The embargo of the great powers was not lifted," Peres wrote. "The independent, sovereign State of Israel has to buy its weapons through dealers, bring them to her territory by clandestine ways, and keep their very existence in utmost secrecy."[3] The IDF of those days was a patchwork army using equipment left over from the War of Independence, refurbished aircraft coming from different sources, tank chassis and turrets bought separately and clumsily welded together, cannons of different calibers using various kinds of ammunition. The only modern weapons the IDF had were a dozen British-made Meteor jets. Israel had been allowed to purchase them only because her Arab neighbors had purchased Vampire jets, also of British manufacture.

There was no other choice but to return to the old, half-clandestine methods that Peres knew so well from the days of the War of Independence. "In matters of arms acquisition," Peres said to his aides, "we should cast as many fishing lines as we can; perhaps something will bite. Everywhere we go we should try to get in by the door, and if we are thrown out, by the window, and if they close the window, too, keep looking for a crack, any crack, in order to get in."[4]

Peres proceeded to analyze the possible sources of weapons. The United States was closed to Israel since the War of Independence. The hostile attitude of Great Britain, and its pro-Arab policy, left no place for illusions. Peres described the British to his aides as "the worst enemy of Israel today." Peres found out how right he was when he visited London in mid-1955. He was received for talks by Defense Secretary Selwyn Lloyd and Deputy Foreign Secretary Evelyn Shuckburgh, but England kept delaying the dispatch of six Centurion tanks to Israel as retaliation for a raid by the Israeli Army on the Gaza Strip in February. Notes prepared by the British defense ministry and the Foreign Office warned against supplying the tanks to Israel because "it is against our interest to supply Israel with heavy weapons against which we may ourselves have to fight one day."[5] The British government also tried to prevent the French from selling Mystère jets to the IDF, arguing that Israel was Great Britain's "potential enemy" in the Middle East.[6] England agreed to sell two destroyers to the Israeli Navy, but only after having signed a similar contract with Egypt. The British government tried very hard to conceal the Egyptian deal from the Israelis, but when Peres and his team arrived in Cardiff to take possession of the ships, the British officers candidly asked him if they were "the Egyptians."[7]

France, Peres realized, was the only other European nation that fabricated most of its own weapons, including tanks, cannons, and jet aircraft. France needed markets to finance its military industry. It was also less dependent on the United States than other Western nations, and often disagreed with the directives coming from Washington. Peres decided to turn to France.

He didn't know France and didn't speak French. Still, it was a fascinating destination for the intellectual and the lover of culture that he was. Paris of the early fifties oozed art and culture. Even the arms deals in France had a romantic aura about them. Israel bought small quantities of arms through a picturesque dealer, a Polish count named Stefan Chernitsky. He lived with his lover, a stunning actress, in the Malmaison Palace, the former home of Empress Josephine. Elegant and fussy, the count threw lavish parties in his opulent domicile, or invited his guests to his king-sized swimming pool in the hot summer days.

Chernitsky received a commission on every deal he made with the French, and received additional sums "to soften" certain cabinet ministers. Peres wasn't enthusiastic about this arrangement; he preferred to establish direct ties with the weapons producers and the French government ministers. He asked Chernitsky to set up a meeting with the deputy prime minister, Paul Reynaud, who was in charge of foreign sales, but Chernitsky delayed the meeting, trying to prevent Peres from speaking directly with the French. Peres flew to Paris and phoned Reynaud, who immediately received him in his office. Reynaud was warm and friendly; they started a negotiation for the purchase of 155-mm. cannons. Peres finalized the deal with an aging colonel in the Ministry of Defense. Everything went fine, except for a moment of confusion concerning the payments. Peres had no idea how one government paid another. He therefore suggested to the French officer that Israel deposit one million dollars in the bank account of the French Ministry of Defense, and they would settle their bills later. "To my surprise he agreed to that suggestion, and the cannons started to move."[8] The era of dealers and brokers between France and Israel was over.

Peres's superiors were doubtful. Defense Minister Pinhas Lavon sent him a cold letter. "It would be silly to harness ourselves to the French cart," Lavon wrote. "Practically—it is not worth it. We have no reason to give up the purchase of arms in England. And if the United States opens its military pocket—that would be even better."[9]

But the United States didn't open its military pocket; neither did England. The British animosity bolstered Peres's determination to storm France. "I came as an uneducated kibbutznik, who had no idea about France," he said. "I entered the most beautiful palace in the world, without the right clothes, without the proper behavior, just like that, and with the intention of conquering the palace."[10] Peres was rather rough; he didn't have any manners, and Yossef Nahmias, the defense ministry's envoy to Paris, tutored him on French culture, fashion, table manners, and courteous behavior.[11] "I was captivated by France," Peres noted in his diary. "In France there was a deep sympathy for the Jewish people, to its fate, to the terrible tragedy that it suffered . . . . We received many negative answers, but we never had the feeling that the answers were final. These clever people, with their open minds, are people of perpetual dialogue. And even though you may lose a debate—their formidable training to use logic guarantees them an advantage from the start—you can suddenly subdue them with a sentimental argument."[12]

Peres went to France during the stormy days of the Fourth Republic (1946-58). The regime was utterly unstable, with governments rising and falling one after another. Many thought that it was impossible to maintain working relations with a government that could fall at any moment. But while for others the turbulent French politics were a hazard, for Peres they were an opportunity. He realized that in the disorder reigning in France it was possible to navigate between the various institutions, organizations, and people. The establishment of personal ties and a network of friends among the politicians, government employees, and army officers could be very helpful.

In the Fourth Republic, Peres discerned two schools of thought about Israel. One group was located in the foreign ministry, the other in the army and the defense ministry. Peres decided to establish close ties with both camps, although the "Quai d'Orsay"—the foreign ministry—seemed lost from the start. Whenever he visited Paris he studied the names of the officers and the high officials who shaped France's policy in the Middle East. Then he would call his aides and say, "Let's meet them." He would spend days rushing from one office to another, without giving up on anyone—industrialists, military officers, government aides, ministers, members of parliament, journalists. During his flights to and from Israel, he would study French with stubborn diligence. True, he didn't overcome his accent, and many of the secrets of French grammar still eluded him, but he achieved a basic knowledge of the language. One day his friend Jean Frydman, the director of the radio station Europe One, told Peres he wanted to introduce him to an aide of the French president. "But in what language would you speak with him?" Frydman asked.

"What?" Peres asked with false innocence. "Doesn't he speak French?"[13]

PERES HAD STARTED knocking on France's doors in early 1954. One time he was to meet with Diomede Catroux, the air minister in the French cabinet. Peres arrived at Catroux's office surreptitiously, but to his surprise the minister was waiting for him with a military band and a guard of honor.[14] "When Dayan and Peres told me about their problems," Catroux said later, "and about the weapons they needed, I said to myself that I couldn't become an accomplice to a new crime and not help the Israeli people to defend itself."[15]

On August 23, 1954, "the young man in the blue suit" signed an agreement with Diomede Catroux for the purchase of Ouragan and Mystère-2 jets, and a Noratlas cargo aircraft. Peres signed other deals with the defense ministry for the purchase of AMX-13 light tanks, radar equipment, and 75-mm. cannons. The agreements were approved by Prime Minister Pierre Mendès-France.[16] Peres, though, was aware that the agreement would have to be reviewed and approved by the NEACC, and all the chances were that it would be killed there.

In the spring of 1955, after Ben-Gurion's return to the defense ministry, the negotiations entered a new phase. Peres asked to meet with the new French defense minister, General Pierre Koenig, and Ben-Gurion immediately agreed. Peres left for France, carrying a letter from Moshe Dayan to the French minister.[17]

General Koenig was the hero of the Battle of Bir-Hacheim in the Western Desert, where his soldiers courageously fought Rommel's army. At the battlefield he met an armored column of soldiers in British uniforms who impressed him deeply. Their Shield of David tags indicated that these were soldiers of the Palestinian Jewish Brigade. Koenig halted his men, made them stand at attention, and saluted "the proud Palestinian soldiers."[18]

Now Koenig received Peres warmly; when Peres mentioned the purchase of weapons, Koenig interrupted him: "Can I have this in writing?" Peres promised that the "shopping list" would be in his hands the following morning at 10 A.M. Exactly at 10 A.M. the phone rang at the Israeli embassy. Koenig's chief of staff was on the line. "Where is the list?" he asked.

"It's on its way to you," Peres answered.[19]

On May 20, 1955, the French interministerial committee for arms sales approved the deal. Nevertheless, Peres didn't halt his search for friends and allies. He met with Foreign Minister Antoine Pinay; two directors general of cabinet ministries; seven generals and colonels from the army staff and the defense ministry; three managers of weapons-producing companies; and Daniel Mayer, the chairman of the parliamentary Foreign Affairs Committee. Even though some of them weren't directly involved in the current deals, Peres believed that his efforts would pay off in the long run.[20]

He meticulously prepared for each meeting. His aides would gather every bit of information on the people he was going to meet—their life stories, their habits, their political careers, their hobbies and areas of interest. When Peres met them, he knew how to steer the conversation toward his hosts' favorite subjects. He knew how to charm his interlocutors, and many of them became his personal friends.[21]

In July 1955, Peres learned that production of the Mystère 2 was being discontinued; the French offered to replace the jets with the more advanced Mystère 4; for the time being they were ready to send to Israel some obsolete Ouragan aircraft. Israel agreed. But the rejoicing was premature. In early October Koenig was forced to resign. Israel lost an important ally in the French cabinet at a moment when dramatic events taking place in the Middle East were turning Israel's efforts for arms acquisition into a question of survival.

DAVID BEN-GURION had returned from Sde Boker during a period of growing tension between Israel and its neighbors. The infiltration of terrorists from Gaza and Jordan was on the rise; Egypt's President Nasser created units of Palestinian terrorists in Gaza, the "Fedayeen," who started sneaking into Israel and attacking civilian and military targets. Ben-Gurion clashed with Prime Minister Sharett on the policy Israel should adopt. Ben-Gurion, supported by Peres and Dayan, was convinced that the Arab nations, led by Egypt, were getting ready to attack Israel.

A few days after the Old Man's return, a group of Fedayeen crossed the border, broke into the Institute for Biological Research in Ness Ziona, and assassinated a civilian cyclist. Another squad of terrorists got in a firefight with an Israeli patrol, and one of the Palestinians was killed. In his pocket the soldiers found a report on the road traffic in the south. On February 28, Ben-Gurion launched a retaliatory raid against Egypt. One hundred and forty-nine paratroopers under the command of Ariel Sharon attacked an Egyptian Army camp in the Gaza Strip. Thirty-eight Egyptian soldiers and eight Israelis were killed.

Shimon Peres hailed the operation as "a brilliant military victory."[22] The operation painfully shook the Egyptian leadership. Gradually, a vicious circle emerged: every terrorist penetration in Israel was followed by a retaliatory raid and vice versa. It looked as if an all-out war was about to break out.

After the July 1955 general elections, Ben-Gurion resumed the functions of prime minister and minister of defense, and Moshe Sharett returned to his former position as foreign minister. But on September 27, the astonished world learned about a huge arms deal between Egypt and Czechoslovakia, acting as front for the Soviet Union. Egypt was to receive 120 MiG-15 fighter jets and 50 II-28 bombers, 20 cargo aircraft, 200 tanks, 230 armored troop carriers, 100 self-propelled artillery pieces, and 500 more cannons of different calibers, as well as torpedo boats, destroyers, and six submarines.

Israel was horrified. Many of her leaders regarded "the Czech deal" as a death sentence on the Jewish state. Israel was unable to face such tremendous power. Late that night, Peres cabled Yossef Nahmias in Paris: "The supply of Russian weapons to Egypt changes our situation completely. There is no doubt that the French would be submitted now to unbearable pressure by the British and the Americans to suspend any supply of weapons to us. We shouldn't spare any effort to assure that the aircraft will be delivered to us on time."[23]

Sharett flew to Europe in a desperate effort to obtain weapons that would balance the Czech deal. On September 29 he met with the foreign ministers of the Great Powers, who were holding a summit in Geneva, but failed to win their support. France's foreign minister, Antoine Pinay, showed compassion for Israel's predicament, but refrained from any promises.[24] Sharett received a more sympathetic response from Edgar Faure, France's prime minister, who promised twenty-four Mystère aircraft to Israel.

In the meantime, Peres was meeting with the heads of the French Ministry of Defense. The new minister, General Pierre Billotte, told him clearly, "We want to see a strong Israel; Israel with weapons in her hands is an Israel of peace, even though there are many Frenchmen who wish that you would defeat the Egyptians."[25] Peres was familiar with the right-wing ideas of Billotte; he therefore chose the appropriate arguments. "We have a common enemy," he said to the French minister, "and that's England. . . . If England learns about the agreement between us, she would sabotage it." Billotte knew that a large part of the weapons sales, in particular the airplanes, depended on the consent of the

United States. He said he was willing to fly to Geneva and talk to Secretary of State John Foster Dulles.

Peres missed a heartbeat. He knew that the Americans might stop all the arms shipments from France. He persuaded Billotte to conclude the deal directly with Israel, without the Americans. Billotte explained, however, that the delivery of the Mystère aircraft was not possible at that time, and a second shipment of Ouragan aircraft was problematic. As for the bazookas that Israel had requested, France had stopped manufacturing them, and if Billotte wanted to supply them to Israel, he would have to take them from the French Army.

Peres didn't despair. He decided to convince the army chiefs of the urgency of Israel's demands. First, he persuaded the ground forces commander to release the tanks that Israel had requested and talked him into disarming several battalions of their bazookas and transfering them to Israel. He then rushed to the air force chief, who was in a bad mood.

"You took away twelve of my Ouragans," he said to Peres, "and you broke up an entire squadron"—a squadron numbered twenty-four aircraft.

"We can solve your problem," Peres retorted. "We'll take another twelve Ouragans."

The general didn't appreciate the joke and said to Peres that he wouldn't give up the Ouragans, but he was ready to release a number of Mystère-4 aircraft. Peres barely concealed his joy. These were the airplanes that the Israeli Air Force was dreaming of!

It seemed that the road had cleared all of a sudden. In the following meeting with Deputy Defense Minister Crouzier and Minister Billotte, they informed Peres that Israel would receive both the Mystère 4s and the other weapons on her shopping list. Peres couldn't believe that. "It looked so good, that the only trouble was that it looked too good," he noted.

"When do we sign?" he asked.

Crouzier checked his diary. "Day after tomorrow, at 5 P.M."

Two days later, Peres, Nahmias, and the Israeli ambassador went to Crouzier's office. "We were in a festive mood, we were wearing our blue suits, ready to conclude the deal," Peres recalled.[26] Crouzier welcomed them with a smile.

"How's the weather in Israel?" he asked.

The Israelis were puzzled. After all, they hadn't come to talk about the weather. They exchanged some niceties with their host.

Still smiling, Crouzier went on: "So, what's new?"

"We came to sign," Peres said.

"Ah, sign? Well, there are some problems."[27]

It turned out that the delivery of the aircraft had run into the firm objection both of the French foreign ministry and of the United States. The first 225 Mystère aircraft to come off the production line belonged to NATO forces, according to an American "Off Shore" order. They had been ordered by the United States for NATO and couldn't be sold to another country without an explicit American authorization. That authorization had been refused.[28]

That day, Peres and his colleagues signed an agreement for an arms purchase that included all their demands, except one—the Mystère-4 aircraft.[29]

Peres left the meeting deeply depressed. To his friends in Israel he said, "I failed my main mission."[30]

HE HAD FAILED, but he didn't give up. He met again with General Billotte. But shortly afterward another crisis erupted: the French government fell and France faced new elections.

Shimon Peres feared that Israel might lose everything she had obtained so far. He went to Ben-Gurion with a new idea: Israel should launch a "private" electoral campaign in France. He suggested sending to France several people who would meet with the various parties' candidates and try persuading them to commit themselves to Israel. Ben-Gurion approved Peres's idea, and he immediately flew to France.

In Paris, Peres diligently carried out his private campaign. He and his aides met the major political figures. Two men seemed to have a good chance: Foreign Minister Antoine Pinay and former prime minister Pierre Mendès-France, who attracted liberal and left-wing supporters. Defense Minister Billotte created a new party and campaigned in the provincial areas, far from Paris.

But in the French capital, Shimon Peres obtained some unexpected help. A friend introduced him to a Jew of Algerian origin, George Elgosi, a senior economist at the prime minister's office. Elgosi invited Peres to his home. Peres was deeply impressed by the astounding art collection that filled the apartment.[31] In the living room an elderly woman, well dressed, sat on a tall chair resembling a throne. "That's my mother," Elgosi said, and introduced his guest. She looked at Peres with sharp, penetrating eyes, and asked him to give her his hand, which she thoroughly examined. Finally she turned to her son. "Do whatever he asks," she said, and raised her eyes to the sky, as if she had received a direct message from the Almighty.[32] Peres felt awkward, but Elgosi took her words seriously. "Come to my office tomorrow," he said.

The following day, still somewhat confused by his meeting with the old lady, Peres went to Elgosi's office, very close to the personal office of the prime minister. Peres was amazed. Elgosi offered Peres the use of his office. He went to see one of his colleagues, a young man named Valery Giscard d'Estaing, who was in charge of the Israeli file. "Do you mind if I take care of the Israelis?" Elgosi asked, and Giscard agreed.[33]

"This guy, Elgosi," Peres said later, "called right away twelve ministries, spoke to ministers and directors general, and in an hour we had a full picture of the situation." From his new headquarters in Elgosi's office, Peres kept trying to release the Mystère aircraft and made appointments with senior officials in the government ministries. He crossed the few yards that separated his office from Prime Minister Edgar Faure's office and asked to buy not twelve, but seventy-two aircraft. "Whatever you conclude with Billotte is fine with me," Faure said to the young Israeli. "He and his deputy Crouzier are your friends."

Peres found Billotte campaigning in Dijon, 200 miles away

from Paris. They stood in the shadow of a truck laden with loudspeakers. Billotte spoke with deep emotion. "I am Catholic," he said. "My father commanded an armored division, and was killed in the First World War. But my mother is Jewish. My wife is Jewish, too, from the Rothschild family. I have sentiments for the Jews. In my district people are calling at me circumscription—Down with the Jews! They say that I work more for the Jews than for France."[34] Billotte promised to help Peres get the aircraft after the elections.

"Ben-Gurion knows how troublesome it is to lead a political party," Peres said, "but he sent me to you, to your electoral district, because the MiGs are already in the air."

"Everything will be over by January 19," Billotte repeated. He and Peres together wrote a telegram to Ben-Gurion.[35]

Meanwhile, Israel's foreign ministry was striving to obtain weapons and political support from the United States. But the American State Department kept procrastinating and leading Israel astray. In private conversations with his colleagues, Secretary of State Dulles said that France should give the aircraft to Israel. However, he refrained from giving France the formal authorization to do so.[36] Another possibility was that Canada or Italy could sell Israel twenty-four F-86 Sabre jet fighters that they produced under American license; but the secretary didn't authorize that deal, either. The United States was determined to stick to a neutral position, even if that endangered Israel. To the Israeli ambassador, Abba Eban, Dulles said that in any case Israel wouldn't be able to withstand the numerical might of forty million Arabs, therefore "she must rely upon the good will [of other nations] which would make available outside strength, and not on its own strength alone." [37]

Dulles even tried to take advantage of Israel's weakness and force her to make territorial concessions to the Arabs.[38] In a memorandum to Sharett, Dulles wrote that the "territorial adjustments" needed in order to achieve peace in the Middle East were in fact "concessions in the Negev in order to create an Arab territorial link between Egypt and the rest of the Arab world."[39] England supported his initiative.[40] The Israeli foreign ministry experts who had assumed that the United States would supply Israel with defensive weapons turned out to be absolutely wrong.[41]

January 2, 1956, was election day in France. Edgar Faure, Antoine Pinay, and Pierre Billotte were beaten at the polls. The right-wing leaders who appeared to be friendly to Israel were removed from power. Mendès-France was defeated as well. The Socialist leader Guy Mollet was charged with forming the new government.

"We failed at the elections in France," a dejected Peres declared at a meeting of the IDF General Staff. He then assembled his aides and told them grimly, "Now we have to start everything from scratch."[42]

But this time Peres was mistaken. The historic reversal in the relations between France and Israel was about to happen—and quite unexpectedly.

FOUR MONTHS BEFORE, on September 3, 1955, the defense ministry's envoy in Paris, Yossef Nahmias, had been invited for drinks to the home of a French tennis champion. He was discreetly informed that some of the guests would be people of extreme right-wing convictions who had belonged in the past to the notorious subversive terrorist organization La Cagoule—"the Cowl." Nahmias was tense and suspicious when he crossed his host's threshold. "I realized that I was going to meet with dangerous people who wanted to establish a connection between the French right wing and Israel, which was fighting the Arabs." In the living room Nahmias saw about ten people and to him "the whole thing smelled like Mafia."[43]

His host introduced him to a young, stocky man, ordinary looking, slovenly dressed, wearing shoes without laces. "This is Abel Thomas," the Frenchman said to Nahmias, "the director general of the interior ministry." He added that his friend Thomas, unlike the other guests, was a Socialist. Nahmias barely restrained himself from bursting into laughter. This untidy and absentminded man with no shoelaces was the director general of the interior ministry? "I wouldn't have bet one franc that this was true; it seemed unreal." Out of caution, Nahmias decided not to reveal his real function, and only said that he was "an Israeli working for the government." Thomas didn't trust the Israeli, either. "In the home of Couiteas de Faucamberge, a famous tennis player, I was introduced to a man named Nahmias," he said later. Thomas thought that the "intelligent, wily man with the glinting black eyes" was an arms dealer.[44]

Nahmias spoke briefly about his efforts to obtain weapons for Israel and the two men parted. The following morning, Nahmias decided to check out Thomas. He called the Ministry of the Interior and asked to be connected to the director general. In a moment, his interlocutor was on the phone. "I recognized his voice; this was the man!"

In the afternoon, he drove to the Ministry of the Interior and asked to see Mr. Thomas. The usher respectfully led him to a posh office. At the door he was met by an admiral in resplendent uniform. Thomas greeted him warmly. "Come in, Mr. Nahmias," he said, and led him to a large office, lavishly furnished; the windows offered a pleasant view of a lush garden. Thomas laughed: "I know why you came. You wanted to find out if it was me."

On the wall, Nahmias saw a large map of Algeria, which was being torn by a bloody war between the French and Arab rebels. He suddenly understood: Thomas was in charge of the war operations! "I realized that I had stumbled on a fabulous treasure," Nahmias said.[45]

The war in Algeria, as strange as it seemed, was the responsibility of the minister of the interior, Maurice Bourgès-Maunoury. The war had broken out on November 1, 1954, when Arab rebels attacked several French settlers and cut their throats. They distributed flyers calling for a revolt against the French regime. Soon the rebellion spread throughout Algeria and turned into France's major political and military problem. The French

Constitution stipulated that Algeria was an integral part of France and had the legal status of a French province. The rebellion, therefore, was an "internal" problem and, according to the Cartesian logic of the French, the war had to be conducted by the Ministry of the Interior.

The French secret services found out that Nasser's Egypt was training the Algerian rebels and supplying them with weapons, funds, and political support. The rebellion's leader, Ahmed Ben Bella, and his acolytes found political shelter in Cairo.

The French refused to accept the simple truth that Algeria's Arabs were waging a war of national liberation. They preferred to cultivate the naive illusion that the Algerians wanted to remain French subjects; but Nasser, the devious fiend, incited them and fomented the rebellion. That drove many French, mostly in right-wing circles, to a logical conclusion: if they succeeded in stopping Nasser's support of the rebels—or got rid of him—the rebellion would collapse.

The Ministry of the Interior's officials sincerely believed that France had to destroy Nasser. They regarded Israel as their natural ally, and a major key for victory in Algeria. In Thomas's office, Nahmias described his mission in France, and Thomas offered to help him. Thomas spoke to Bourgès-Maunoury, and the minister espoused a firm pro-Israeli stand.[46]

A few months later, Peres arrived in Paris and met Thomas at a Parisian restaurant. Thomas was deeply impressed by Peres. "The discussion with him was clear, frank and practical," Thomas wrote, "exactly like his character. All of Israel spoke through his mouth."[47] Thomas told Peres that he was speaking in the name of Bourgès-Maunoury. "So why don't we go to meet him?" Peres suggested.

Late that evening, they entered Bourgès-Maunoury's house. Peres saw a young, brilliant, and dynamic man. Bourgès's conversation sparkled with a subtle sense of humor and a rich imagination. He was surprised by the unexpected visit, but regained his spirits and offered Peres a glass of aged port left to him by his grandfather, Marshal Maunoury.

Bourgès left a lasting impression on Peres and mutual sympathy immediately sparked between them. Nahmias regarded Bourgès as "the French Shimon Peres."[48] The future would prove that Bourgès-Maunoury was the most important among the French leaders who established the de facto alliance with Israel. He was regarded as the enfant terrible of the Radical Party. A hero of World War II, he had been wounded, decorated, and promoted to colonel. At the age of forty-two he had already served fourteen times as a cabinet minister.

Peres and Bourgès-Maunoury soon became close friends. "We used to go on the town in the evenings," Peres recalled. They would often meet at the home of Bourgès's mistress, and the Frenchman appreciated the discretion of his Israeli friend.[49] That friendship was to become the cornerstone of French-Israeli relations in the mid-fifties.

On January 31, 1956, a new government was established in France. The Socialist Guy Mollet was elected prime minister. The foreign minister, Christian Pineau, was also a Socialist; during World War II he had been imprisoned by the Nazis at the Buchenwald concentration camp. Maurice Bourgès-Maunoury was appointed defense minister.

Thus, a new era started in French-Israeli relations.

BALD, BESPECTACLED, with a firm body and a thin mustache hovering over an eternal cigarette, Guy Mollet was a self-controlled but decisive man. He was eager to solve the Algerian problem, but after a tumultuous visit to Algeria he realized that his ideas about a compromise solution wouldn't work. He therefore adopted a tough line of outright war against the rebels.

At first, Mollet tried to achieve an agreement with Egypt and put an end to its support for the rebels. Foreign Minister Pineau flew to Cairo and met with Nasser, who gave him his "soldier's word" that he would stop the incitement against France. The solemn promise was kept for barely three days, and the anti-

French broadcasts coming out of Egypt became even more virulent. The French government, realizing that Nasser was unreliable, moved toward an open confrontation with Egypt—and closer ties with Israel.

The partners in the new French coalition each supported Israel for his own reasons. Mollet, Pineau, and the other Socialist ministers sympathized with Israel and Ben-Gurion's Mapai Party. Guy Mollet was determined to help Israel overcome the danger of destruction by her Arab enemies.[50] Christian Pineau, the former concentration-camp inmate, had sworn to do all in his power to help the survivors of the Nazi camps.[51] "Shimon Peres," he said, "was the first to inform me about the grave danger threatening Israel. We couldn't ignore his warnings."[52]

The Socialists' partners in the government were Bourgès-Maunoury's radicals. Their main goal was winning the Algerian war. The new French government, therefore, turned out to be the most pro-Israeli ever. One of its first initiatives was to request from the United States a final answer about the sale of twelve Mystère-4 aircraft to Israel.[53] If an answer was not received by March 15, the French said, the aircraft would be sent to Israel without further delay.

The French kept their word. The first Mystère jets landed in Israel on April 11, 1956.

But by then Peres had ventured far beyond the purchase of twelve airplanes.

IN FEBRUARY AND MARCH 1956, Peres and Bourgès-Maunoury discussed, for the first time, the possibility of a joint French-Israeli operation against Egypt. Those meetings, which also included contacts between officers of the two armies, had an immediate result: the decision to bypass the foreign ministries of the two countries and establish a direct link for joint planning and exchange of intelligence.

That decision exacerbated the tension between Ben-Gurion and Sharett. The two men were in deep disagreement concerning Israeli activities in France. The tightening of the secret contacts with France was bound to result in a bitter confrontation between the prime minister and the foreign minister.

On April 3, 1956, the United States rejected Israel's request to buy American weapons. At an emergency meeting with Sharett, Dayan, and Peres, the Old Man vented his frustration. "Dulles's words are base hypocrisy," he said. "We should stop right away all efforts in the United States, and not even try to use its good services to obtain weapons in other countries; we should turn to them directly."[54] Sharett desperately clung to his policy of relying on America, and claimed that the U.S. response was not definitive yet.[55] Ambassador Yaakov Tzur, Sharett's friend, sadly admitted that Sharett kept "underestimating France."[56] Moshe Dayan congratulated Peres for obtaining the twelve Mystère aircraft that were on their way to Israel. Ben-Gurion gave Peres a free hand to continue his activity in France.

Sharett was deeply offended, and after the meeting sent Ben-Gurion an angry letter, attacking both Dayan and Peres. He maintained that he—and not Peres—had obtained the Mystère aircraft from France and that Ambassador Tzur had been promised twelve more aircraft by Pineau.

"I don't see any importance in the question—who obtained more or who was the first," Ben-Gurion answered the following day. "I'll be as happy at the success of Ambassador Tzur as at the success of Shimon, for what matters is to succeed .... But Shimon, too, can meet with Pineau or some other Foreign Minister. All this inter-departmental rivalry seems somewhat bizarre to me."

Sharett got even angrier. "When the Chief of Staff attributes all the successes to the Ministry of Defense people"—he meant Peres—"without admitting that others have contributed something too—and when you refrain from rebuking him—I react as I did."[57]

Sharett wasn't aware of the secret relationship between Peres and Bourgès-Maunoury and between the IDF and the French Army. The foreign minister had been removed from the decision-making circle; he disagreed with Ben-Gurion, criticized Dayan, but most of all was furious with Peres, who kept bypassing his ministry.

Indeed, the relentless Peres had just dispatched a letter to Bourgès-Maunoury: "I would like to place an order in France for 60 aircraft Mystère A-4." Peres got into details. "According to the offer of your Ministry," he wrote, "the government of Israel agrees that the aircraft be delivered in a few shipments throughout 1956." Peres also asked to purchase 36 more Ouragans or Mystères 2s and 15 Vautour light bombers—all in all, 111 aircraft beside the 12 whose sale had been already approved.[58]

But before the first Mystère landed in Israel, a new crisis broke out.

ON APRIL 9, the French foreign minister was expected to come to Israel on an official visit. But on April 5, the Egyptian Army opened fire on an Israeli patrol on the Gaza Strip border, the IDF returned fire, the Egyptians shelled Israeli settlements, and the IDF shelled Gaza. But the Egyptians got what they wanted—Pineau canceled his visit to Israel. He also informed the chargé d'affaires at the Israeli embassy in Paris that he wouldn't sign any more agreements on the supply of weapons before the meeting of the NEACC. He added that because of the Algerian war, France couldn't be the exclusive supplier to Israel, and set a new condition: if—but only if—England and the United States supplied at least 25 percent of the weapons to Israel, France would supply the rest. In a closed meeting, Shimon Peres declared that Pineau was leading Israel astray by his declarations of friendship. "Pineau is wishing us well," he said, "but he is not a great friend of Israel."[59]

Sharett was deeply disappointed by the cancelation of Pineau's visit. "He already had planned what red carpet would be laid for Pineau and which band would play for him," cracked Ambassador Tzur.[60]

Actually, the crisis was not as terrible as that. The shipment of the first twelve Mystères was not put off, and they were expected to land on April 11.

On April 10, Ben-Gurion again called for a meeting, to discuss relations with France. Sharett and Tzur insisted on sticking to the traditional procedures. Dayan interrupted Tzur: "Don't you think we can reach an arrangement with the defense ministry people, in order to put an end to all these hesitations and overcome the objections of the foreign ministry?"

Tzur answered: "Only with the army and the defense ministry? No."[61]

Peres intervened: "We have to ask France for a double quantity of weapons. We should stop speaking about seventy-two Mystères and start talking about one hundred and fifty; we should talk about two hundred tanks instead of sixty. We are getting ten tanks now, and that's our fault, the defense ministry's fault. At first, when we asked for sixty tanks, it seemed something huge, but if we had asked for two hundred tanks in the first place—they would have talked with us for other proportional quantities."[62]

Sharett was skeptical. "And if they wouldn't play the game?"

Peres answered, "When they hear this for the first time—they'll laugh. At the second time—this will be the figure that the world will accept. Considering the huge numbers of MiGs and Ilyushins that Egypt is receiving, seventy-two aircraft won't be enough . . . ."

"The main question now is how we make the French believe that we are ready to act together with them . . . . We must take dramatic steps, to make France understand that we are ready to engage in a far-reaching cooperation."

"I propose finding an unconventional way to negotiate with the French, and make them offers that they would consider as real accomplishments."[63]

At the end of the meeting, Ben-Gurion made a final decision about the quest for arms in France; he transferred it to the defense ministry.

The following day, April 11, the twelve Mystère aircraft landed in Israel.

A confrontation between the Ministries of Defense and Foreign Affairs, strikingly similar to the angry clashes in Jerusalem, took place in Paris. During the months of April through June 1956, Bourgès-Maunoury and his people exchanged angry letters and accusations about the arms sales to Israel with Pineau and his aides. The direct negotiations between Israel and the defense ministry infuriated Pineau;[64] Bourgès-Maunoury criticized the Quai d'Orsay for delaying the supply of aircraft to Israel;[65] senior Quai d'Orsay officials bitterly complained to their minister about Bourgès-Maunoury's people, who signed new agreements with Israel disregarding their reservations.[66] The Quai d'Orsay strongly protested against France becoming the only supplier of weapons to Israel,[67] but Bourgès-Maunoury didn't care. A few days later, his aide Colonel Leveque calmly notified his colleagues at the Quai d'Orsay of a new Israeli request for 100 tanks and 142 fighter and bomber aircraft.[68]

During the hectic days of that spring, a secret agreement was forged between the defense ministries of France and Israel to bypass, at all costs, their foreign ministries.

ON APRIL 12, after midnight, Shimon Peres was urgently called to Ben-Gurion's office. Moshe Dayan was already there. The clashes with the Egyptian Army at the Gaza Strip were threatening to turn into an all-out war. Ben-Gurion sent Peres on an urgent mission to France and gave him a letter to deliver to Prime Minister Guy Mollet. He described "Nasser's intentions to attack Israel," and stressed the "huge quantities" of Soviet weapons dispatched to Egypt. They were, in his words, "a terrifying threat to the State of Israel." Finally, he asked Mollet to urgently supply arms to Israel "in order to guarantee the survival of our State."[69]

Upon his arrival in Paris, Peres was received at the Hotel Matignon, the prime minister's official residence. He knew Guy Mollet from the electoral campaign, when the two had met in a Parisian restaurant. He had been impressed with Mollet's personality. He disagreed with those who claimed that Mollet was dry and dull. "Quite often," he later said, "a smart smile, rather a Parisian wink, sparkles in his eyes."[70] Mollet told Peres that some of Mollet's rivals accused him of anti-Semitism; that accusation stemmed from his disagreements with Daniel Mayer, a Socialist leader of Jewish origin. "The opposite is true," Mollet said. "I have been a witness to the Nazi persecutions. The greatest Frenchman I knew was [the socialist leader] Léon Blum. He was my mentor and my teacher. You know that Blum was a courageous man and a proud Jew."[71]

At that first meeting, Peres told Mollet that his socialist party, Mapai, always felt "both hope and anxiety" whenever a socialist party abroad acceded to power. On one hand, Peres said, we are thrilled by the hope that a sister party is going to be in charge; on the other hand, we deeply fear that the socialist party, once in power, might abandon its principles and promises. [72] Peres cited the example of the British Labour Party: when it was in opposition it declared its support for Israel, but when it acceded to power, Foreign Minister Ernest Bevin became a staunch enemy of Zionism.

"I shall not be Bevin," Guy Mollet answered.[73]

Several months had passed, and today Mollet was prime minister. During their meeting, he tried to be informal and relaxed. "I am not a diplomat," Peres said, and Mollet retorted, "Neither am I." They spoke of the American position about the sale of weapons to Israel, and Mollet remarked that "Dulles is a very hard man to rely on."

When they parted, Mollet said to Peres, "I believe that we can help you." Then he added, almost in a whisper, "Did I tell you that I was not Bevin?"[74]

PERES ALSO MET WITH Bourgès, and afterward said to his friends, "The French Defense Minister is a better ambassador of Israel than any Israeli ambassador."[75] He added cynically, "Our affair with France will go on as long as French people are being killed in Algeria, and Egyptians are killed in Israel."[76]

Shimon Peres spent the following few days in Paris in intensive meetings with scores of officers, politicians, and senior officials in the defense ministry. But at night, Peres was reborn, urging his aides to go out to a restaurant, a night club, or a discotheque. His appetite for Parisian nightlife and cultural events was insatiable. This became a characteristic trait of Peres, and in his travels abroad, he often towed his assistants to late-night tours of clubs and restaurants, while the only good time they could dream of was going to bed.[77] Several times, after a long and exhausting day, Peres fainted while in a restaurant or a club.[78] After one of these collapses, the doctors ordered a few days of complete rest. Mordechai Limon, the defense ministry's envoy to Paris at the time, took him to a pleasant hotel, about an hour's drive from the capital. "At 4 A.M. the phone rang," Limon recalled. "Shimon was on the line. 'I can't sleep,' he said, 'I'm returning to Paris.' "[79]

On April 19, Bourgès promised Peres that in two or three weeks he would release the second dozen Mystères, without asking the Americans and without waiting for the Quai d'Orsay's authorization.[80] And on April 23, at a festive ceremony at the French defense ministry, Shimon Peres signed the contract for the sale of the jets to Israel. Bourgès-Maunoury and the minister of the air, Laforet, signed in the name of France. The only request the French made was to keep the deal secret, so that the Quai d'Orsay people wouldn't know about it.

The aircraft left for Israel on the 15th and 25th of May.

"Good work, Shimon!" Ben-Gurion cabled.[81]

TO PRESERVE THE SECRECY, the phone conversations between the defense ministry in Tel Aviv and the ministry's envoy in Paris were carried out in code. Back in Israel, Peres would often phone Yossef Nahmias; their conversations sounded like an exchange between two naughty boys.

Nahmias: Shimon, our two friends traveled to a far-off country.

Peres: And what about the horse?

Nahmias [who forgot the meaning of the code and hurriedly looked for its meaning in the coded instructions leaflet]: Oy, the horse, the horse, what number?

Peres: Three.

Nahmias: That's the same thing .... Shimon, about the place that we visited together there are some questions: our guys have to answer them [the French] what fuses we need for the 25 pounders.

Peres: Yossef, be more careful on the telephone.

Nahmias: Okay .... Shimon, what quantities of food do you need?

Peres: From one hundred, six, and from forty, four.

Nahmias: Good.

Peres: Carmen Miranda—did she get married or not? [The "marriage" of actress Carmen Miranda was the code name for one of the top-secret operations in France.]

Nahmias: Who?

Peres: Carmen.

Nahmias: She went out.

Peres: She still didn't find a groom?

Nahmias: We don't know yet if there will be a wedding or not.[82]

While Peres was waiting for the marriage of Carmen Miranda, Ben-Gurion's relations with Sharett were on a collision course. Ben-Gurion feared a war with Egypt, yet he wanted it, in order to smother in the cradle the building of Egyptian might. Sharett objected, and did all in his power to thwart Ben-Gurion's plans. Finally, Ben-Gurion forced Sharett to resign, and appointed Golda Meir foreign minister.

Golda was an activist on security matters, exactly like Ben-Gurion, and totally approved his policy. She was also devoted to him heart and soul, and often used to say, "If Ben-Gurion asks me to jump from the fifth floor, I'll do it right away."[83] Ben-Gurion didn't ask her to jump, but Golda's assuming the foreign minister position removed a formidable obstacle from his path. Now, his hands were free for the following stage.

That stage was not long coming. Barely three days after Sharett's resignation, at night, a French Nord aircraft took off from an Israeli military airfield; twelve hours later, it landed at the Persan-Beaumont air base near Paris. Three important passengers were on the plane: Moshe Dayan, Shimon Peres, and General Yehoshafat Harkabi, the IDF's head of intelligence. They were met by Colonel Louis Mangin, Bourgès-Maunoury's chief of staff, and several high-ranking French officers. Yossef Nahmias also joined the small delegation.

The group drove in a convoy of cars to an old castle, north of Paris, that was surrounded by a park and an ancient wall. It had been chosen by the French government for the secret conference. Peres, who loved colorful formulas, named the secret meeting "the Loading Conference," meaning that France and Israel were loading their weapons.

The discussions started that very day. On the French side the main participants were Generals Maurice Challe, deputy chief of staff; Pierre-Cyrille Lavaud, member of the general staff; and the heads of the SDECE, French intelligence agency.

Dayan spoke for Israel. "We shall be ready," he said to the French, "to act together with you against Nasser to the extent that you will be ready to cooperate with us." He believed that Nasser was about to launch an onslaught against Israel. "It is important for us to know if France is willing to fortify Israel against the Egyptian attack."[84] The French officers agreed with Dayan. They were ready, they said, to act with Israel "to foil Nasser's schemes."

The participants agreed that some immediate steps had to be taken—a massive rearming of Israel, an exchange of intelligence, a close cooperation in secret projects, and a common execution of subversive actions, including sabotage and unconventional operations. Israeli intelligence dispatched to Paris Colonel Yuval Ne'eman, and charged him with the planning of operations "which, had they become known, would have politically embar-rassed Israel."[85]

Now Peres presented the new shopping list he had prepared: zoo AMX tanks, 72 Mystère-4 aircraft, 40,000 75-mm. shells, 10,000 antitank missiles. Peres thought that these were "fan-tastic" figures, and that nobody would take them seriously. But the French didn't bat an eyelash. They immediately started dis-cussing how to ship the weapons to Israel. The tanks, they said, could be brought to Israel on LSTs (tank-landing ships) that would unload their cargo during the night. The aircraft would arrive in direct flights from France. The entire deal amounted to $80 million.

The Israelis hadn't yet recovered from the shock caused by the French agreement when Louis Mangin bent over Peres. "Are you ready to sign?" he asked.

Peres reached for his pen and signed the agreement.

Moshe Dayan "almost fainted" and Yossef Nahmias was flab-bergasted. "Are you crazy?" he whispered to Peres. "Why did you sign? We didn't get an authorization!"[86] The amount that Peres committed to by his signature was equivalent to 20 percent of the total yearly budget of the State of Israel![87]

When the conference ended, Moshe Dayan was elated. "In a year," he wrote, "we'll have a new air force and a new armored corps.... We'll be out of the danger that was brought upon us by the alliance between Egypt and the Soviet Union."[88]

The delegation returned to Israel on June 25 and reported to Ben-Gurion, who approved the agreements. "This is a somewhat risky adventure," the Old Man sighed, "but what can we do? All our existence is like that."[89]

On July 24, at night, the first ship loaded with weapons arrived at the port of Haifa. Ben-Gurion, Dayan, and French ambassador Pierre Gilbert went to watch the unloading. In less than an hour, thirty tanks moved on shore and disappeared. In the following months phantom ships kept docking in Israel in utmost secrecy. The Mystère jets arrived in large formations. Peres convinced the French to add to the deal some self-propelled 105-mm. guns and Sherman tanks. France stopped reporting to the NEACC, to England, and to the United States about the arms shipments to Israel.

It was not until August 19 that Ben-Gurion informed the cabinet about the shipments from France. A few ministers went to Haifa to watch the unloading of the French ships; others were invited to an air base, where the Mystères landed on their last drops of fuel. Shimon Peres took the poet Nathan Alterman to the port of Haifa. Alterman wrote a moving poem in his *Davar* column. And in mid-October, when the operation was drawing to its end, Ben-Gurion read Alterman's poem from the Knesset podium.

Perhaps that is a night that was or just a dream. And in that dream—iron could be seen, a lot of iron, iron new,

Pointing long barrels. Thundering on chains of steel,

From far away it comes. It climbs ashore, and while still a fantasy, it turns out to be real,

And as it touches our land, a Jewish force it becomes.

That is a night that was—or that will be. If so or so, it's not a false mirage.

An unknown night it is, a festive night

To be remembered far beyond the boundaries of our time

Happy is the people that lives that way . . . . Its flaws are bare to eyes of friends and eyes of foes—

But its fine, boldest feats are hidden and concealed, for darkness them should cover.[90]

On July 26, two days after the first French ship arrived in Israel, President Nasser announced the nationalization of the Suez Canal.

That was the first shot of the Sinai Campaign.

CHAPTER 11.

SUEZ

ON AN ELEVATED platform in Alexandria, facing thousands of cheering Egyptians, stood Gamal Abdel Nasser, proud and confident.

A few days before, Secretary of State Dulles had dealt Nasser a painful blow by declaring that America wouldn't finance the building of the Aswan High Dam, which was the key for reviving Egypt's economy.

In his speech that night, July 26, 1956, Nasser boasted that he had found a source for the financing of the high dam—the Suez Canal. The canal, which was owned by an Anglo-French company, would be nationalized. The money for the dam, he said, would come from the duties and tolls paid by ships sailing through the canal. The crowd in the Alexandria square listened to Nasser with admiration and pride. Nasser was giving back to Egypt its national treasure. Nasser stood up to the corrupt West; he was a hero.

The Western world reacted with rage to Nasser's speech. Europe regarded Egypt's ambitious ruler as a great danger. The French blamed him for the Algerian rebellion. The socialist movements in Europe compared him to Hitler: a dictator determined to annihilate Israel. For many he was an imperialist of a new kind, aspiring to create an Islamic empire in the Middle East, in Africa, and even in parts of Europe. England was worried; it had evacuated its army from Egypt, but couldn't rely anymore on Nasser's loyalty. The United States watched helplessly as he fell into the open arms of the Soviet Union. Nasser's agents undermined the pro-Western regimes in the Middle East while he openly opposed the Washington-inspired Baghdad Pact.

But this time he had gone too far. The first reaction in London and Paris to Nasser's speech was a call to go to war and defeat him. Nasser had carried out an act of piracy, France and England claimed, that hurt large companies and small investors.

But behind the defense of the small investors other interests were looming. England wanted to preserve control of the waterway to the Far East. As for France, it saw in the Suez crisis a golden opportunity to destroy Nasser and put an end to the Algerian rebellion.

In the night of July 26 and during the following days, hectic activity reigned in the general staffs of the French and British armies. Senior officers met in London, and operational plans succeeded one after another. Generals declared a state of high alert, reserve soldiers and officers were urgently called to the service—and it seemed that in a few weeks the French and British forces would invade Cairo and Alexandria.

But soon the French-British expedition got mired in a diplomatic imbroglio. The United States wasn't interested in a new war. It faced a presidential election in early November. President Eisenhower was running for a second term and believed that no military adventure overseas should threaten his reelection. Dulles, a master of procrastination, called for several international conferences, established a "Canal Users' Association," and directed lengthy negotiations—but blocked the use of force. France and England were compelled to bring the matter before the United Nations Security Council, while Dulles decided it was a good time to take a vacation in Bermuda.

The British resolve started waning. The French didn't give up, however; when they realized that the British were unreliable, they turned to their alternative ally. Israel.

THE SUEZ CANAL was nationalized a few days before Shimon Peres's thirty-third birthday. He happened to be in Paris, negotiating a deal for the purchase of some Vautour bombers. He was urgently invited to see Colonel Louis Mangin, one of Bourgès's closest aides. In Mangin's office he met the deputy chief of staff of the army, General Maurice Challe. Mangin and Challe told Peres that Christian Pineau was about to fly to London to meet with Prime Minister Anthony Eden. They asked Peres for some intelligence reports about the capacity and the deployment of the Egyptian Army.[1]

A few days later, Peres was invited to an urgent meeting with Bourgès-Maunoury. Peres and Nahmias rushed to the defense ministry, at Rue Saint-Dominique, and were ushered to a map room where a large group of French generals were holding a conference. Bourgès turned to Peres without any preamble: "How long will it take your army to cross the Sinai and reach the Suez Canal?"[2]

Between five and seven days, Peres replied.

Skeptical smiles flourished around the room. Bourgès, too, thought that Peres's estimate was too optimistic. "Our people believe that you'll need at least three weeks," he said. Then he asked Peres: "Does Israel intend to take action one day on her southern border? And if she does—where would that action take place?"

"Our Suez is the port of Eilat, on the Red Sea," Peres said. "We shall never agree to its blockade, and that would be the target of an Israeli operation, if we decide to act."

One of the generals fired another question: "If France goes to war against Egypt, will Israel join us?"

"Yes," Peres said without hesitating.[3]

When they left the building, Nahmias turned to Peres: "You should be hanged for talking like that. How can you say such a thing? You don't have the authority!"

"If I had given a negative answer," Peres said to him, "that would have been the end of our relations with France. I said yes, but it is evident that such an operation must be approved by Israel's government. We can always change our mind."[4]

Peres returned to Israel and reported to Ben-Gurion, but the Old Man was vague in his responses.[5] Dayan and Peres decided to coordinate their activities. They both wanted to establish an alliance between Israel and France and launch a military operation that would remove the Egyptian threat for years to come. They both had the feeling, Peres wrote later, "that a great historic moment in the French-Israeli relations was approaching, but if we failed to act, there would be no second chance."[6]

In their meeting, Peres and Dayan made several decisions: 1. To suggest to the French that they invite Israel for formal talks on their cooperation. 2. To make sure that England, which had a defense treaty with Jordan, wouldn't act against Israel if Jordan intervened in a conflict between Israel and Egypt. 3. That after the war Israel should get control of the Straits of Sharm al-Sheikh (Tiran), to defend free navigation to Eilat; she should also keep the strategic crossroads of Nakhal, Abu-Ageila, and Rafah, in the Sinai.[7]

Peres arrived in Paris on September 18 and met with Bourgès-Maunoury. Bourgès was pessimistic; he doubted the resolve of the British to go to war and wanted to propose an alternative plan to his government.

"There are three possible timings," he said. "The French timing—that insists on an immediate action against Nasser; the English timing—that prefers political activity for two more months; and the American timing—that is based on repeating the Mosaddeq episode"—a subversive process that would topple Nasser in the long run, the same way the Iranian prime minister, Dr. Mohammad Mosaddeq, had been overthrown in 1953.

Bourgès gloomily added, "Apparently, the English timing is closer to the Israeli timing than the French one. France has to decide before the end of the year, before the winter, before a possible downfall of the present government."[8]

Peres reported to Ben-Gurion and flew to London for some

unrelated meetings. But soon after his arrival in the British capital, he received a telegram from Ben-Gurion that included a historic sentence: "As for the three timings, we prefer the French timing."[9]

BOURGÈS-MAUNOURY ASKED to meet Peres at once.

Peres landed in Paris on Sunday, September 23, at dawn. Nahmias was waiting for him and they drove through the empty Parisian streets. But at the defense ministry they were told that the minister had gone for the weekend to a hunting lodge in Sologne, and expected them there. The two Israelis scrutinized the map and discovered the place in a wooded area north of Paris. They drove for 125 miles, but on arriving found out that the minister was in another town of a similar name—and that this town was located 125 miles *south* of Paris. They set off again, lost their way, stopped for directions, and arrived, exhausted and mortified, at the right address, after an eight-hour delay Bourgès welcomed them warmly. The room where their conversation took place looked like a movie set—a fire burned in the fireplace, leather-covered armchairs and heavy wooden tables were arranged around it, and on the walls hung weapons and stuffed animal heads. A mysterious man stood by Bourgès, who addressed him, very respectfully, as "Mr. President." Peres and Nahmias wondered who that strange "President" was; only when he left the room did Bourgès reveal that he was the president of the local hunting club.

Bourgès and his Israeli guests started discussing a joint operation against Egypt. Peres asked whether "the French-Israeli relations would be based on absolute equality," and Bourgès gave an affirmative answer. Peres kept asking about the expected reactions of England, America, and Russia, and Bourgès answered that "England will have no choice but to act; with America we can argue and we can influence her; as for Russia—her reaction can't be assessed." Bourgès agreed to the suggestion that Peres had made a few days before "to call for a conference at the highest level to discuss the relations between France and Israel."[10]

Late at night, on their way back to Paris, Peres and Nahmias stopped for a drink at a picturesque inn, built in the shape of three huge wine barrels adjoining one another. The two Israelis decided to put down in writing the details of the conversation with Bourgès-Maunoury, but they had no paper. Peres tore his pack of cigarettes and noted on the small square of cardboard the main points that were discussed. That was the first written document of the Suez-Sinai Campaign.[11]

Nahmias drove Peres straight to the airport, where the director general boarded the first flight to Israel. The following day, Dayan and Peres drove to Jerusalem with Ben-Gurion in his car. Ben-Gurion turned to Peres. "How are your French friends?" he asked.[12]

Peres told him about his conversations with Bourgès-Maunoury. Ben-Gurion was visibly agitated. In his diary he wrote that Peres's report was "perhaps fateful." He diligently noted down Peres's account: "Bourges-Maunoury said that ... he is ready to act against Nasser—with the knowledge and the consent of the British. They want Israel to participate—that too with the consent of the British. They [the British] have one condition—that we wouldn't attack Jordan. The French ask that a delegation of three people—among them at least one Minister—go there next Saturday for talks with Guy Mollet, Pineau, and Bourgès-Maunoury about cooperation based on equality."[13]

Ben-Gurion told Peres: "Your report fundamentally changes the situation." He also divulged some of his territorial dreams: "Israeli control of the western shore of the Red Sea and of the Straits of Eilat."[14]

In Jerusalem, Ben-Gurion invited the Mapai and Ahdut Ha'avoda ministers to his office and informed them of the talks with the French. "Here is being born the first serious alliance between us and a Western power," Ben-Gurion added, "and in no case should we refuse to accept it."[15] In his diary, Ben-Gurion wrote with wonder, "The French demand that the 'action' should start on October 15!"[16]

At the end of that week a French Navy Neptune bomber landed at the Israeli air base of Hatzor. On September z8, in the late evening, five people boarded the aircraft: Foreign Minister Golda Meir, who was the delegation's leader; Transport Minister General (res.) Moshe Carmel, an Ahdut Ha'avoda member; Moshe Dayan; Shimon Peres; and Colonel Mordechai Bar-On, who headed Dayan's office.

Before she set on her way, Golda received a detailed letter of instructions from Ben-Gurion. With an almost prophetic sense, Ben-Gurion firmly demanded that the United States be informed of the projected operation. "We deem it vital, that the operation should be carried out with the [prior] knowledge of the United States," the Old Man wrote, but he also stressed: "We don't think she should participate. On the contrary, it would be better if she does not."

Ben-Gurion specified, in writing, the war goals of Israel: "Israel's control of the Tiran [Sharm al-Sheikh] straits . . . Demilitarization of the entire Sinai Peninsula, except for the Israeli positions on the Red Sea shores; we shall propose that the new regime that would be established in Egypt will enter peace negotiations with us. In any case we shall demand free passage through the Suez Canal." At the end of the letter, Ben-Gurion advised Golda to speak positively, to stress Israel's will to take part in the operation, and to express her gratitude for the French aid so far; but he added that she shouldn't be too humble and submissive.[17]

THE NEPTUNE flew along the illuminated Egyptian coastline and after midnight landed at the French Navy base at Bizerta, in Tunisia. After a fine dinner and a few hours of rest, the five Israelis continued their voyage, this time aboard a DC-4, the personal plane of General de Gaulle, which had been a present from President Harry Truman.

The Israeli delegation landed at the Villacoublay military air base in France. General Challe and Colonel Mangin were waiting for them and drove them to Pavilion Henri IV, a former palace converted into a luxury hotel, in the Parisian suburb of Saint-Germain-en-Laye.

In the morning of September 30, Yossef Nahmias drove the Israelis in his car to an apartment building at 4 Rue de Babylone, in Paris. They got out of the car one by one, and sneaked into one of the apartments. They were in Colonel Mangin's private residence.

A group of French leaders was waiting for them: Ministers Christian Pineau and Maurice Bourgès-Maunoury, Abel Thomas, General Challe, and their host, Louis Mangin. At a later stage more senior army officers were to join them.

For Golda Meir, the conference started with a disappointment, as Prime Minister Guy Mollet didn't come. That made her assume, from the start, a negative attitude toward the very idea of an alliance with France. "She never liked the Frenchmen and France," her biographer Dr. Meron Medzini stated. "Their culture and their language were alien to her."[18] She was also hostile to Peres. She didn't trust his reports about the building of an alliance with France. Golda inherited from Sharett an animosity toward Peres for his bypassing of the foreign ministry and conducting his own foreign policy. Some said that her jealousy of the special relations between Peres and Ben-Gurion made her loathe Peres from the very beginning. A Mapai politician had tried to dispel Golda's hatred of Peres. "He is a very gifted man," the Mapai activist said. "So was Al Capone!" Golda retorted.[19]

Now, on arriving in Paris, Golda adopted an attitude of suspicion and mistrust. The absence of Guy Mollet from the meeting was for her proof that the French were not serious. Peres wrote, "For Golda, who was curt and morose throughout the trip, this was instant confirmation of her suspicion that I was leading her and the whole Government up the garden path."[20]

Peres rushed to the parliament, found Mollet, and set up a meeting between him and Golda, but her attitude didn't change.[21] "She remained skeptical and dour as the talks proceeded," Peres wrote.[22]

The first meeting at Mangin's apartment dealt with political issues. As the debate in the U.N. Security Council hadn't ended yet, neither France nor England could commit to an offensive against Egypt. Israel hadn't made any definitive decision, either. It was clear, therefore, that the political results of the meeting would be limited. Yet most of the Israelis realized that holding a conference with one of the Great Powers was in itself an important achievement.

Pineau opened the debate, stressing France's determination to launch a military operation. France, he said, wanted to go to war in mid-October, before the presidential election in the United States. The Americans wouldn't dare object to the operation for electoral reasons. He was pessimistic about the British, however, and wanted to know whether Israel alone would join France if the British decided not to.[23]

Golda Meir expressed Israel's will to act together with France. She asked about France's assessment of the American and Soviet reactions. Pineau answered that in his opinion the Soviet Union wouldn't intervene, and the United States would assume a passive position.

The scenario that the French favored was an Israeli attack on Egypt and, later, the intervention of France, or France and England. Pineau said that if the British were assured that Israel would act alone in the opening stage, they might be more willing to join the operation. Moshe Dayan made it clear that Israel could destroy the Egyptian Air Force on her own, but if the Soviet Union sent to Egypt Russian "volunteers," the situation would change.[24]

After a quick lunch, cooked by Mangin, the debate moved to military questions. It continued the following morning when General Paul Ely joined the small group. The French spoke with Dayan of a possible D-day: October 20. But nothing was concluded; Dayan was disappointed with the French officers, who refused to reveal their operational plans.

The Persky family, outside their Vishneva house. Shimon is sitting on the right, beside his brother Gigi. PERES ARCHIVES (HENCEFORTH PA)

Shimon (center seated on the floor) made it to the mandolin school ensemble, but that was the end of his musical career. PA

Before Sarah Persky and her sons departed for Palestine the Meltzers and the Perskys gathered for a family photograph. Shimon, third from the right in the back row, stands beside his mother (center). Grandfather Zvi Meltzer (second row, far left) and many of Shimon's relatives perished in the Holocaust. ISRAEL GOVERNMENT PRESS OFFICE (HENCEFORTH GPO)

Shortly after their arrival in Palestine, Shimon's father took the boys to the photographer. They were far from looking like Sabras, the Israeli-born youths they wanted to emulate. PA

With Sonia, the love of his life. GPO

His father, the here. PA

The enlarged Persky family. Seated, from the right: Getzel, Sarah, and Shimon. Standing: Carmela (Gigi's fiancée), Gigi, and Sonia. PA

The Peres family in the Holy Room. From the right, Sonia holding Hemi (Nehemia), Shimon, Yoni (Yonathan), and Tziki (Zvia). IDF Archives

Some said Ben-Gurion had divided his legacy between his two young protégés. He had given the leadership to Moshe Dayan, and the vision—to Shimon Peres, PA

The Ministry of Defense director-general occupied a place of honor in the official photo of IDF's General Staff. Peres, Ben-Gurion, and Chief of Staff Moshe Dayan are seated in the center. Standing, between Peres and Ben-Gurion, is Yitzhak Rabin. On the far right, Nehemia Argov, who was to meet a tragic death, GPO

The road to Suez. Peres at a meeting with France's Prime Minister Guy Mollet. On the left, Yossef Nahmias, the Defense Ministry's envoy in Paris, PA

"There was nothing that Bourgès wouldn't do for me." Peres with his great friend, Defense Minister (and later prime minister) Maurice Bourgès-Maunoury. PA

Change of the guard at the IDF. General Laskov (far right) is replacing Moshe Dayan as chief of staff. Behind Ben-Gurion is Teddy Kollek, future mayor of Jerusalem. Golda is visible behind Dayan, PA

Atonement: Franz Josef Strauss, West Germany's defense minister, secretly provided Israel with large quantities of weapons, free of charge, GPO

Peres's folly"—the nuclear reactor, near Dimona. When asked, the Israelis claimed that they were building "a textile factory." PA

In 1978 Peres met Egypt's President Sadat in Vienna (seated between Germany's Chancellor Willy Brandt and Austria's Chancellor Bruno Kreisky). But Peres was the leader of the opposition, and Sadat made peace with Prime Minister Menachem Begin, PA

Golda Meir and Shimon Peres. There was no love lost between those two. Courtesy of the LAVON Institute

Rabin and Peres with the author. BAR-ZOHAR Archives

Peres had no reasons for disappointment. He presented a new shopping list for the operation: 100 Sherman tanks, a cargo aircraft squadron, 300 four-wheel-drive trucks, 1,000 bazookas,

300 halftracks, 50 tank carriers, ammunition, and protective equipment. The French agreed to most of his demands, and Peres tackled three subjects connected with the arms purchase. First, he asked that the agreements made at 4 Rue de Babylone would be final, and no more authorizations from the French foreign ministry would be needed. Second, that some of the weapons France would send to Israel would be American made. Third, that the weapons wouldn't be sold, but "leased" to Israel. This request was intended to bypass the interdiction the United States had laid on her allies against selling weapons of American manufacture to third parties. Bourgès-Maunoury agreed. "We signed a personal agreement, between Bourgès-Maunoury and me, stipulating that no matter if we remain in our positions or not, Israel commits herself to return the 'leased' tanks in the 24 hours following a French request."[25]

The conference was over. On the night of October 1, de Gaulle's plane took off again, on a direct flight to Israel. Besides the Israeli delegation the plane also carried a surveying mission of the French Army, headed by Challe and Mangin. They were charged with examining the needs of the IDF and the military infrastructure in Israel.

"The other members of our delegation were somewhat disappointed," Peres admitted. "They thought that the conference had been premature or that we had expected too much of it. They believed I was too optimistic about the possibility of cooperation with France. At the conference it became clear that France would indeed stand by Israel if Israel acted alone; France's assistance, however, wouldn't be direct military assistance, but only a strengthening of Israel's army. We also found out that the United States rejected all the suggestions made to her by the British and the French. The delegation came back to Israel with mixed feelings."[26]

The one delegation member whose feelings were not mixed at all was Golda Meir. "Her frustration was great," wrote Dr. Medzini. "She believed that Peres deceived Ben-Gurion by trying to convince him that he definitely could count on the French. On their return, she told Ben-Gurion that the chances of the French cooperating with Israel were not good. The entire matter looked to her like an unripe fruit that had not matured enough." Medzini added, "This wouldn't be the last time when Golda doubted Peres's judgment and character; she still couldn't decipher the secret of his influence on Ben-Gurion."[27]

Ben-Gurion didn't say a word to Peres about Golda's harsh criticism; Moshe Dayan, however, backed his friend all the way.[28]

The naked truth was that Golda Meir didn't understand the heart of the matter. She didn't realize what a tremendous achievement the very convening of the conference was for the tiny, eight-year-old State of Israel. She didn't appreciate the contribution of Peres, who had succeeded, alone, in establishing a real alliance between Israel and France. Fortunately, the other participants in the Rue de Babylone conference understood the situation better than the foreign minister. As soon as he landed in Israel, Chief of Staff Moshe Dayan issued an order to the IDF to prepare for a possible campaign against Egypt. Probable date: October 20, 1956.

BEN-GURION WASN'T HAPPY with the French plans. He told Peres and Dayan that he was reluctant to launch an operation of the Israelis and the French alone. The French would need the British airfields in Cyprus, and Ben-Gurion doubted if the British would let the French use them if Great Britain didn't participate in the operation. He also feared Egyptian bombing raids on Israel's cities. He asked Peres over and over again, "Are you sure that Mollet knows we have not committed ourselves?"[29]

On October 13, the debate at the U.N. Security Council drew to its end. A British-French draft resolution calling for the internationalization of the canal was defeated by a Soviet veto. The following day, October 14, General Challe and Minister Albert Gazier flew to London and met with Prime Minister Anthony Eden at his country residence at Chequers. Challe told Eden,

"The Israelis will start a war against the Egyptians. We'll come and separate them." Israel, Challe explained, should attack and conquer most of the Sinai. England and France would then require that the two warring parties retreat from the canal. Right after, the two powers would occupy the canal under the pretext that they had to protect it from the combatants.[30]

"Good idea!" Eden exclaimed.

On October 16, Anthony Eden and his foreign secretary, Selwyn Lloyd, flew to Paris and met Guy Mollet and Christian Pineau. For five hours, the four leaders debated in Mollet's office; Don Quixote and Cardinal Richelieu watched them from the magnificent tapestries hanging on the walls. The prime ministers finally approved "the Israeli pretext." Eden handed the French a written declaration to be conveyed to the Israelis. Fie agreed that a British representative would participate at the forthcoming talks between the Israelis and the French.

The same day, a telegram summing up the talks reached Shimon Peres, who brought it to Ben-Gurion. The Old Man reacted "furiously and decisively."[31] He was very suspicious of the British, and so he rejected "the Israeli pretext." Still, he finally suggested a tripartite meeting between France, Israel, and Great Britain. Peres cabled Paris, and the following morning received Guy Mollet's answer. He invited Ben-Gurion to come to Paris, adding that "if necessary, a British Cabinet member will also be invited."

At a restricted meeting in Jerusalem, with the participation of Golda Meir, Levi Eshkol, Peres, and Dayan, Ben-Gurion took a strong position against the idea of the Israeli pretext. He thought it was another devious British scheme, meant to undermine the French-Israeli alliance. Yet he was ready to fly to Paris and meet with the French leaders. Golda, as usual, didn't approve of the plan. "It seemed," Peres wrote, "that Golda was skeptical about the [Paris] meeting. Eshkol didn't conceal his support. Moshe barely concealed his enthusiasm. Ben-Gurion himself wanted to participate in the meeting. There was no enthusiasm in his words, hut his position was firm."[32]

On October 18, at 1 A.M., Nehemia Argov woke up Ben-Gurion and brought him a message from Guy Mollet. The French prime minister had been briefed about Ben-Gurion's reservations; nevertheless he reiterated his invitation to Ben-Gurion for a summit meeting in Paris. "They'll send an aircraft on Sunday," Ben-Gurion wrote in his diary. "I ordered to reply that I accept the invitation."[33]

Ben-Gurion had the firm intention of objecting to the Israeli pretext scheme. But Dayan, in a sober and wise analysis, expressed a different opinion. "In the military campaign," he pointed out, "England and France don't need us. The five hundred aircraft they intend to use will annihilate the Egyptian Air Force, and the same will happen at sea and on land. The only advantage we have in this matter, which is the only one England and France don't have, is our ability to give them the needed pretext for entering the campaign. Only this ability can serve us as an entrance ticket to the Suez Campaign Club."[34] Peres fully agreed with him.

Ben-Gurion's delegation for the talks included Dayan, Peres, Nehemia Argov, and Mordechai Bar-On. Arthur Ben-Nathan, who was going to replace Nahmias as the defense ministry's envoy in Paris, also joined the delegation. Ben-Gurion didn't ask Golda to join him, even though the French foreign minister and a British representative were going to participate in the talks. "She didn't believe in cooperation with the French," said Avraham Ben-Yossef, a senior defense ministry official.[35]

On Sunday, October 21, 1956, de Gaulle's plane landed in Israel again; from its door emerged, smiling, Challe and Mangin. In the evening, the Israeli delegation met in Ben-Gurion's office and set off for the Hatzor air base, where the plane was waiting. The trip was shrouded in secrecy. An official communiqué announced that Ben-Gurion was going to spend three days watching IDF maneuvers in the Negev. "Ben-Gurion was in an excellent mood," Peres wrote, "lively and vigorous and oblivious of his age, as usual. But on the way, in the car, his good mood evaporated. Moshe and I reported to him about our conversations with Challe and Mangin [concerning the Israeli pretext] and he was furious .... The Old Man even said: 'If they don't understand that our negative answer is final, the entire trip is worthless.' At that moment the driver should have turned back and returned home."[36]

But Ben-Gurion didn't stop the car, and it continued on to the big aircraft that waited in the dark. At 8 P.M. the plane took off. In its cabin it carried a handful of Israelis who had set off on the most fateful mission in their country's history.

CHAPTER 12.

THE SECRET CONFERENCE AT SÈVRES

DURING THE LONG FLIGHT, Ben-Gurion was immersed in a book by the Byzantine historian Procopius, describing an ancient Jewish kingdom on Yotvat Island—today's Tiran, in the strait of the same name. Ben-Gurion's book, Peres thought, revealed his secret dreams.

As the plane landed on the rain-swept runway at Villacoublay, several cars approached the gangway. Ben-Gurion wore a wide-brimmed hat to conceal his famous shock of white hair. Moshe Dayan was wearing dark glasses over his black eye patch. One car took Ben-Gurion to the suburb of Sèvres, and the Old Man entered a beautiful villa whose walls were covered with vines. The villa had been put at the disposal of Bourgès-Maunoury by the Bonnier de la Chapelle family, whose son, Fernand, had been executed during World War II for resisting the Vichy regime.

Dayan, Peres, and Bar-On checked into the Reynolds Hotel in Paris. Dayan signed as "Mosh Day." The reception manager asked for the guests' passports. Peres, who had stayed at the Reynolds before, shook his head. "Forget about the passports," he muttered.

At 4 P.M. Peres and Dayan arrived at the villa. In a side room they saw "an unforgettable scene." Ben-Gurion faced Mollet, Pineau, and Bourgès-Maunoury. "The French, who were young in comparison with Ben-Gurion, looked like students sitting before their rabbi. Ben-Gurion was wearing a blue suit that enhanced his white mane. He looked relaxed, and was smiling. In spite of the respectful attitude of the French, the ambiance was informal and intimate. Ben-Gurion introduced us to the French as a father introducing his sons, and his words were tinted with fatherly pride."[1]

It turned out that Ben-Gurion had already expressed his objection to the Israeli pretext and now presented to his hosts, instead, a rather far-fetched plan for the reshaping of the Middle East by redrawing Israel's boundaries and even wiping Jordan from the map. The French listened politely, then steered the discussion back to the projected invasion of Egypt.

Pineau described the advantages of immediate action. The United States, he said, was immersed in its electoral campaign; the Soviet Union had to deal with the rebellions that had broken out in Poland and Hungary. The weather, too, said Pineau, demanded immediate action.

Ben-Gurion said that he objected to any plan that could result in Israel's condemnation by the international community. He also feared the Soviet-made bombers in Nasser's air force and an attack on Israel by Soviet "volunteers." Most of all, he kept repeating that it was imperative to secure American neutrality, even if that meant delaying the operation.

"At Day One of the three days of negotiation," Peres wrote, "Ben-Gurion behaved as a man who hated hasty decisions, a man who understood how dangerous Nasser was, but didn't cling to the proposed dates as a fatalist. The French realized that instead of pressuring him, they should put pressure on the British, who always undermined any sincere cooperation."[2]

Ben-Gurion's insistence on informing the Americans irritated the French and some of the Israelis.[3] Bourgès said firmly that if the operation was not launched in a few days, France would have to abandon the idea. France couldn't keep scores of ships mobilized and thousands of soldiers on reserve for very long. He offered Israel warships and aircraft to protect her civilian population, but stressed that the beginning of November was "the last deadline."[4]

Shimon Peres didn't participate in the talks. He was the producer and the director of the play, but not one of the leads; on center stage stood Ben-Gurion and Dayan. Peres knew his position in the hierarchy and didn't intervene in the talks without Ben-Gurion's permission. He preferred short, informal exchanges with his French friends in order to settle practical issues. After the first round of talks was over, he quietly asked Guy Mollet to send French planes and pilots to Israel right away, so that the defense of Israel's airspace would be assured from the very beginning. Mollet agreed.[5]

A few hours later, the British representative to the negotiations arrived in Sèvres. It was the foreign secretary, Selwyn Lloyd, who was accompanied by his secretary, Donald Logan.

With Lloyd's arrival, the Israelis felt as if a cold wind had penetrated the villa and dispelled the friendly atmosphere. Ben-Gurion and Lloyd exchanged a formal, reserved handshake, and behaved toward each other with open distrust. "Britain's Foreign Minister may well have been a friendly man, pleasant, charming, amiable," Dayan wrote. "If so, he showed near-genius in concealing these virtues. His whole demeanor expressed distaste—for the place, the company, and the topic."[6] Shimon Peres described him as "a man with no brilliance and no human warmth. His phrasing was cautious but lacking feeling and imagination."

A small group moved into a side room—Ben-Gurion, Dayan, and Peres; Pineau, Bourgès, and Challe; Selwyn Lloyd and Logan. The real talks started in an informal setting. Moshe Dayan presented a plan that he thought could satisfy both Ben-Gurion and Lloyd. He proposed parachuting a small Israeli force close to the Suez Canal and having it engage in military activity. That would be the pretext for the French and the British to send an ultimatum to both sides and intervene to "separate the combatants." Selwyn Lloyd didn't reject the idea; he demanded, though, that it not be "an isolated attack by Israel" but "a large-scale military operation."

The debates continued till midnight, amid continued sparring between Lloyd and Ben-Gurion. "It seems that Lloyd didn't fall in love with Ben-Gurion," Peres noted at the end of the dinner, "but there is no doubt at all that this feeling was mutual from the moment they met." Late that night Lloyd flew back to England to present to the British cabinet the new plan that had started taking shape, based on Dayan's idea.

But in the meantime an unexpected event occurred, plunging France into extreme turmoil.

THAT DAY, OCTOBER 22, a Moroccan plane with a French crew had taken off from Rabat, Morocco, on its way to Tunis. After takeoff, the crew found out that five leaders of the Algerian rebellion, with Ahmed Ben Bella at their head, were on the plane; they were on their way to participate in a conference of the Algerian underground. On discovering the identity of his passengers, the pilot veered from his programmed route and landed in Algiers, where the rebellion's leaders were promptly arrested. Anti-French strikes and protests broke out in Morocco and Tunisia.

On October 23, the unrest reached the French parliament, and the cabinet was convened in an emergency meeting. Some feared it wouldn't survive the controversy. The government was deeply embarrassed by the accusations of "air piracy" that the world hurled at France. It looked as if the ministers wouldn't be able to go to Sèvres. But the situation calmed down by midday, and Pineau arrived at the villa. "I drove my car myself," Pineau said, "to protect the conference's secret from the Quai d'Orsay officials."[7] The French foreign minister shared his relief with Ben-Gurion: "Thank God, we finished the Cabinet meeting with the same number of ministers who were there at the start."[8]

On that second day of the conference, Ben-Gurion wanted to go to Paris to buy philosophy books at one of his favorite stores, on the Boulevard Raspail, but, worrying that he might be recognized, Peres and Nahmias drove to the store in his stead, and purchased some Greek books for the Old Man.

They were back in time for lunch, and met with Bourgès, Pineau, and Thomas. During the lunch, General Challe came up with a new, chilling idea. He suggested that the Israeli Air Force stage a night attack on Beersheba and bomb the city. Egypt would be accused, and the Anglo-French forces would intervene immediately. Ben-Gurion jumped from his seat, his face flushed with fury, and angrily rejected the idea of such a provocation. "Israel is strong because she fights for a just cause," he said. "I cannot lie, either to the world public opinion or to anybody else." He demanded that his answer be translated, phrase by phrase.

"A sepulchral silence descended on the dining room," Peres wrote. "Challe became as red as a beet. It suddenly became clear to everybody that the man they were sitting with was not a professional politician and an opportunistic tactician. The hardships in the present situation wouldn't make him give up his moral values."[9]

Ben-Gurion's hosts hurriedly changed the subject, and Peres dolefully wrote, "That lunch turned out to be one of the worst moments of the conference."

Pineau was about to fly to London, and the Israeli delegation met by themselves for a last consultation. That meeting, in the early afternoon of October 23, turned out to be the most important in the entire conference.

Peres and Dayan presented their ideas to Ben-Gurion. Peres suggested that Israel send a test ship to the Suez Canal. The Egyptians would stop the ship, and Israel would launch an attack on Egypt. That would be the pretext for the British and the French to intervene.

Moshe Dayan developed his original idea. On D-day, shortly before nightfall, a battalion of IDF paratroopers would be dropped over the Mitla Pass, thirty miles west of the Suez Canal. A communiqué of the General Staff would be released to the media. Simultaneously, an IDF armored column would cross the

Israeli-Egyptian border into Sinai, conquering the enemy forts on its way, and join the paratroopers at Mitla. On the first day, the Israeli Air Force would limit its activities to dropping the paratroopers and protecting them. Thirty-six hours later, the French and British forces would intervene, and then all of the IDF would be thrown into the battle.

Ben-Gurion gave his permission for both Peres and Dayan to present their ideas to Pineau and Bourgès, but did not express his own opinion.[10] Then he retired to his room.

The two French ministers were waiting for the Israelis in the den. Peres gave his idea of dispatching a test ship to the canal.[11] Dayan described his plan, and Pineau diligently wrote down its details. Dayan also demanded that England and France recognize Israel's right, once the war was over, to keep certain parts of the Sinai under her control.

Pineau then flew to London to meet with Anthony Eden—and the second day of the Sèvres conference was over.

DAYAN, PERES, ARGOV, and their aides made an effort to escape the tension of the previous couple of days and went to watch a striptease show at a Parisian nightclub. But they were restless, and very soon gave up the shapes and the curves that the pretty ladies generously exhibited before their weary eyes. They opted for the more solid ambiance of a café, where they spent the evening complaining of Ben-Gurion's refusal to tell them what he thought. "We wondered," Peres said. "We had no idea if the man had decided or not."[12]

At Sèvres, Ben-Gurion was left completely alone after Arthur Ben-Nathan escaped to Paris as well. What would Ben-Gurion's decision be? Peres wrote, "One man, alone, had to make a decision, when a part of the facts were unknown, blurred, frightening in their blindness. Here stood a lonely man, holding a cruel watch, disposing of a few hours that were running out fast—and he had to make a momentous decision, tainted with horrible dangers."

"None of us envied him for the long evening that lay ahead."[13]

ON THE MORNING of October 24, the phone rang at the Reynolds Hotel. Dayan and Peres were urgently summoned to Sèvres. They arrived at the villa after 11 A.M. It was a golden autumn day and Ben-Gurion was sitting under a tree in the garden, a soft wind playing with his hair.

In his hands, Ben-Gurion held a list of questions, which he started reading to Peres and Dayan. On hearing the first questions, Dayan understood: Ben-Gurion had decided to go to war.[14]

Indeed, that morning Ben-Gurion had written in his diary, "I considered the situation, and if effective aerial measures are taken for our defense in the day or two before the British and the French bomb the Egyptian airfields—I believe the operation must be carried out."[15]

Ben-Gurion asked Dayan to draw for him a map of the projected campaign. Nobody had any paper, and Peres had to sacrifice his second pack of cigarettes. Dayan sketched on it the Sinai Peninsula and drew a dotted line across its center, representing the flight of the planes that would drop the paratroopers at Mitla. He then drove three arrows through Sinai's north, center, and south. The arrows represented the main axes of the offensive. Ben-Gurion, Dayan, and Peres signed the small sketch. Peres dropped it in his pocket. That was the first map of the Sinai Campaign.[16]

In the afternoon, Pineau returned from London in an excited mood and told the small group that Eden had agreed to Dayan's plan. Ben-Gurion agreed to go ahead, even without a provocation from the Egyptian side. He accepted the idea of the Israeli pretext, not because of the French and British pressure, but mostly because of Dayan's and Peres's support of the operation.

WITH PINEAU CAME Lloyd's secretary, Donald Logan, and the foreign secretary's assistant, Patrick Dean. Ben-Gurion insisted that a protocol should be drafted, signed by the three parties, and ratified by the three governments. A drafting committee was appointed, including Dayan and Nahmias for the

Israeli side, Dean and Logan for Great Britain, and Abel Thomas and Challe for France.

While the document was being prepared, France's leaders promised Peres to alleviate the financial burden on Israel, and to veto any anti-Israeli resolution at the U.N. Security Council. Peres also spoke with the three ministers about Israel's project of building a nuclear reactor.

Two hours later, the Sèvres Protocol was ready.

The agreement described the plan: Israel would attack Egypt on October 29, in the evening hours; the following morning, France and England would send Israel and Egypt a demand to stop any military action and retreat to a new line ten miles from the canal. That meant that Egypt was being asked to evacuate the entire Sinai Peninsula, while Israel was allowed to conquer it and advance up to a line ten miles east of the canal. It was obvious that Israel would accept these conditions and Egypt would reject them.

If the Egyptian government rejected the Anglo-French demand, the French and the British would launch a military operation against Egypt in the early hours of October 31.

Two paragraphs in the written agreement were of major importance to Israel:

The Israeli government will send forces to occupy the western coast of the Gulf of Aqaba and the islands Tiran and Sanafir, in order to assure free navigation in the Gulf of Aqaba.

Israel undertakes not to attack Jordan . . . . But if Jordan attacks Israel, the British government undertakes not to come to the aid of Jordan.

The contents of that agreement, the document concluded, would be kept in utmost secrecy, and it would take on legal status after the approval of the three governments.[17]

In an appendix to the protocol, the French government undertook to position in Israel a reinforced squadron of Mystère-4 aircraft and a squadron of fighter-bombers; ships of the French Navy would be sent to Israel's ports.

In an improvised ceremony at 7 P.M., the protocol was signed by Christian Pineau, Patrick Dean, and David Ben-Gurion. The Old Man carefully read his copy, folded it, and put it in his vest pocket. Shimon Peres heaved a sigh of relief and lit a cigarette. The complex structure that he had tried so hard to build since the hectic days of the summer materialized before his eyes. Would it withstand the storm that was about to break out? Bourgès-Maunoury approached Peres and shook his hand. "The greatness of your Ben-Gurion," he said, "is that even though being a philosopher, he is capable of making decisions."[18]

The Sèvres conference was over. At midnight, de Gaulle's plane took off, on its way back to Israel. Inside the aircraft, Peres scrutinized the faces of his companions. "The dominant person in the conference is of course Ben-Gurion," he noted. "Moshe Dayan also achieved remarkable recognition. Over and over again he surprised [his interlocutors] by his wisdom or his courage. The French listened to him attentively not only on matters concerning Israel, but were eager to get his advice even about their own decisions . . . ."

"Me, I think, the French regarded as an unconditional friend who totally supported the cause; they often came to ask me how to overcome a small obstacle or a more significant gap. The Israeli delegation was very impressive by its original mix—a great man, rich with experience, and around him a young, enthusiastic team."[19]

While Peres wrote in his diary, Dayan drafted the first order for "Operation Kadesh."

CHAPTER 13.

ONE HUNDRED HOURS

ON OCTOBER 29, 1956, at 4:59 P.M., Major Rafael (Raful) Eitan jumped from a Dakota aircraft near the Mitla Pass. Another 394 paratroopers jumped after him. Moshe Dayan released a carefully worded communiqué, in accordance with the Sèvres agreements.

"The IDF spokesman announces that IDF forces entered and attacked Fedayeen units at Ras el Nakeb and Kuntila, and took positions west of the Nakhel crossroads, in proximity to the Suez Canal."

The Sinai Campaign had begun.

Up to the very last moment, grave problems had surfaced, fueling the suspicions of Ben-Gurion, Dayan, and Peres toward the British. When the Sèvres Protocol was brought to Anthony Eden, on the morning of October 25, the British prime minister was furious. Determined to erase any trace of Britain's collusion with Israel, he ordered the document destroyed immediately. He also demanded that the French destroy their copy of the protocol, but Paris ignored his request.

Eden sent Guy Mollet a vague, odd letter, confirming England's participation in the operation.[1] The letter didn't mention the Sèvres Protocol. Eden also refrained from sending Israel any message about his agreement.

On receiving Eden's letter, Mollet photocopied it and sent it to

Ben-Gurion, together with a personal letter confirming France's and Great Britain's agreement to the operation, and a letter from Bourgès-Maunoury confirming the dispatch of French fighter squadrons and warships to Israel. The documents were rushed to Ben-Gurion, who sent Mollet a letter confirming the agreement of Israel's government "to the results of the Sèvres talks and the conditions of the Sèvres Protocol of October 24."[2]

On October 28, Ben-Gurion got cabinet approval for an operation against Egypt. He told his amazed colleagues that two days after the launching of the Israeli offensive, the French and the British would intervene as well. He didn't say a word, though, about his secret trip to France and the signing of the protocol.

The Israeli war machine was revving at high gear. Ninety thousand reserve soldiers were mobilized and joined their units. The French jet-fighter squadrons landed at Israeli Air Force bases. Noratlas cargo aircraft of the French Air Force took off from their bases in North Africa and brought to Israel equipment and ground crews for the jet squadrons. Three French warships, the *Kersaint*, the *Bouvet*, and the *Surcouf*, patrolled the Israeli coast.

At the last moment, President Eisenhower dispatched two urgent messages to Ben-Gurion, warning Israel against a military operation. The American administration erroneously thought that Ben-Gurion intended to attack Jordan. It had no idea about the secret alliance between Israel, France, and Great Britain.

Ben-Gurion's answer to Eisenhower was carefully worded, so as not to lead him astray. Ben-Gurion didn't include in his answer any promise that Israel would refrain from military action. "With Iraqi troops poised in great numbers on the Iraq-Jordan frontier," Ben-Gurion wrote, "with the creation of a joint command of Egypt, Syria and Jordan, and with the renewal of the incursions into Israel by Egyptian gangs, my government will be failing in its essential duty if it were not to take all necessary measures to assure that the declared Arab aim of eliminating Israel, by force, should not come out."[3] This message actually hinted that Israel intended to take military action.

The same day, at 5 P.M., Shimon Peres spoke with the French ambassador, Pierre Gilbert, and divulged to him the secret of the forthcoming operation. At 1 A.M. Peres held a press conference, together with Ben-Gurion's political adviser Dr. Yaakov Herzog, and spoke to the foreign press about the Sinai Campaign and its official purposes.

A few hours after the paratroopers' drop at Mitla Pass, the Sèvres scenario was enacted. The British and the French summoned Israel and Egypt to back away from the canal. Israel accepted the ultimatum, Egypt rejected it. Now the bombings of the Egyptian airfields were to start.

But nothing happened. Late at night, a telegram from Yossef Nahmias confirmed Ben-Gurion's suspicions of the British. Despite French pressure, Nahmias reported, the British had decided to postpone their bombing until 5 P.M.

Ben-Gurion, seething, called Peres, who immediately cabled Nahmias: "The Egyptian superiority affects our forces, and places our units in a dangerous situation. We regard the delay of the bombings as a grave sabotage and strongly demand that immediate action be undertaken." Peres dispatched a second telegram, in the name of Ben-Gurion, to the French government. "At this moment all the power of the Egyptian Air Force is being used against us, and in particular against our forces in the Sinai. Your two squadrons stationed here do not participate in the defense of our units in the Sinai, claiming they have not been instructed to do so. Our Cabinet Ministers are asking me if we have been abandoned to our fate."[4]

Ben-Gurion even wanted to pull back the paratroopers from Sinai, but Dayan convinced him to wait another twenty-four hours.

After an urgent call from Peres, Nahmias called Christian Pineau at home, in the middle of the night. "Monsieur Pineau," Nahmias said, "there are no bombings."

"No bombings?" Pineau was astounded. The bombings were to be carried out by British bombers operating from their bases in Cyprus.

"No bombings," Nahmias repeated. "The British are not fulfilling their promise."

"I'll fly to London right away," the French foreign minister decided. "You'll hear from me before sunrise."[5]

The bombings indeed started the following day. But it soon turned out that the feared Egyptian Air Force was a nonexistent threat, and Nasser's pilots were unable to carry out a single operation against Israel. The IDF forces in the Sinai were not in danger.

With lightning speed, the Israelis pursued the Sinai Campaign. On October 30, three Israeli armored columns invaded Sinai. One stormed the Gaza Strip and northern Sinai, another one plunged into the heart of the peninsula, and the third descended along the Red Sea coast toward Sharm al-Sheikh.

The swift victories astounded even the IDF General Staff. Long convoys of Egyptian vehicles, artillery, and armor fled the battlefields and were annihilated by the Israeli Air Force. The roads and passes of Sinai were jammed with hundreds of burning trucks, tanks, and cannons. Thousands of Egyptian soldiers escaped into the desert, and many of them were taken prisoner. Israeli Navy destroyers, supported by the French ship *Kersaint*, captured the Egyptian destroyer *Ibrahim el Awal*. The only tragic news came from the Mitla Pass. The combat-thirsty Ariel Sharon led his paratroopers into an Egyptian ambush and lost scores of men in a needless battle.

The French and the British hadn't started their invasion yet—while Israel had almost completed the conquest of the Sinai Peninsula. On November 1, Peres cabled Nahmias: "Total collapse of the Egyptian Army in Sinai. Brilliant and complete victory of the IDF on all fronts. Tremendous quantities of booty are in our hands, including heavy tanks of various makes, cannons, ammunition etc."

"Now is the time to save every penny. Stop all orders, except for those we mark as top priority."[6]

A wave of enthusiasm swept Israel. The world realized that Nasser was nothing but a paper tiger. Now that Egypt's weakness had been exposed, the French desperately tried to advance the date of the landing. But the war machine they had built with the British moved with exasperating slowness. According to the original plan, the landing in Egypt was to take place eleven days after the ultimatum—November 9. After frantic efforts, the French finally persuaded the British to start the invasion on November 5. But on that very day, the IDF completed the conquest of Sinai and all combat stopped.

Israel rejoiced. The Sinai Campaign had been crowned with total victory. The blockade of the Strait of Tiran had been shattered, and Israeli soldiers blew up the long Egyptian cannons controlling the approach to the Gulf of Aqaba. The IDF had captured 6,000 Egyptians, while only 4 Israelis were in Egyptian hands. Between 1,000 and 3,000 Egyptian soldiers had been killed; Israel had lost only 172 lives.

Israel's victory triggered a surge of admiration for the small Jewish state throughout the world. The United Nations, though, fired salvoes of condemnation at Israel's action. The U.N. Secretary General, Dag Hammarskjöld, threatened Israel with sanctions. The General Assembly demanded that Israel withdraw from the Sinai without delay.

The United States and the Soviet Union brought tremendous pressure to bear against Israel, Great Britain, and France, demanding that all military operations stop immediately. President Eisenhower, just reelected with a large majority, furiously lashed out at the three Sèvres allies; he singled out Anthony Eden, who had "stabbed him in the back."

On November 5, the Soviet prime minister, Nikolay Bulganin, sent menacing messages to France, Britain, and Israel. The message to Ben-Gurion included brutal threats against Israel's very existence. "The Government of Israel," Bulganin wrote, "is criminally and irresponsibly playing with the fate of the world and with the fate of its own people. It is sowing hatred of the State of Israel among the Eastern peoples, such as cannot but leave its mark on the future of Israel and places in question the very existence of Israel as a state .... The Soviet government is at this moment taking steps to put an end to the war and to restrain the aggressors."

What "steps" did Bulganin have in mind? Terrifying rumors spread throughout the world about Russian "volunteers" who would fly to the succor of Egypt and destroy Israel. Simultaneously, the scary rumors became more precise—Soviet airplanes were detected overflying Syria, Soviet submarines and frogmen arrived in Alexandria, a Soviet fleet crossed the Dardanelles on its way to the Middle East.

Ben-Gurion's elation gave way to anxiety. He was deeply worried by the threat of a Soviet offensive that could annihilate Israel. He decided to send Golda Meir and Shimon Peres to Paris on an urgent mission: to find out what France would do in the case of a Soviet attack on Israel.

The odd couple—Golda and Peres—flew secretly to Paris aboard a special El Al plane on November 6. They met with Bourgès-Maunoury and Pineau.

"Mr. Pineau," Peres wrote, "told us in deep sadness that France would stay by Israel 'with everything she's got' and would share with us her military resources; but the Russian military superiority cannot be ignored. They have got missiles and unconventional weapons and that demands that we draw conclusions."[7]

Pineau viewed the Soviet threat with extreme gravity. He also took seriously the news about Soviet volunteers who were already operating in the Middle East.[8] Golda intervened in the conversation, and offered Pineau a share in the exploitation of oil fields in the Sinai. Pineau looked at her "as if she had lost her mind" and said, "Soviet pilots are flying over Syria, the Soviets want to intervene in the Middle East, and you still think of the oil in Sinai?"[9] On leaving Pineau's office Golda was "desperate."

After the talks, Bourgès-Maunoury called Golda and Peres at their hotel. He told Peres that he agreed with Pineau, but he personally thought that the Russian menace was "a psychological threat" and nothing else.[10]

Peres took the Soviet threat very seriously. "Look at what they have done in Budapest," he said to his colleagues. The Russians "sent 6,000 cannons that fired into civilians' apartments, so why wouldn't the Russians bomb Tel-Aviv? There is no doubt that Russia hates us, perhaps she doesn't hate us as much as she is determined to gain a foothold in the Middle East; and she doesn't mind doing this on a bridge of two million [Israeli] bodies."[11]

In the end, though, the threats were not carried out. The Anglo-French invasion of Egypt ended in a debacle; they landed, indeed, in Alexandria and Port Said, but international pressure forced them to cut short their operation a few hours after it had started. Israel, too, realized that it had to face a new and harsh reality. After painful soul-searching, Ben-Gurion announced Israel's decision to withdraw from Sinai. In his replies to the Great Powers' leaders, he preferred to yield to the American pressure and not to the Soviet threats.

Bourgès-Maunoury had been right: the story about the Soviet "volunteers" turned out to be nothing but a smart bluff by Moscow's disinformation services.

The Anglo-French invasion armies were forced to retreat from Suez. France failed to achieve its secret purpose, the toppling of Nasser.[12] Israel, too, finally retreated from Sinai. She didn't keep control of the Strait of Tiran, but she obtained freedom of navigation. U.N. peacekeeping forces were stationed in Sinai and along the Gaza Strip, and the southern border of Israel became peaceful for eleven years.

"The French wanted to overthrow Nasser," Peres concluded, "but failed because of the hesitations of the British. The British wanted to gain control of Suez—but instead were expelled from Suez for the second time. Israel wanted to foil the danger of an imminent attack—and succeeded. She wanted to do that with a minimum of casualties—and succeeded. In this war there were three partners, France, England, and Israel; only one of the three achieved a hundred percent of its goals, and that's Israel."[13]

Peres heaped praise on Moshe Dayan, whose brilliance had made the Sinai Campaign a classic in the art of war. His words about Dayan sounded like an ode to a mythological hero: "In a minimum of time—one hundred hours; with a minimum of casualties—a few scores killed; with brilliant planning—starting the war at its final objectives; with total surprise—for only at the end of the battle did the enemy perceive its full intent; with an amazing exploitation of the terrain—moving where he was the least expected; with psychological savvy—to collapse an entire army without needlessly massacring its soldiers; with restraint vis-à-vis the media—minimizing the scope of the battle; by employing the existing means—[transporting troops] even on milk trucks; and finally, displaying the rare talent to sew together one campaign from complicated political materials and clear-cut military capacities—all these resulted both in the admiration of the world and in achieving the real goals of the war: annihilation of the Fedayeen bases in the Gaza Strip, opening of the Red Sea Straits, destruction of the Egyptian Army with its modern and awesome weapons."[14]

CHAPTER 14.

NEW HORIZONS

FOR SHIMON PERES, the Sinai Campaign had an unexpected result. He suddenly emerged from the shadows as the real architect of the French alliance. So far, he had operated in secrecy. Now the veil was lifted slightly—but enough to crown him with laurels. On his desk reigned a photograph of Guy Mollet with a warm dedication; Peres himself was incessantly shuttling between Tel Aviv and Lod Airport, welcoming or sending off delegations of senior French officers, past and present ministers and deputy ministers of defense, air, and armaments.

In 1957, Peres was awarded the high distinction of "Commander of the Legion of Honor" by the French government. Bourgès-Maunoury pinned the medal on Peres's chest and ceremoniously kissed him on both cheeks.

Peres kept striving to reduce Israel's heavy foreign debt. And like a master juggler, he kept getting from the French leaders more discounts and rebates.

On his return from France in February 1957, he reported to his colleagues, "They offered us discounts we had never dreamed about. The purchase of weapons before the Sinai Campaign amounted to 60 million dollars. Out of that we paid 20 million, which left us with a debt of 40. From those 40 million, they accepted to subtract 12 million as 'Lend-Lease equipment.' That left us with 28. On those 28 they gave us a discount of 6 million—for taxes and subsidies. We were now at 22 million dollars. They said that out of that sum, 6 million dollars is for 'legal' deals, and gave us a loan for five years to pay it. We had 16 million dollars left. On these 16 million they said that 3 million we should pay, that left us with 13 million. Of these 13 million they said: 'We cannot give you any more discounts, so we have an offer for you: pay us in cash and we'll give you a cash discount of 25 percent.' We said: 'Give us the discount.' We got it and we had 9 million dollars left. We said that the prices were too high, and they took 2 more million off the price. We were left with 7 million dollars. We told them we had no dollars but we would pay them with Israeli Pounds (Liras), which would be spread over two to three years . . . . We feared we would have to pay 20 million dollars this year, but now we'll have to pay only 3 or 3.5 million, and we said that we shall start paying this amount only after April."

"The bottom line is," Peres summed up—"that they erased 28 million dollars of our debt."[1]

The friendship with France spread through all walks of life. The French press was full of enthusiastic reports about "brave little Israel." "France is ready to sell Israel all the weapons she needs," declared Pierre Montet, the president of the French parliament's Defense Committee.[2] The French, indeed, agreed to sell to Israel Super-Mystère fighters, Vautour bombers, Noratlas cargo aircraft, and Alouette helicopters. They also granted Israel the license to produce Fouga Magister training jets. One day, the heads of the French aeronautical industry showed Peres a strange contraption: "A plane that has no wings," Peres reported. "It is delta-shaped, flies at 2,500 to 3,000 kilometers an hour, and its name is Mirage III." The French promised Peres that the airplane would enter the production stage in two or three years.[3] The Mirage III would become the backbone of the Israeli Air Force.

Israeli officers trained at French academies and military schools in Paris. Others attended courses at air force and navy bases and at the armor-training facilities at Saumur and Treves. At the Ministries of Defense in Tel Aviv and Paris, liaison bureaus were established to monitor the contacts between the two armies. Direct relations were also established between the intelligence services of the two nations.

On May 27, 1957, Dayan and Peres were secretly flown to Colomb-Béchar, in Algeria, on the fringe of the Sahara. There they watched tests of the new guided missiles that the French Army had developed. That was another avenue in the alliance with France: cooperation in the research and development of air-to-air and surface-to-surface missiles. Peres was somewhat skeptical about the effectiveness of the French missiles.[4] He suggested developing an independent Israeli missile program, but Dayan strongly objected.[5] It was one of the rare cases when Dayan and Peres disagreed. Peres was determined to create a purely Israeli missile and electronics industry, fearing that one day France might turn its back on Israel or get its missiles from the United States and close its own facilities.

At this point, though, Israel was the darling of French public opinion. In both France and Israel a league was created to work toward achieving a formal alliance between the two nations. Some of the most eminent French leaders joined the league. The venerated statesman Edouard Depreux declared at a meeting in Paris, "If a party of national unity could be ever created in France, its name would bear the initials I.S.R.A.E.L."[6]

FRANCE'S PRO-ISRAELI policy stemmed, of course, from its vital interests at that time. But if Peres hadn't been able to detect those interests and harness them to the needs and goals of Israel, the alliance between the two nations might never have been born.

The Sinai Campaign opened a golden era in French-Israeli relations that lasted for several years. France's arsenals were wide open before the IDF. France stood by Israel at international forums, first and foremost at the United Nations; researchers and scientists of both countries worked together on joint projects. Peres's personality played a central role in the strengthening of the ties between Paris and Jerusalem; he had turned Mollet, Bourgès, Thomas, Mangin, and so many others into his personal friends. When Mollet's government fell in May 1957, and Bourgès-Maunoury was elected prime minister, Israel reached her most amazing achievements in France, thanks to the close friendship between Bourgès and Peres.

Yet not all of Peres's initiatives were successful. In some cases his bubbling creativity tested the confines of wild imagination and even wandered up and beyond those confines, as was shown in the French Guyana episode.

French Guyana was a neglected and gloomy colony in South America. It had gained its grim notoriety by serving as a penal colony for thousands of hardened French criminals, most of whom died in what was a living hell. Guyana's most famous prisoner was Captain Alfred Dreyfus, who had spent a few years on Devil's Island, off Guyana's coast. Another prisoner, who became world-famous thanks to his book and the motion picture that was based on it, was Henri Charrière, known as "Papillon."

In 1957, a high-ranking visitor from Guyana toured Israel, and said to Peres, "If we were associated with Israel instead of France, our situation would have been different."[7]

That phrase fired up Peres's fertile imagination. French Guyana, he was told, was a large country of thirty-five thousand square miles, and the number of its inhabitants barely reached thirty thousand. Guyana was terra incognita that had never been fully explored. Rumors described fabulous natural resources hidden under its impenetrable jungles. On learning all of this, Peres visualized an Israeli colony overseas where Israeli experts would perform wonders.

"Do you need Guyana?" Peres asked the minister of colonies, his friend Jacques Soustelle. "We can do a lot of things there." He suggested that France lease Guyana to Israel for thirty to forty years, or that Israel and France, together, establish a company for the development of the country. Soustelle didn't say no—and Peres took off. He already planned to bring to South America scores of thousands of Jews who would settle there, creating a sort of branch of Israel. He shared his idea with Ben-Gurion, and convinced some leaders of the Histadrut labor union that the idea was worth exploring. They sent a mission of seven experts to tour the faraway land. Ben-Gurion was skeptical. "They dream of settling a Jewish majority (around 40,000) in Guyana," he noted, "and establish a Hebrew State as Israel's estate."

"Isn't this on the expense of Israel? And how can we be sure that the Guyana Jews would want to stay connected with Israel? I advised Shimon not to go too far in his talks with Soustelle, but rather speak of common ventures . . . . When the members of the delegation return, I'll check the aridity of that land, and find out if there is a possibility of settling it."[8]

The idea, of course, was too far-fetched. On its return, the delegation submitted a detailed report and a film that was screened before the cabinet ministers. The reaction was one of fear and indignation. Minister Pinhas Sapir said to Peres, "This is a disaster, this is colonialism, this is imperialism. It will be terrible for our relations with Africa, and it will stir objections in South America. Golda will not let this thing pass, only over her dead body. The Old Man has promised her that as long as she is foreign minister, this thing will not happen."[9]

Ben-Gurion, too, agreed that Israel had nothing to do in the jungles of Guyana, and discarded the idea of turning Israel into a colonial power. Peres bowed to his leaders, but was sadly disappointed. "The French were ready to give us Guyana," he kept repeating.[10]

On ideas like this, Yossef Nahmias, Peres's friend, used to say, "If only five percent of Shimon's ideas come true—that's enough!"[11]

PERES'S "IMPERIALISM" OVER Guyana was related to some other projects of his that were also tainted with fantasy. In a lecture before his colleagues he spoke about one of Israel's goals. "I'll call this, on purpose, by a somewhat funny name. On my opinion we should strive to establish a Hebrew Empire, an Israeli Empire." For that purpose, he thought, Israel should find friends in the United Nations. She should obtain markets for her products and new sources of raw materials, partners for the war against Nasser, pan-Islamism and, communism, and a strong position in Africa and Asia.[12] The Sinai Campaign had instilled in him an intoxicating feeling of success and power that loosened his self-restraint. "We have to aspire to alter the State of Israel's borders," he said in a closed meeting. "I wouldn't suggest invading the West Bank or Sinai or Lebanon in order to take the Litani [River]. . . . I don't suggest war and conquests. I suggest that . . . if certain developments occur in the Middle East we would be ready to review again the boundaries of the State."[13]

In these days Peres's self-confidence soared and his political initiatives reached a global scope. He bluntly told the foreign ministry's senior officials that there were areas and countries where the defense ministry could be more successful. Many Third World nations began courting Israel after the Sinai victories and applied for military, technical, and agricultural assistance. Peres's emissaries reached remote lands in Asia and Africa. They operated in many African nations—Kenya, Congo, Uganda, Ethiopia, Tanganyika, Zanzibar, and Sudan. In the Far East they were active in particular in Nepal and Burma. Israeli experts trained local armies, or established units mirroring the Israeli "Nahal" unit—soldiers who spent half of their time working the land and creating agricultural settlements.

In South America, the defense ministry's endeavors were less glorious. Peres's people exported surplus weapons, and Peres maintained that he needed the money in order to buy new equipment for the IDF.[14] In most cases, the buyers were shady South American dictatorships. A delegation that came to Israel from Nicaragua in February 1957 and bought weapons worth $1 million was led by Colonel Anastasio "Tacho" Somoza, the future dictator of his country.[15]

But the main target of Peres's foreign policy remained Western Europe. The director general of the Ministry of Defense controlled a vast organization of permanent representatives and special envoys that operated in France, Germany, England, Italy, Holland, and Belgium. In his trips he often established purely political contacts that had nothing to do with his official functions. In France he met with Jean Monnet, a famous economist and ideologue, the former president of the High Authority of the European Coal and Steel Community and the founder and president of the organization considered a precursor of the Common Market. Years later, Peres confessed that he had exceeded his authority and had gone too far by meeting Monnet.

Peres objected to the theory that Israel should "integrate in the Middle East." He maintained that the connection of Israel to that part of the world was geographical only, and that Israel should ignore the area and seek permanent association with Europe. "I am not an ardent admirer of the Middle East culture," he said, "and I don't need music records from Yemen or books from Egypt . . . . We should follow the world's big blocks and the only natural place for us—distance-wise—is Europe."[16]

Peres's initiatives raised the tension between the Ministries of Defense and Foreign Affairs. That tension reached new heights in Paris. The direct connections between Peres's people and France's leaders frustrated the Israeli diplomats, who bitterly complained to Golda Meir. Golda, in turn, would immediately fly into a rage and rush to Ben-Gurion's office.

Over and over again, Ben-Gurion had to calm her down; yet he kept supporting Peres's moves. "The Director of the Defense Ministry is coming to Paris for matters concerning the purchase of weapons," Ben-Gurion wrote to the Israeli embassy staff in the spring of 1958. "He will let you know who he is meeting, but in order to succeed he should meet these people alone. Some things between us and France have been done—and will be done—in an unorthodox way, sometimes by ignoring this or that Minister, including the Finance Minister. The members of the French Cabinet prefer, because of this, to talk to us informally and in private. The French are skipping diplomatic protocol, so you should give it up as well."[17] Ben-Gurion couldn't reveal to the

Israeli diplomats in France the real purpose of Peres's talks in Paris—unconventional research and the building of a nuclear reactor.

IN 1958, GENERAL Charles de Gaulle became France's new prime minister and later president. He was welcomed with enthusiasm as the man who had saved France from dictatorship after the collapse of the Fourth Republic. De Gaulle put an end to the close cooperation with Israel in several domains. He appointed as foreign minister Maurice Couve de Murville, a cold and distant diplomat who was not Israel's friend. Couve de Murville immediately launched an effort to restore France's relations with the Arab world.

These were worrying signs; nevertheless, five of the ministers in de Gaulle's government were members of the League for a France-Israel Alliance. And de Gaulle approved of the sale of weapons to Israel and authorized the supply of Mirage fighter planes to the IDF, in spite of the objection of Couve de Murville. Ben-Gurion publicly praised General de Gaulle; Peres wrote the foreword for the Hebrew edition of de Gaulle's memoirs. When he visited Paris, at a later date, he received from de Gaulle a copy of his book with the dedication, "To Mr. Peres, in memory of a world drama, as a testimony of my heartfelt appreciation, and as an expression of my feelings of deep respect and friendship toward Israel."[18]

On July 14, 1958, a bloody coup took place in Iraq. An army officer, General Abdul-Karim Kassem, seized power and massacred the royal family in their Baghdad palace. The coup shook the Middle East. Subversive groups, inspired by Egypt's Nasser, revolted against Jordan's King Hussein and besieged the royal palace in Amman. Hussein's rule and his very life hung on a thread. With Ben-Gurion's consent, an airlift over Israel's territory carried two thousand British paratroopers to Amman. The prompt British operation saved the king. Israel's relations with Britain were dramatically improved.

The result was not late in coming. Golda Meir and Shimon

Peres visited Britain; London agreed to sell Israel submarines and Centurion tanks that were partly financed by a secret American fund.[19] The United States, too, sold Israel a thousand recoilless rifles. The turmoil in Iraq and Jordan made the United States realize how important Israel could be as a rampart against Nasser and his subversive policy. Gradually, the American suspicion toward Israel changed into growing cooperation. The State Department started encouraging Israel's activities in Asia and Africa.[20] John Foster Dulles was very impressed with "the Peripheral Pact," which Ben-Gurion had built secretly after the Sinai Campaign. The pact grouped several states—Turkey, Iran, Israel, Ethiopia, and Sudan—that had two things in common. They were all nations located geographically on the periphery of the Middle East, and they were all threatened by Nasser's subversion. Shimon Peres was very active in establishing the pact, and secretly traveled to the member nations' capitals.

The new reality in the Middle East now made Peres a frequent visitor to London.[21] Yet, in spite of the director general's efforts, Great Britain never became "a second France" in her relations with Israel.

But in the meantime, Peres had detected a new potential ally in Europe, and he stormed it with audacity and zeal.

PART 3.

AGAINST ALL ODDS

CHAPTER 15.

A BLIZZARD IN GERMANY

ON THE NIGHT OF December 26, 1957, in A howling blizzard, a car coming from Paris crossed the German border. It skidded on the black ice, left the road, and got stuck in a heap of snow. The engine stalled. The three passengers got out of the car, and the driver tried to restart the engine. After long efforts, the engine coughed into life, and the driver tried to pull out of the snow mound by going into reverse. As the car darted backward, it almost hit one of the passengers, who flung himself to the side and miraculously escaped. That was General Haim Laskov, the IDF deputy chief of staff, who was accompanying Shimon Peres and Arthur Ben-Nathan on a secret trip to Germany.[1]

The perilous journey continued in the dense fog covering the countryside. "The fog stayed with us all along the trip," Peres wrote in his notebook. "For some reason, I had the impression that the German fog is utterly different from the French. In France the fog is more delicate, soft and transparent like a diaphanous scarf, and through it one can see the characteristic details of the ornate French landscape. . . . In Germany the fog was very heavy, massive, opaque like the smoke spewed by the many stacks of the coal and steel plants in the Sarre region. One could draw the odd conclusion that climate has a national I.D . . . ."

"For us, the trip to Germany was like a parting from reality. We didn't see trees, houses and people. We saw memories, sights and goals one can't forget."[2]

Finally, at noon of the following day, the car arrived at the village of Rott-am-Inn, about forty miles south of Munich. The men knocked on the door of a small house near the village church, the country home of Franz Josef Strauss, the defense minister of West Germany.

THE SECRET TRIP of Peres to Germany was the culmination of a long process that Ben-Gurion had initiated in the early fifties. He conceived a controversial policy toward Germany, based on reconciliation between Israel and the newly democratic Germany that he called "the other Germany." Ben-Gurion's position was largely influenced by the personality of the German chancellor, Konrad Adenauer, an old and wise statesman.

In 1952, Israel had obtained from Germany $822 million in reparations for the property pillaged from the Jewish people during the Nazi era. The issue divided the Israeli public; protests, stormy debates in the Knesset, and clashes between Holocaust survivors and the police underlined the Israelis' dilemma: should they accept or reject restitution money from the nation of their former murderers? Ben-Gurion carried the day, but he didn't try to normalize relations between Israel and Germany.

Shimon Peres agreed with Ben-Gurion's policy, but learned from experience that ties with Germany had another meaning, one that could be vital for Israel. In his frequent visits to Paris he witnessed the building of the European Union. Germany and Italy played an important part in the process. Peres's French friends advised him to tighten his ties with these two countries.

In early 1957, when Peres had met with the famous French economist Jean Monnet, Monnet told Peres that Israel should try to join the Common Market.[3] In this new structure, Monnet said, West Germany would have a major role.[4]

On his way back to Israel, Peres met with an Israeli cabinet minister, Zalman Aran, who told him, "The German nation is indebted to us more than any other. We should demand that Germany include in her constitution a commitment to come to the help of Israel if it is attacked!"[5]

Peres knew well that there was no chance that Germany would make such a constitutional commitment, but he believed that Germany couldn't expiate her past just by paying reparations to Israel. Germany, he thought, should help Israel to defend itself.[6]

Peres was deeply impressed by Chancellor Adenauer, and felt that his policy toward Israel was based on "a pure religious element, without a shade of opportunism. He regards Israel as a nation toward which he has a moral debt, and not a common and routine interest from the viewpoint of his foreign policy." Two other ministers stirred his interest: Foreign Minister Heinrich von Brentano and Defense Minister Franz Josef Strauss.

Von Brentano was a very cautious politician. His attitude toward Israel was reserved; like other senior officials in Bonn, West Germany's capital, he feared that any pro-Israeli step might lead to the recognition of communist East Germany by the Arab states. Peres also noted that "on top of the fear from the Arabs, there is no doubt that strong pro-Arab tendencies prevailed in Bonn."[7]

It was evident that no good tidings for Israel could be expected from Minister von Brentano. On the other hand, Peres was impressed by the power and influence of Strauss. He was a dynamic man of forty-two with a lot of political clout in the state of Bavaria. In World War II he had served in an artillery unit on the Russian front. He was said to believe in right-wing ideas and to symbolize the new German militarism. Rumors maintained that his view of Israel was less than tepid, and that he even objected to the reparations.[8]

The only way to find out the truth about Strauss was to meet him. Peres got Ben-Gurion's approval, learned all he could about Strauss, and on July 3, 1957, flew to Bonn to meet with him.

The trip to Germany was not easy for Peres. He couldn't suppress the thoughts about so many of his relatives, his beloved grandfather among them, and millions of other Jews who had been massacred by the Nazis. He always thought that "in America live 6 million Jews and in Germany are buried 6 million Jews."[9] In a rare interview during a later visit to Munich, he exposed his feelings: "How do I feel here [in Germany] as a Jew? Objectively, the German people don't stir my enthusiasm. Subjectively, my entire attitude is permeated by a feeling of reservation, and I almost fear, physically, the touch of a German. [I get] a guilty feeling, if I like something here . . . . And yet it is almost painful to see how much the Germans are humane like us. Is there in this people a source of danger that cannot be changed? Is it inevitable that this people would beget hatred and arrogance, oppression and murder? Or is this people repentant?"[10]

STRAUSS RECEIVED PERES in his house at Venusberg, an affluent suburb overlooking Bonn. The director general met "a mountainous man of more than 100 kilograms, a man who loves very much to eat, a man with blue eyes that exude energy, and a brilliant debater."[11]

The two men plunged into an absorbing conversation that lasted for five hours. Peres started by reviewing Israel's political and military situation, and he discussed with his host the possibility of buying two refurbished German submarines. Nazi Germany had sunk seven of its own submarines at the end of the war; the Germans had now raised two of them and refitted them for service. Peres offered to buy them through a French intermediary.[12]

Strauss promised to give the idea positive consideration and pointed out a subject that preoccupied him: "We want to learn from the Israeli experience of fighting against Russian weapons."[13] That turned out to be Strauss's main worry as defense minister—the danger of a confrontation with the Soviet Union. He knew that in any war between the East and the West, Germany would become the main battlefield. He stressed that Turkey, Israel, and the American Sixth Fleet could play a major role in rescuing Europe from a Soviet attack.[14] Strauss kept praising Israel for her victory in the Sinai Campaign, and asked over and over again "that you teach us how to destroy Soviet weapons."[15]

Peres discussed relations between the German and the Jewish peoples. These relations, he said, couldn't be based only on financial commitments. Strauss answered that he was ready to help build a bridge over the terrible chasm lying between the German people and the Jewish people. He would do it, he said, in spite of the objections he might encounter on the cabinet level and in public opinion.

This was the first of several meetings. A rapport of mutual trust developed between the two men; their common projects were about to affect not only their countries, but also faraway regions in Africa and Asia.

By the end of 1957, Peres and Strauss decided to improve the ties between the defense establishments of the two countries by a visit of the IDF chief of staff, Moshe Dayan, to Strauss's country home in Bavaria. The trip was scheduled for the end of December and was supposed to be kept secret.

But a few days before it took place, some information about it leaked out and infuriated the ministers of the left-wing parties in the Israeli cabinet, Mapam and Ahdut Ha'avoda. Both those parties objected to any relations with Germany; they also had allies in Mapai, led by Golda Meir.

At a cabinet meeting, the left-wing ministers demanded to know the reason for Dayan's visit to Germany. To purchase submarines, Ben-Gurion answered. But the left-wing parties strongly objected. The cabinet voted to approve Dayan's trip by one vote.

The leaders of the left wing didn't give up. Ten days before Dayan's departure, a report was published in Ahdut Ha'avoda's daily paper, *Lamerhav*. It described the preparations for the visit of "a senior defense personality" to Germany. The report triggered a storm of public opinion. The newspapers published emotional articles for and against the projected journey. Finally, Ben-Gurion convened the Committee of Defense and Foreign Affairs of the Knesset and made the shortest announcement in its history: "The chief of staff will not go to Germany," Ben-Gurion said, and left the meeting.

The government crisis was solved after the left-wing ministers formally pledged not to leak secret information anymore. In the middle of the crisis, Peres left for Germany, and this time the Mapam and Ahdut Ha'avoda ministers kept silent. Their only achievement was that instead of Moshe Dayan, Peres took with him Dayan's deputy and designated successor, General Haim Laskov.

And so, on December 27, 1957, the Israelis' car reached its destination. In Rott-am-Inn, Strauss's wife received the exhausted visitors and offered them a hearty lunch. Strauss himself arrived twenty minutes later, red-cheeked and short of breath after a morning jog with his two dogs. ("One of them is Bavarian, allegedly absolutely loyal to him, and the other Hungarian—black and treacherous," Peres noted.)[16]

Strauss told Peres that he had reported to Adenauer about their meeting, and Adenauer had given him his full approval. They exchanged views on the Soviet threat, which was Strauss's main concern. Strauss spoke with admiration of Turkey's positive attitude toward Israel. He didn't know that Israel was in the process of establishing her secret Peripheral Pact with Turkey, Iran, Ethiopia, and Sudan.[17] (Peres revealed to Strauss the existence of the Peripheral Pact only at their following meeting, three months later.)

Peres mentioned the submarines, and Strauss offered to sell Israel submarines of the next generation, built in Germany.

The discussion moved to another subject: the weapons in use by the German Army. The idea behind the discussion, even if not expressed in so many words, was that some of those weapons would be supplied to Israel free of charge.[18] Peres spoke of the Uzi submachine gun that Israel was trying to export to Europe; Strauss answered that the Uzi was being tested by his experts, and that it was on the short list of two submachine guns that suited the purposes of the German Army.

The effort to sell Israeli arms to Germany was to continue in the future. In 1960, Israel sold to Germany twenty-five G-25 (Gavriel) sea-to-sea missiles. In the following years, Israel sold Germany Uzi submachine guns, hand grenades, mortars, and other military equipment.

At the Rott-am-Inn meeting, it was also agreed that Israeli officers would visit the German Navy and armor installations. At the end of the meeting, Laskov presented Strauss with an album of photographs from the Sinai Campaign. He spread a map on the table and explained Israel's moves in the war to his fascinated host. When the Israelis left Strauss's home, it was clear that the meeting would result in closer cooperation with Germany. Strauss asked them to keep their contacts in total secrecy.

Back home, Peres reported to Ben-Gurion and Dayan. Strauss's motives, he said, were probably several: his fear and hatred of the Soviet Union, his admiration for the IDF, his support for building a common European force, and the strengthening of Germany's allies in the Middle East and Africa. Apparently, Peres said, Strauss had been empowered by Adenauer to manage relations with Israel instead of Foreign Minister von Brentano.[19]

Peres called the secret relations he had set up with the German military establishment "a friendship for a rainy day." His initiative was motivated by his tendency to look beyond the horizon. "He believed that the climate of the Fourth Republic in France might change," said his aide Avraham Ben-Yossef. "The friendship with France could end one day and Shimon was looking for an alternative."

THREE MONTHS LATER, Peres and Strauss met in Bonn and agreed on an exchange of intelligence between the two countries. Strauss told Peres that von Brentano had been upset about the meeting on December 27, but now he had agreed with Strauss that those meetings would be pursued, and officially labeled as "meetings with the director general of the Israeli defense ministry."[20] Peres secretly brought Strauss's secretary to Israel and introduced him to Ben-Gurion.

The relations between Peres and Strauss evolved into a friendship, somewhat similar to the friendship between Peres and Bourgès-Maunoury in France. Peres was often a visitor at Strauss's home, and once was a guest at a summer residence that the Strauss family had rented on the French Riviera. When he visited Strauss in March 1958, he asked his German friend if there was any truth in the newspapers reports that Strauss might replace Adenauer as chancellor of Germany. Strauss replied: "I read this in the papers too, and I am not so stupid as to deny it. But in Germany only the young people die. The old ones live forever."[21] Peres chuckled; Strauss didn't know how much his words reflected the situation in Israel.

Peres and Strauss reached a major agreement: Germany would lease—actually supply to Israel, free of charge—weapons of various kinds. The two men spoke about cargo planes, helicopters, artillery, air-to-air missiles, and other sophisticated matériel.

In another secret meeting, Strauss gave Peres an American Sidewinder air-to-air missile for examination. It was one of two missiles the United States had delivered to West Germany. The missile was returned after the defense ministry experts had examined it thoroughly. Strauss also agreed to "lease" to Israel six Noratlas cargo planes for parachuting purposes.[22] Yet, in order for the weapons deliveries to continue on a regular basis, Adenauer's approval was needed. The matter became urgent for Peres and Ben-Gurion after the ascent of de Gaulle to power in France. Worrying signs started to appear in the French policy toward Israel, and "the friendship for a rainy day" became even more vital. "Who knows," Ben-Gurion grimly noted, "if Germany wouldn't remain the only country from which we would be able to purchase weapons in the coming years."[23]

ON MARCH 7, 1960, Ben-Gurion visited the United States and met with its leaders. The meetings took place in a pleasant atmosphere but Ben-Gurion was disappointed by his meeting with President Eisenhower. After visiting Washington and Boston, he flew to New York and checked into the Waldorf-Astoria hotel.

On March 14, at 9 A.M., Ben-Gurion descended from his suite to another suite a few floors beneath his, where Germany's chancellor Adenauer was expecting him. It was a historic meeting between the prime minister of the Jewish state and the leader of the nation that only fifteen years before had been engaged in insane efforts to annihilate the Jewish people.

Adenauer warmly received Ben-Gurion and expressed his desire to help Israel; he agreed to loan Israel $500 million for the development of the Negev. Ben-Gurion then asked for the supply of military equipment to Israel, free of charge, following the conversations between Peres and Strauss. Adenauer had been briefed about the talks and immediately promised Ben-Gurion that large quantities of weapons would be supplied to Israel for free.

Adenauer's decision had been meticulously prepared by Peres and Strauss. Three weeks before the meeting of the two "Old Men," Peres had flown to Germany with Moshe Dayan, who was now a minister in the Israeli government. Strauss was deeply moved when he met the legendary Israeli general. Dayan spoke of the dangers facing Israel, and in clear, direct words asked Strauss that Germany supply Israel with military equipment. Peres read a list of the weapons that Israel needed from Germany. Strauss agreed right away. Now he needed Adenauer's stamp of approval; that was given at the Waldorf-Astoria meeting.

Ben-Gurion was deeply impressed by Adenauer's personality and returned to Israel with a feeling of elation. Still, he didn't lose his sense of proportion. On March 31, Peres showed him the draft of his letter to Strauss, thanking him for getting Adenauer's agreement to the arms supply. Peres added that "Ben-Gurion was deeply impressed by the chancellor, by his personality, his statesmanship, and his philosophy." Ben-Gurion asked Peres to strike out "his philosophy."[24]

THE PROMISE OF Adenauer and Strauss was fulfilled in absolute secrecy. The chancellor and his defense minister decided to bypass the government and the defense establishment. But they couldn't circumvent the Bundestag, the West German parliament. Strauss suggested to Peres that he meet with the leaders of the three major parties in Germany—the Christian Democratic Union, the Socialists, and the Liberals—and present to them the agreement they had reached.

So it was. The talks with the leaders of the Christian Democrats and the Liberals proceeded smoothly. But the most complicated conversation was the one Peres had with Dr. Fritz Erler, a leader of the Socialist Party.

Erler was Israel's friend, but he believed that Germany shouldn't provide her with weapons. At the end of a long conversation with Peres, however, he admitted that Israel had no choice but to acquire weapons for her defense—and Germany couldn't evade its duty to help her. "When you face two conflicting demands," Dr. Erler concluded, "choosing the less immoral of the two is a moral choice." Peres thought he was hearing "a quote of Martin Buber's teaching." He felt great respect for Dr. Erler, one of the few politicians who believed that political considerations should be subjected to moral judgments.[25] Yet Erler demanded that the United States be informed of Germany's assistance to Israel. Peres revealed the secret to President John Kennedy during a visit to the White House on April 2, 1963. When he was about to leave the Oval Office, Peres said to Kennedy, "Chancellor Adenauer, in the name of his government, and Prime Minister Ben-Gurion want you to know that the German government is assisting the Israeli government in the areas of defense and transports."

"What is the size of this assistance?" the president asked.

"It is large and very important."[26]

Kennedy remarked, "The relations between Israel and Germany are not ordinary relations, in any case." He didn't have any objection, he added, to that assistance.[27]

On Adenauer's initiative, a secret committee was created in the Bundestag; its members represented the three major parties. Adenauer and Strauss briefed them about the weapons deliveries to Israel. The committee secretly appropriated the necessary funds. In Israel, the supply of weapons from Germany was also kept in total secrecy.

In September 1960, the supply of weapons intensified. During another visit at Strauss's home in Bonn, Peres asked him for twelve Fouga Magister planes and ten 155-mm. "Long Tom" cannons, "on lease"—the formula for the supply of weapons free of charge. Strauss agreed immediately.[28] In less than two years, Israel received from Germany twelve Nord cargo aircraft, twelve Fouga Magister jets, some Sikorsky helicopters, 40-mm. antiaircraft guns with ammunition, Cobra antitank missiles, and large quantities of ammunition and spare parts. The value of those deliveries was about $25 million.[29] In June 1961, during a visit by Ben-Gurion to Paris, Peres organized a top-secret meeting between him and Strauss, in the home of the defense ministry's envoy.

SHIMON PERES MET with Chancellor Adenauer in Bonn in June 1962. The sight of the chancellor who rose to greet him in his private office had a profound impact on Peres: "From behind a medium-sized desk in a clean and severely furnished room rises a tall, erect man, well dressed, skinnier than he looks in his pictures; his face is fresh, and in its center two blue eyes shine that change [their expression] from a cunning smile into a serious look full of unshaken authority. His walk is agile, his hearing good, he reads without glasses, and his movements are devoid of any sign of fatigue or old age. He who hasn't seen this sight with his own eyes—wouldn't believe that this is the eighty-six-year-old Adenauer."[30]

The meeting lasted for two hours. Why do the Arabs hate Israel so much, Adenauer asked as soon as they had settled down. Peres answered that "the emotions of the Arab world are stronger than the intellectual discipline of the West. The Arab feels separately, thinks separately, speaks separately and acts separately .... Besides, Islam is an aggressive religion where hatred always played an important role." Adenauer wasn't satisfied with the answer and wanted to know if there hadn't been periods of calm and fraternity in the development of Islam, but Peres stuck to his guns. "There almost were not such periods," he said. "Islam always wielded its sword." He stressed, nevertheless, that there were many Muslim and even Arab countries whose relations with Israel were not hateful, and gave as examples Turkey, Iran, Jordan, and Lebanon.

Adenauer expressed the opinion that the hatred of the Arabs stemmed from jealousy of Israel's achievements, and from their inferiority complexes. The chancellor then mentioned the trial of Colonel Adolf Eichmann and his execution. Eichmann, the one responsible for the "final solution of the Jewish problem" in Hitler's Germany, had been captured by Israeli agents in Argentina, brought to Israel, tried, and hanged. "Please convey to my friend Prime Minister Ben-Gurion," Adenauer said to Peres, "my deep appreciation for the way the Adolf Eichmann affair was managed and concluded. I couldn't imagine a more dignified way of dealing with that matter. And I am, personally—for reasons I won't elaborate—grateful for that." He had been a prisoner of the Nazis during the war, Adenauer added, and wasn't aware of the scope of the horrors; he had learned the full extent of the tragedy from the Eichmann trial, and he was shocked by the atrocities.

Peres spoke of the danger to Israel's existence because of her neighbors, but also of the danger for the West resulting from the brutal penetration of the Soviet Union into the Middle East. He said that Israel had decided to turn for help to three nations—the United States, France, and Germany.

Adenauer answered that Germany was a friend of Israel for two reasons. "I don't see any need to explain the first reason," he said. "The second reason is that we are facing a common enemy

.... No matter if the situation is calm or full of tension, Israel must be strong. What is the aid you need, military or financial?"

Peres answered that the country needed not only military and financial aid, but a clear and firm policy. France, he said, gave Israel weapons and no money, America gave it money and no weapons; from Germany it wanted something in the middle. Like the mermaid, he said, smiling: "the flesh of the fish and the taste of the lady."

Peres enumerated Israel's requests: helicopters, torpedo boats, submarines, and assistance in military research and other subjects. Adenauer approved the request and promised to brief Strauss. He then reviewed the world situation, stressed the dangers represented by China and the Soviet Union, and spoke warmly of General de Gaulle. At the end of the meeting he said to Peres, "We helped you and we'll help you in the future as well. We have common problems and a common enemy. I also believe there is a debt that we owe Israel." The suave Adenauer turned to Dr. Felix Shinar, Israel's representative in Germany, who had accompanied Peres. "I want to thank you in particular," he said, "for bringing me a visitor whose descriptions and conversation I enjoyed thoroughly."

Peres noted with admiration: "These leaders, how generous they are in heaping praise on foreign visitors!"[31]

Adenauer wrote to Ben-Gurion: "Shimon Peres made a very good impression on me. I hope he is satisfied with the results of his talks here."[32]

LATE IN 1962, Peres introduced to Strauss a young leader from Kenya, Tom Mboya, whom the Ministry of Defense had taken under its wing. He talked Strauss into supplying military equipment to Kenya, which was fighting a subversive pro-communist rebellion in the country. Peres told Strauss that Israel trained Kenya's army. Strauss was excited by his common projects with Israel in Africa, which had started when Peres let him into the secret of the Peripheral Pact and asked for Germany's help for Sudan. Now Strauss told Peres, "Following your suggestion, we got involved in Sudan, and I hope that neither you nor we are going to be sorry. We shall now move along the eastern shores of Africa in coordination with you."[33]

Germany's involvement in Israel's initiatives in Sudan, Kenya, and other lands was not the result of a chance whim of Peres. During the years he developed a policy concept that became a cornerstone of his activity: creating common interests with foreign countries that would tie those countries to Israel. The partnership with France was forged by the Sinai-Suez Campaign, nuclear development, and the joint development of missiles. He operated the same way in building a common anti-Soviet front with Strauss.

In September 1960, Shimon Peres spoke with Strauss about the penetration of the West into the new African and Asian countries and the checking of Soviet subversion. It is difficult to win the sympathy of the common people, with their lack of education and contact with the wider world, Peres said. "The only way is to win the sympathy of the existing leadership, even though it is corrupt. We should gain their support by quick, spectacular acts and achievements that the leaders could be proud of. For instance: Israel established an air force academy in Ghana, and [President Kwame] Nkrumah is proud of it." Peres couldn't refrain from firing a jibe at his French friends. "The French are very sensitive," he said. "They think that by contributing some of their French culture to these nations they have done everything for them, and are offended if these peoples demand something else, like factories, ports, or roads."

Strauss agreed "with every word," Peres reported later.[34] It was decided that he would arrange a meeting for Strauss with the Kenyan leaders; Peres also obtained Strauss's help for another of Israel allies, Nepal, whose geographic position between China and India gave it strategic value. Peres described Israel's assistance to Prime Minister Bishweshwar Prasad Koirala, and asked Germany for help in building the Nepalese Air Force. Strauss immediately agreed to present Nepal with ten cargo aircraft.[35]

At that meeting in September, Strauss was so impressed by Peres's views that he organized another meeting at his home, to which he invited the Bundestag chairman and the secretary of state in the foreign ministry. Peres warned his interlocutors that the nascent states in Asia and Africa might become an easy target for Soviet subversion, "if the West doesn't act right away by unconventional means." He spoke of five states in need of immediate assistance where Israel was involved: Nepal, Iran, Ethiopia, Mali, and Kenya. In each of those countries, he said, Israel would be willing to provide experts and instructors. He suggested that Germany supply the equipment. The Germans agreed and promised to create a special committee to plan activities in these countries.

Both nations benefited from that cooperation. Israel was warmly welcomed in the new nations, and sent over experts and instructors, but didn't have the means to supply equipment. Germany didn't enjoy the same status, but could achieve considerable influence by supplying vital equipment. By establishing that cooperation, Peres created a solid base of common interests with Germany.

But sometimes, the Israelis and the Germans went too far.

IN 1961, ISRAELI and German officials held top-secret negotiations about a treaty that went beyond anything Israel had signed with any other country. In the spring, senior officials of the two defense ministries drafted a secret agreement between the countries. The treaty, in effect for five years, was defined as top secret; its contents were not to be revealed to a third country. Paragraph One stated that Germany would supply to Israel, for free, torpedo boats, 350-ton submarines, medium-size helicopters, Noratlas cargo planes, and other equipment. Other paragraphs dealt with regular consultations between the defense ministries of the two countries and with enlarging the fields of cooperation.

But Paragraph Two was a time bomb, and if that agreement had been signed it could have toppled the Israeli government.

It read, "The Government of Israel is ready to consider, in case of need, the request of the Government of the German Federal Republic to put at her disposal military bases for the purpose of the defense of the West." This paragraph expressed Strauss's strategic thinking; he wanted to make Israel a bastion of the Western bloc against Soviet penetration. But the deep meaning of that paragraph was revolting: the very thought that Israel, the land of the Holocaust survivors, could even consider giving bases on her territory to the German Army was terrifying. Those who had drafted the agreement were devoid of any understanding of the Israeli psyche. The Israeli people would never have allowed such a paragraph to be included in an agreement with Germany.

After the agreement was drafted, Strauss was supposed to present it to Adenauer and get his approval, but the relations between them turned sour after the German election in the summer of 1961, and the draft treaty was not brought to the chancellor.

When Peres prepared for his meeting with Adenauer, his assistants had the draft treaty in mind; they included it in the written notes detailing the topics he should discuss with the chancellor.[36] "It was nothing but a German draft that was never signed," stressed Arthur Ben-Nathan. Years later, Peres said he didn't remember that draft.

Peres had been lucky. If he had brought the agreement to the Israeli government, his political future would have become a thing of the past.[37]

IN NOVEMBER 1962, Strauss resigned from the position of defense minister following a political scandal. In his last meeting with Peres, Strauss promised to supply Israel with missile boats, helicopters, and two submarines that would be built in Britain. Peres thanked him for his help to Israel. "Adenauer is an old man," he told Strauss. "He has proven his moral courage, at least in the eyes of the world, by his decision on the reparations. You are a young man, and your future lies ahead of you. Don't miss the opportunity that History has offered you."[38]

Strauss was succeeded by Kai-Uwe von Hassel. On his next visit to Bonn, Peres was received with full military honors: a large honor guard, a military band, and a string of official visits at German Air Force bases. Von Hassel continued his predecessor's policy toward Israel, and even intensified the weapons shipments. Peres and von Hassel worked out an ambitious program for common action in Africa that planned the building of flight academies and navy schools in Ethiopia, Tanganyika, Uganda, Kenya, and Congo.

Peres and von Hassel also agreed that Israeli soldiers would train in Germany in the handling of sophisticated weapons; von Hassel decided to keep purchasing Israeli-made arms. "Fifty percent of the potential of the Israeli military industry is based on Germany," Peres said later.[39]

Some German friends warned Israel that she should obtain tangible commitments from the German cabinet. Adenauer was about to resign, and his designated successor was the economics minister, Dr. Ludwig Erhard. One of Peres's friends told him that "he was not sure that the triangle Erhard-Schröeder-von Hassel would be as friendly to Israel [Gerhard Schröeder was foreign minister at the time]."[40] But even after the transfer of power, the secret assistance to Israel continued.

In 1963, Peres told his colleagues at the defense ministry, "Lately we reached an agreement with the Germans on substantial aid to Israel, both in matériel and in money. The worth of the project is two hundred fifty million marks. One hundred fifty million out of this [is] in the form of weapons from the German arsenals, and the remaining one hundred million marks [are] payments that Germany will make for weapons we are buying."[41]

The secret supply of weapons continued until 1964, and Peres candidly declared, "If I were asked what was better—relations between the defense ministries of Germany and Israel without diplomatic recognition or diplomatic recognition without military relations—I believe the answer is clear. Diplomatic relations are not always the solution. Sometimes they are a substitute and a camouflage."[42]

The harrowing night journey in the December 1957 blizzard had been fruitful beyond Peres's wildest dreams.

CHAPTER 16.

THE HOLY ROOM

SHIMON PERES'S PRIVATE realm was called the "Holy Room." That's what Sonia and Tziki had named the living room in the family apartment. A sofa, a few armchairs for guests, and a desk stood beside a wall covered with bookshelves. The apartment was small. In one room slept Tziki and Sonia's mother; in the second slept Yoni and, later, his younger brother Hemi, who was born in 1958; Shimon and Sonia had a small bedroom. Shimon used to withdraw to the Holy Room almost daily.

When Peres entered the Holy Room to write or talk with a guest it was forbidden to open the door. Once in a while, he would ask Tziki to serve refreshments and the girl would be thrilled; she would bring drinks, drag her feet, and listen to part of the conversation. For her it was a way "to be in, to provide a service to the nation."[1] Peres's guests were usually defense ministry officials or visitors from abroad. But there were times when secret visitors would come, people whose faces she didn't see either when they arrived or when they left. Tziki knew that her father was doing very important work, but she couldn't say a word about it to anybody. She had a very strong feeling of "a secret mission."

She liked, in particular, to sit by her father when he came back from his trips abroad. He would sip some tea, then a glass of whiskey, and when he felt relaxed he would start his stories. He would tell her about France—that Israel has friends there, but nobody knows they are Israel's friends; that it is a totally different country. In Israel, he would say, there is white cheese and yellow cheese, but in France, hah, there were hundreds of sorts of cheeses—a cheese that was covered with pepper, another cheese that was wrapped in vine leaves, and whatnot. He would describe the places he had visited, the food and the wines; how the French prepare a meal, how they serve the hors d'oeuvres, how they pour wine, how they change the glasses during the meal, and what they talk about while eating. The French, he told his daughter, talk about two things—food and books. He would then tell her about French books and French writers, about France's splendid culture, and she listened, fascinated, to those stories about "another world."

Some family friends also used to visit, and the most frequent visitor was Colonel Nehemia Argov, Ben-Gurion's military secretary and her father's beloved friend. Argov always came in uniform, and always alone; he spent many hours with her parents, who loved him dearly. Often Argov would sit by Sonia and watch her with such admiration that Tziki suspected he was in love with her.

In October 1957, a terrible disaster happened. During a debate in the Knesset, a feeble-minded man, Moshe Duek, stood up in the Visitors' Gallery and threw a hand grenade at the government seats. The explosion wounded Ministers Moshe Shapira, Golda Meir, Moshe Carmel, and David Ben-Gurion. They were rushed to the hospital. For days on end, Nehemia Argov sat by Ben-Gurion's bed. On November 2, on the Jerusalem-Tel Aviv road, he hit a cyclist, David Kadosh; Argov took him in his car to the hospital, where the doctors said he was dying (David Kadosh finally survived).

When Argov failed to report for work the following day, a security officer was sent to his home, a small apartment on the ground floor. Through the slits in the shutters the officer could discern Argov sitting in a chair, his upper torso lying motionless on his desk. His service revolver was beside him. The officer called Peres right away: "Shimon, come quick. The worst has happened."[2]

Peres saw Argov through the window. He felt "a stab in the heart."[3]

Argov had shot himself. On his table his friends found two letters—one to his friends and one to Ben-Gurion. He feared Kadosh wouldn't survive, he wrote, and even if he did, he wouldn't be able to take care of his family. Argov therefore willed all his property to the Kadosh family. "I am sorry, but I cannot go on living."[4]

Peres knew that his friend had been going through a depression. He had suffered a romantic setback and lately felt very lonely. Sonia and Shimon smothered him with warmth and affection, but in vain. A day before his suicide, they had taken him to a bar mitzvah at a friend's house, hoping to distract him.

Three days after Argov's death, Moshe Dayan, Teddy Kollek, and Shimon Peres entered Ben-Gurion's hospital room. Dayan told Ben-Gurion about Argov's death and handed him his letter. The Old Man read the letter of his beloved assistant and broke into tears.

Sonia was in the late months of her pregnancy. When Shimon told her the terrible news, they decided that if their child was a boy, they would call him Nehemia. It was a boy.

"He was a valiant soldier," Shimon eulogized his friend, "a passionate friend, and a fierce lover."[5]

THE PERESES' OLDER SON, Yoni, loved Saturday mornings, when his father would invite over friends, writers, artists, and journalists. Yoni sat among them and listened, captivated, to their conversations about art, philosophy, and literature. Peres always brought him a present on his return from a trip abroad. He would arrive late at night and carefully thrust the package under the sleeping child's pillow. Yoni would wake up to the scent of the present's wrapping, mixed with his father's aftershave. Peres knew that Yoni loved animals. "He used to bring me entire farms, with cows and horses and all the rest."[6]

Peres also brought new books from his trips. Reading was his favorite occupation; he would spend two hours reading every night.

"My love of books is a love of wisdom," Peres wrote. "I travel with the books to faraway worlds, real and imaginary. I meet there wonderful characters that God has blessed with an enchanting, enthralling spirit. I love a book even more than the theater, the cinema or a music record. When I start reading it, I decide to do this as my own master, who is not accountable to anybody. I free myself from any kind of submission, including the submission to what the book itself tells."

"I take a book, I say good-bye to the world, and appoint myself producer, director, actor, a new man."

"I allow the first page to sound the first note, to check if the sound is well tuned. Then I start sketching in my mind the characters, the tastes, the odors, the dialogues, the events and the emotions, the victories and the defeats . . . ."

"In the company of books I feel that I can walk about naked, without a shirt, without being interrupted, and fill my belly and my imagination with the fruits of the trees of knowledge, taste and fantasy."[7]

Peres claimed to be a reader of a special kind. Not a passive reader, who lets the book lead him to the author's destination, but an active participant, who faces the writer, sometimes agrees with him, sometimes confronts him, and sometimes even "corrects" the book's message. "I argue with the story, sometimes I am captured by its logic, and sometimes I reject its sentences. And I improve, as a free man, all that needs to be improved."[8]

But at the same time, while delighting in the magic of books, Peres also discovered the power of the press.

"IT IS FOUR P.M.," a five-page article in the *Bamahane* weekly started. "Out of the gates of the giant building of the Defense Ministry in Tel-Aviv a crowd of employees flows toward the bus stations . . . . In an adjacent house, surrounded by a well-tended garden, the lights are still on." In that small house, dwarfed by the towering building of the ministry, operates "the heart and the brain" of the huge defense establishment.

"This is a formidable kingdom, that supplies to the IDF all its weapons ('from a bullet to a Vautour') and its equipment ('from a soldier's gear to a giant bulldozer'), drafts its soldiers and assures their reintegration in society after their discharge; builds camps and paves runways; controls the giant plants of the Aircraft Industries and the Military Industries; it employs hundreds of scientists in the development of new weapons; acts to prevent espionage, sabotage and terrorism; provides pioneering education to the young generation . . . ."

"A large part of the bodies and institutions of this kingdom were conceived and born in the last six years, since Defense Minister David Ben-Gurion put in charge of this complicated organization a man who was still under 30—Shimon Peres."[9]

The message was clear—while the Israelis returned to their routine, that young and wonderful man, Shimon Peres, kept working for their defense, down in the small house by the big building. The article's author, Yossef Levite, heaped praise on Peres, told of his quest for arms, delved into his views on the European Union, Asia, and Africa, and his plans for assistance to developing nations. The article included an interview with Peres and described his way of life.

Quotes from the article appeared in the daily papers and came to the attention of Ben-Gurion. The Old Man didn't like what he read. Since *Bamahane* was the IDF weekly, published under the auspices of the Ministry of Defense, Ben-Gurion summoned its editor in chief. "I reprimanded him for the publication of the article on Shimon Peres," Ben-Gurion wrote in his diary. "The editor told me that this article was being planned for a long time. Shimon himself had read the text before its publication."[10]

Ben-Gurion didn't raise the matter with Peres. In the Mapai leadership circles, though, voices were raised against Peres's self-publicity initiatives. And those voices were many. The Sinai Campaign and the successes of the Ministry of Defense carried Peres's name to the newspapers' headlines. He apparently enjoyed that; he gathered around him a cluster of senior journalists who sang his praise constantly. Articles about Peres appeared in the foreign press as well, and several European papers delighted in his calm and intelligent character, and "his modest behavior."[11]

Peres also spoke a lot throughout the country, and devoted spokesmen kept the media well informed. Peres's lectures were not factual reviews by a civil servant, but the speeches of a statesman, analyzing Israel's problems, achievements, and social perspectives. His articles in the papers detailed his political concepts and his views on current topics. Many people were impressed by Peres's public appearances, but the older generation of Mapai leaders and Peres's political rivals reacted with outbursts of anger and jealousy. The controversial weekly *Haolam Hazeh* named him "Shimon Pirsomet"—Shimon Publicity. Elhanan Yishai warned him, "Your achievements generate hostility and jealousy, and you should cautiously weigh your moves."[12]

Peres, though, didn't try to reduce his exposure in the media. In a speech at the Mapai bureau, Golda Meir mocked him and some other young leaders. "They don't have ideas for publication," she cracked, "only ideas for self-publicity."[13] Moshe Sharett, who was utterly hostile to Peres, breathed fire on the director general. Yet Peres was the first Israeli politician who grasped the immense potential of media exposure and harnessed the press to his own carriage. He kept enlarging his court of trusted reporters, who believed in him and knew that he was a fountainhead of exclusive information and headlines for their papers.[14]

That method of attracting sympathetic journalists continues to this very day, and can be illustrated by a much later episode in Peres's career. When he was elected prime minister in 1984, he had his media adviser call five senior reporters from the newspapers *Davar, Haaretz, Yediot Abaronot, Maariv,* and *The Jerusalem*

Post. They came to Peres's temporary residence in the King David Hotel in Jerusalem. Peres removed his shoes, poured them whiskey, and had a long talk with them about his government policy. That was the first meeting of what would be called "the Five." The Five would secretly meet once a month, as long as Peres was prime minister, minister of foreign affairs, or minister of the Treasury. Peres's secretary would phone them and say, "Tonight—Five," and they would flock to the prime minister's home. "In that forum, Peres behaved in the most uninhibited way one could imagine—he would curse, besmirch [his opponents], and speak as someone who feels quite relaxed," said the journalist David Landau. Peres spoke with the reporters on current subjects, without restrictions. It was a forum for consultation and the shaping of new ideas.[15]

In this way, Peres maintained secret contacts with a group of senior opinion-makers. He could influence them, prevent the publication of sensitive information, and learn what they thought of his policy. The Five were eager to participate in these meetings in spite of the conflict of interest they represented.

Peres himself had a clear-cut answer when he was asked about his wooing of the major reporters. "I was attacked all the time," he said. "Papers like *Lamerhav, Haolam Hazeh* [and others] hurt me all the time. I had to defend myself."[16]

That self-defense was the subject of a conversation that Peres had with Ben-Gurion in mid-1958.

"I ASKED SHIMON—what were his plans," Ben-Gurion wrote in his diary in May 1958.

Peres answered, "I cannot remain a civil servant. I have no right to talk, and the [new] law of Government Service rules will impose even more restrictions on me."

Ben-Gurion was aware of the criticism directed at Peres from all sides, and knew that as a government official he couldn't defend himself publicly.

"I don't see anybody else who could direct the defense ministry," he said.

Peres suggested resigning, returning to Alumot, and presenting his candidacy at the Knesset elections. When elected to the Knesset, he would be appointed deputy defense minister and would continue directing the ministry. "But I shall be free like all the Knesset members."

Ben-Gurion agreed.[17] On June 22, 1959, Peres resigned from his position as director general of the ministry.

Thus, at the age of thirty-five, he officially started his political career. He believed he was attacked mostly because of his closeness to Ben-Gurion. Those who wanted to sling mud at Ben-Gurion refrained from directly attacking the Old Man; those who ground their teeth at Dayan's aggressive statements since he quit the army couldn't challenge him because of his hero image; the one left, therefore, was Shimon Peres, who became the punching bag of all the critics. That was a simplistic explanation, but it carried a ring of truth.

Peres entered political life together with a group of young talents that Ben-Gurion decided to promote to the nation's leadership. Number one in that group was Moshe Dayan, who had been replaced as chief of staff by Haim Laskov. From the United States returned Abba Eban, with an impressive record as ambassador in Washington. Several other promising young men, including the famous writer Yizhar Smilanski (S. Izhar), were also picked by Ben-Gurion.

The decision to entrust the leadership of the country to the hands of the younger generation took shape in Ben-Gurion's mind after the Sinai Campaign. He was impressed by the achievements of Dayan and Peres; at the same time, he was disappointed with his friends of the old guard. He divulged his thoughts in a conversation with the party secretary, Dr. Giora Yosseftal. "A new generation should be promoted to leadership .... They fought at the Independence War and the Sinai Campaign and proved their abilities. They should be charged with the leadership of the party and the nation; at first—together with the old guard, but that wouldn't last long. There would be opposition in the party to that change, but it should be rejected."[18]

"During the Sinai Campaign," wrote Dr. Meron Medzini, "the names of Peres and Dayan were glorified, while the names of Golda Meir, Abba Eban and the Israeli diplomats were left in shadow . . . . Golda never remembered the Sinai Campaign as an event she could be proud of."[19]

Thus began the ruthless war of succession that was to shake Mapai's very foundations. The old guard was not ready to give up that easily. They were alerted when Dayan started attacking them in public, saying that young people should lead the country. Peres supported him, quoting President de Gaulle: "De Gaulle says: I am today 67 years old. Unlike the Mapai members, he believes that 67 is not the age when the fervor of youth begins, but the age when one should retire from political life."[20] Thus spoke Peres at the age of thirty-five, in 1958; later he would reconsider the recommended retirement age.

The old guard counterattacked by fiercely criticizing the young men. Ben-Gurion retorted by defending "the young generation that is the future of our nation," and the elders got even more upset.[21]

Golda Meir joined the chorus and informed Ben-Gurion that she wouldn't join the next cabinet. "I know that the youth should revolt against the old, but I revolt against the youths who think that there is no need of ideology." She added a jab at Ben-Gurion: "And I revolt against the old who defend youths who have no ideology."[22] Her friend Minister Zalman Aran added a hinted threat: "When the Eskimos get old and lose their teeth, they are taken far into the snow to die. But we, the old guard—we have teeth!"

Ben-Gurion organized a "reconciliation meeting" between the old and young generations; some party leaders warned him that Lavon wouldn't come to the meeting if Peres took part in it. "I would be sorry if Lavon didn't come," Ben-Gurion answered, "but Shimon shouldn't be ostracized. Nobody succeeded like he did at the Defense Ministry."[23]

Indeed, Lavon didn't come to what he called "the young generation's coronation ceremony," and together with Aran he spread the rumor that Dayan was preparing "a military coup."[24] Moshe Sharett, who couldn't forgive Ben-Gurion for firing him from the foreign ministry, now became Lavon's ally, in spite of the painful Lavon affair.

At the November 3, 1959, election, Mapai gained seven more seats in the Knesset and achieved the highest total in its history: forty-seven seats. Ben-Gurion reached the apex of his power. Six of the young leaders were elected to the parliament. But Ben-Gurion didn't exploit his success thoroughly; he couldn't part ways with his longtime friends and convinced the old guard leaders—Golda Meir, Zalman Aran, and Pinhas Sapir—to join the government. By acting so, he defeated the same young leaders he was trying to promote. They were given only four government jobs: Dayan became minister of agriculture, Yosseftal minister of labor, Eban minister without portfolio, and Peres deputy minister of defense.

The new government was sworn in on December 17, 1959. From his Knesset seat, Peres watched his friend Dayan with admiration. "Moshe Dayan looks very solemn in his dark suit, adorned by a red tie. He is amazingly handsome and his personality stands out again, in totally different circumstances. For him this is not the apex of his life, but an important turning point."

Peres looked at the government table, which Dayan, Eban, and Yosseftal had joined. "The government table offers a new sight," he wrote. "The government has become younger, but the young ministers seem to have become older." He added, "At once, the leadership of the party changed."[25]

He was wrong. The leadership of the party didn't change; the struggle for power had just started.

NOW THAT PERES had started climbing the political ladder, his rivals intensified their attacks. Golda Meir took the lead.

"Golda's antipathy towards me hung like a dark shadow over my own political career. My relations with her were always complex and ambivalent, and usually unhappy. With Golda, as I learned over the years, there was no such thing as middle ground: either you were 100 per cent for her, or she was 100 per cent against you. Teddy Kollek once said of her, 'She doesn't so much conduct a foreign policy as maintain a hate-list.' " Peres occupied a place of choice on Golda's list.[26]

When she was appointed foreign minister, in 1956, Golda was more of a Ben-Gurionist than Ben-Gurion himself and was totally devoted to him. She accepted the Old Man's authority, did not pretend to conceive an international strategy, and didn't try, like Moshe Sharett, to shape Israel's foreign policy. Perhaps her approach resulted from her lack of vision and her inability to develop her own political thinking; perhaps her self-disparagement resulted from her total identification with Ben-Gurion. Except for the German issue, on which she was at odds with Ben-Gurion (and Peres), she never argued with him on Israel's policy; she was mostly concerned about personal appointments of ambassadors abroad, and Ben-Gurion, as a rule, agreed to her demands. But the deteriorating relations between the Ministries of Foreign Affairs and Defense took their toll; she developed a deep resentment toward Peres and a growing frustration for Ben-Gurion and his young protégés.[27]

When Golda was appointed foreign minister, Peres was thirty-three years old. He was creative, with a soaring imagination and endless ideas, some of which, indeed, were far-fetched and even absurd. But he knew well the political map of Europe and established personal relations by unorthodox means; the foreign ministry, of course, couldn't employ the same methods, and its diplomats had to be much more cautious. Peres had created secret relationships with some European nations, France in particular, but when these relationships came into the open he continued to manage them; the frustration of the Israeli diplomats soared and infected Golda as well.

Peres would travel to Paris, meet with France's ministers—some of whom were his personal friends—then spend the evenings with them at restaurants and nightspots. He negotiated with them on arms purchases, loans, and strategic policy coordination. Most of the agreements were kept secret, and Peres reported only to Ben-Gurion. On two secret subjects at least—nuclear research and missile development—he would speak to nobody else. "I spoke with Golda on Shimon's voyage to Paris," wrote the Old Man in his diary. "He may meet Prime Minister Mollet about arms purchases. She suggested that he inform Tzur [Israel's ambassador to Paris] and take him to the meetings. I agreed to the first thing but not to the second. That may be harmful, for the issues are very secret."[28]

That didn't happen only in France. Peres traveled throughout Europe and the world, established relations with Asian, African, and South American nations, signed agreements for the purchase and the sale of weapons, and carried out diplomatic negotiations. Golda couldn't stand that. Over and over again she angrily clashed with Peres; over and over again she complained to Ben-Gurion and threatened to resign. In most cases Ben-Gurion backed Peres, and that infuriated Golda even more. Sometimes it was a small thing that enraged her. Once she told Ben-Gurion that she was flying to Europe the following day.

"What is your flight?"

She gave him the flight number and the time of departure.

"Great," Ben-Gurion said, "you will be on the same flight as Shimon." Golda was beside herself with anger.[29]

Another time, when she was on her way to Vienna, Peres again happened to be on the same flight. Ben-Gurion had asked him to report to her on the plane. But Golda got so mad when she saw him approaching that she told him she was not feeling well and couldn't talk to him.[30]

Sometimes her wrath was justified, as after Peres's meeting with Jean Monnet, the French economist. Golda was about to meet Monnet in July 1957, but on learning that Peres had seen him earlier, she canceled the meeting. She summoned Arthur Ben-Nathan, the defense ministry's envoy in Europe. "I was present when Golda burst into tears," said Ben-Nathan. "She cried hysterically because of Shimon delving into affairs that had nothing to do with the defense ministry, like that meeting with Jean Monnet. It was a painful emotional outpour; she bitterly complained about Shimon mixing in affairs that are not related to defense."[31] Ben-Nathan felt that Golda used him as a "lightning rod," and he barely succeeded in calming her. He stressed, though, that Peres had acted "with the full backing of Ben-Gurion."[32] Indeed, Peres described his meetings with Jean Monnet to Ben-Gurion, who diligently noted down his report.[33]

Ben-Gurion suggested to Golda that she have a frank conversation with Peres; that conversation took place at the end of 1959. "I want to avoid the feeling of bitterness," Peres said. "I dare to disagree with you [on certain subjects, like the policy toward France], and even more, I also may make mistakes. I ask you to point these mistakes out to me right away, for I don't want to make them." But shortly after this conversation, Golda Meir and Peres described to Ben-Gurion their differences of opinion about the policy toward France. Ben-Gurion ruled in favor of Peres, and Golda was furious.

In the company of close friends, Golda described Peres as a reckless adventurer, an intriguer lacking credibility. On every step she saw the secret manipulations of Peres and his dark schemes. Once in a while she received enthusiastic reports about his political contacts abroad, and that angered her even more. When Peres visited the Italian minister of defense, Paolo Taviani, in Rome, Ambassador Eliahu Sasson sent a detailed report to Golda. He concluded, "I'll allow myself one remark: Mr. Peres conducted the conversation with great talent, and in a very clear way; he won the trust and the sympathy of our interlocutor and made him speak openly .... Minister Taviani greatly appreciated [Peres's exposé] and asked Mr. Peres to drop in and see him whenever he happens to visit Italy."[34] That report was circulated by Sasson at the highest levels of the foreign ministry and certainly didn't fire up Golda's enthusiasm.

But Golda Meir's frustration had deeper reasons. In name she was Israel's foreign minister, but in practice foreign policy was managed by Ben-Gurion, who sometimes used the foreign ministry, and sometimes Shimon Peres and the defense ministry. Golda held the official title, but some major issues of Israel's policy were out of bounds for her. The relations with France had been taken away from her; she visited the Elysée Palace once and met with de Gaulle, but wasn't invited to join Ben-Gurion and Peres on the official visits of the prime minister to the French capital. She was not involved in relations with Germany; her role in the establishment of the Peripheral Pact was marginal. She actually objected to most of Ben-Gurion's initiatives that were conceived by his brilliant young men—the alliance with France, the moves toward the Sinai Campaign, the building of a nuclear reactor, the connection with Germany. It seemed that she had a free hand only in Africa, but that, too, was an illusion: while she spoke and toured, participated in independence festivities, and danced with the newly liberated women of Africa, or had her picture taken dressed in their colorful boubous, Peres was concluding agreements with the governments, dispatching experts and equipment, creating local paramilitary units, and bringing ministers, officers, and senior leaders to Israel.

How could Golda live with all this?

GOLDA'S OLD GUARD friends didn't lag behind. Pinhas Sapir didn't stop criticizing Dayan and Peres, whom he called "a cheat and a charlatan"; only when they got to know Peres did some of Sapir's friends realize, to their amazement, that Sapir had led them astray.[35] Sapir, too, was infuriated by Ben-Gurion's praise of Peres. After all, Sapir had been the defense ministry's director general before Peres, but Ben-Gurion didn't stop saying that "Shimon was the best director general to this day."[36]

Eshkol's attitude was vague. True, he had brought Peres from Alumot to the defense ministry and had worked with him in total harmony; yet during the Lavon affair he had been ready to sacrifice him to Lavon. On one hand, he told his relatives that Peres was a potential prime minister;[37] on the other, he kept speaking of Peres with hostility and harshness.[38]

Sharett filled his diary with terrible explosions of anger against Peres. "I reject Peres absolutely," he told the Mapai secretary, "and I regard his ascension as an utterly malignant moral corruption. I shall sit in mourning for the State of Israel if I ever see him sitting in a minister's chair."[39]

BUT NEITHER SHARETT nor Peres's other critics could even imagine that while they mercilessly sniped at him, Peres was building, in the utmost secrecy, the most amazing enterprise that Israel had ever undertaken.

CHAPTER 17.

AGAINST ALL ODDS

ON THE EVENING of October 24, 1956, Shimon Peres and David Ben-Gurion stood in one of the spacious rooms in the villa at Sèvres. Across the room, the French foreign minister, Christian Pineau, and Defense Minister Maurice Bourgès-Maunoury were conversing in low voice. In a nearby room, Moshe Dayan, along with several Frenchmen and Englishmen, was drafting the Sèvres Protocol. Shortly before the signing ceremony, Peres said to Ben-Gurion, "I think I can get it approved now." Ben-Gurion nodded in agreement.

The director general crossed the room and approached Pineau and Bourgès-Maunoury.

"Israel is undertaking a formidable risk," Peres said. "She is joining France and Great Britain and may attract the hostility of the entire Arab world. Our very existence may be in danger. We need a force of deterrence. France can give us this deterrent."

The two Frenchmen moved aside and held a short consultation. Even though nothing specific was said, they understood what Peres meant. By mentioning a "deterrent," Peres meant the acquiring of nuclear capacity, while the raising of the subject shortly before the conclusion of the conference was a hint to the French that this was an Israeli condition to the entire operation. If the French rejected Israel's request, she might reconsider her position.

Peres wanted to get the consent of France's leaders to a draft agreement for the building of a nuclear reactor in Israel. The agreement also included a paragraph about the continued supply of French uranium to Israel for the reactor's operation. Peres had worked out the draft agreement with the heads of the French Atomic Energy Commission.

Earlier that day, Peres had discussed the agreement with Prime Minister Mollet. Mollet had answered that there was the issue of Euratom, the European organization for atomic research. The problem, he said, was in the paragraph about the sale of uranium to Israel.[1]

Peres's request was without precedent. Never before had one country built a nuclear reactor for another nation, or supplied uranium and know-how for its operation. Mollet and Pineau didn't want to get involved in a long-term commitment. But on October 24 the situation was different. The French realized that "the Israeli pretext" had a price; besides, they sincerely believed that Israel's existence was in danger. Finally, Peres knew well that of the three French leaders, one was an almost unconditional ally—Bourgès-Maunoury.

The two Frenchmen came back to Peres. Pineau was the one who spoke: "Our main problem is the uranium," he said. He meant that France couldn't supply uranium to another country.

Peres had a ready solution. "Don't sell us any uranium," he answered. "Lend it to us, and we'll return it to you after use."

"In that case," Pineau said, "I am ready to draft the agreement right away."[2]

Peres barely concealed his joy. The French leaders' agreement crowned his long and stubborn effort to endow Israel with atomic power.

IN EARLY JUNE 1956, Peres had instructed the defense ministry's heads to launch a nuclear program that would provide Israel with atomic capacity. Among the men Peres spoke to in the ministry were his friend Munia Mardor, who was to become the director of the Rafael Armament Development Authority, and

Professor Ernst David Bergman. Peres gave concise directions to his aides on how to carry out the plan, stage by stage, until the final step. He established a committee to manage the project, and appointed Professor Amos de-Shalit, a nuclear scientist, as its head.

Ben-Gurion regarded the building of a reactor as a means to guarantee Israel's survival and a way to wipe out the formidable gap between his tiny nation and the huge number of Arabs surrounding Israel. For Peres, the atomic project became a top-priority goal.[3] He was barely thirty-three. He knew that most of his colleagues regarded his addiction to the nuclear project as "reckless adventurism,"[4] but he strongly believed that it was the right thing to do; with Ben-Gurion's support he undertook what seemed to be an impossible mission.

Israel's first step in the nuclear field was the building of a one-megawatt baby reactor, supplied by the United States. But when Peres met with the heads of the French Atomic Energy Commission, he found out that there was a good chance of getting a much larger reactor from France.[5]

A French foreign ministry memorandum disclosed that a 1953 technical agreement between the two nations established nuclear cooperation in two main fields: uranium enrichment from low-grade ore that was discovered in the Negev, and laboratory production of heavy water.[6] The process of producing heavy water had been developed in the Weizman Institute by Professor Israel Dostrovsky.

In 1956, the cooperation between France and Israel suddenly accelerated. Abel Thomas, Bourgès-Maunoury's aide, claimed that Israel persuaded France to help her by means of an impressive argument. The French scientists, he said, had difficulty conceiving the last formulas needed for the assembly of a nuclear weapon. According to Thomas and Bourgès-Maunoury, Israel undertook to obtain from Jewish-American nuclear scientists the information that France needed to build its bomb.[7] Thomas claimed that he conveyed the promise about the formulas to the scientific chairman of the Atomic Energy Commission, Francis Perrin, and convinced him to support the agreement with Israel. Peres firmly denied this allegation. "That's what they thought," he admitted years later, "but we never got anything from Jewish scientists in America and never passed any formulas to the French."[8]

Yet the cooperation between France and Israel was not a oneway street. Years later, Bourgès-Maunoury declared that the cooperation with Israel was an exchange of know-how between the two countries.[9] Professor Yuval Ne'eman, Israel's former military attaché in Britain, claimed that "the heads of the Israeli Atomic Energy Commission traded with the French and the British the few achievements Israel had attained" and got in return "important know-how that contributed largely to the Israeli nuclear project."[10]

In the nuclear matter, once again, the Israeli envoys succeeded in forming a group of devoted French friends. The chairman of the French Atomic Energy Commission was Pierre Guillaumat, an admirer of Israel.[11] Francis Perrin supported the Israeli connection for scientific reasons. Two other senior scientists at the commission were sworn supporters of cooperation with Israel. They were Bertrand Goldschmidt and Jules Horowitz, both of them Jews and friends of Israel. Horowitz, the head of the department for mathematical physics and a friend of Peres and Professor Bergman, had envisaged immigrating to Israel in the early fifties.[12]

In the summer of 1956, the talks between the Israelis and the French were upgraded again. A new Israeli scientific attaché arrived in Paris. He was Shalheveth Freier, Peres's personal envoy, who reported to Peres directly.[13] On September 21, the Israeli and the French Atomic Energy Commissions reached an agreement on the sale of a French reactor to Israel. All that was needed, at this stage, was the French government's consent.

And on October 24, in Sèvres, Peres obtained the approval of the French leaders.

As soon as the Sinai Campaign was over, Peres was back in Paris. The French Atomic Energy Commission was inclined to sell Israel an EL-102 model reactor, but the Israelis asked for far-reaching modifications.[14] Peres got in touch with the French enterprises that were supposed to build the reactor in Israel. The major company in this field was Saint-Gobain, which had built the French reactors. Peres was interested in reaching a draft agreement with these companies so that they, too, would exert pressure on the government. Moreover, several front companies were created in France; their purpose was to participate in the building of the reactor in Israel, but at the same time conceal and camouflage their connection with the Israelis.[15]

On December 12, 1956, the first agreement between France and Israel was signed.[16] This was actually an agreement between the French and the Israeli Atomic Energy Commissions. France undertook to supply Israel with "technical and industrial assistance" by building a research nuclear reactor. The reactor would use natural uranium. According to the French foreign ministry documents, France agreed to supply Israel with a 40-megawatt reactor (in another French document the reactor is rated as 25 megawatts) and assist the Israelis in building it. France also agreed to supply to Israel 385 tons of uranium according to a detailed timetable: the first 10 tons would be supplied in 1960, to be followed by five yearly deliveries of 45 tons each, and five yearly deliveries of 30 tons each. Israel pledged to use the reactor and the uranium for peaceful purposes only, and to return the radiated uranium to France.[17]

But the second agreement was kept deeply secret, even from the members of the French cabinet. That agreement was signed on August 23, 1957, between Peres and Bourgès-Maunoury, who in the meantime had been elected prime minister. It stated, in so many words, that the two nations would cooperate in research and production of nuclear weapons.[18]

This agreement amounted to a veritable alliance between the two countries in the nuclear field. Without the input of Bourgès, this agreement would never have been signed. Shimon Peres himself admitted later that "there was not a thing that Bourgès wasn't ready to do for me."[19]

The third and final agreement was scheduled for signing in October 1957. It covered every aspect of the building of the reactor, but included a new, astounding element: a French commitment to assist Israel in building a plant for the separation of plutonium.[20] The agreement was supported by Bourgès, but he needed the approval of the Socialist Party, whose representative in his cabinet was Foreign Minister Pineau. Both Pineau and the party chairman, Guy Mollet, had told Golda Meir that they opposed the agreement.[21] The French feared that if the Americans found out about the agreement they might stop supplying France with the materials necessary for its own nuclear project. Mollet and Pineau advised Israel to reveal the secret to the United States and ask for its consent. Golda realized that such a step would be a death blow to the project.

Golda came back from Paris and reported to Ben-Gurion. The project seemed doomed.

In the gloomy atmosphere that descended on Ben-Gurion's office, Peres was the only one who didn't give up. He convinced Ben-Gurion that there was still a chance to save the agreement. At the end of September 1957 he flew to France, to try changing its leaders' opinions. But now a new problem surfaced.

The opposition parties in the French parliament presented a motion of no confidence in Bourgès-Maunoury's government. The government had been unstable for quite a while, and Peres assumed it might fall at any moment.

He arrived in Paris on a Sunday. He expected the cabinet to fall on Monday evening. He had a little less than twenty-four hours to change the minds of France's leaders and to sign the agreement. No future government, he knew, would be as pro-Israeli as Bourgès and his ministers had been. If the present government didn't sign, all hope was lost.

On Monday morning, September 30, he rushed to the office

of Pierre Guillaumat, the French Atomic Energy Commission chairman, who had to sign the agreement in the name of France. But Guillaumat couldn't sign the document without cabinet approval. Peres therefore hurried to the Quai d'Orsay for the decisive conversation with Pineau.

Peres was familiar with the main reasons for Pineau's objection. The first was that there was no precedent to what Israel was asking from France. If the existence of the agreement became known it could engender American sanctions and a harsh reaction by NATO and Euratom. The Soviets, too, might retaliate by introducing atomic weapons in Egypt.

While waiting for the meeting, Peres rehearsed his answers to Pineau's arguments. When he finally entered Pineau's office, the foreign minister told him outright that his position was negative.

Peres answered Pineau's arguments one by one. He stressed that the reactor would be used for peaceful goals only. In order to dispel Pineau's fears, Peres solemnly promised that when the moment came for Israel to choose—or not—the military option, she would first consult with France. He also overturned the argument about the Russian reaction. What would happen, he asked Pineau, if the Soviets introduced nuclear weapons to Egypt on their own initiative? Did Pineau really believe they needed a pretext for that? What would the West do then?

Pineau thought for a long moment. Finally he said to Peres: "I accept your arguments; you convinced me."[22]

Peres couldn't believe his ears. Pineau withdrew his objection to the agreement! Now that this obstacle had been overcome everything would fall into place. Yet he didn't get up and go on his way but kept firing questions at Pineau. "If the cabinet fell, what would your consent be worth? Why don't you call Bourgès and inform him that you agree?"

Pineau picked up the telephone, but Bourgès was not in his office.

"Give me your consent in writing," Peres said to Pineau, "and I'll bring it to Bourgès myself."

That was utterly irregular. A representative of a foreign country wanted to take a letter from the foreign minister on a divisive matter and bring it to the prime minister by his own hand. Yet Pineau agreed to Peres's request. He dictated to his secretary a short letter summing up the agreements between him and Peres. After the secretary had typed the letter, Pineau destroyed its copies. The letter was actually a paragraph to be added to the agreement. The Israeli commission, Pineau wrote, agreed that the plutonium extracted in the separation plant would be used for peaceful purposes only. If the above research assumed a different character, the Israeli government would consult the French government; France would have the right, after informing the government of Israel, to bring the matter before the members of NATO. Pineau added in his own hand: "This text has been approved by me," and signed it, together with Shimon Peres.

With the miraculous letter in his pocket, the director general now set off to find Bourgès-Maunoury. The prime minister was at the parliament, where he was leading a cabinet meeting. Peres established a momentary contact with him; Bourgès returned to the cabinet meeting room and got the ministers' approval of the agreement. Now Bourgès himself had to sign the agreement; but he was called to the plenum, where the opposition assault reached a new peak. He asked Peres to wait until 6:30 P.M. He would then propose a break in the debate, so that he could meet with him and sign the agreement.

At 6:30, Peres entered the prime minister's office, but Bourgès wasn't back yet. His aides offered Peres a glass of whiskey. But the hours and the whiskey glasses came and went—seven, eight, nine, ten, ten-thirty—and Bourgès didn't come. Peres realized that Bourgès wouldn't be back before the vote. But he also knew that if Bourgès didn't sign the agreement before his government fell, everything was lost. He therefore sent one of his aides to Bourgès with a suggestion—to sign the agreement tomorrow, but to backdate it to today, before the government's eventual defeat. Bourges agreed.

That same night, the government fell.

In Israel, Ben-Gurion followed the death throes of the Bourgès government. "The radio announced," he wrote, "that Bourgès-Maunoury's government fell in a vote on the Algerian issue. I am afraid that Shimon's journey to Paris was in vain."[23]

The following morning at nine, Peres was back in the office of the defeated prime minister. Bourgès received him. "After a sleepless night, with red eyes and with no government—he had lost it during the night—he took out his pen and said: 'I understand that my Socialist friend [Christian Pineau] has agreed.' " Bourgès then wrote to Atomic Energy Commission chairman Guillaumat that the government had approved the agreement on the building of a nuclear reactor in Israel, and Guillaumat was asked to proceed with the matter.[24]

On the letter they wrote the date of the previous day. Actually, Bourgès wasn't allowed to sign the letter, as his government had already fallen. But he did it out of friendship for Peres and Israel. If that fact had become known at the time, the agreement would have been annulled.

"Such a date, another date, what difference does it make?" Peres said years later. "What is such a thing between friends?"[25]

Elated, Peres and his assistants headed for Guillaumat's office. They gave him Bourges's letter and asked him to sign the agreement.

But things turned out differently.

"I AM NOT SIGNING," Guillaumat said.

He told his visitors that the foreign ministry was furious about the way Peres had obtained Pineau's signature. Guillaumat added that because the agreement included political issues that had been inserted by Pineau and Peres, the Atomic Energy Commission couldn't sign those paragraphs, as it was not a political commission. Without the consent of the foreign ministry, Guillaumat concluded, he wouldn't sign the agreement. He also disapproved of Peres's unorthodox methods. He said to Peres, his voice heavy with criticism: "You are good for war, but not for peace. I wish France had a few people like you, for times of war."

The mayhem started all over again. Peres dashed to Bourgès's office. The defeated prime minister immediately called Pineau and the ministry's secretary, Louis Joxe, and angrily reprimanded them. "There is an agreement, and nothing comes out of it. Why did we need a government resolution?"

Another day passed, and Peres again climbed the marble staircase at the Quai d'Orsay. He met with Joxe in order to finalize the agreement. They agreed that the French and Israeli Atomic Energy Commissions would sign several technical agreements—on the building of the reactor, the supply of uranium, and the construction of the separation plant.[26] Joxe stressed, however, that on the political subjects agreed between Peres and Pineau the two governments should sign a separate accord.

The two governments? Peres knew that if the French insisted on this, the agreement was lost. In France there was no government anymore, and they would have to wait for the next government to be instated. That government would certainly refuse to sign. Again Peres started looking for a solution, and he finally agreed with Joxe that the accord would be finalized by an exchange of letters between the two foreign ministries.

On Thursday, four days after Peres had arrived in Paris, the agreement with the French Atomic Energy Commission was duly signed. Now he expected to receive the foreign ministry letter, signed by Pineau. It was agreed that Yaakov Tzur, Israel's ambassador to Paris, would sign the letter confirming the agreement in the name of Israel.

Again Peres appeared at the door of Pineau's office. The afternoon hours ticked away—but Pineau had vanished.

The wait was harrowing. Apparently Pineau was at a meeting. The letter from the foreign ministry was already on his desk, but had not been signed yet. It was after 6 P.M. already. At any moment, a new government could be sworn in, and Pineau would lose his authority to sign the letter. The Israelis felt that their project's fate would be decided in hours, perhaps minutes.

They finally persuaded the political director at the Quai d'Orsay, Jean Deridan, to interrupt the meeting and have Pineau sign the document. "Ten minutes later, the letter was in our hands," Peres recalled. On the spot, the letter of agreement of the Israeli government was prepared and signed by Yaakov Tzur. "Five minutes later, our letter was in their hands."[27]

A secret Quai d'Orsay memorandum entitled "Nuclear Cooperation" reveals that in the exchange of letters it was agreed that France would give Israel technical and industrial assistance for the building of the reactor and the separation plant; Israel would use the plutonium only for peaceful purposes; in case the character of the Israeli research changed, the two governments would consult with each other in order to reach a mutual understanding about the steps that should be taken; and finally, each of the two governments had the right to put an end to the agreement. The untreated and special materials that were exchanged between the two governments according to the agreement—uranium and plutonium—would then be returned to their lawful owners.[28]

This was a strange agreement whose essence contradicted its wording. According to the agreement that was declassified years later by the Quai d'Orsay, France undertook to assist Israel in constructing a plutonium separation plant. But the same agreement stipulated that the plant would serve only peaceful purposes. That was, to say the least, a strange assertion, since it was obvious that a separation plant could serve one purpose only—the production of plutonium, the material needed for nuclear weapons. The French government apparently hoped that the wording of the agreement would shield it from the eventual accusation that it had helped Israel to become a nuclear power.

Now, at last, Peres could breathe a sigh of relief. He held all the documents in his hands. He cabled Ben-Gurion: "We signed the agreement this afternoon."

In Sde Boker, Ben-Gurion read Peres's telegram with amazement. He hurried to cable back: "Congratulations on your important achievement."

ON DECEMBER 16, 1957, France set up a credit line of five billion francs (about $10 million) to finance the purchase of the equipment for the construction of the reactor.[29] In Israel, Peres started building a huge organization of manpower, scientific personnel, construction companies, budgets, and, primarily, weaving a watertight cover of concealment that would hide the daily activity of thousands of people. The success of the project depended on preserving absolute secrecy; any leak might set off heavy international pressure that could kill the project.

First, Peres chose the location of the reactor—the arid plateau of Dimona, which was a rather secluded area in the north of the Negev. Then, he handpicked the members of his team. The major figure at his side was the prime minister's scientific adviser, Professor Ernst Bergman. "He was one of the most impressive people I ever met," Peres wrote. "I never stopped admiring him, in spite of his personality flaws, which made working with him difficult."[30] Bergman believed that the entire reactor, including all its components, should be built in Israel. That was very patriotic, but far from practical. Peres preferred the advice of Pierre Guillaumat. "Don't try to reinvent the wheel," Guillaumat had told him. "Don't try to build from scratch what others have already built."

For the key role of directing the entire project, Peres needed somebody special—"a pedant, a man who would not compromise over detail, whether vital or ostensibly marginal."[31] Peres finally chose for the job Manes Pratt, an army colonel with three university degrees, whom he had known since the War of Independence. Peres brought Pratt from Burma, where he was serving as a military attaché. "Within a few months," Peres wrote with admiration, "he had become Israel's foremost expert in nuclear engineering."[32]

Among the other members of the team were Saul Friedlander, who then changed his name to Shaul Eldar, and Binyamin Blumberg, a close-lipped young man who became the head of the Bureau for Scientific Relations. The bureau, established by Peres, was a top-secret unit that collected scientific and technological information in Europe and the United States. According to foreign media, the bureau had placed "scientific attachés" in most Western capitals. Some observers claimed that the bureau was "an 'entrepreneur' of technological thefts for the Israeli military industries."[33]

In contrast to Peres's enthusiastic team, a coalition of relentless opponents to the nuclear project emerged in the highest political and military circles. "The idea and its execution made many people furious with me," Peres complained. "Some claimed that nothing would come out of this, others wanted to prove that the plan could not be carried out, and some even predicted that if we tried to take the road that I suggested the whole world would rise against us, and Dimona would cause a terrible war intended to thwart the project."[34]

On the government level, most ministers opposed the project. Foreign Minister Golda Meir strongly objected on the grounds that the project would harm Israel's relations with the United States. Finance Minister Levi Eshkol and Trade and Industry Minister Pinhas Sapir feared that the grandiose project would swallow the entire state budget. Sapir regarded Dimona as an adventure; he didn't believe that the project had any chance of success. Besides, he was haunted by fears of the American reaction. "We were called charlatans," Peres said, "we were accused of promising something that could not be realized, that only the Great Powers could accomplish."[35] Moshe Dayan supported the project but was skeptical about its feasibility. The head of the intelligence community, Isser Harel, objected for several reasons; first, because he hadn't been involved in the decision making; second, because he didn't like Peres;[36] and third, because he feared that the Soviets might take action against Israel.

Some senior IDF officers, one of whom was Yitzhak Rabin, thought that the project would divert most of the defense budget and the military would be left with very little money for weapons purchases.[37] Abba Eban called the project "an enormous alligator stranded on dry land."[38] The leaders of Ahdut Ha'avoda, Israel Galili and Yigal Allon, believed that Israel shouldn't acquire nuclear capability,[39] and ought to invest her money and her efforts in conventional weapons instead.[40]

Shimon Peres was left alone. True, Ben-Gurion supported him, but Peres was exposed to the virulent attacks of the body politic. In closed meetings, some of Israel's public figures angrily assailed the project. Labor leader Eliezer Livneh prophesized that the Americans and the Russians would land forces at Dimona or bomb it from the air. The venerated Professor Yeshayahu Leibowitz said that nothing would remain of the Dimona reactor but a new name on the map: "Shimon's Ruins."[41]

From the start, Peres decided that his name shouldn't be mentioned in connection with the reactor. "I felt that if I were exposed, the press could quickly destroy both me and the program. After all, I was politically controversial, known as a reckless fantasizer, and the program itself seemed so fantastic."[42]

Peres was shocked to find out that a large majority of Israel's nuclear scientists were opposed to his plan. A group of professors, headed by Amos de Shalit and others, refused to cooperate in the project. "They didn't believe it would ever be completed," said one of their colleagues.[43] For most scientists, the project seemed a fantasy. They couldn't imagine that the small State of Israel, with its limited resources, would be able to undertake a giant venture like the building of a nuclear reactor. Anyone with an inkling of knowledge about the Manhattan Project—the American nuclear program during World War II—knew what a huge price the United States had paid in money, raw materials, manpower, and scientific research.

Faced with recalcitrant scientists, Peres decided to look for manpower among the young engineers who had recently graduated from the Technion (Israel's prestigious Institute for Technology) and were inspired by youthful enthusiasm and ambition.[44]

The financial issue was of major concern, as it was evident that the price of the reactor was going to be much higher than the funds previously allotted. Ben-Gurion and Peres launched a secret fundraising effort among Israeli industrialists and friends of Israel throughout the world. The money raised that way didn't bring glory and recognition to the contributors, and no plaques with their names were affixed to the reactor's walls. But they all contributed out of the feeling that they were partners in a momentous project that would ensure the very existence of Israel.[45] Peres maintained that this effort brought in $40 million—about half of the reactor's cost.[46] But some estimated that the project's cost was much higher.

While the building of the Dimona reactor progressed, Peres chose to direct media attention toward the small research reactor that was being built at Nebi Rubin. "We must create a focal point for diverting the [public] attention from the [nuclear] affair," he told some of his colleagues. "That's why we built a small reactor at Nebi Rubin, open to the public, open to visitors, open to the press, and we direct the public attention to it." In February 1960, Peres declared that the research reactor at Nebi Rubin would be completed and inaugurated in two months' time.

But while Nebi Rubin was preparing for a celebration, Dimona was suddenly threatened with total failure.

CHAPTER 18.

DEPUTY

ON A SUMMER DAY in 1953, Ben-Gurion summoned his political secretary, Yitzhak Navon, and Shimon Peres. He complained about the demographic situation in Galilee. We shall lose the Galilee, he said, because most of its inhabitants are Arabs. Nazareth is an Arab city; we have to build a Jewish city in Galilee as well. Ben-Gurion said that he had spoken with the directors of the Histadrut contracting company Solel Boneh, with Jewish Agency officials, and others, but nobody had done a thing.

Suddenly he turned to Peres. "I want you to build a city in Galilee!" he said. Navon stared at him with surprise. What did Peres know about building cities? He expected Peres to answer "I'll look into it" or "We shall need a big budget." But instead, Peres said "All right."[1]

Peres regarded Ben-Gurion's request as a compliment. "In those days," he boasted to some friends, "Ben-Gurion thought I could do anything. He even asked me to set up a soccer team that would travel abroad, defeat the foreign teams, and cover Israel with glory."[2]

Peres didn't organize a soccer team, but the city in Galilee was another matter. After the meeting with Ben-Gurion he summoned two defense ministry officials, Yossef Dekel and Mordechai Allon. "You'll be in charge of the project," he said to Dekel; then he told Allon, "And you'll be the mayor."

That was how Peres started building Upper Nazareth.

"That infuriated many people," Peres noted. "When we built the aircraft industry we also had to face a huge commotion. El Al got mad, the air force got mad. The minister of transportation got mad, Pinhas Sapir was always mad .... The same thing happened when we started working on Upper Nazareth. The building of the city was a matter of daring, of committing yourself. And I believed that he who doesn't commit himself doesn't do anything. I told myself, there are enough cautious people in Israel. I read somewhere once that pessimists never discovered a star in the sky."[3]

That was how a trio of defense officials, who had never dealt with construction, set off to build a city in Galilee. Peres pressured other ministries for construction budgets and asked businessmen to establish factories in the new city. "I talked with industrialists and company directors who had defense ministry contracts and asked them to create jobs in Upper Nazareth."

Allon and his wife, Shoshana, were among the first to move to the new site. It was a barren, cold mountain, lashed by fierce winds. The local Arabs didn't want to go near it and called it Goosebumps Mountain. When the construction work was under way, Allon himself brought the first immigrants from Europe. And in 1956, Upper Nazareth was born.

"On November 2, 1956," Peres proudly announced, "three days after the start of the Sinai Campaign, the Defense Ministry started another campaign—making the Galilee Jewish. The first family of immigrants settled in Upper Nazareth." The first immigrant, Peres said, was a shopkeeper who kept buying from himself because he had no customers yet. But by 1959 the new town already numbered three thousand people.[4]

In 1960, Peres summed up the operation: "The Nazareth venture cost us only one hundred thousand Israeli pounds, and that was an important contribution to our security. The question is, can we reach a majority in Nazareth in four years? In Nazareth today there are twenty-five thousand Arabs and in Upper

Nazareth there are five thousand Jews. The question is, can we bring, in four years, twenty-five thousand more Jews to [Upper] Nazareth?"[5]

In 2004, Upper Nazareth numbered fifty-two thousand inhabitants.

"Shimon is a man of action," Yitzhak Navon summed up, "and he made it."

After the building of Upper Nazareth, Peres and his aide Elhanan Yishai helped build the town of Mitzpe Ramon, in the Negev.[6]

IN AN INTERVIEW for the Galei Tzahal radio station, a reporter asked Shimon Peres, "In what [way] is your new job as a deputy minister different from your former functions as director general?"

"There is no big difference," Peres admitted. "My present job is a continuation of my former one. The real difference is the Knesset."[7]

Peres was appointed deputy defense minister during the golden era that started after the Sinai Campaign. Israel dwelled secure in her borders; her foreign relations had dramatically improved, she had no difficulties purchasing military equipment in France, Britain, and Germany. True, some worrying signs could lately be discerned in France's policy toward Israel. The French were trying to improve their relations with the Arab countries, while turning down the volume of their pro-Israeli declarations. They refused to renew a flight agreement with El Al; the Renault automobile company closed its factory in Israel; the signing of a cultural agreement was delayed. But the defense ministry's envoys in Paris repeated the same answer to the inquisitive Israeli reporters: "Why do you worry?" they would say. "We are getting all the arms we want. That's what matters, isn't it?"[8]

The nuclear project, too, was on track, or so it seemed. For the first three years after the signing of the agreement, the French assistance continued at full steam. As set out in the Quai d'Orsay documents, French industrial architects prepared the blueprints of the reactor and the separation plant.[9] French experts took an active part in the construction at Dimona. Most of them lived in Beersheba under assumed names. Engineer Robert Galley, who was France's minister of defense in the eighties, spent a year in Beersheba, working on the nuclear reactor under the name of Durand.[10]

With de Gaulle's rise to power, a process of change began. He closed the Israeli liaison offices at the French Army and intelligence services; he also decided to stop assisting the building, "close to Beer-Sheba, of a plant for the transformation of uranium to plutonium, which, one day, could produce atomic bombs."[11]

De Gaulle convened the Ministerial Committee for National Defense and instructed the French government to freeze any cooperation with foreign nations in the production of nuclear weapons.[12] He didn't know, though, that his instruction wasn't implemented, and the nuclear cooperation with Israel even intensified. That happened thanks to the new minister of atomic energy, Jacques Soustelle. Soustelle was a major leader of the League for a France-Israel Alliance. "Soustelle is even more Zionist than us," Peres joked. "Every time I meet him, I feel an inferiority complex."[13] In spite of the inferiority complex, Peres met with Soustelle as soon as he was appointed a minister in de Gaulle's cabinet. Soustelle told Peres that de Gaulle had only some general knowledge about the nuclear agreement between France and Israel. Couve de Murville opposed it, Soustelle added; Pierre Guillaumat, too, was reluctant. Both of them were worried about the American reaction if the involvement of France in Israel's project became known; therefore total secrecy was necessary. Following their conversation, Soustelle instructed France's Atomic Energy Commission to restore the cooperation with Israel according to the 1957 agreement for the joint research and building of nuclear weapons.[14]

Soustelle instructed the heads of the Atomic Energy Commission to report to him alone about the cooperation with Israel. He also ordered his assistants to meet with Israeli scientists and answer all their questions about the construction of the French nuclear bomb, which was to be ready in early 1960.[15] These orders were implemented, and the Israelis presented to the French lists of detailed questions. But the "father of the French bomb," General Albert Bouchelet, claimed that "the Israelis didn't need us and they apparently knew even more than us." Bouchelet believed that the Israelis' knowledge resulted from the fact that many Jewish scientists had been involved in building the American atomic bomb at Los Alamos.[16]

The members of the French Atomic Energy Commission, deeply alarmed by Soustelle's instructions, complained to Prime Minister Michel Debré, who sent to the maverick minister two stern letters demanding that he "put to sleep" the agreements with Israel right away. Debré hinted that very soon France would develop her own atomic weapon and would have to conduct talks about it with the United States; it must be able to promise the Americans that the French know-how would be kept in absolute secrecy. "We contributed to the progress of the Israeli scientists' knowledge," Debré wrote to Soustelle on June 8, 1959. "The national interest compels us to stop here. France cannot endanger her entrance to the Nuclear Powers' 'club' by maintaining special relations with a foreign nation."[17] Soustelle, however, ignored the letter and didn't even reply to it.[18] "When I was atomic energy minister, I did all I could to help Israel in every possible way," Soustelle admitted later.[19]

The scientific chairman of the Atomic Energy Commission, Professor Perrin, decided to complain to President de Gaulle. In the past, Perrin had cooperated with Israel, but now he changed his mind, either because he felt the icy wind blowing from the Elysée Palace or because of the preparations for the first French atomic test. He wanted, therefore, to end any cooperation with another country that could dwarf France's achievement. In July 1959, Perrin wrote a top secret report to de Gaulle about a forthcoming atomic test in the Sahara. Under the subtitle "Military Nuclear Assistance to Other Countries," Perrin stressed that France had no interest in other countries developing nuclear weapons, because in that case it wouldn't be the world's fourth nuclear power, but only the first among the small nuclear powers. France, Perrin argued, shouldn't assist any foreign country in developing nuclear weapons.

"This is in particular the situation with Israel," Perrin pointed out, "with which France signed a secret agreement, allegedly for peace purposes, to help her build a plutonium-producing nuclear reactor, and a plant for plutonium separation." Perrin complained about Soustelle's having given the Atomic Energy Commission the written directive to restart common research with Israel for the production of nuclear weapons.[20]

Perrin and the Atomic Energy Commission also rejected Peres's latest request that France sell Israel the uranium she needed, instead of lending it to her as per the agreement. "If France had conceded to that request," a senior French official wrote, "the Israeli government would have obtained, in a few years, enough plutonium for intensifying the military research, and producing, finally, several nuclear weapons."[21]

But all the meetings, the memoranda, and the declarations didn't change a thing on the ground. In Dimona, the construction project progressed as planned. Huge bulldozers and hundreds of workers dug the foundations for the nuclear installation, and thousands of tons of concrete flowed into the entrails of the Negev. In Beersheba, a special suburb was created for the French experts, and comfortable apartments were built for the young engineers Peres had hired. Many of the engineers' families objected to settling down in Beersheba. Peres spent long hours trying to convince the engineers' wives. He promised that a modern hospital would be built in Beersheba; and indeed, less than two years later the Soroka modern hospital was inaugurated. Peres even guaranteed to the ladies that there would be a beauty salon at least as good as those in Tel Aviv.[22]

The French experts stationed in Israel reported to their government that the building of the reactor was progressing according to plan, and Israel would soon start assembling its most delicate parts. Israel's friends at all levels erected an invisible barrier that stopped these reports from reaching the Elysée Palace. They also took care that the new governmental instructions concerning the Israeli connection would get lost somewhere in the labyrinths of French bureaucracy.

In February 1960, France carried out its first atomic test at Reggane, in the Sahara, and joined the atomic club. Shortly after, the French government decided to impose severe restrictions on its assistance to Israel and to reexamine the conditions of cooperating with her. On March 18, the cabinet met at the Elysée Palace and discussed the possibility that Israel might use her nuclear installations, and the French uranium, to build weapons. It was decided to stop all supplies of uranium to Israel immediately.[23] Some of de Gaulle's advisers, however, pointed out that stopping the uranium deliveries didn't guarantee that Israel wouldn't use her reactor for military purposes; she might be able to get the uranium elsewhere, and France would still be held responsible for the military use of the reactor.

De Gaulle had no intention of harming the close relations between his country and Israel; he thought very highly of David Ben-Gurion and intended to keep providing Israel with weapons for its defense. Nevertheless, he believed that the cooperation with Israel shouldn't include nuclear affairs. He decided to put an end to France's involvement in Israel's atomic program. At that time, he also dismissed Soustelle from his ministerial post because of his extremist views on the Algerian issue, and, as a result, Israel lost her major ally in the French government. True, Soustelle's successor was another friend of Israel, Pierre Guillaumat, but he wouldn't go as far as Soustelle had.

On May 12, the French government informed Israel's ambassador, Walter Eitan, that Israel's atomic facilities should be submitted to international control.[24] "Upsetting news arrived from

France," Shimon Peres wrote in his diary. "Couve de Murville called Walter Eitan on Saturday and informed him of the decisions of the French government about the reactor. First—that it is time to make public the Dimona project . . . . Second—foreign, perhaps international, control should be implemented. Third—till then they wouldn't supply the uranium that they promised."[25]

Ben-Gurion and Peres knew that international control would put an end to Israel's atomic projects. Ben-Gurion at once asked to meet with de Gaulle. The president of France agreed, and the meeting was set for June 14. Ben-Gurion knew that this meeting might be fateful; he therefore sent Shimon Peres ahead to Paris.

ON JUNE 6, the thirty-seven-year-old Peres flew to Paris. He met with General Nicot, the prime minister's military adviser, and the two of them together planned the subjects of the conversation between Ben-Gurion and de Gaulle. Nicot also advised Peres about what Ben-Gurion should say to the French president. Peres's next meeting was with General Lavaud, the French chief of staff, who briefed him about the positions of the new defense minister, Pierre Messmer. Those two generals and some of their assistants, whom Peres also met, were among Israel's most devoted friends.[26] So were Generals Challe and Jouhaud, and a large group of parliament members and government ministers.

On June 8, Peres met with Pierre Guillaumat, the atomic energy minister. He tried to persuade Guillaumat to cancel the government's decision. He refused. "The matter can't be kept secret anymore," Guillaumat told him. "And a leak may occur at any moment because of the scope of the activities and the number of Frenchmen employed at Dimona. In their employment contracts it is specified that they will be sent to 'a hot climate and desert conditions,' and it is not difficult to guess where."[27]

Peres, dejected, met again with Foreign Minister Couve de Murville, the man who blew an icy breath toward Israel. In Couve's office, Peres was told that France had never helped another nation to build an atomic reactor; the secrecy on this subject couldn't be kept anymore. Peres told Couve that there was no way to stop the project now. He reminded him of Israel's huge investments in the project. Couve listened politely, but didn't accept Peres's arguments.[28]

Peres firmly told Couve that Israel rejected the idea of international control. Five days later, he came to Couve with another idea—to charge Euratom, the European organization for nuclear cooperation, with supervising the reactor.[29] Peres knew that Euratom was an impotent organization, incapable of exerting effective control over Israel. Couve stressed that the nuclear cooperation with Israel had gone too far. Peres answered that "Israel is now in the middle of the lake, and to swim back is as hard as to keep swimming forward."[30] The talks stalled, and it was decided to wait for the meeting of Ben-Gurion and de Gaulle. Peres and his aides, "depressed and unhappy," drove straight from the Quai d'Orsay to the airport to meet Ben-Gurion, who was arriving from Israel.[31]

Ben-Gurion spent the rest of the day with Peres and his advisers in the Bristol Hotel in preparation for his meeting with de Gaulle. On June 14, Ben-Gurion met with de Gaulle at the Elysée Palace. "An Honor Guard expects us," Peres wrote. "They are dressed in blue and red uniforms, Napoleonic hats and large belts; they hold drawn swords in their hands." Everything seemed perfect—the meeting between Ben-Gurion and de Gaulle, the lavish lunch in the Elysée dining hall, the coffee served in the lush garden. De Gaulle invited Peres to join his table. "You must know well Paris and its ways," de Gaulle said to Peres, and the younger man reminded the general of his visit to Kibbutz Geva. As Peres watched Ben-Gurion and de Gaulle, it seemed to him that a current of sympathy and mutual esteem flowed between the two leaders.[32]

All this was very nice, but the nuclear subject didn't come up in their conversation. At the end of their meeting, de Gaulle invited Ben-Gurion to a second one.

Later in the day, Ben-Gurion met with Prime Minister Michel Debré, who told him that France was ready to assist Israel in nuclear research for peaceful purposes, but wouldn't go beyond that. Ben-Gurion promised him to consult with France before deciding to choose the military option, but Michel Debré's position didn't change. On the other hand, Debré was anxious to know if the veil of secrecy surrounding the nuclear project was still intact. He seemed haunted by the fear that the French-Israeli nuclear cooperation might be exposed and that France's status might be harmed.

At their second meeting, on June 17, de Gaulle bent toward Ben-Gurion: "Tell me, truthfully, why do you need a nuclear reactor?" Ben-Gurion explicitly told the French president that Israel had no intention of developing nuclear weapons.[33] He also suggested that Peres meet with Guillaumat, and the two could try to find a solution to the crisis.

After that meeting, Ben-Gurion left France—with the problem between the two countries still unsolved.

ON AUGUST 1, the Quai d'Orsay sent an official memorandum to the Israeli embassy in Paris. During Ben-Gurion's talks in Paris, the memorandum stressed, Israel's consultation with France, mentioned in the 1956 and 1957 agreements, had taken place. "Because of France's negative position," it went on, "Israel decided that the plutonium to be produced in the nuclear installations she is building would not be used for military ends."[34] A few weeks later, Defense Minister Messmer informed the Israelis that "the agreement for French-Israeli nuclear cooperation" of August 21, 1957, was canceled. The joint development of nuclear weapons was a matter of the past.

Messmer's letter and the Quai d'Orsay memorandum were supposed to put an end to the crisis with Israel, but the French government also demanded that the 1956 and 1957 agreements about the assistance in building the Israeli reactor be canceled. It insisted that the existence of the reactor be made public, as well as the conditions of France's past assistance to Israel. France also requested "the establishment of control, whose character is to be determined, on the installations and future production."

The French government asked Israel to declare that she accepted these conditions. "It is obvious," the Quai d'Orsay memorandum added, "that France wouldn't be able to assist Israel in the building of a plutonium separation plant."[35] France offered to pay an indemnity to Israel for the cancellation of the agreement.[36]

The French demands were a serious blow to Israel's nuclear project. The publication of the agreement, on the one hand, and the acceptance of international control, on the other, would have prevented any possibility of completing the Dimona project. Golda Meir was convinced that the nuclear project was therefore dead and buried, and Ben-Gurion hesitated as to the steps to take. "I felt that we couldn't capitulate without a struggle," Peres wrote, "and asked Ben-Gurion to send me to Paris to talk with Couve de Murville."[37]

On November 8, Shimon Peres returned to Paris. "I knew that this time a delicate and almost hopeless negotiation awaited us," Peres wrote in his diary, yet he admitted, "Couve de Murville, by his objection to the continuation of the French assistance, represents authentic French interests."[38] On November 10, Peres and Israel's ambassador, Walter Eitan, met with Couve de Murville and Guillaumat. Peres informed the French ministers that Israel refused to place her nuclear installations under international control. The confrontation that Ben-Gurion and Peres had tried to avoid in June seemed imminent.

The decisive meeting was with Couve de Murville. As always, Peres meticulously prepared for the meeting and tried to assess the character of the man whom he was about to face. Couve de Murville, a calm, self-controlled man, wasn't a friend of Israel. Some regarded him as the cornerstone of the "Arab policy" of the Quai d'Orsay. Shortly after his appointment to the post of foreign minister, Couve de Murville had recalled France's ambassador to Israel, Pierre Gilbert, a great friend of the Jewish state.

He had also objected to the sale of Mirage jet fighters to Israel. Peres understood that Couve's approach to the issue of the reactor wouldn't be favorable. He knew Couve as a serious man whose thought processes were neat and orderly. Diplomacy for him, Peres thought, was like a game of chess, where one planned one's moves and tried to guess the moves of one's opponent.[39]

Peres and Eitan arrived at the Quai d'Orsay and were led to the sumptuous waiting room. Exactly at 12 P.M., the wall clock chimed and the guests were invited to the foreign minister's office. Couve de Murville repeated the main arguments that had been expressed in his memorandum. Peres answered that this was reneging on former decisions of the French government, and that it denied Israel the reactor that she was building, depriving her of a five-year-long effort. No financial indemnity, Peres said, could ever compensate Israel for her tremendous endeavor.

Peres quietly added that Couve intended to break, unilaterally, the joint decision of the two nations to refrain from revealing their agreement to the Arab world. The Arab Boycott Bureau, he said, would be delighted to punish the French companies that had cooperated with Israel.

Couve de Murville interrupted him. France had no intention whatever, he said, of breaking that agreement, and it wouldn't reveal anything about the nuclear cooperation between the two countries.

Peres replied that if Couve unilaterally abrogated the agreement's essence, "we would be unable to maintain those aspects of it that he wished to be maintained, namely the non-publication provision."[40]

That was a subtle hint of blackmail. Couve de Murville suddenly realized that the cancellation of the agreement would result in the exposure of all the secret cooperation between France and Israel so far. That would mean the blacklisting of some of France's largest industrial companies by the Arab Boycott Bureau and the vilification of France throughout the Arab world for giving atomic capability to Israel.

"What do you suggest?" Couve asked. Peres answered that France could abrogate the agreement "from this moment on." But as for what had been done in the past, "he had no right to abrogate any of these decisions retroactively."[41] Peres had in mind the written agreements between Israel and the French companies, with the government's approval, on the building of the Dimona reactor.

Couve thought for a moment, and finally said, "You have a point."

"The chess game had ended," Peres wrote contentedly.[42]

PERES OFFERED A COMPROMISE to Guillaumat and Couve de Murville.[43] In a letter to Peres, the two ministers made clear that the 1957 agreement was canceled. Nevertheless, France undertook to complete the plans for the Dimona reactor's construction and to supply the equipment that Israel had already ordered. In the future, Peres was told, Israel would be allowed to buy in France "ordinary" equipment only. The industrial architect would continue his work for a transition period of three to four months, then the plans would be delivered to Israel. France would continue supplying Israel with uranium that would be returned to France after its use. Israel would complete the building of the reactor by herself.[44]

Peres and Eitan agreed to the French offer, and the two French ministers instructed their staffs to prepare an exchange of letters with Israel.

On December 29, 1960, the French foreign minister summed up the new agreement in a letter to the Israeli ambassador.[45] This compromise agreement that Peres had negotiated saved the Israeli nuclear project from total ruin. Ben-Gurion was pleased with it, but the usual opponents objected, as always. Golda Meir maintained, with astounding naïveté, that Israel should reveal all the facts about the reactor to the Americans. Isser Harel again expressed his fears about the Russians. Eshkol and Sapir feared the supplementary burden that might crush the Treasury. The powerful finance committee in the Knesset also joined the project's opponents. Peres therefore invited the committee members to visit the reactor site; they were awed by what they saw in Dimona, and the budget was approved.[46] After a while, Ben-Gurion told the Knesset member Amos Degani, "The Jewish people doesn't know what it owes Shimon."[47]

But in the meantime, a dramatic event took place, and Israel's nuclear program was thrown into another crisis.

A FEW DAYS after concluding his agreement with Guillaumat and Couve de Murville, Peres was urgently called back to Israel. From Lod Airport he was flown at once to Sde Boker for a meeting with Ben-Gurion. Isser Harel and Golda Meir were also there. The tense atmosphere fringed on panic. Ben-Gurion turned to Isser: "Explain the situation," he gravely said.

Isser Harel reported that Dimona had been photographed from the air, and the secret had been exposed. Moreover, the Soviet foreign minister, Andrei Gromyko, had flown urgently to Washington to discuss with the Americans what action should be taken against the Israeli reactor. Harel demanded that Ben-Gurion, or at least Golda, fly to Washington right away, and reveal to the Americans what was being done at Dimona.

Ben-Gurion asked Golda if she had anything to add. Israel should act at once, she said, in order to thwart Gromyko's efforts to persuade the Americans to act against Israel.

"There was a sense both of certainty and of hopelessness in the air," Peres wrote.[48] It was clear to him that the move suggested by Golda and Harel would terminate the nuclear project. He therefore started by saying that he was not overly alarmed by the aerial photographs of the reactor. From the air, he said, it was impossible to see what Israel was really building. We could always pretend that we were pouring the foundation of some big building. As for Gromyko's flight to Washington—nothing proved that it had been caused by the reactor. There could be a thousand reasons for his visit to the United States. If the two superpowers asked us, then indeed we could give them the explanations that Golda and Isser suggested. "But why should we run to them now?"

Peres also discussed the suggestion that Ben-Gurion fly to Washington. He couldn't do that, Peres said, without coordinating such a move with the French. After all, the affair concerned them, too. Peres stressed that Israel couldn't expose the secret about the nuclear project on her own, as she had an agreement with France, and she had undertaken to keep it secret. "One thing I could promise: if we were looking for a way to destroy our relations with France, this was the way."[49]

Ben-Gurion found himself in a very delicate situation. He had to choose between Shimon Peres, with whom he secretly agreed, and Golda Meir and Isser Harel, two of his closest colleagues. After a long hesitation, Ben-Gurion made a vague statement. The situation is very serious, he said, and could become even worse. But Shimon is right—we don't have to act at once, and anyway, we have to be coordinated with the French.

Golda didn't hide her disappointment, and the head of the Mossad was furious.

"I swallowed hard and kept quiet," Peres wrote.[50]

CHAPTER 19.

LAVON'S REVENGE

ON SEPTEMBER 26, 1960, Pinhas Lavon went to Ben-Gurion's office. For years, he had carried the scars of the 1955 humiliation, when he had been forced to resign as defense minister following the fiasco in Egypt. True, he was now the Histadrut general secretary and was regarded as one of Mapai's leaders, but the "affair" had been haunting him all these years.

Lately, new facts about the debacle in Egypt had emerged, including proof that certain documents blaming Lavon had been forged by Binyamin Gibly's assistants. Lavon therefore rushed to see Ben-Gurion and presented him with this new evidence. He asked the Old Man to clear him of any responsibility for the tragedy in Egypt and put the blame on Gibly. Ben-Gurion said to Lavon: "I didn't condemn you then, and I don't condemn you now. But I am not authorized or empowered to clear you, because I am neither judge nor investigator."[1]

Lavon was upset by the Old Man's answer and threatened to bring the matter before the Knesset's Defense and Foreign Affairs Committee. Ben-Gurion advised him not to do so. Lavon left the Old Man's office angry and furious.

That was the beginning of Act Two of the Lavon affair.

Ben-Gurion believed in the judiciary, and strongly objected to politicians interfering with judicial procedure. Even if the allegations about the forging of documents were true, Ben-Gurion still believed that only a court or a judicial board of inquiry was qualified to find who did or didn't give the order for the tragic operation in Egypt.

Lavon's testimony before the Knesset's Defense and Foreign Affairs Committee caused a sensation that set the whole country in an uproar. Before the legislators he appeared to be a martyr and the victim of a dark plot. The central topic of his testimony was his version of "the 1954 mishap in Egypt." He launched a vile attack on Peres and Dayan, who were identified with the defense establishment. He hinted that they took advantage of the "plot" to settle their accounts with him. Lavon maintained that he had resigned in 1955 because of Sharett's refusal to fire Peres and Gibly, "these two men that no person with self-respect could have continued working with, after that affair."[2]

Then he launched a fierce attack against the entire defense establishment, slaughtering en masse Israel's sacred cows. He assailed the aircraft industries, the ship-repair installations, and the "economic imperialism" of the defense ministry. He spoke of corruption in the defense establishment, of scores of defense ministry employees and IDF officers who worked full-time to slander him. He attacked the IDF for allegedly carrying out operations behind his back when he was defense minister.

Lavon's testimony set off a political earthquake. The opposition parties immediately seized on it to attack Mapai, hoping to bring about the government's fall. Sources close to Lavon provided the newspapers with detailed accounts of his sensational testimony. Many newspapers virulently criticized Ben-Gurion and his young followers and demanded the rehabilitation of Lavon, even though they were not allowed by military censorship to publish the details of the 1954 affair. The public at large read in the papers enigmatic articles full of strange code words, and had not the foggiest idea of the real nature of the "mishap."

Many statements Lavon made to the committee were untrue, and most of his accusations were baseless. Moshe Sharett testified before the committee and refuted Lavon's arguments about the reasons for his resignation. He also confirmed that Shimon Peres hadn't communicated his testimony to Lavon on the explicit order of the Olshan-Dori board. Peres himself brought to the committee meeting documents and letters and repelled Lavon's accusations one by one.[3] But nobody cared about the facts, and the political hurricane reached a monstrous might.

Lavon's incendiary testimony forced Ben-Gurion to abandon his passive position and plunge into the melee. Now he wanted to crush Lavon, who had deviously attacked the most sacred Israeli value: national security.

Lavon's press campaign made it a point to attack Peres every day with partial or distorted information. At a meeting with friends, Peres described his private battle with the press. "I read in an inside page of *Lamerkav* that Shimon Peres had flown to the Isle of Rhodes for a fun vacation, and on the front page I read that Shimon Peres spoke in the Jordan Valley. I wondered how I could be at two places on the same day. I called them and asked, and it turned out that the man who flew to Rhodes was my brother, but they didn't bother to check this." Peres added a long list of examples of lies and falsehoods about him in the papers and admitted, "That hurts like hell!"[4]

In articles and letters to the newspapers, Ben-Gurion heatedly defended Peres, claiming that "he managed the defense ministry with a rare talent; there are not many who have done so much for the country." Peres was very grateful. "I never asked Ben-Gurion to defend me," he told the heads of the defense ministry. "I was moved by the extraordinary comradeship that Ben-Gurion showed to a man whose case looked quite gloomy. I don't know another example of a man who clears his busy schedule to defend the honor of his student, friend, or subordinate as did Ben-Gurion."[5]

Yet Peres was critical of the Old Man's feeble reaction to Lavon's campaign. For the first time he was disappointed in discovering a different Ben-Gurion, a man getting weaker and losing his grip on the leadership of the country. "I recall being unpleasantly surprised, time after time," Peres wrote, "by Ben-Gurion's decisions and public pronouncements. At the time, people thought that each morning we, his close aides, would hold a 'council of war' with Ben-Gurion, reporting to him on the state of the battlefield and offering our tactical advice. But that was far from the case. Often he consulted no one and took decisions which all of us thought were ill-advised."

"I believe that, had he allowed me into his heart, I could at least have prevented the isolation."[6]

MAPAI'S LEADERS, FRIGHTENED about the snowballing scandal, decided to put an urgent end to the affair before Lavon did more damage. In the cabinet, a "Committee of Seven" was established. Seven ministers, headed by Levi Eshkol, barely glanced at the documents brought by Lavon and pronounced him "not guilty." "We hereby conclude," the seven wrote, "that Lavon didn't give the order to the 'senior officer' [Binyamin Gibly] and that the 'mishap' was carried out without his knowledge."[7]

Ben-Gurion read the committee's report "and didn't believe his eyes." At the cabinet meeting on December 25, 1960, he had harsh words for his colleagues. "There is a certain procedure that is the only way to find the truth. [Only a court or a board of inquiry] have the power to interrogate witnesses, confront testimonies; both sides have lawyers who question and plead. Why were you afraid of a judicial inquiry board?" Ben-Gurion declared to his stunned comrades that he was resigning. "I am not your partner; I am not a member of this government."[8]

Peres tried, in vain, to prevent Ben-Gurion's resignation. "Dear Ben-Gurion," he wrote to him on December 30,

In a few years you would be able to bring the nation to a safe haven.

In four major fields you have laid the foundations for a serious and far-reaching change.

1. In Defense—with the atomic deterrent.

2. In the Political regime—with the chance to reform the electoral system.
3. In the Negev—with its industrial and agricultural settlement (that has been greatly furthered by the German loan).
4. In Foreign affairs—by our ties with Africa and Asia.

I am afraid that all those things would be shaken, harmed, perhaps even eradicated if you leave your functions today.

For a people that is in danger of destruction—there is no replacement for your faith, your vision, and your experience.

I can imagine what you have been through in the last three or four months. I had never seen such disgrace, distortion and disloyalty before. It is not the people who did this—but its petty politicians.

You're not allowed to drop the hope and the shield at the most crucial moment.

A man like you cannot leave.

ON JANUARY 31, Ben-Gurion resigned.

He was determined to win the battle for a judicial inquiry of the Lavon affair; he also wanted to get rid of Lavon, whom he regarded as disruptive and negative. But he hadn't realized until now that the protagonists in the Lavon affair had regrouped along the lines of either the old guard or Ben-Gurion's young protégés. The old guard now objected to any judicial inquiry; the young leaders supported it. Golda Meir, Moshe Sharett, and their friends who had so fiercely fought in 1955 against the "devious" Lavon now objected to Ben-Gurion's views. The Lavon affair had turned into the battlefield on which the War of Succession was being waged.

In an attempt to prevent a disastrous election, Ben-Gurion proposed that a new government be created with Eshkol as prime minister. He had a favorite candidate for defense minister. "I would have proposed Peres as Defense Minister," he wrote in a draft letter to the Mapai Bureau, "but if some important comrades objected, I wouldn't insist."

"We could take Dayan and appoint somebody else as Agriculture Minister. . . . Or perhaps ask Yigael Yadin."[9] Under the pressure of the old guard, he finally dropped the names off the final draft of his letter.

But even his old guard opponents wouldn't let him quit the political arena. Golda Meir, in particular, fought with all her power to keep Ben-Gurion at the helm. She and her friends insisted on new elections, once again under Ben-Gurion's leadership.

The elections took place on August 15, 1961. Mapai lost five seats. Ben-Gurion returned as prime minister, embittered and weakened, secretly determined to establish a judicial board of inquiry into the Lavon affair.

During the tumultuous days of "the affair," Peres and Ben-Gurion were in dire need of nerves of steel, for in those very same days a new drama erupted, once again caused by Israel's nuclear project.

IN THE SECOND WEEK of December 1960, sensational news exploded in the world press: a "small nation" was developing the ability to build nuclear weapons.[10] Banner headlines announced that a mysterious country was about to become a nuclear power. On December 16, the London *Daily Express* named the country: Israel, and on December 18, on the television program *Meet the Press*, the information was confirmed by John McCone, the chairman of the U.S. Atomic Energy Commission. Israel, McCone said, was secretly building a nuclear reactor. The newspapers published photographs of the building site in the Negev; some of them had been taken by American spy planes. *The New York Times*, in its December 20 edition, stated that Israel had misled the United States about the reactor.

The press campaign had been triggered by intelligence reports that the United States had received from various sources. In early December, the American government pressured Israel to explain what was happening in Dimona. First the Israelis answered that the building was "a metallurgic complex" or a "textile factory," but they fooled nobody. The international exposure and the American pressure finally forced Ben-Gurion to make a public announcement in the Knesset, where he declared that Israel was building a nuclear reactor for peaceful purposes. The Quai d'Orsay denied the rumors that France was helping Israel to build a reactor for military use, and stressed that the reactor was going to serve exclusively for peaceful purposes. In Cairo, President Nasser announced that he would attack Israel with an army of four million soldiers and destroy her atomic installations.

In Washington, Israel's ambassador, Abe Harman, heard some very harsh comments from senior State Department officials. On January 3, the U.S. ambassador to Israel, Ogden Reid, presented five questions to Golda Meir on behalf of the State Department. He requested that answers be delivered to him before midnight:

1. What was Israel planning to do with the plutonium generated by the reactor?
2. Would Israel consent to inspection of the plutonium produced in the reactor?
3. Would Israel permit authorized scientists from the International Atomic Energy Commission, or some other friendly body, to visit the reactor?
4. Was Israel building or planning an additional reactor?
5. Could Israel declare unreservedly that she had no plans to manufacture nuclear weapons?[11]

Golda informed Ben-Gurion right away, and he called an urgent meeting in Jerusalem, with the participation of Golda, Shimon Peres, and Ambassador Harman, who had been called back from Washington. The Old Man was infuriated by the disrespectful character of the American demand, which he regarded as pressure of the crudest kind. He therefore decided not to answer the questions by the midnight deadline. The following day he summoned Ogden Reid. He spoke firmly, bridling his fury. He first answered the questions. As to the first question, the plutonium would be returned to France. As to the second question, Israel wouldn't accept foreign inspection. "We don't want hostile states meddling in our business." On the other hand, he gave an affirmative answer to the third question, and expressed willingness to allow a visit by scientists from a friendly country or an international organization, but not right away. "There is anger in Israel over the American action in leaking the matter." As to the fourth question, he answered that Israel did not intend to build another reactor, and he replied to the fifth question by declaring that Israel didn't intend to build nuclear weapons. He ended by forcefully protesting against the offensive character of the American demands. He stressed that if the United States wanted to talk to Israel, "even though we are a tiny state, you must talk to us as equals, or not talk to us at all."[12]

That conversation didn't solve the crisis. The American secretary of state, Christian Herter, met with Couve de Murville, who presented him with detailed information about France's assistance to Israel. A few weeks later, John F. Kennedy was sworn in as America's new president. Kennedy was haunted by deep fears about nuclear proliferation. He exerted a growing pressure on Israel that reached its peak a few months before his assassination.

In Israel, Peres knew no respite from the cross fire directed at him from all directions. Saul Friedlander, a future scholar of world renown who was Peres's assistant for scientific affairs, was astounded by the way Peres faced all the crises that assailed him simultaneously. "He had to face an internal political crisis—the Lavon affair—that rocked the nation. The crises with the French followed one another. The French informed him over and over again that they were terminating the cooperation agreements. The people close to him argued and engaged in stormy debates. The United States was infuriated by the discovery of the reactor. Major leaders like Golda Meir were in a panic. And Peres absorbed all these blows, and went on. This matter could have ended in a terrible catastrophe. In the middle of the crisis, I would come to his office, he would put his feet on the desk in his ill-mannered way, make a toothpick out of a folded piece of paper, and hold a casual, relaxed conversation for hours on every possible subject—starting with the reactor's latest crisis, and ending with philosophical theories and books he had read. Never in my life had I seen a man who withstood such severe crises with such calm and cool."[13]

After the international storm, the new agreements between France and Israel were completed. At the end of January 1961, a tense conversation took place between Couve de Murville and Peres. Couve tried again to sever the French assistance to Israel in the nuclear field, and even to put an end to the sale of equipment and instruments by French companies to Israel; Peres fought against what he saw as a discrimination of Israel vis-à-vis any other country. Finally Peres prevailed. On February 21, 1961, binding diplomatic letters were exchanged between Ambassador Walter Eitan and the Quai d'Orsay's secretary general Eric de Carbonnel. In these letters it was agreed that France would put an end to its assistance in the building of the nuclear reactor, but Israel would continue to employ French companies in its construction, without the government's aid. The supply of uranium would continue, and until 1963, 145 tons of uranium would be delivered to Israel.[14] The plutonium produced by the reactor would be returned to France.[15]

As the American pressure continued, Ben-Gurion decided to visit the United States and meet with President Kennedy. Before leaving, he sent a letter to de Gaulle describing what he intended to tell Kennedy. "I intend to tell him the truth as it is," Ben-Gurion wrote. "I. In 1956 we signed an agreement with France on the assistance in building an atomic reactor. 2. In a meeting with you in Paris, in June 1960, I told you we wouldn't produce nuclear weapons without your approval. 3. If the French would sell us uranium, we agreed that the French would have the right to control its use."[16]

In his answer, de Gaulle suggested that Ben-Gurion not tell

Kennedy about the 1956 accord; he also asked Ben-Gurion to inform the president that the reactor was being built for peaceful purposes and the uranium would be returned to France after being irradiated. Finally, according to these documents, de Gaulle mentioned the separation plant. That was a purely Israeli project, de Gaulle wrote, and it was Israel's business; he wouldn't comment on the answer Ben-Gurion would give to Kennedy. De Gaulle concluded his letter by inviting Ben-Gurion to visit him again after meeting Kennedy.[17]

On the eve of his journey, Ben-Gurion authorized two American experts to visit Dimona. They visited the site and reported to President Kennedy. At the same time, the opponents of the nuclear project in the Israeli cabinet stepped up their pressure, so that if serious problems emerged at the Ben-Gurion-Kennedy talks, the project would definitely be scrapped. Ben-Gurion and Peres were, once again, completely alone.

But the meeting with Kennedy was a success. The president told Ben-Gurion, with satisfaction, that the American experts were very content with their visit to Dimona. He added, "But it is not enough for a woman to be virtuous, she also should look virtuous." Kennedy therefore asked Ben-Gurion's permission to show the report of the American experts to other nations. He also requested that neutral experts be allowed to visit the reactor. Ben-Gurion agreed. Still, he was keen to preserve Israel's freedom of action. "As for now, the reactor will be used for peaceful purposes only," he said to Kennedy. "In three or four years we'll have a reactor. [Then] we'll see what happens in the Middle East. It doesn't depend on us. Perhaps Russia wouldn't give [atomic] bombs to China or to Egypt, but perhaps Egypt would develop them herself."[18] That was actually a hint that Israel might reconsider the reactor's purposes.

At the end of the meeting with Kennedy, Ben-Gurion felt enormous relief. The reactor had been saved, at least for now.

On his way back to Israel he stopped in Paris, where Peres joined him. Ben-Gurion had a long talk with de Gaulle and briefed him about his conversation with Kennedy. De Gaulle didn't conceal his deep appreciation for Israel's leader. It seemed that the disagreement with France about the reactor had simmered down and the tension between the two countries had been defused. The ties in some fields were even strengthened: Israel had recently learned of a plot, concocted by the French right-wing underground group OAS, to assassinate de Gaulle and had warned the French president; de Gaulle had asked his son-in-law, Colonel Alain de Boissieu, to convey his deep gratitude to the Israelis.

And at an Elysée Palace lunch with David Ben-Gurion, de Gaulle raised his glass in a toast to Israel. "Long live Israel," he solemnly declared, "our friend and our ally."

DURING THE VISITS of American experts to Dimona that followed, nothing unusual was discovered, but the suspicions of the Kennedy administration kept increasing. According to foreign press reports, false walls were built in Dimona, concealing empty spaces; doorways were built "that didn't lead anywhere and windows that didn't open." Abba Eban was quoted as saying, "It had cost us a lot of money so that their inspectors wouldn't discover what was really taking place."[19] But the inspectors assumed that they were not seeing everything. The CIA head of station in Israel was instructed to photograph the reactor and collect samples of water, soil, and plants so that their radioactivity could be tested.

In early 1963, President Kennedy dispatched some harsh letters to David Ben-Gurion and instructed his ambassador in Tel Aviv to keep the Israeli government under constant pressure. He demanded twice-a-year visits to Dimona and sent barely veiled threats to Israel saying that the relations between the two countries would be gravely damaged if Israel didn't yield to his demands. His heavy pressure continued after Ben-Gurion's resignation in June 1963 (because of a crisis unrelated to the nuclear issue), and his blunt letters were now addressed to Ben-Gurion's successor, Levi Eshkol. Kennedy instructed White House and

State Department officials to conceive of ways to prevent a possible development of nuclear weapons by Israel (and by Egypt, even though it didn't have the capability of doing so).

On April 2,1963, Shimon Peres visited the White House. He was in Washington to conclude a groundbreaking deal for the purchase of Hawk antiaircraft missiles. This deal augured a change in the American policy toward Israel, because for the first time Washington agreed to supply Israel with sophisticated weapons. During his visit, Peres met with Mike Feldman, Kennedy's adviser, and was invited to the Oval Office. In order to avoid angering the Arab countries, the White House informed the press that President Kennedy had bumped into Peres "by chance" in one of the hallways and invited him to a meeting. The truth was that Feldman led Peres to Kennedy "to say hello," and the president invited him into the Oval Office.

Kennedy asked Peres, "You know that we follow with great concern any indication of the development of nuclear capacity in that area. That would have created a very dangerous situation; that's why we were so keen in maintaining contact with your nuclear efforts. What can you tell me on this subject?"

"I can tell you clearly," Peres said, "that we shall not introduce atomic weapons to the region. We certainly shall not be the first to do so. We are not interested in that—quite the contrary; we are interested in a decrease in the course of armaments, even in total disarmament."[20] According to the American report about that meeting, "Peres had given an unequivocal assurance that Israel wouldn't do anything in that field unless it finds that other countries in the area are involved in it."[21] In any case, at this visit to the White House Peres coined "the ambiguity formula," which was to become Israel's official slogan up to this very day. It states that Israel will not be the first nation to introduce nuclear weapons to the Middle East. On his return to Israel, Peres was attacked by some of the nation's leaders for the formula he used in his meeting with Kennedy. That didn't prevent them—Levi

Eshkol and Golda Meir in particular—from using the same formula when they reached the position of prime minister.

Kennedy apparently wasn't convinced by Peres's assurances and tried to apply indirect pressure on France; foreign reports indicated that it was still supplying uranium to Israel. In May 1963, Couve de Murville visited Washington, and Kennedy raised the subject in their conversation. He spoke of the atomic danger facing the world and in particular the Dimona reactor. "The Israeli problem causes me grave concern," he said to Couve.

The French foreign minister tried to play down the gravity of the matter. After all, France was still deeply involved in Israel's nuclear project. He said to Kennedy that "the Israelis would be able to produce at the most one or two devices that cannot be considered as real weapons. That would cause unrest in the Middle East, but there would be no real threat to the survival of mankind."[22]

That answer didn't satisfy the president, and a few minutes later he returned to the subject. "I want to return to the problem of Israel," he said. "We are extremely worried about the atomic possibilities of this country."

"As far as we are concerned," Couve answered, "we have taken all the necessary precautions. We have undertaken to supply them with certain quantities of uranium for their reactor, but they have to return it to us as soon as they have treated it, so they will have no possibility of extracting plutonium out of it. Unfortunately, the Israelis may obtain uranium elsewhere, without control." He admitted that that was a "danger."

"If Israel obtained atomic weapons," Kennedy remarked, "we and you would be blamed, you for providing her with uranium and we because of our financial aid to Israel. The position of that country is stupid, because they give a pretext to the Russians—who are in a state of retreat from that region—to accuse us before the public opinion, and perhaps not without reason."

On May 25, the French diplomat Charles Lucet told the director of the Central Intelligence Agency that there were parts of

Dimona that even France didn't know about; he also proudly informed the director that France had succeeded in foiling the purchase of uranium by Israel in Gabon and some other former French colonies.[23] On other occasions, President Kennedy and Secretary of State Dean Rusk questioned the French about the missiles they were selling to Israel.[24]

Kennedy intensified the pressure on Israel; Peres complained about that during a meeting with Couve de Murville. "In the past," Peres said, "the Americans asked twice to visit the reactor, in May 1961 and in October 1962. We agreed, in order to be at peace with the Americans. They must be able to say that their files are being properly updated."

"But last April they came with new demands. Now they want to visit the reactor twice a year. We didn't conceal our anger, because we don't agree to their demand to maintain a permanent control on us. After Prime Minister Ben-Gurion's meeting with President Kennedy, the Americans seemed satisfied. At that time we agreed to a second visit. But we are not [American] satellites. We don't accept a permanent control. Afterwards President Kennedy wrote a personal letter to Mr. Ben-Gurion where he stressed his worries from the spread of unconventional weapons."

"Didn't the United States supply you with missiles lately?" Couve asked.

"Yes, they gave us Hawk missiles, but this is not the problem .... Mr. Ben-Gurion very recently answered Kennedy's letter. He doesn't accept the control, but he is ready to authorize another visit. We pointed out that we have an agreement with you and you control the uranium that you supply us with. We believe that the construction at Dimona would be completed by the end of December, and then we'll invite the Americans to come and see the finished reactor. Simultaneously, we'll call off the secrecy surrounding this installation .... Starting early next year, the reactor will be open for all."

"Actually," Couve said, "everybody knows well what you are

building there. I must tell you that we revealed to the Americans the sort of agreement we have with you. Therefore it can be said that the building of the reactor is not a secret, even if it is not officially public."

"I agree," Peres said, "and we said this to the parliament as well. What we have not divulged yet in our public statements is the control agreement that exists between our two countries."

Couve replied: "If we are asked by other countries, like England, we'll tell them the same thing we told the Americans."

"We agree to a bilateral French-Israeli control," Peres said, "but we don't agree that it should be an American control. The Americans should deal only with the other reactor, the one we are building with their help"—the Nebi Rubin baby reactor.[25]

THE CONVERSATION COULDN'T be more polite—but under the surface a storm was brewing again. The truth was that Shimon Peres had no intention of placing Israel's atomic project under French control. And Couve de Murville succeeded in concealing from Peres the secret move he had initiated a few months before. The general feeling in de Gaulle's government was that France was being drawn into an impossible situation because of its nuclear assistance to Israel. The French watched Peres's international contacts, especially with the major producers of uranium. They suspected that Israel was looking for uranium on other markets as well.

During 1962, as Quai d'Orsay documents reveal, Couve de Murville received reports about Israel buying large quantities of uranium on the free market, in Gabon, in South Africa,[26] and later in Argentina as well.[27] The contract with Argentina dealt with the supply of "yellow cake" uranium. The French also learned that Argentina had authorized the sale to Israel of a hundred tons of uranium during three years, starting in January 1963.[28] France realized that Israel could obtain uranium from other sources and wouldn't be compelled to return it after use, she could extract plutonium and build atomic bombs, and finally

France would be accused of having turned Israel into a nuclear power.

France charged her intelligence agency, the SDECE, to report on the activity at the Israeli nuclear site. In May 1963, the SDECE informed the French foreign minister that Israel was continuing to build the reactor, and in spite of the termination of French assistance, there were no delays in the working pace. The SDECE's conclusion was unequivocal: the reactor would reach its maximum power in early 1964; the extraction of plutonium would probably start at the beginning of 1965.[29]

The only way of stopping Israel, for Couve de Murville, was to halt the supply of French uranium, in blatant violation of the February 1961 agreement. The French minister well knew that he was breaking a duly signed agreement; he also knew that the agreement didn't include any commitment by Israel not to buy uranium from other countries. But he was determined to stop Israel, even if he had to bend the rules. In April 1963, Couve put his plan down in writing: "In my opinion," he wrote to the heads of the French Atomic Energy Commission, "it is preferable that you [don't] supply the quantities of uranium to Israel—as it was agreed in the exchange of letters between France and Israel on February 21 1961—without a new consultation with my office .... The efforts of Israel's government to obtain uranium without control in Gabon and in other countries like South Africa makes me assess that we should be extremely prudent in supplying uranium to this country, even with all the control guarantees that we have imposed. Therefore I believe it is most important that after the first delivery, which was carried out in January, we should stop for a while, and the second delivery shouldn't be carried out without my agreement."[30]

The deliveries stopped. Couve de Murville and his entourage were convinced that Israel would cave in under the pressure; they estimated that all the uranium Israel had purchased on the free market so far "was 15 tons all in all"; the amount of plutonium that could be extracted from it was only a small part of the total needed "for the activation of a plan of military experiments." The Quai d'Orsay's experts assumed that the situation might change if Israel succeeded in purchasing larger quantities of uranium on the free market. That's why, they concluded, "we have to prevent Israel from loading the Dimona reactor with any other uranium but the French . . . . The quantities of uranium we supply and the rate of the deliveries assure us of practical control on the activity of this reactor for the next ten years. Israel should respect and implement her commitments that give us a monopoly on the supply of uranium for the period in question."[31]

The French foreign ministry also planned the following stages. Israel would ask France to resume the uranium supplies. France would answer that the future deliveries depended on Israel's guarantee that she wouldn't bypass her commitments anymore; any Israeli attempt to obtain uranium on the free market would result in the immediate termination of France's assistance. "We have every reason to think that this warning will be heard and followed," the foreign ministry experts firmly stated. "The realization of the Israeli nuclear program, as we know it, depends largely on us."

To that statement, the French added an ominous threat: "The Israelis would certainly understand that the cessation of our assistance might be the first in a series of measures of the same kind in other fields as well"—meaning the supply of weapons.[32] Those warnings were soon followed by a demand that Israel guarantee, in writing, that she wouldn't buy uranium in other countries.

But Israel didn't satisfy France's demand, and didn't provide the written guarantee it had asked for. France waited in vain. According to the foreign media, Israel obtained large amounts of uranium by secret methods, not always strictly legal; it used front companies and intermediaries from other countries—Belgium, South Africa, even the United States. Some deliveries simply vanished from the control of the states where they were bought, as in a much publicized affair in Pennsylvania: a load purchased in Belgium and placed aboard an Italy-bound cargo ship in Antwerp was transferred at night to an Israeli ship in the middle of the Mediterranean. The final result was that Israel obtained enough uranium for her needs. The investigations carried out by Western security services didn't discover a trace of the vanished uranium.'[33]

Only on February 11, 1964, almost a year after France had stopped all uranium exports, did Israel's scientific attaché come to the Quai d'Orsay. He inquired why the uranium deliveries had been stopped. The French explained the reasons and asked for the commitment in writing they had decided upon, but the attaché only promised to convey the demand to his government. On his way out, he told the French that some American nuclear scientists had visited Dimona, and that "they seemed very pleased with what they saw and were convinced that Israel's research there was for peaceful purposes."[34]

The Quai d'Orsay was deeply disappointed. The cessation of the uranium deliveries hadn't worked. Israel didn't ask France to resume the uranium deliveries. "We got the uranium elsewhere," Peres said.[35]

France was at a loss. At a meeting in the prime minister's office on October 22, 1963, it was decided to ask Israel to implement the agreement between the two nations and return immediately the thirty tons of uranium that France had leased to her. The ministers also discussed the measures France could take if Israel didn't return the uranium. Couve de Murville stopped short of threatening Israel with a cessation of the arms sales. According to French documents, Israel returned to France a first shipment of irradiated uranium only on November 18, 1967.[36]

Israel won this round and pursued her nuclear project in spite of the French measures. However, Israel's atomic policy greatly irritated the upper layers of the French administration. What had started as sincere assistance by France to "her little sister," Israel, now turned into a crushing burden for the French, who feared the reactions of the Western world and of the Arab nations, and were infuriated by Israel's maneuvers. The Quai d'Orsay had to lie to concerned Arab diplomats, and to maintain that "France is cooperating in nuclear research with several countries, and Israel is only one of them."[37] Couve de Murville had to lie to President Kennedy about the missiles that France was selling to Israel, by saying that "these were short-range missiles that cannot carry nuclear war heads."[38] President de Gaulle had to lie to Arab statesmen by saying that the Israeli nuclear reactor "is not equipped for the production of plutonium."[39] In 1967, de Gaulle learned about the common production and testing of Israel's Jericho missile, which could carry nuclear warheads; the French president was furious.[40] The French leaders felt cheated and frustrated; there is no doubt that de Gaulle bitterly regretted the agreement that his predecessors had signed with Israel. We may assume that the anger of de Gaulle and Couve de Murville, caused by the nuclear imbroglio, influenced to some extent the anti-Israeli decisions that France made during the Six Day War.

CHAPTER 20.

THE DEATH RAYS

ON JULY 21, 1962, President Nasser stunned the world by launching four missiles: two with a range of 175 miles, the other two with a range of 350 miles. The missiles were named Al-Zafer ("the Winner") and Al-Kaher ("the Conqueror").

The launchings came as a complete surprise to the defense community in Israel. In a speech in Cairo, Nasser boasted that his wonder weapons could hit any target "south of Beirut." Isser Harel, the head of the intelligence community, was immediately summoned by Ben-Gurion and promised to deliver a complete report on the Egyptian missiles in the near future. A few weeks later, Shimon Peres revealed in a restricted meeting that the missiles had been built by German scientists.[1]

There were hundreds of German scientists and engineers secretly hired since 1959 by Nasser, as Isser Harel soon reported. According to Harel, they were working on a devious plan to destroy Israel: they were developing doomsday weapons, supersonic aircraft, huge missiles, radioactive warheads that could "kill any living thing" and poison the air in Israel for many years; they were even working on death rays and all kinds of hellish contraptions.

Harel launched an all-out campaign against the scientists, while in Israel the public reacted with panic to the horror stories screaming from the headlines. Harel, supported by Golda Meir, requested that Ben-Gurion contact Chancellor Adenauer at once and demand that he take immediate action to thwart the scientists' extermination plans.

Ben-Gurion refused. The relations between Germany and Israel were very fragile, and he didn't want to risk a rejection by Adenauer. He preferred that Shimon Peres intervene with his friend Franz Josef Strauss.

On August 17, Peres cabled an urgent message to Strauss. "The seriousness of the matter that I see as my duty to raise before you made me ignore conventional diplomatic etiquette, and turn to you personally about a matter that is, actually, of national importance." Peres described the launching of the missiles by Nasser and the role played in the project by German scientists. He named the German companies and the German experts involved in the Egyptian project. He also expressed his certitude that both Strauss and Dr. Adenauer would certainly be shocked by the idea that the Germany of today might cooperate, directly or indirectly, with Egypt's and Russia's efforts to annihilate the State of Israel.

Peres asked that Germany act decisively to end her citizens' activities in Egypt. "[This is] a situation that neither you nor we are interested in; to open a scarring wound and transform it into a tragedy of horrifying scale and meaning."

"We thought," Peres concluded, "that Israel had the right to live in security and the new Germany would do all in her power to contribute to her security . . . . I know that this is also the Chancellor's thinking as well as yours."[2]

IN THE FOLLOWING MONTHS, Isser Harel informed Ben-Gurion that the Germans intended to fill their warheads with radioactive materials such as cobalt 60 and strontium 90; he also spoke of uranium enrichment using centrifuges Egypt had acquired in Germany and Holland. The hysteria reached its peak with stories published by the newspapers about "death rays that destroyed everything in their path" and other similar accounts that, in retrospect, seem borrowed from Flash Gordon's adventures. The foreign press accused the Mossad of carrying out a wave of attempts on the lives of leading German scientists in Egypt; some of them were in fact killed or wounded.

Ben-Gurion didn't want to make the German scientists' affair a major issue in Israeli-German relations, for in those very days Israel was receiving large deliveries of weapons from Germany. Peres and Israel's envoy in Germany, Pinhas Shin'ar, were in the middle of a secret negotiation with Germany for another arms deal and the establishment of diplomatic relations. Ben-Gurion was determined not to jeopardize these efforts.

Harel's stand toward Germany, however, was hostile and distrustful. Since he had captured the Nazi criminal Adolf Eichmann in Argentina, his anti-German feelings had turned into deep hatred. He sharply criticized Ben-Gurion's policy toward Germany. Golda Meir shared Harel's feelings. The German issue was the only one on which Golda openly opposed Ben-Gurion. Golda and Harel were joined, in their anti-German campaign, both by the left-wing parties in the government and by Menachem Begin's opposition party, Herut.

But the Mossad director was also jealous of Peres because of his close relations with the Old Man. Amos Manor, former director of the Shabak, the General Security Service, said, "The relations between Isser and Shimon deteriorated because of their permanent contest—who of them was more appreciated by Ben-Gurion, who had more influence on Ben-Gurion. Isser wasn't involved in the preparations for the Sinai Campaign. Whom did he accuse? Not Ben-Gurion, who had kept him out of it, but Shimon Peres. Shimon didn't like Isser, either, and was quite happy that he hadn't been let into the secret." After Peres was appointed deputy defense minister, Harel's animosity toward him soared; he used to say that Peres was some sort of Rasputin at Ben-Gurion's side.[3]

PERES WAS THE first to sober up from the hysterical fears that had swept the nation. In closed testimony at the Knesset he tried to instill some sanity into the affair. "What we know so far," he said, "is that the Egyptians have built a missile of an obsolete model that was used in World War II. To our best knowledge, this missile still does not have a navigation device, and only next March or April, if everything works well, would they be able to build a model with a navigation system." The Egyptians, Peres added, were investing great efforts in building radiological warheads, or cobalt bombs; but these warheads presented only a limited danger, and Egypt had acquired only a tiny amount of cobalt. He stressed that the danger of a radiological warhead was more psychological than practical. Peres even hinted that it was better for Israel that the "obsolete" scientists in Egypt kept developing obsolete missiles of the World War II V-2. type.[4] He knew what he was talking about; according to French sources, in April 1963 he signed an agreement with the Marcel Dassault company in Paris for the development of medium-range missiles.[5]

Harel, on the other hand, intensified his attacks on Germany. On January 1, 1963, he told Ben-Gurion, "In Germany they all knew about the German scientists' activities—Adenauer knew, and so did Strauss, and Erhard [the German minister of economics]. They ignored the issue on purpose."[6] Ben-Gurion refrained from comment. And for good reason: a few weeks later, Germany transferred to Israel another $24.3 million from the $500 million loan Adenauer had promised Ben-Gurion. That same week, Adenauer himself wrote a letter to his foreign minister, Gerhard Schröeder, informing him of his decision to establish diplomatic relations with Israel in the near future.[7]

But in Israel, the storm raged. At the Knesset, Golda Meir declared that hundreds of German scientists and technicians were developing offensive missiles in Egypt, "and even weapons forbidden by international agreements, that serve the exclusive purpose of the extermination of any living being."[8] Golda's words triggered a wave of unbridled attacks on Germany and its government, with Menachem Begin leading the pack. Herut's leader accused Ben-Gurion of "providing Germany with an alibi" and shouted: "You're sending out Uzi submachine guns to Germany, and the Germans send microbes to our enemies!"[9] The tide of anti-German feelings threatened to destroy Ben-Gurion's German policy. Only too late did Ben-Gurion realize that he shouldn't have left the stage to Golda Meir and Harel.

On March 24, Peres returned from a trip to Africa and immediately went to work to put an end to the frenzy. He realized that the stories about the weapons "that kill any living thing" were simply ludicrous. The IDF's intelligence branch presented him with a totally different estimate. "We gathered all that we could collect," said the IDF intelligence chief, General Meir Amit, "and slowly a picture emerged: this story has been blown out of any proportion .... Our people said that this couldn't be true; it couldn't be something serious."[10] With the help of a former SS colonel, Otto Skorzeny, Amit's men recruited the security officer of the German scientists in Egypt and obtained firsthand information about their activities.[11]

Amit's people didn't find any indication that the German scientists were developing chemical or bacteriological weapons; the stories about doomsday weapons seemed borrowed from Baron Munchausen's adventures; the quantities of cobalt bought by Egypt were infinitesimal.

Peres and Amit reported to Ben-Gurion that the panic that had swept the nation in the last few months was absolutely unfounded. The truth was that Egypt had recruited a team of mediocre scientists who were building obsolete missiles.[12]

Ben-Gurion summoned Harel and questioned him about his sources; he told him that he doubted the accuracy of his reports. An angry confrontation followed; the Mossad director returned to his office and wrote Ben-Gurion a letter of resignation.

THE FUTURE WAS to prove that Peres and Amit had been right; Golda and Harel had been wrong. The Egyptian missiles were not dangerous; their navigational system failed, and Egypt didn't develop unconventional warheads. Ben-Gurion and Peres discreetly acted behind the scenes to get the German scientists out of Egypt. The German government brought back home many of the scientists by offering them employment and good salaries. In his letters and speeches, Ben-Gurion qualified the campaign against the scientists as "a commotion, partly exaggerated and partly the fruit of demagogy" that harmed the State of Israel.

Yet most of the harm befell Ben-Gurion himself. For him, the affair of the German scientists resulted in a threefold crisis: in his German policy, in his relations with Golda Meir and Isser Harel, and with the parliamentary opposition. That crisis was to cause his downfall ten weeks later.

Peres turned the crisis into a means to accomplish one of his secret designs. He established the "Missile Fund" and charged the defense ministry's director, Arthur Ben-Nathan, to raise money throughout the world for the financing of Israel's missile project and the Dimona reactor.[13]

During 1963 and 1964, Israel's leaders, including Peres, based their repeated requests for American military assistance on the German scientists' misdeeds. It seems puzzling, therefore, that years later Peres totally denied the German scientists affair, and claimed forcefully that "there had never been German scientists in Egypt."[14]

ON JUNE 15, 1963, Golda Meir went to Ben-Gurion's house in Jerusalem. She seemed very upset. She urged Ben-Gurion to instruct the military censor to prevent the publication of a news item about Israeli soldiers training in Germany. The publication of that report, Golda said, would only cause "superfluous trouble." Ben-Gurion said that he was not empowered to interfere in the decisions of the censor, who followed very clear and strict rules.

Golda was infuriated by the answer. At eleven o'clock that night, she returned to the Old Man's house, accompanied by Teddy Kollek, the director of the prime minister's office. The three of them sat down in the kitchen, and Ben-Gurion and Golda plunged into a heated argument about the German issue. Golda harshly criticized Ben-Gurion's German policy and, as usual, attacked Shimon Peres.[15] Ben-Gurion was irritated and impatient, and Teddy Kollek felt "that he was fed up."[16]

The following day, Ben-Gurion resigned from office.

Peres learned about the Old Man's sudden decision during a visit to Paris. He flew to Israel at once and tried persuading Ben-Gurion to cancel his resignation, but the Old Man's decision was final. He refused to divulge his reasons, but in his diary he wrote harsh passages about Lavon, Harel, and Menachem Begin.[17] It was the end of an era.

Ben-Gurion's departure hurt, most of all, his young supporters. His impulsive decision put an end to his efforts to entrust Israel's leadership to the hands of a new generation. Dayan, Peres, and their comrades lost their bid for power, and the war of succession ended with the absolute victory of the old guard.

BEN-GURION'S RESIGNATION was a heavy blow for Peres. He was deeply attached to the Old Man. His career had flourished largely because of Ben-Gurion's support and protection. Peres depended on that support, as his leadership hadn't yet been publicly recognized. He wasn't a charismatic hero like Moshe Dayan. He was the punching bag for all those who opposed Ben-Gurion but didn't dare to confront him. Only Ben-Gurion's backing protected him from many leaders of Mapai and other parties who fiercely fought against him. He also allowed himself to take initiatives that infuriated many leading figures, out of certainty that he could count on Ben-Gurion. Peres had accomplished his major achievements—the relations with France and Germany, the building of the nuclear reactor, the penetration in Africa, the transformation of the defense ministry into an empire—in spite of Golda Meir, Isser Harel, Pinhas Lavon, Pinhas Sapir, Moshe Sharett .... He couldn't have done any of this without Ben-Gurion's support. "He let me dare," Peres said.[18]

Their personal relations were more complex. Peres admired Ben-Gurion; Ben-Gurion held Peres in high esteem and supported him almost automatically. Yet he didn't show him love; that was reserved for others, like Moshe Dayan or Yigael Yadin.

Ben-Gurion was aware of Peres's unique talents, as well as his political limitations. Peres was his first choice for defense minister when he wanted to resign in 1961, but he shelved the idea because of the objections that such an appointment would have stirred up.

Peres was an unconditional disciple of Ben-Gurion's political thinking. "I support David Ben-Gurion because I agree with his ideology," he wrote in 1965. "I agree with most of his views, and I admire his personality, which has defeated his age."[19] All the great leaders of the twentieth century, Peres pointed out—Lenin, Churchill, de Gaulle, Mao Tse-tung—had been born in the countries that they eventually ruled, and had to cope with situations that existed in their lands or with enemies that threatened them from the outside. "Ben-Gurion was the only one among them who wasn't born in his country. He was born before he had a homeland; he was the bearer of an idea before he was the leader of a nation; he fought a war before he had an army; he was a statesman before he had a state. In the span of two generations he led his people along a stretch of history that other leaders and other peoples need hundreds of years to traverse."

Even Ben-Gurion's outward appearance stirred Peres's admiration. "A small man, who for some reason seems so great; on his shoulders rests a big head, from which two penetrating eyes smolder; his chin is determined, rebellious. There was in him something leonine and deterring, and yet magnetic. His legs seemed to have been made for running, not for walking. His big hands were the hands of an artist—expressive and capable. There was no tenderness in his person, which exuded a strange and captivating personal charm. His figure seemed to be molded out of one block, and his only decorative feature was his mane of [white] hair."[20]

But the Ben-Gurion he so admired, the spiritual teacher, the political leader, the personal patron, had now stepped down, and Peres had to face a new reality.

BEN-GURION'S CHOICE for successor was Levi Eshkol. A

former minister of agriculture and finance, Eshkol was not the least bit like Ben-Gurion: he was a friendly man with a great sense of humor, casual, relaxed, a master of compromise. He was not resolute, but rather hesitant; before any decision he would hold long meetings and ask many people's opinion before he made up his mind. He wasn't charismatic like his predecessor. Like Peres he also was a kibbutznik, from Degania, in the Jordan Valley. Peres loved Eshkol's humor and would often quote one of their first conversations, when Eshkol had divulged to him his political philosophy. *"Jungermann,"* he had cracked, "get into the ocean and swim. If you make it, good. If you drown, it's even better."[21] Eshkol's public image was of a warm, humane leader. He supported Ben-Gurion's policy, and Ben-Gurion trusted him completely.

Right after Mapai elected Eshkol to succeed Ben-Gurion, he sent Peres a note in his large, rounded handwriting: "Would you work with me as Deputy Defense Minister? Of course, I'd like to be involved in the running of things. I'll try to bridge matters with Golda. Eshkol."[22] Peres met with Eshkol on June 18, and Eshkol agreed to Peres's written demands:

1. The political and defense issues will be discussed in a restricted forum—you, the Foreign Minister and me.
2. The special relations with Germany will be pursued and developed.
3. You'll try to put an end to all the misunderstandings between the Foreign Ministry and the Defense Ministry.
4. I shall be invited to the Cabinet meetings when they deal with matters of defense.
5. I shall join the Ministerial Committee for Defense matters.
6. The chain of command in the Defense Ministry will be the following: The Prime Minister and Minister of Defense, the Deputy Defense Minister, the IDF Chief of Staff.

Two other paragraphs dealt with the Dimona reactor and the development of missiles.

The fifth paragraph in the agreement between Eshkol and Peres raised fierce opposition in Ahdut Ha'avoda, Mapai's coalition partner. The leader of Peres's opponents was Yigal Allon, the young Ahdut Ha'avoda leader. Eshkol tried to keep his promise to Peres, but Ahdut Ha'avoda's leaders launched a crusade against the deputy defense minister. Some newspapers ridiculed Allon's relentless endeavors, pointing out that Shimon Peres was the only leader who really understood defense matters; his presence at the committee meetings was nothing short of vital.[23]

Peres, deeply hurt, informed his Mapai colleagues that he had decided to resign,[24] but they persuaded him to stay. Finally, he announced that he wouldn't seek a seat at the Ministerial Defense Committee. In his letter to Eshkol, Peres bluntly accused the Ahdut Ha'avoda leaders of sabotaging his candidacy for "sectarian interests."[25]

His letter was published in the *Davar* newspaper. Among the many letters of sympathy he received about his decision was a warm letter from David Ben-Gurion. He defined Peres's decision as "wise and courageous, which gives you more prestige than any alleged right to vote. Your opinion carries more weight than any raising of your hand [to vote in the committee]."[26]

In spite of this initial storm, Peres established good working relations with Eshkol. Still, the prime minister often taunted him about "the Young Guard" and kept asking him, "What it is that you want, exactly?" Peres answered him in a seventeen-page letter, in which he presented his outlook about the need for reforms, "a vision for the future, and not a glorification of the past." Peres also coined a phrase, which utterly unnerved the old guard. Israel, he wrote, should strive to ensure that "a simple worker—not only a lord—would own a car and would be able to afford buying a painting for his home."[27]

These words were considered iconoclastic by Mapai's elders. In their view, an automobile was a "luxury" item that no socialist worker in an egalitarian society should ever dream about. But

Peres stuck to his formula that the socialist ideologues wouldn't forgive: "a car for every worker."

AS SOON AS ESHKOL was elected prime minister and minister of defense, he radically changed his attitude toward the Dimona project. Before, he had systematically objected to the project, and to Peres's activity promoting it. But as prime minister, Eshkol became a devout supporter and ably led the struggle for its completion. He took up Peres's formula that "Israel wouldn't be the first to introduce atomic weapons into the Middle East." Eshkol was the one who received the harshest letter from Kennedy on the nuclear issue, and he answered it wisely but firmly. He also set up rules and timetables for American experts' visits to Dimona that the American president had required.

Yet Kennedy continued his crusade against nuclear-arms proliferation in the world, and especially in Israel. The president's compulsive warnings, letters, and messages threatened to cause a grave deterioration in relations with Israel. Kennedy's pressure on Israel was at its peak in November 1963 when he was assassinated in Dallas. It seems that the untimely death of the president spared Israel a grim and painful confrontation with the United States.

Kennedy's successor, Lyndon Johnson, gradually eased the pressure on Israel; Levi Eshkol, too, maneuvered prudently, and the nuclear obstacle was relegated to the sidelines of Israeli-American relations. The improved relations with the United States were celebrated on June 1, 1964, when Eshkol went to America on an official visit and was warmly received by President Johnson. The visit was very intensive, but its practical results were few. So was Eshkol's visit to Paris a few weeks later. His meeting with de Gaulle produced mostly flowery phrases and reheated statements. Nevertheless, these visits were the beginning of a turnabout in Israel's policy—from a European, mostly French orientation, which had been conceived by Ben-Gurion and Peres—to an American orientation, which was Eshkol's idea.[28]

The change had an unexpected result: it lessened Peres's impact on Israel's policy He still held the levers of power in the defense establishment, as in the time of Ben-Gurion. But America, unlike France, wasn't his exclusive domain. In Israel's governing circles there were quite a few people who knew America, its language, its customs, and the Washington scene; while in France, Germany, Italy, and other European nations Peres had no equal.

This change didn't happen overnight. At the time of the 1964 visit of Eshkol to Washington, America still supplied very small quantities of weapons to Israel. The only memorable experience that Peres went through during the Washington visit happened during the White House dinner. A rather tasteless meal (Peres blamed the kosher cooking for that) was followed by music, an endless piece by Bach that almost collapsed the entire Israeli delegation, and for cause—Eshkol and his aides hadn't slept for thirty-six hours, since they had landed in the New World.

But even Bach and the kosher meal had been but a preamble to what awaited them—dancing in the spacious hall of the White House. "The band," Peres wrote in his diary, "strikes the first notes of a Viennese waltz and a shocking, critical moment in the American-Israeli relations befalls us. The President, tall and cheerful, picks up Miriam Eshkol [the prime minister's wife] and in fast, large steps, leads her on the waxen floor. What about Mrs. Johnson? Eshkol doesn't dance. 'Ich tantz nicht' [I don't dance, in Yiddish], he declares and then points at me. 'Jungermann, you dance.' From the darkness suddenly emerges, tired and worried, Ambassador Abe Harman, and approaches me with threatening steps. 'Shimon,' he says, 'you must invite Lady Bird to dance.' It is as if the skies fall upon me. I am not sure if they're playing a waltz or a tango (and from my point of view there is not a big difference between the two), but beside that professional hesitation, I can envision already the headlines of tomorrow's papers in Israel: 'Mapai's Young Guard elbows its way to America's First Lady.' ... My stubbornness grows, but Abe is not a defeatist either and he keeps hitting me with his elbow and saying: 'Come on . . . come on . . .' " Finally, Peres resorted to a typical Mapai compromise. "I saw I couldn't resist him much longer, so I invited Zinna Harman [the ambassador's wife] to dance in the President's wake."

"Slowly the dancing area filled with couples and I finally decided that it was a waltz. At that moment we were told it was time to leave. So we left."[29]

THE MOST IMPORTANT result of that visit to Washington turned out to be an arms deal with . . . Germany. During his visit, Eshkol asked the United States for Patton tanks. The Americans refused to supply them directly to Israel, but agreed to a revolving deal: they would supply "improved Pattons" to West Germany, which would transfer to Israel 150 outdated Pattons that were still used by its army. Germany seemed worried that the transaction would leak to the media—and that it might result in a harsh reprisal by the Arab nations. Peres therefore suggested involving in the deal a third country—Italy.

Peres was on friendly terms with Italy's defense minister, Giulio Andreotti, and obtained his permission for the tanks to be transferred from Germany to Italy without engines and cannons; they would be outfitted in Italy and sent to Israel. The deal was carried through, but was almost exposed when the train carrying the tanks got stuck in an Italian tunnel, and the papers described at length the sensitive cargo loaded on the freight cars.[30] The Israelis succeeded in hushing up the affair and the tanks arrived in Israel as planned.

This was, however, the swan song in the secret relations between Israel and Germany. In October 1964, *The New York Times* published an extensive report about arms deliveries from Germany to Israel, and Chancellor Ludwig Erhard decided to discontinue all weapons shipments to the Middle East. Israel received a monetary compensation for the canceled shipments, and the German government decided to offer Israel the establishment of full diplomatic relations. The United States helped solve the crisis by supplying to Israel directly—for the first time—110 Patton tanks.[31]

Peres was very active in the negotiations with Germany. He also was deeply immersed in the nuclear endeavor and in the missile project; he had conceived both of them and was determined to see them through to their full completion.

But the gloomy shadow of the Lavon affair emerged from the recent past and swept the country again, like a huge tidal wave carrying away all that it encountered. And Peres was right there in its path.

CHAPTER 21.

SIX DAYS IN JUNE

THE LAVON AFFAIR haunted Ben-Gurion without respite. Soon after his resignation in 1963 he formally asked Eshkol for a judicial investigation of the affair.

But Eshkol refused. He wanted to put the affair behind him; he even sent Lavon a letter of rehabilitation, which angered Ben-Gurion. Eshkol also created a parliamentary block with Ahdut Ha'avoda, whose leaders were bitter rivals of Ben-Gurion and Peres. Eshkol had deviated from his old leader's views, knowing that the nation was tired of the "affair" and wanted to turn the page.

Ben-Gurion, though, felt that the moral foundations of the state would crumble if the principles of justice and the rule of law were abandoned. When he found out that Eshkol, his former loyal aide, refused to follow him, he attacked him as well. An important group of Mapai members—not the majority, however—supported his struggle.

The confrontation inside Mapai caused a rapid deterioration in relations between Shimon Peres and Levi Eshkol. Eshkol now regarded his deputy minister with growing suspicion, mostly because of Peres's absolute loyalty to Ben-Gurion.[1] Peres felt caught between a rock and a hard place, and tried to work out a compromise between Eshkol and Ben-Gurion. "In spite of all the tension," he wrote to Eshkol, "is there a possibility and a hope for a meeting between you and Ben-Gurion? Perhaps there are between you two differences of opinion, and perhaps some of them are just 'typing errors.' Perhaps they could be prevented?"[2]

Eshkol didn't answer; on the contrary, his anger at Peres, who was openly on Ben-Gurion's side, kept growing. In January 1965, on the eve of Mapai's tenth congress, Eshkol sent Peres an acrimonious "top secret and personal" letter. "From rumors that are reaching me I see that you ignore the limits on the rights of a Deputy Minister to organize political activities that are contrary to the Prime Minister's position."

"Of course there is no ban and no censorship on opinions," Eshkol continued. "[But] I am talking about a large-scale campaign, whose echoes are going far and whose ricochets are reaching me in the form of questions, reactions of surprise and displeasure by comrades and circles outside the party. You must work out a balanced approach. It is hard to accept the fact that colleagues at the government are engaged in relentless efforts to topple their Prime Minister."[3]

"Dear Eshkol," Peres wrote back. "The country is full with rumors, in all directions, and that doesn't surprise me." He presented the subjects of disagreement between them. "I am against the parliamentary block" with Ahdut Ha'avoda. "I believe that the Lavon Affair should be dealt with by the appointment of a judicial board of inquiry." Peres stressed, "You know well my feelings for D. Ben-Gurion, which stem from a combination of reasons: the deference of a party activist to his mentor; my admiration for the man, and also a deep personal attachment that I cannot and want not to discard."

Peres added that at political meetings, held on the eve of the party congress, "it is only natural that I express my views, with utmost clarity, on what I believe is right." He rejected, however, Eshkol's accusations about his "efforts" to topple the prime minister. "I continue to support you as Prime Minister," he stated. Yet he hinted that he wouldn't stay at his position at all costs. "If I am asked to choose between abandoning my views and abandoning my functions, my choice is clear."[4]

The final confrontation between Ben-Gurion and Eshkol took part at the Mapai congress, in mid-February 1965. Ben-Gurion demanded a judicial inquiry; the old guard fiercely rejected his request. The three principal speakers against Ben-Gurion were Eshkol, Golda Meir, and a dying Sharett, who was brought to the podium in a wheelchair to attack Ben-Gurion with unprecedented ferocity. At the end of his speech, Golda walked to Sharett and kissed him on the forehead. Golda herself delivered one of the harshest speeches anyone had made against Ben-Gurion. She couldn't resist launching an attack on his young protégés. "The first curse lying over the threshold of our home," she said, "occurred when people began to talk of 'favorites' and 'non-favorites.' " She then went on to a fierce attack on Ben-Gurion. The Old Man, dazed by Golda's animosity, got up and left the dais. "The ugliest thing at the Congress," he wrote in his diary, "was Golda's venomous speech. I was sorry to hear her speaking in this manner, pouring out hatred and poison.... I think she lives in a contaminated environment and drinks from muddy springs."[5]

When the congress finally voted, Ben-Gurion's motion for the judicial inquiry received 841 votes, about 40 percent, while Eshkol's motion against it got 1,246. After the congress, Eshkol adopted a harsh and hostile position toward Ben-Gurion's young supporters. As for Ben-Gurion, he declared that Eshkol was not worthy of being prime minister; he hinted that he might split Mapai and create an independent list for the following elections. (A "list" was a list of candidates running together at a parliamentary election.) Eshkol turned to Ben-Gurion's supporters in the government and demanded them "to draw the obvious conclusions."[6]

Shimon Peres realized that his days at the head of the defense ministry were drawing to an end. He didn't want to resign. In those very days, according to foreign reports, the first Jericho missiles that Israel had ordered from France arrived safely and the construction of the nuclear reactor was completed. He wanted to stay on his job. But finally, he and Yossef Almogi, another minister who supported Ben-Gurion, had to tender their resignations.[7]

For the first time in eighteen years, Peres found himself unemployed, and detached from the defense establishment.

PERES NOW DECIDED to organize the "minority"—the 40 percent of Mapai activists who had voted for Ben-Gurion's motion at the party congress. He succeeded in getting a large suite at the El Al building in Tel Aviv and established there the minority headquarters. Very quickly a group of young leaders formed around Ben-Gurion. Among them were Moshe Dayan, Yitzhak Navon, Teddy Kollek, the writer S. Izhar, and others. The "minority" leaders were opposed to splitting the party; they disagreed with Ben-Gurion's harsh attacks on Eshkol and his entourage. But Ben-Gurion decided to split Mapai anyway and run for the Knesset at the head of an independent list. To Haim Israeli, his devoted aide, he said, "What really matters for me is whether Moshe and Shimon will come with me."[8]

Moshe and Shimon, however, were determined to prevent a schism in Mapai. When the Old Man realized that Dayan and Peres might foil his plans, he took things into his own hands. He invited the minority leaders to an urgent meeting at his home. On the evening of June 29, forty-five people met in Ben-Gurion's modest house at Keren Kayemet Boulevard, in Tel Aviv. Peres chaired the small assembly gathered in the library. Right after his opening remarks, Ben-Gurion intervened and declared, "This meeting is a meeting of people who want to establish an independent list."[9] He then read to his guests a platform of nine paragraphs that he had prepared beforehand.

Peres objected to the unusual procedure, but Ben-Gurion dismissed him and appointed somebody else as chairman of the meeting. Peres paled, deeply hurt by the Old Man's behavior. Dayan and a couple of other leading activists firmly objected to the proposed split, but Ben-Gurion ignored them. "Most of the comrades present wish to establish an independent list," the Old Man forcefully said, "and so it was decided."[10] Ben-Gurion named the newborn party Rafi—a name formed by the initials of Reshimat Poalei Israel (Israel Workers' List). He also decided to release a statement to the press. Peres tried in vain to postpone the press release, hoping that he and his friends might still prevent the split. But Ben-Gurion didn't give him a chance. Finally, Peres and another minority leader sat in a corner and drafted a short statement about the creation of Rafi. That same night, the sensational news was broadcast on the radio.

Peres went home, mortified and deeply offended. True, he disagreed with Eshkol, but he also disagreed with Ben-Gurion's attacks on his successor. Besides, he knew a great secret: the Dimona reactor was about to enter the stage of advanced activity. According to the French historian Pierre Péan, the first experiments in extracting plutonium began "in the second half of 1965."[11] Could Peres leave all that and the defense work he loved so? And yet, could he forsake Ben-Gurion, whom he had admired and followed since his youth?

In the early morning he was awakened by a telephone call. It was Ben-Gurion. He wanted to come to Peres's home right away to apologize for his conduct the previous night. He was in a state of utter tension, he said. That was why he had behaved so rudely.

"You shouldn't bother to come to me," Peres answered. "I'll come to you." When he entered Ben-Gurion's house, the Old Man embraced him and again apologized profusely. Ben-Gurion added that he wouldn't be able to set up the new party without Peres and Dayan. Peres decided on the spot "that my loyalty to Ben-Gurion took priority over everything else—including my belief that he was making the wrong decision."[12]

It turned out that there was nobody else to manage Rafi. Moshe Dayan hurriedly set out on a long trip to Africa. Peres became Rafi's secretary general, with the task of preparing the new party for the elections, slated to occur in three months.

In an article he wrote a few days later, Peres called Ben-Gurion's struggle "a moral combat, a combat to repair an injustice and a distortion of the law." He also defended Ben-Gurion's attacks on Eshkol. "Many would have loved to see Ben-Gurion fight without really fighting," he wrote. "They are pleased seeing 'a tiger' on the battlefield, but they are disappointed when their caresses don't transform him into a house kitten."[13]

RAFI'S COFFERS WERE EMPTY and Peres had to find contributors. The first check that arrived in the mail, for 150 Israeli pounds, was signed by a young paratrooper officer, Rafael (Raful) Eitan.[14] Eitan was a future IDF chief of staff and a minister of agriculture. Al Schwimmer, the aircraft industries' director, came to Peres with a check for fifty thousand pounds. Peres returned the money after learning that Schwimmer had secretly mortgaged his home to help Rafi. Peres himself had to mortgage his refrigerator to get a few pounds for expenses.[15] Ben-Gurion, too, contributed large sums of money from his own pocket to finance some Rafi events.

From the day of its creation, Rafi raised two flags. One was Ben-Gurion's campaign for investigating the Lavon affair and restoring the nation's moral fiber. The other was Peres's platform pointing toward Israel's future: development of science, industrialization of the country, bridging social gaps, promoting higher education, populating desert areas, reforming the electoral system—in short, Peres had conceived a dream of building a new, better Israel than the one described in Mapai's obsolete slogans. Mapai's leaders doggedly attacked Peres for "not being a socialist." As in the past, he was ahead of his time. Only a few years later, his ideas about science and research, or "a car for every worker," turned into a typical component of Israel's social profile.

Shimon Peres started building Rafi all alone. After a short while, though, Moshe Dayan returned from Africa and joined as well. The summer of 1965 was Rafi's finest hour. It sparked hope, attracted young people, and impressed the public with the exceptional group of people who had joined it. Peres was the major figure at every Rafi event, and Sonia was with him wherever he went. She even sewed the window curtains for the Rafi headquarters, which had been established in an old building on Ha Yarkon Street, a stone's throw from the Mapai Center.

Peres was a one-man show in every sense: he spoke at countless meetings, wrote articles in the papers, supervised the drafting of the party platform, raised money, and represented the party at any public forum, debate, or media event.

The electoral campaign soon became an ugly and bitter combat. The leaders of Mapai and Rafi kept slinging mud at one another, and the nation watched, stunned, the brutal dispute between these former friends and allies.

When the campaign was at its peak, things got worse. At a parlor meeting in Tel Aviv, Ben-Gurion revealed classified information about a reprisal raid on the West Bank village of Kibiya in 1953, where fifty Jordanian citizens had been killed. That was upsetting, but not in the least like what Shimon Peres apparently did. When he learned that Eshkol had authorized visits of American experts to Dimona, Peres assailed the government, using veiled hints about the reactor and Israel's nuclear policy. Both Peres and Ben-Gurion were treading on very risky ground, as the public discussion of sensitive matters could be very harmful to Israel. A very upset Eshkol dispatched a letter to Peres. "Are you out of your minds?" he wrote. "What is Ben-Gurion doing by speaking about Kibiya, what are you doing by speaking about Dimona?"

"I even received information in your name—from different sources—that you say I intended to sell Dimona! Is there no limit to setting fires and poisoning wells?"[16]

Peres wrote back, claiming that the information quoted by Eshkol was nothing but "malicious libel."[17]

The election took place on November 2. Its results stunned Rafi. The new party that had hoped to win between fifteen and twenty-five seats barely got ten seats in the Knesset. The united front of Mapai and Ahdut Ha'avoda, on the other hand, achieved a significant victory: forty-five seats. The masses had turned their backs on Ben-Gurion and expressed their confidence in Levi Eshkol.

And Peres, the man of action, of vision, of great dreams and great projects, was exiled to the opposition benches and paid the heaviest price for the creation of Rafi.

PERES ENTERED A SAD and depressing period in his life. He had to manage a small, poor party and devote valuable time to petty politics; at the Knesset he didn't stop attacking the government, causing Eshkol to remark that he was even worse than Begin. He watched from afar his successor at the defense ministry, Tzevi Dinstein, carry out extensive reforms in the ministry structure and in the rules he had established. Rabin, the IDF chief of staff, rejected Peres's views on Israel's capacity to produce her own weapons and halted the efforts he had initiated.

The nuclear project continued without Peres. According to foreign sources, on November 2, 1966, the secret test of a nuclear device took place.[18] American intelligence sources assumed that Israel was assembling an atomic bomb. And Shimon Peres, who had devoted to the Dimona project almost ten years of his life, now had to watch, from the outside, the realization of his dream. Instead of managing the gigantic complex he had built, he now had to wander between seedy party branches, solve the personal problems and petty quarrels of branch secretaries and undersecretaries, and preach Rafi's message to sparse and skeptical audiences. When a friend would come to visit, Peres would sit with him on the sundrenched roof of Rafi's decrepit headquarters and declare that "he felt free and full of energy, like a colt."[19] The truth was that he felt bitter and frustrated for being away from the reins of power and the vital functions that once had been his.[20]

During these bitter years, Peres became convinced that being in the parliamentary opposition was a sterile and worthless occupation. He was a man of action, not of flowery speeches from the

Knesset podium. True, he made pertinent speeches; he knew how to be blunt, sarcastic, and brutal when needed. But his heart was not there. "Shimon was ready to form a coalition with anybody," Minister Haim Ramon said of him years later, "only to get away from the opposition. 'If I am there, I exist,' Shimon said about participating in the government—'and if I'm not there, I don't exist.' "[21] Because of this attitude, Peres didn't spare any effort in the coming years to join the government or form an alternative coalition. Any ally was good for that purpose, and any alliance preferable to the frustration of a man of action watching others do the job—and knowing he could do it better.

ON MAY 15, 1967, while Israel was celebrating its Independence Day, Egypt's President Nasser suddenly ordered his armored divisions to advance into Sinai and boastfully threatened Israel with annihilation. MiG jets landed in droves on Sinai's airfields, and the media was inundated with photographs of planes, tanks, and Egyptian commandos on their way to destroy "the Zionist entity." Israel, which had gotten accustomed to a relatively calm existence, was stunned by Nasser's moves. For almost eleven years the southern border had been peaceful; now, suddenly, the nation had to face a grave crisis that threatened its very existence.

Nasser had been alerted by Soviet intelligence that Israel intended to invade Syria, with whom she had clashed several times that spring. The information was absolutely false, but Nasser didn't bother to verify it and rushed his army to the Sinai to deter Israel. From that moment on, Nasser's bravado dimmed his sense and he crossed the point of no return: he expelled the U.N. peacekeepers from Sinai and Gaza, closed the Strait of Tiran to Israeli shipping, and signed a military pact with Jordan and Syria. On the television screens, throngs of Egyptians danced in the streets like possessed beings, chanting slogans about Israel's destruction, while a confident Nasser intensified his threats. On May 19, after additional armor moved toward the

Israeli border, Chief of Staff Rabin ordered a partial mobilization of reservists.

A large majority of Israelis felt that Egypt's moves endangered their existence and that the only way to survive was by going to war against Nasser and crushing him in the Sinai. That was Moshe Dayan's opinion as well. But Ben-Gurion, fearing a new war and settling old accounts, bluntly accused Eshkol of causing the crisis. He even summoned Rabin and harshly criticized him for having mobilized the reservists. The truth was that the eighty-one-year-old Ben-Gurion was no longer the farsighted statesman he had once been. "He lives in a past world," Dayan wrote. "He admires de Gaulle, exaggerates Nasser's power, doesn't appreciate the tremendous force of the IDF." Ben-Gurion feared a long war on three fronts, with many casualties; he therefore concluded that Israel shouldn't risk a war at this time.[22]

Ben-Gurion's position, though, wasn't known to the public. On the contrary, the media again depicted him as a courageous, decisive leader, perhaps the only man capable of facing Nasser at this fateful hour. Worried by Eshkol's indecision, many influential figures launched the idea of bringing Ben-Gurion back to the helm. On May 24, the day after Nasser blocked the Strait of Tiran, Menachem Begin approached Peres in the Knesset. Begin, for years a fierce opponent of Ben-Gurion, now asked Peres if Ben-Gurion, at his age, would agree to resume the leadership of the country. Peres answered, "I have no doubt that Ben-Gurion is capable to lead the country." The leaders of the right-wing Gahal bloc, the National Religious Party, and Rafi met to discuss a common policy, including reinstating Ben-Gurion as prime minister. Peres then tried to persuade Ben-Gurion to take on the job, in a national unity government, with Eshkol as his deputy. The Old Man finally agreed.

The man who refused, though, was Eshkol. "These two horses," he said to Begin, "won't pull that cart together."

Ben-Gurion continued expounding his pessimistic views; Dayan and several Rafi leaders rejected his analysis outright.

Once again it was Peres, the last loyalist, who flew to the succor of his mentor. In a long speech before the Rafi parliamentary group, Peres explained why he objected to Israel's going to war. His arguments mirrored Ben-Gurion's analysis to the smallest detail and starkly contradicted Dayan's opinions. Peres also stressed that Eshkol wasn't the right person to be prime minister and defense minister now. "I want a prime minister and defense minister," Peres declared, "who, in spite of everybody saying yes to going to war, can be brave enough to say: not now!"[23]

PERES RELENTLESSLY STRIVED to form an alternative coalition, but his initiative was doomed from the start. Moshe Dayan rebelled against the Old Man and rejected his ideas. The people wanted a strong, decisive government that would lead Israel to war and dispel the nightmare that had descended upon the country.

Peres had convinced the doves in the body politic to support Ben-Gurion, but other leaders moved away from him. On May 27, Menachem Begin and his colleagues went to Ben-Gurion's house, but on hearing his views they were deeply disappointed. They dropped the idea of making Ben-Gurion prime minister again.

That evening was the moment when Peres, unconsciously at first, started moving away from Ben-Gurion. He realized that the Old Man couldn't assume the nation's leadership anymore. He now focused all his energy into making Moshe Dayan defense minister.

The following day, May 28, Peres and another Rafi leader, Yossef Almogi, met with Golda Meir. She was now secretary general of Mapai. Peres said to her that for the good of the nation, Dayan should be appointed defense minister. He added a phrase that infuriated Almogi: "If the independent existence of Rafi prevents the realization of our proposal, Rafi would be ready to return to Mapai without conditions."[24]

In the meantime, the turmoil in Israel intensified. Officers in the IDF High Command learned that on May 23, Chief of Staff

Rabin had collapsed and had to recover at home for more than a day. After thirty-six hours, on May 25, he finally returned to his job, but he was now crestfallen and insecure.

In Mapai a veritable rebellion took place when major leaders demanded of Eshkol that he entrust the defense portfolio to Dayan's hands. Eshkol and his people used every possible maneuver to deny Dayan the defense position. Eshkol sent a message to Peres, inviting him to join the government as minister without portfolio.[25] It was a tempting offer—Peres could now return to the select group of the nation's leaders, this time as a government minister!

But he rejected the idea at once. Rafi has one candidate for minister, he said, and that was Moshe Dayan.

Finally, Eshkol gave up, and on June 1 he asked Moshe Dayan to join a national unity government as minister of defense. Menachem Begin and Yossef Sapir from Gahal joined the government as ministers without portfolio.

NOW PERES HAD to carry out a most painful task: obtaining Ben-Gurion's approval. He went to the house on Keren Kayemet Boulevard.[26] "Ben-Gurion," Peres said, "I did all that I could, but except for Rafi, no party supports the idea of removing Eshkol. The appointment of Moshe Dayan as defense minister is the maximum we can achieve. The war is imminent, and with Moshe as defense minister we have the best chance to win."

"And Eshkol will remain prime minister?" Ben-Gurion asked.

"Yes," Peres said.

Ben-Gurion's expression suddenly changed, and Peres felt a wave of fury surging in the Old Man. He exploded "like an eruption of lava."

"I thought you were a friend—and you're not," Ben-Gurion roared. "I thought you were a statesman—and you're not. I thought you knew how to negotiate—and you don't. How could you give up the most important change that had to be made, Eshkol's replacement?" The Old Man kept furiously lashing at

Peres, who stood in front of him, his face chalk white. Ben-Gurion had never yelled at him like this.

This was "one of the worst moments" in Peres's life. He had done everything to satisfy Ben-Gurion's demands. "I had worked tirelessly, making new enemies, losing old friends, creating a weird coalition of disparate parties, rejecting the various temptations and blandishments that had been offered to me—and this was my reward? To hear from the man I so much admired that I was no longer his friend?"

"Ben-Gurion," Peres quietly said. "I want to ask you a question. You have often said that if all the ideals of the world were to be placed on one scale of the balance, and on the other, Israel's security, security would prevail. Is this rule binding for us only, or for you as well?" The threat to Israel's security was the primary concern right now, Peres added.

Ben-Gurion looked stunned. "Perhaps you're right," he finally said.

That evening, Ben-Gurion opened a meeting of Rafi's leaders by saying, "Shimon did a great job for the country's sake, and did it successfully. He was the only one who acted without even a drop of self-interest." Ben-Gurion added: "I don't remember anybody who refused an offer to be a minister—so that his friend would be one."[27] Ben-Gurion expressed his support for the appointment of Dayan as defense minister.

Rafi agreed to Eshkol's offer and the news spread through the country like wildfire. But Peres's via dolorosa wasn't over yet. Ben-Gurion insisted that Peres tell Eshkol that Rafi still maintained that he was not worthy of being prime minister; in spite of joining his government, Rafi would pursue its efforts to replace him.

"There was no option for me but to swallow this final indignity," Peres wrote.[28] The following day he went to Eshkol's office with Yitzhak Navon. "My knees felt weak," he wrote. "I was about to do something that made me heartily uncomfortable."

First, Peres and Navon informed Eshkol that Rafi had decided to join his government with Dayan as defense minister.

"But there is something I must add," Peres said and fell silent. Eshkol noticed he was sweating and his face had suddenly flushed. Peres knew he was going to hurt a man whom he loved and respected.

"Well, *Jungermann*," Eshkol urged him, "say what you want to say."

"I have to tell you, in the name of Rafi, that we think you are not worthy of being prime minister."

Eshkol took Peres's words rather lightly. I understand that's your position, he said. Perhaps you'll change it one day.[29]

Peres felt emboldened and asked to remain alone with Eshkol for a few minutes.

"Eshkol," he said, "you and Ben-Gurion have fought enough. There is going to be a war. Go to Ben-Gurion, ask him to fly to America, to France, and explain our views to the presidents and the governments of these countries."

"*Stenna shwoie*"—"Wait a moment"—Eshkol said in Arabic. "And what if Ben-Gurion refuses?"

"If you agree," Peres said, "I'll go to him right away and I'll talk to him."

But Eshkol's answer was negative. Peres understood: the quarrel between the two men would last till their deaths.[30]

PERES ALSO REALIZED that Dayan's ascension to the position of defense minister signified a change in Rafi's leadership. "I knew in my heart," he wrote, "that the inevitable had happened. The scepter had been passed from the man we all admired the most—to his disciple, the man who [Ben-Gurion] felt, as did almost the entire nation, should lead our group in the future."[31]

A few days later, Peres had a last-minute idea to prevent the war. According to certain sources, he went to Eshkol and suggested that Israel carry out a widely publicized nuclear test. It would show the Arabs and the world how powerful Israel was, he said; that way, the Arabs might be deterred from any aggressive action, and perhaps the war could be avoided.[32] His suggestion was rejected.

Faithful to the strategy conceived by Peres, Israel never admitted that it had become a nuclear power. Years later, though, a strange event seemed to crown Peres's relentless efforts and to mark Israel's joining the atomic club. A flash in the southern Indian Ocean, detected by a satellite on September 22, 1979, was allegedly the result of an Israeli-South African nuclear test. Israel, however, kept firmly denying the sensational news.*

On June 5, Israel went to war. Peres followed with excitement the stunning victories of the IDF. Dayan often briefed him on the situation in the war theaters, and Peres learned about the success of the "Moked" operation—the annihilation of the Arab air forces on the ground, and about the IDF victories in the Sinai, the West Bank, the Golan, and Jerusalem. He pursued his political activities, but now he played a different tune. Since he had transferred his support to Dayan, he didn't repeat anymore the moderate, Ben-Gurion-inspired views against going to war.

Yet he felt deep frustration. He was now merely an observer at the great drama that shook the Middle East and the world. His friend Moshe Dayan led Israel to a brilliant victory and reaped its fruits, while he sat on the sidelines, deprived of any official function, far from the decision-making meetings and the war rooms.

At the end of the Six Day War, Peres went to Jerusalem with David Ben-Gurion. Together they stood, facing the Western Wall, and raised their eyes to its ancient stones. And the picture of the two, looking at the eternal Wall and at thousands of years of Jewish history, is perhaps the most fitting to conclude the chapter of their close association. From now on, Peres wouldn't be Ben-Gurion's devoted aide; he would follow Dayan, with the same loyalty and the same devotion, for Dayan was the man he admired the most after Ben-Gurion.

A few months later, on January 21, 1968, the Israel Labor Party was created. Shimon Peres and Moshe Dayan led Rafi back to Mapai. Moshe Dayan remained minister of defense, and Shimon

Peres was elected deputy secretary general of the united Labor Party; Golda Meir was elected secretary general.

Ben-Gurion didn't join the Labor Party.

ESHKOL DIED SUDDENLY on February 26, 1969. Golda Meir was elected as his successor and led the Labor Party to victory at the October 1969 elections, even though she lost seven Knesset seats. On December 15, Peres was appointed minister in Golda Meir's cabinet.

Golda didn't appoint Peres out of excessive love or appreciation. The appointment was a result of the blunt pressure of Moshe Dayan, which was accompanied—all along the electoral campaign—with heavy hints about a new split and the possibility of Dayan's running at the head of a new party. After the Six Day War, Dayan had become the most admired man in Israel. Alarmed by his popularity, Mapai's leaders were ready to pay any price to satisfy him, and Golda had no choice but swallow the bitter pill and promote Peres to a ministerial position.

On his return to the country's leadership, Peres realized that the political setup had radically changed since he had left in 1965. Israel after the Six Day War was a different country—strong, confident, controlling vast territories. The IDF was now fighting a bitter war of attrition on the eastern front against terrorists coming from Jordan, and on the Suez Canal with the Egyptian Army, supported by the Soviet Union. The Israelis were still intoxicated by the Six Day's victories and felt invincible; that was why they rejected any concessions for peace, and spoke in biblical terms about the rebirth of King Solomon's empire. Only the old Ben-Gurion maintained that in exchange for peace, Israel should give back all the occupied territories, except for Jerusalem and the Golan Heights.

The international scene was unrecognizable as well. France's President de Gaulle didn't conceal his anger toward Israel for not having listened to him on the eve of the war, when he advised it "not to fire the first shot." He imposed a strict embargo on the sale of weapons to Israel; in a few years, the French sources of military equipment would totally dry up. But by ending its alliance with Israel, France also lost its influence in the Middle East. That error of de Gaulle's was never corrected.

Unlike de Gaulle, President Lyndon Johnson started supplying Israel with modern weapons, which was a revolution in American foreign policy. The tiny stream turned into a mighty surge after the Six Day War, and the United States soon became the main weapons provider to Israel. The European orientation of Shimon Peres was therefore seriously eroded; his prestige as the man who could obtain weapons and friends for Israel was eroded as well. The United States had become the main source for weapons and financial support for Israel—and that was not Peres's doing.

IN GOLDA MEIR'S cabinet, Peres was appointed minister without portfolio.

But the minister without portfolio soon became the portfolios champion. At first, Dayan charged him with the development of the West Bank and Gaza. At the same time, Golda appointed him acting absorption minister. Eight months later, she appointed him minister of transportation and postmaster general.

Peres left his thumbprints at each of those ministries. As absorption minister he started planning an international university in Jerusalem and worked on settling new immigrants in the capital and a speeded-up housing program for new immigrants, financed by American Jewish investors.[33] As minister for West Bank affairs he initiated a project for improving the living conditions in the refugee camps, and built industrial parks on the former borders to provide work for the Palestinians. In the Gaza refugee camps he built hundreds of new houses. He also promised the Gaza inhabitants that he would build a new wharf at their port. They told him, "We are tired of all the promises we've heard in the past from the Turks, the British, the Egyptians—and now from you." Peres answered, "Let the stones talk, not the mouths." Four months later, the new wharf was inaugurated.[34]

When he moved to the postal ministry he changed its name to the Ministry of Communications, built a satellite-communication installation at Haela Valley, installed emergency phones along the roads, and introduced electronic sorting of mail. He suggested to Golda that the telephone and mail departments be turned into autonomous public companies. "Who is going to support that idea?" Golda asked in wonder.[35] Today, both the telephones and the mail service are managed by autonomous companies.

In the transportation ministry he was among the initiators of Ayalon Freeway, a fast highway system serving the Tel Aviv metropolitan area. He conceived a system of fast train service in the center of the country, and started raising funds for a subway system in Tel Aviv; he persuaded Japanese and Canadian investors to join the project.

"As far as ideas were concerned, he was a fountainhead," his chief of staff, Aliza Eshed, said. "But as soon as he moved to another ministry, he would discard [what he was doing] and didn't care if somebody else continued implementing his plans after him. Why didn't he keep fighting for his ideas at the government level? He was minister till 1977. He really had wonderful ideas that could have been carried out."

"That's the problem with Shimon. He doesn't bring things to completion, to a finish. I would ask him, why didn't we do this or that? It was a wonderful idea. He would answer, let it be, the past doesn't interest me."[36]

* Nuclear Weapons Database, Israeli Nuclear Delivery systems, http://www.cdi.org/issues/nukef&f/database/isnukes.html, Dec. 1996.

PART 4.

_____

THE FANTASY COUNCIL

_____

CHAPTER 22.

THE LONG DUEL (I)

ON THE DAY OF ATONEMENT, October 6, 1973, at 6 A.M., the phone rang at Shimon Peres's home. Haim Israeli, the defense minister's aide, asked him to come to Moshe Dayan's office right away. Peres rushed to the Ministry of Defense. At 4 A.M., Dayan told him, intelligence reports had arrived that indicated that Egypt and Syria were about to attack Israel. He asked Peres to mobilize the two ministries he managed—transportation and communications—and make them a part of the emergency military setup.

At 2 P.M., the Syrians launched an offensive on the Golan Heights, and the Egyptians crossed the Suez Canal into Sinai. The Yom Kippur War had started.

This war was different from Israel's previous wars. Israel suffered heavy blows along the fortified line at the Suez Canal; in the Golan, the Syrian Army almost succeeded in breaching the last Israeli line of defense. Peres was shaken by the heavy casualties. Many of his closest friends, such as Elhanan Yishai, Rafael Vardi, Arthur Ben-Nathan, and Sam Avital, lost their sons in battle.

Peres was impressed by the crossing of the Suez Canal by General Ariel Sharon. The Labor ministers kept vilifying Arik Sharon and named his unit "the Likud Division," after the Likud right-wing bloc that he had founded. Sharon had then abandoned politics to return to army service. But Peres, as always, had warm feelings for Sharon. "As for myself, I trust Arik and believe in him," he wrote. "He is a formidable doer, his inventions cannot be ignored, he loves battle and in battle he loves to advance. The gist of the battle in his eyes is pressing forward."[1]

During the war Dayan's image was somewhat tarnished in Peres's eyes. He heard from Dayan some overly pessimistic statements, and didn't get satisfactory answers to his questions about the IDF deployment and the plans to defend the Sinai against an Egyptian attack. He also rejected Dayan's glum forecasts. In one cabinet meeting, after Israel had checked the enemy's advance, Dayan again presented a dark report to his colleagues. He then asked Peres if he hadn't sounded too pessimistic. "Yes," Peres answered. "You should be more balanced in your reports. I love your devotion to the truth, but there is also the issue of morale."[2]

But Peres himself was not immune to the depressing news about the deaths of his friends' sons. His heart "was broken" when he learned about the death of Amnon Ben-Nathan, "tall and handsome like his father." He wrote in his diary: "That's the end of a young man full of promise, the destruction of a family and the misery of a nation."

And from the personal tragedy of his friend, he turned to the national mourning. "The number of casualties is on the rise, day by day .... This is the high and horrible price paid by a generation of Israelis who were allegedly born in our most splendid age—and were cast into the crudest war, where they showed supreme courage and intelligence."

"I return home, barely holding back my tears, and Sonia bursts out crying at the sight of our prisoners of war, shown on Jordanian television. Their hands are tied behind their backs, they are barefoot and unshaven." Peres was very worried for the soldiers captured by the Syrians, "who are absolutely inhuman."[3]

But when the war ended, the IDF had advanced deep into Egyptian territory and surrounded Egypt's Third Army; in the Golan Heights, Israeli armor and artillery had moved close to

Syria's capital, Damascus. Now a long and tough negotiation was about to start while the nation was mourning its twenty-seven hundred soldiers fallen in battle. It also mourned David Ben-Gurion, who died a few weeks after the end of the war. The myth of Israel's invincibility had been shattered; many Israelis were convinced that the government was guilty of a momentous mishap by not foreseeing the enemy's preparations for war, and by its delayed reactions during the fateful hours of October 6.

Many accused the government, in particular the defense minister and his generals, of terrible miscalculations that had brought a bloody war upon Israel. Articles in the newspapers, protests in the streets, heartbreaking sights during the funerals—all those foretold the approaching storm. True, at the December 31 elections, the Labor and Mapam alignment won again, but the long-contained fury exploded in early 1974. The nation demanded a board of inquiry that would establish who was to blame for the lack of foresight that led to the war. Golda Meir objected at first, but finally the board was created, under the chairmanship of Supreme Court justice Shimon Agranat.

Dayan was downcast and restless. People protested against him, shook their fists at him, spat in his direction. He didn't know how to cope with the harsh criticism that also reached the Labor Party's higher levels; many party activists demanded his resignation. Dayan refused to join the new Golda Meir government, and Peres—loyal to the very end—declared that he wouldn't join the government, either. Golda Meir was desperate, but also furious. She threw at Peres and Dayan, "You have no right to go, not at this time and not away from your jobs!"[4]

Golda decided to appoint a new defense minister, and chose Yitzhak Rabin, who until recently had been Israel's ambassador to the United States. At the very last moment, though, Dayan changed his mind. He told Peres that IDF intelligence had compiled a report about threatening movements of the Syrian Army that could herald the resumption of combat operations. Dayan and Peres went to Golda and informed her that because of the danger of the war continuing, they had decided to stay in the government. Many thought that Dayan's decision resulted from the imminent appointment of Rabin as his successor. But Golda was deeply moved and burst into tears. "That's the best present I could have asked for," she said to Dayan and Peres.[5]

Golda Meir's new government won the Knesset confidence vote on March 10, 1974. Peres was appointed minister of information, Rabin minister of labor. But this was not the end of the crisis. When Golda and Dayan arrived at the military cemetery at Mount Herzl to participate in a memorial service for soldiers fallen in the war, they were heckled by bereaved parents shouting at them, "Murderers!"

These shouts, more than anything else, proved that Golda Meir's government had reached the end of the road.

ON APRIL 10, 1974, in the Knesset caucus room, Golda faced her rebellious parliamentary group. The tension was high, the Knesset members were in turmoil, and angry shouts echoed throughout the room. A few days before, the Agranat inquiry board had published its report on the Yom Kippur War, but the public wouldn't accept its findings. The chief of staff, the head of intelligence, the head of the Southern Command, and other senior officers had been fired. The military leadership had been severely punished, but the political one—which meant in particular Moshe Dayan—had sailed through the drama with flying colors. The protest spread throughout the country, and many demanded Dayan's resignation. Golda tried to protect him, but became entangled in an impossible situation. The rebellious spirit finally pervaded the Labor parliamentary group as well; some demanded Dayan's resignation, others the resignation of the entire government and new elections.

Golda got up to answer her critics. "I ask the comrades to believe me that even if Dayan had decided to resign or to move to another position, I would have announced what I am about to announce now . . . . I am resigning. I cannot carry that burden anymore. Don't try to convince me. I've reached the end of the road."[6]

So saying, she left the room.

The news of Golda's resignation sent shock waves throughout the nation. Pinhas Sapir, a close friend of Golda's and the most powerful old guard leader, seemed her likely successor. The very mention of his name, though, triggered angry opposition among ex-Rafi members. Sapir had fought Rafi all along the way and was a stark opponent of Peres and Dayan. For many he symbolized Mapai's moral degradation.

Many Rafi activists again started speaking of splitting the party and going their own way. But it was clear to them that Dayan, whose image had been badly damaged, wouldn't be a major figure in the confrontation with Sapir. For the first time since 1967, Dayan didn't lead. Thus a vacuum was created at the head of Rafi. Shimon Peres, by a bold move, jumped into that vacuum.

He informed his friends that he intended to run against Sapir for the premiership. The electors were the 560 members of the Labor Party Central Committee.

To many, Peres's decision seemed sheer madness. Sapir, after all, controlled the entire party apparatus; former members of Mapai and Ahdut Ha'avoda would certainly vote for him. Rafi was nothing but a small faction, with only 24 percent in the Labor Party institutions. But Peres was determined. His time had come to reach for the leadership.

This was also a symptom of his liberation from Dayan and Ben-Gurion. He said to a Rafi colleague, Gad Yaacobi: "Since the days of Working Youth this is the first time when I can act according to my own judgment, and not by the judgment of Ben-Gurion and Dayan. For the first time I feel that I am standing on my own feet."[7]

Sapir, though, announced that he didn't want the job that everyone expected him to take. In a long talk into the night with Yitzhak Rabin, Sapir said to him, "If I had to choose between being Prime Minister and jumping from the tenth floor, I would have jumped . . . . I am telling you, Yitzhak: I shall not be Prime Minister! Run for Prime Minister, and I shall support you!"[8]

Golda agreed, without excessive enthusiasm, to support Rabin; other major Mapai figures also joined the Rabin camp. The old guard decided to support Rabin; for the first time in Israel's history they had no candidate of their own. Rabin had several important advantages: he had just returned from Washington and was not involved in any way in the Yom Kippur mishap. Rabin had an impressive military record and international experience, which he had acquired during his diplomatic service in Washington. He was gifted with a clear and organized mind, even though he was utterly conventional and lacking imagination. He had the authentic roughness of a Sabra. He was sincere and frank, even blunt, in his public declarations; he was basically honest and fair, always said what he thought, and stuck to the truth even if it was unpleasant. Many people loved him most for his brutal honesty and truthfulness. Aliza Goren, who was both Rabin's and Peres's adviser, noted that "Yitzhak always impressed people who met him with the idea that he was real: what they saw and heard was what they got. With Shimon, it's always packaged, sophisticated; he is multilayered and multifaceted."[9]

During the War of Independence, Rabin was a handsome, blond, and blue-eyed officer who served as Yigal Allon's deputy at the head of the Palmach. He married the beautiful Leah and they emerged as the typical couple of the new Israelis, like those who appeared on the posters of the United Jewish Appeal. Golda Meir and Ben-Gurion liked Rabin mostly because of his mother, Rosa Cohen, a workers' leader and former Russian revolutionary who had carried her dreams and her ideology to the Land of Israel.

Yet Rabin's candidacy was not devoid of doubts. He was not an active member of the Labor Party and was supposed to be close to Ahdut Ha'avoda because of his service in the Palmach. He had no political experience and only recently had been appointed minister for the first time in his life. He was a distant, introverted man, lacking warmth and patience with people; he was of a cynical and utterly suspicious character. He was interested only in issues of foreign affairs and security. He despised politicians and said so more than once. He was a mediocre speaker and his sense of humor was rather poor. His rivals claimed that his main flaw was his strange lack of sensitivity to human and social problems; some of them sarcastically labeled him "autistic." Some accused him of giving lectures during his tour of duty as ambassador to the United States for honorariums that he kept for himself; he didn't deny that.[10] Golda Meir also feared that he might not be able to function well under pressure, as had been the case on the eve of the Six Day War.[11] But she finally decided to back him for another reason that to her was crucial: he seemed to be the only candidate who could defeat Shimon Peres.

Rabin's throwing his hat into the political arena was received with enthusiasm. He carried about him the aura of having been the Six Day War chief of staff, and of a talented diplomat who had reaped many a success in Washington. When he made his maiden speech to the central committee of the party, the audience cheered and applauded him warmly.

There was no love lost between Rabin and Peres. In the past, Peres had confronted Rabin on the issues of research, development, and local production of weapons in Israel.[12] The two also clashed on the issues of purchasing a mega-computer for the IDF and Mirage jets for the air force. Rabin was skeptical about the nuclear project. Before the Six Day War they disagreed on foreign-policy issues as well. Peres was committed to the French orientation, and wanted to buy as much equipment as France could provide; Rabin, however, preached an orientation toward America, even though at that time Washington rejected most of Israel's requests.

In January 1963, Peres suggested to Ben-Gurion that he not appoint Rabin as IDF chief of staff. He didn't say so explicitly, but pointed out that there were two disadvantages in the appointment: One, he said, Rabin was indecisive; and two, you would be handing the army over to a political group.[13] He knew that Ben-Gurion would listen to that kind of argument. Ben-Gurion also thought that Rabin was "too cautious,"[14] and his connections with Ahdut Ha'avoda disturbed and angered him. Yet Ben-Gurion liked Yitzhak Rabin. Because of his political connections, Ben-Gurion had delayed his promotion; but when Tzvi Tzur was appointed chief of staff, Ben-Gurion appointed Rabin as his deputy and head of operations.

Peres wrote in his diary: "Lunch with Cherra [Tzvi Tzur]. He is worried by Rabin's appointment—and he is right."[15] Very soon, Tzur and Rabin were at odds, and Tzur even tried to fire Rabin from his position. Still, Ben-Gurion promised Rabin that he was next in line, and indeed, in January 1964, Eshkol appointed him chief of staff. Rabin wrote in his *Memoirs* that when he told Peres about Ben-Gurion's promise, "Peres paled."[16] In an interview, Peres fired back. "Rabin must be color-blind," he said.

When Rabin was chief of staff and Peres deputy defense minister, they often clashed. "Shimon had a problem with the chiefs of staff who refused to accept his authority," said Avraham Ben-Yossef, a former director general of the defense ministry. "I wouldn't say there was hatred between them at that time; it was mostly a rivalry, a struggle for status."

But their diverging views were not a secret. "The objection to the building of the nuclear reactor was stronger during Yitzhak's term," Tzvi Tzur said. "He didn't fight against it, but his support couldn't be acquired. And as a matter of principle, anything that Shimon started was wrong in Rabin's eyes."[17]

PERES, INDEED, DISLIKED RABIN. But according to Dov Goldstein, the coauthor of Rabin's autobiography, Rabin felt "a crazy hatred" toward Peres. Goldstein said that "the loathing and the hatred of Rabin toward Peres were one thousand times fiercer than Peres's feelings toward Rabin." Their rivalry had started years before. Rabin suspected that Peres, because of his close ties with Ben-Gurion, had delayed Rabin's promotion to the chief of staff position. He also accused Peres of helping to make Tzvi Tzur chief of staff ahead of him.

When Rabin was informed that Peres would run against him, he reacted with spite and disdain. One of the major reasons for his deciding to run, he said, was because he saw with "utmost gravity" the possibility of Peres becoming prime minister. He was of the War of Independence generation, Rabin added; and "the possibility of the Labor Party electing a candidate, who had not worn the IDF uniform, to the most important political position, was in his view a moral flaw of the highest order." All the Labor Party leaders had worn military uniforms, Rabin continued: "Ben-Gurion and Eshkol in the Jewish Legion, Sharett in the Turkish Army; and Golda Meir 'angrily protested' against the exclusion of women from the Jewish Legion. The Prime Minister bears the supreme responsibility for the most fateful decisions, and a man who had not served the people as a soldier and fought the people's wars—is not worthy of bearing that responsibility."[18]

From the first moment, Rabin didn't consider Peres worthy of even running for prime minister. "In Rabin's world," Dov Goldstein remarked, "there was nothing as important as the Independence War . . . . His terrible experiences [during the war] left in his flesh a scar that had an overwhelming influence on his political and military views. Therefore, beyond the emotional conflict between him and Peres, he never forgave Peres that during that terrible period he didn't serve in the army. For him, he had evaded his duty."[19]

This attitude wasn't shared by the leaders of the Labor Party. Even Golda, who couldn't be suspected of any sympathy toward Peres, asked one of Rabin's friends, "Tell me, why does Rabin think that he is the chosen prince? There are no princes in political life. Shimon has the right to run against him."[20]

Beside their personal rivalry, Rabin and Peres differed in their views on matters of policy. Rabin supported the Allon plan, which was based on a far-reaching territorial compromise in the West Bank. Peres was much more hawkish. He followed Dayan's idea of "a functional compromise," which was in favor of keeping the entire West Bank in Israel's hands, but giving its inhabitants Jordanian citizenship.

Shortly before the election, Peres invited Rabin to lunch in a Jerusalem restaurant. Afterward, Peres had the feeling that they had understood each other.[21] But Rabin described it quite differently. "Peres spoke mellifluously .... 'Let us learn something from the experience of our older friends—Allon and Dayan fought each other, wasted their forces—and neither of them became Prime Minister. Let's conclude a gentlemen's agreement, that we would deliver a fair fight [very shortly I learned what a fair fight in Peres's eyes was and the worth of his words]. One of us will win—and the other will accept the result and the winner's authority.' "

"I knew Peres already," Rabin continued. "I didn't believe one word he said. I was determined, that if Peres was elected Prime Minister—my foot wouldn't cross the government's threshold. I was reserved in my answer: 'We'll run, if we run, fairly. The loser will accept the winner's authority.' "[22]

The Labor leaders decided that the election would be by secret ballot. As election day approached, Peres launched an intensive campaign of a new kind. He didn't rest for one moment; he met with hundreds of central committee members, telephoned all of them, even his opponents; he inspired favorable articles in the press.

Rabin acted differently. He didn't wage a vigorous campaign, and he left all the hard work to Pinhas Sapir and his people. Rabin himself had his own doubts that he didn't reveal in public. "I was a 'rookie' in the party. Only the energetic support of Sapir and his friends bridged the gap in time; I started campaigning only a week before the election at the party's central committee. Some of my supporters were quite pessimistic. I was not involved in the party's activities, and didn't know its militants closely .... I had doubts: only in January had I been elected to the Knesset. In March I was elected Minister, and in April I was running for Prime Minister?! Am I ready for that? I had no doubts as far as the issues of defense and foreign affairs were concerned. Here I was treading on solid ground. But would the party support me?"[23]

With his son Hemi, a helicopter pilot, during the bitter War of Lebanon (1982). GPO

Prime minister, at last. Peres signs the "Rotation Agreement" with Likud's leader Yitzhak Shamir (1984) Between them is Minister Moshe Shachal. GPO

A fiery speech at the Knesset. GPO

Sonia and Shimon in the prime minister's residence in Jerusalem. GPO

King Hassan of Morocco was involved in Peres's efforts to achieve peace with Jordan and the Palestinians. GPO

Peres never forgave U.S. Secretary of State Georgy Shultz for the way he handled the London Agreement in 1987. GPO

At secret meetings in London and Amman, Peres laid the foundations of a peace treaty with king Hussein of Jordan (foreground, left). Hussein's brother, Prince Hassan, was present at one of their meetings in Amman. PA

President Reagan warmly thanked Peres for the release of American hostages in the Middle East, which was a part of the Iran-Contra affair. PA

The long duel. Peres and Rabin at the Knesset. GPO

Under the benevolent gaze of President Clinton, Peres signs the Oslo agreements on the south lawn of the White House. Rabin (far left) didn't conceal his aversion for having to shake Arafat's hand. On the far right, Mahmoud Abbas (Abu Mazen), future chairman of the Palestinian Authority, GPO

The Nobel Prize winner. "Without Arafat," Peres said, "the Oslo agreements wouldn't have been signed. With Arafat, they couldn't be implemented. GPO

In the Arava Desert, Peres signs the peace treaty with Jordan. GPO

Prime minister again. Peres speaking at a joint session of Congress in Washington. PA

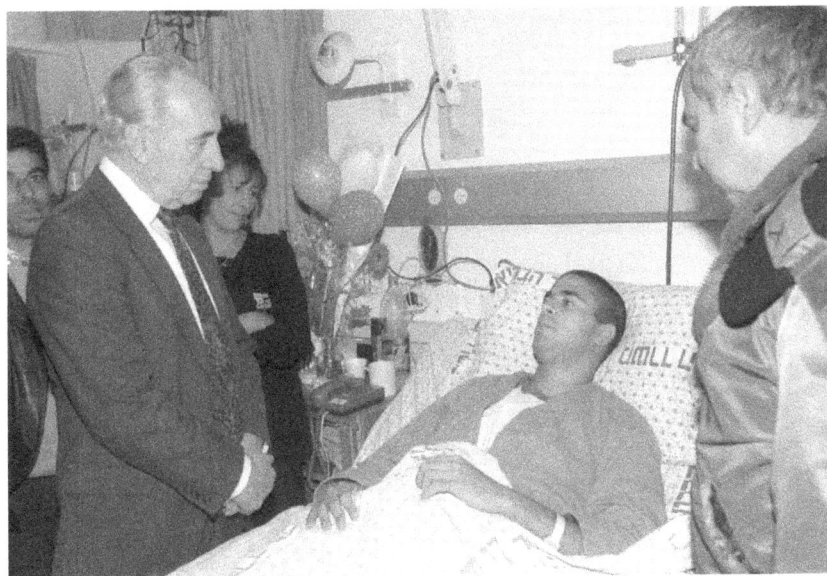

At the bedside of a wounded soldier. GPO

Only Peres could bring together all those world leaders for an antiterrorism summit. Front row from the left: King Hussein (with Great Britain's John Major watching from behind), Shimon Peres, President Clinton, President Mubarak, President Yeltzin, Yasser Arafat, King Hassan of Morocco, President Chirac. Besides flowery speeches, this summit achieved absolutely nothing. GPO

The Last Samurai. At a popular feast in Jerusalem. GPO

Back on the campaign trail (1996). Peres should have called for an early election, but refused to be elected "on Rabin's blood." GPO

Operation "Grapes of Wrath" against the Hezbollah in Lebanon deeply upset the Israeli Arabs who abandoned Peres at the eve of the 1996 election. GPO

The defeated Peres transfers power to Binyamin Nethanyahu. GPO

Ehud Barak, the Labor Party's new leader, tirelessly maneuvered to prevent Peres's election as Labor's honorary president. GPO

"You're the most stubborn man I've ever met," President Clinton said at Peres's eightieth birthday. GPO

The Tel-Aviv Drummers. On Peres's eightieth birthday, the guests are marking the beat of a popular Israeli melody. From the left, President Moshe Katzav, Shimon Peres, Prime Minister Ariel Sharon, President Bill Clinton. Second from right, Dalia Rabin, Yitzhak Rabin's daughter. GPO

From this handshake, the Kadima Party was born, but Sharon would never lead it to victory.
GPO

Peres met George W. Bush, long before he become president, on a Mediterranean VIP cruise,
where Bush spoke about his baseball team. PA

The Peres tribe, at 12 Oppenheimer Street in Tel-Aviv. Sitting: Shimon, Sonia, Tziki. Standing, second row, far left, Yoni. Third row, second from the right, Hemi, and spouses, children, and grandchildren. COURTESY OF PETER HALMAGI

Presidents exchanging medals. Left: Mark Neiman, GPO. Right: Amos Ben Gershom. GPO

Rabin claimed that a lot of harm was done to him by the man whom he mockingly called "Doctor" Ezer Weizman. In Rabin's words, General Weizman "described, with his best story-telling talents, the events of May 23, 1967, on the eve of the Six Day War, and delved into the story of my collapse." Rabin suspected him of acting on Peres's orders, because he had heard Weizman boast more than once, "I am not a Mapai member, but I am Peres's friend."[24]

Political observers estimated that Peres wouldn't get more than 35 percent of the vote. After all, he could only count on the votes of the former Rafi members, and perhaps those of some ex-Mapai friends. But on April 22, 1974, when the ballots were counted, the results came "as a surprise to some and as a shock to the others."[25] Despite the support of Pinhas Sapir and the former Ahdut Ha'avoda and Mapai parties—which were absorbed into the Labor Party in 1968—Rabin got 298 votes and Peres 254. Rabin had won, but by the slight margin of only 44 votes!

Peres didn't win, but proved that he had a strong following in the Labor Party. He had won the support of almost half the members of the central committee. That made him number two in the party.

Peres now demanded the defense portfolio previously held by Dayan. Rabin angrily rejected his request and tried to appoint Yigal Allon instead. Peres's rich record in defense matters didn't impress Rabin.

"I didn't see in Shimon Peres a man suitable to serve as Defense Minister," he wrote. "He lacked any military experience, and his experience in the purchase of weapons didn't tip the scales in his favor. But the choice wasn't mine. There was no doubt that if the defense portfolio wasn't given to Peres the ex-Rafi faction wouldn't support the government and it couldn't obtain a majority."[26]

Actually, it was Yitzhak Navon who made it clear to Rabin that if Peres didn't receive the defense portfolio, Rafi wouldn't support his government, depriving him of the majority he needed. "I gave in with deep regret and gave the defense portfolio to Peres. I was going to be sorry for that; I was going to pay in full the price of this error."[27]

In June 1974, after a nine-year absence, Shimon Peres returned to the Ministry of Defense.

THE NEW DEFENSE MINISTER had to deal right away with two major tasks. The first was to rebuild the IDF, which had been severely crippled during the Yom Kippur War. The second was to complete, together with the prime minister and the new foreign minister, Yigal Allon, negotiations for the disengagement agreements with Egypt and Syria.

In order to rebuild the IDF, Peres had to hit the road again, as in the days in his youth, and travel the world in his quest for weapons. In the United States he negotiated with Secretary of State ITenry Kissinger and Secretary of Defense James Schlesinger. His first talks with Kissinger were quite bumpy; Peres was known as a hawk, and Kissinger didn't like his tough views. Only a secret conversation between the two of them mended the fences, and infused their relations with a feeling of mutual trust. As far as Schlesinger was concerned, Peres's aides warned him that the secretary was hostile to Israel; but right at their first meeting Peres and Schlesinger struck a friendly rapport and even discovered that they could be related; Schlesinger, a converted Jew, was descended from a woman named Persky.

The talks were fruitful. Schlesinger agreed to supply Israel with Lance missiles (but refused to sell Pershing missiles because of their longer range and their capacity to carry nuclear warheads). Peres also persuaded him to sell Israel Cobra helicopters and laser-guided bombs, for antiterrorist operations.

In Italy, Peres negotiated the purchase of troop carriers; in a secret trip to Germany, he met with the defense minister, Georg Leber, and renewed some of the agreements he had concluded years before with Franz Josef Strauss—a massive supply of tanks and other weapons, "on lease"; Israel paid for only a small part of the shipments.

In Israel, Peres incessantly toured army camps, emergency stocks, ammunition dumps, infantry and armor bases. He thoroughly checked the equipment, the ammunition, and even climbed into the tanks to make sure the soldiers had their personal weapons, binoculars, sleeping bags, and other equipment.

In March 1975, during the negotiations for a disengagement agreement with Egypt, a grave crisis broke out between Israel and the United States. Peres had rejected Kissinger's demand that Israel retreat from the strategic Mitla and Gidi passes in the Sinai. Rabin and Allon, although more moderate than Peres, followed suit. The confrontation led to a "reassessment" of the U.S. policy toward Israel. Many arms shipments were delayed or canceled, and Peres was told, in veiled terms, that he'd better cancel his forthcoming visit to the United States.

Peres went to Rabin with a new idea: Israel wouldn't hand over the Sinai passes to Egypt, but she would withdraw from them. The area would be placed under the control of American soldiers on the eastern approach to the passes, and of Soviet soldiers on the western end.[28]

Rabin was "stunned," in his words. "The political thinking of the Defense Minister," he wrote, "had taken off this time to unbelievable heights. Had I not heard, with my own ears, a senior government minister suggest that Israel herself would request the entry of Soviet troops into the Sinai, and insert them as a buffer between her and Egypt—I would have been certain that Peres's vile enemies were spreading lies about him."[29]

Rabin's astonishment was exaggerated. Shimon Peres was well known for his mass production of creative plans and ideas; more than once his creativity had gone too far. That was a typical trait of his character, for which many called him "a man of fantasies" and of far-fetched ideas. One of his fantasies had been the Guyana project—but others had been Dimona, the French alliance, and the German arms deals. Peres himself admitted that he would be satisfied if only half of his ideas came to fruition.[30]

Ben-Gurion used to take from Peres's ideas the creative part and discard the unrealistic elements. And indeed, after severely condemning Peres, Rabin did just that: he dismissed the idea about the Soviet soldiers, which was too risky, but adopted the idea of the stationing of American soldiers at the Gidi and Mitla passes. When he proposed that idea to Kissinger, it ended the crisis with America and, after a lot of refining and redrafting, became the basis for the disengagement agreements of September 1975.

Another idea surfaced in Peres's mind when touring the border with Lebanon, which was in the grips of a civil war. The IDF had established close ties with the Christian villagers in South Lebanon, and had created the South Lebanon Army under the orders of Major Sa'ad Haddad. The South Lebanon Army fought alongside the IDF against the terrorists from the PLO (the Palestine Liberation Organization), who controlled large parts of the country. The IDF also built an electronic fence along the border with Lebanon to prevent the penetration of terrorists.

While touring the fence, Peres suddenly saw a car stopping on the Lebanese side. A woman holding a baby got out and sneaked into Israel through a hole in the fence. Peres asked to speak to her; she told him that she was on her way to get medical care in Israel, because her village was under terrorist artillery fire. "What do you do in such cases?" Peres asked the chief of the Northern Command, General Rafael Eitan, who accompanied him.

"We give them medical assistance," Eitan said.

Peres suggested making that a permanent arrangement. Thus, "the Good Fence" was born. The IDF soldiers built a small gate in the fence and opened a clinic manned by a doctor and a nurse. After a short while, Lebanese men seeking work in Israel started to line up by the gate, too; so did Lebanese farmers who came to sell their produce.

"I presented this to Peres," Eitan reported, "and got his blessing. Motta [Gur], the chief of staff, was against the idea, and Rabin was indifferent. Peres was open-minded and understanding. He realized that this could be an opportunity for breaking the vicious circle of permanent hostility with the Lebanese. He also had encouraged us to establish contact with the Christian Phalange in Lebanon."[31]

As defense minister, Peres also took part in many a secret project. In his efforts to tighten the ties with the Phalange, he secretly brought the sons of the Christian leaders Kamil Sham'un and Pierre Gemayel to his home, now on Oppenheimer Street in Tel Aviv. "Your fathers fought each other for many years," he said to Dani Sham'un and Bashir Gemayel. "It is your duty to become allies and friends."[32] Peres also dispatched military assistance to the Kurdish rebels in Iraq, visited Tehran to upgrade the military relations with the Shah, and, together with Yitzhak Rabin and Yigal Allon, met with King Hussein of Jordan.

But more that anything else, the Rabin government's term was dominated by an ugly and bitter phenomenon—the unending, worsening conflict between Rabin and Peres.

AT FIRST, THE TWO of them tried to maintain a correct rapport, and even used to meet on Saturdays at Rabin's home. But alienation and mutual suspicions gradually took over. Peres realized that Rabin performed poorly as prime minister, and he made his criticism known. Rabin maintained that Peres constantly undermined his position, and his aides suspected Peres of being behind the never-ending media onslaught on Rabin's mediocre functioning. Rabin also suspected that Peres was a major source of leaks to the newspapers. A mini scandal broke out when an employee at a Jerusalem hotel found a top-secret document under a table in the lobby. The employee brought the document to the hotel security officer, who alerted the authorities. It turned out that a short while before, Peres and Dayan had met by that table. Apparently, Peres had shown Dayan classified documents, and one of them had slipped to the floor.[33] Rabin didn't conceal his fury.

At cabinet meetings, Peres and Rabin exchanged angry words. Rabin openly taunted Peres and expressed doubts about the information he presented; the other ministers sat in their places, embarrassed and silent, grimly waiting for the storms to subside. It seemed that there was no issue on the government's agenda that didn't cause a verbal duel or an exchange of acrid barbs between the prime minister and the defense minister.

The political analyst Shlomo Nakdimon reported that at government meetings, "those present . . . see how Rabin treats Peres with impatience, interrupts his words angrily, until at times it seems that the very presence of the Defense Minister infuriates him .... Peres himself doesn't always respond to Rabin's remarks. Sometimes he remains silent, at times he answers quietly. Only seldom does he use tough language. Peres's way of speaking is more refined, and he tries to avoid confrontation at these forums."

Another conflict erupted between the two when Rabin appointed Ariel Sharon as his adviser, humiliating both Peres and General Motta Gur. Sharon resigned after a few months in office.

"In Rabin's hatred of Peres," Dov Goldstein said, "there was a major component of jealousy. He saw in Peres qualities that he didn't have. In his first months as prime minister he didn't realize the importance of the party and treated it with contempt. But he slowly came to realize that the party was a body of support, without which one couldn't remain prime minister. From this stemmed his jealousy of Peres: a man of open character, with excellent party contacts, connected with people, knowing how to win their support, gifted with a sense of humor, quoting books and charming people with his words—in short, everything that Rabin was not."[34]

RABIN HAD BECOME prime minister in the middle of a vast settlement effort in the West Bank that was carried out by the national religious group Gush Emunim ("the Bloc of the Faithful"). The "Gush" clashed over and over again with the government and carried out relentless settlement attempts in Judea and Samaria (the West Bank).

The Gush leaders were impressed by Shimon Peres's favorable attitude. On several occasions Peres declared that they were "true pioneers" and hinted that he would support creating settlements in Samaria.[35]

The Gush leaders liked Peres's hawkish views; they maintained that Peres had told them that Samaria's chain of mountains had a strategic value and that Israel should settle the mountain crest. "In Peres, we found an attentive listener," one of the Gush leaders said. "His door was always open to us."[36] Some even claimed that Gush Emunim had succeeded in driving a wedge between Peres and Rabin, who was much more cautious. In a meeting with the Gush leaders on July 17, 1974, Peres declared that he recognized, in principle, the rights of Jews to settle anywhere in Eretz-Israel; yet he added that a settlement in the Nablus area was not of a high priority.[37]

Peres's sympathy for the Gush was motivated both by his hawkish positions and by the political reality: large groups of Labor Party members, belonging to the Ahdut Ha'avoda kibbutz movement and the moshav movement, supported the idea of Greater Israel. Rachel Yanait Ben-Zvi, the widow of Israel's second president, even suggested to Gush members that they establish "work companies" that would offer their services to the army or to other government-sponsored groups.

Hanan Porat, a Gush Emunim leader, was very excited by the idea and established such a company. It worked at the ancient site of Baal-Hatzor, in Samaria, and received the authorization of the defense minister to stay there overnight; Peres then instructed the army to let them be. Finally, he gave them a formal letter of authorization to remain there. That's how the Ofra settlement was established. Peres was photographed planting a tree in the new settlement. In a debate in the Knesset, Peres admitted openly, "I gave the authorization to establish the work camp at Ofra, near Ramallah, after consultation and approval from the competent authorities. When it seems possible, we'll bring the plan to turn this into a permanent settlement to the government, in full daylight and without apologizing. The debate is not about Greater Eretz-Israel, but about Greater Jerusalem, about Jerusalem and the territories that surround it."[38]

The next goal of the Gush was the biblical site of Alon Moreh. They tried to settle there several times, but the IDF kept expelling them, on firm government orders. On December 1, 1975, thousands of Gush militants started moving to the area. The settlers took over the abandoned train station at Sebastia, about six miles northwest of Nablus. Here stood the biblical Tel-Shomron, the capital of the ten-tribe kingdom of Israel. The Gush leaders established a synagogue there and braced themselves for a confrontation with the army. Throngs of ecstatic young men participated in the prayers and dances by the old station. Chief of Staff Motta Gur wasn't excited at all by the prospect of having to use force against the settlers.

At the Knesset, Peres said that he was seeking a fair solution to the problem. At the same time, Sebastia was submerged by sympathizers from the Ahdut Ha'avoda kibbutzim. The famous composer Noemi Shemer, the author of "Jerusalem of Gold," wrote a song to celebrate the Gush spirit.

Peres suggested a compromise to Rabin: he would propose to the settlers that they voluntarily leave the grounds, and in return, the government would consider the building of another work camp on the eastern slopes of the Samaria Mountains, near the Jordan Valley. Rabin agreed, and the following day Peres flew to Sebastia in a helicopter.

The defense minister and the coordinator of activities in the territories, General Vardi, were welcomed by the settlers with songs and dances. The settlers believed that Peres was about to authorize the Sebastia settlement, but Peres informed their leaders of his compromise plan, and even added a threat: if they didn't leave voluntarily, they would be evacuated by force. A stunned silence followed his words, and then one of the most extreme leaders of the Gush, Rabbi Moshe Levinger, ran toward the crowd, ripping his shirt in a Jewish gesture of mourning and yelling, "Tear your clothes! Tear your clothes! This is a day of mourning!"

An ominous, angry roar erupted from the crowd. Peres left the meeting and walked to his helicopter, surrounded by soldiers who protected him from the furious militants. After he left, the poet Haim Gouri, who sympathized with the settlers, offered them his own compromise: "Will you be ready to consider a government offer that allows twenty-five men to stay, temporarily, in a military camp in the center of Samaria, until the final decision?" The settlers immediately realized that by making such an offer, the government would be accepting the presence of Gush settlers in Samaria. They therefore gave him a positive answer.

Gouri returned home and called some of his friends in the government. The offer reached Peres, and he instructed his adviser Naftali Lavi to discuss Gouri's plan with the settlers. Finally, on December 8, a Gush leaders' delegation went to Peres's office. "We came to him disheveled," Hanan Porat recalled, "after a week in which we hadn't washed, hadn't changed clothes—straight from the field. One of the rabbis was barefoot. There was a casual atmosphere; it was like a meeting of the Palmach."[39] Aliza Eshed, Peres's chief of staff, felt that the minister loved the ambiance created by the Gush Emunim men. "Shimon wanted these guys to like him. He regarded them as true Zionists, as the new settlers of the land. I remember how Hanan Porat and his buddies used to come to the office, and Shimon was so happy that there was such a group of young settlers around him. So in the Sebastia affair he used this a little against Rabin, for he had the power, and Rabin didn't try to stop him."[40]

Peres opened the meeting by declaring that he had been given the authority to reach a compromise. He proposed to the settlers that they leave Sebastia, and some of them would be moved to an IDF camp where they would have freedom of movement. The camp wouldn't become a permanent settlement, and in two or three months the government would hold a discussion on the settlement policy in Judea and Samaria.

During the conversation that followed, something strange happened. The twenty-five settlers that Haim Gouri had mentioned mysteriously became thirty; and from thirty men they inflated into thirty families! That meant not thirty people, but more than a hundred. Shimon Peres was flexible and agreed to thirty families. Yet he kept calling Rabin to update him about the progress of the negotiation and to get his approval. Finally, Peres drafted the agreement, in his own handwriting, on a sheet of paper, his adviser Naftali Lavi brought a bottle of whiskey, and the entire assembly duly celebrated.

The agreement was approved by Rabin, who presented it to the government.

The settlers understood that by agreeing to "thirty families" Peres had agreed that a settlement would be created. They returned to Sebastia exhilarated, and celebrated with the militants for hours. They were right. The defense minister instructed the army to employ the settlers in various jobs in the Kadum army camp, where they had been taken. By doing that he actually established a settlement.[41] He allowed the settlers to build a workshop for spare parts. That was how he interpreted the government's resolution that "the army will find employment for the settlers."

Kadum, like Ofra before it, was a substantial breach of government policy. Since 1968, the government had rejected any initiative for settling the mountains' crests or the eastern slopes of Samaria. An analyst who criticized Peres's decisions concluded that his motives "were a result of his continuous rivalry with Prime Minister Rabin."[42]

At a later stage, Rabin attacked Peres on the Sebastia affair as well. He hinted that Peres and his friends were "Trojan horses" for the Gush inside the Labor Party. He claimed that the defense ministry had bypassed him and created facts on the ground, which was "cheating."[43] Peres denied that allegation.

There is no doubt that Peres considerably aided the efforts to settle Samaria. He also helped build the city of Ariel in the West Bank, and the city notables still speak of his assistance with gratitude.[44] Today Peres is still severely criticized for his support of the settlers and of Gush Emunim.

THE WORST CRISIS between Peres and Rabin occurred on January 29, 1976, while Rabin was on a visit to Washington. In the evening, after meeting several major administration figures, Rabin invited Israeli reporters to his quarters at Blair House. He looked tired and extremely nervous. He suddenly started speaking of the "shopping lists" of weapons he had brought from Israel, and then moved on to a blunt attack on the defense minister.

The lists that had been submitted to the Americans, he said, were inflated, and included needless equipment. He was satisfied that he had been able to put things back in order. The following morning, Rabin's outburst made the headlines of the Israeli papers. It was attributed to "a high-placed source in the Prime Minister's entourage." In his private apartment Rabin used even harsher language. His friend Dov Goldstein was on that trip. "I witnessed an unprecedented outburst of fury, loathing, and hatred of Rabin toward Peres," Goldstein admitted later. "Rabin was trembling with fury. He told me, 'Peres is sabotaging my visit. He does this on purpose. The President and the Secretary of State will laugh at me. I'm going back to Israel and I'll throw him out.'" Goldstein added, "Even though there were some good reasons for that hatred, it resulted mostly from deep, personal motives, and there was nothing one could do against it."

In Israel, Peres and his aides were dumbfounded; the shopping lists had been drafted after long consultations with the prime minister, and had been approved by the government as well as by a restricted ministerial committee. Rabin had never expressed any reservation about the lists before. Some failed to understand the reason for Rabin's flare-up; others maintained that perhaps he had consumed one drink too many.[45]

When Rabin returned to Israel, he had no choice but to retract his statements from the Knesset podium. He had had no intention of offending the defense minister, Rabin said, and admitted that he had participated in the drafting of the "shopping lists." He wrote, "I admit that I made a mistake." He confirmed that he had approved the lists that he later called "inflated."[46]

Crises kept breaking out between Rabin and Peres on various issues. At the Labor Party bureau meeting on May 13, Peres insisted that Rabin should form a new government in which he, Peres, wouldn't participate. This was his reaction to another attack Rabin had launched at him in an interview in *Haaretz*.[47] Scared party apparatchiks frantically shuttled between the two men and succeeded in organizing a meeting; at the end of the day,

Rabin and Peres announced, as expected, that the dispute was over.

But the dispute was far from being over.

That murky atmosphere, poisoned by the Rabin-Peres conflict, became the backdrop of a momentous drama that stunned Israel and the world.

CHAPTER 23.

ENTEBBE

ON JUNE 26, 1976, in the middle of a government meeting, Shimon Peres's military secretary passed him a note. It carried a message: an Air France airliner on Flight 139 from Ben-Gurion Airport to Paris had been hijacked after a stopover in Athens. The plane was on its way to an unknown destination.

Peres passed the note to the prime minister, and they decided to hold an urgent meeting with the participation of the ministers of foreign affairs, justice, transportation, and the minister without portfolio, Israel Galili.

Gradually, details started falling into place. The Airbus carried 246 passengers, 105 of them Israelis. The terrorists had boarded the plane in Athens and hijacked it after takeoff. They were members of the most dangerous terrorist organization—the Popular Front for the Liberation of Palestine, headed by Wadi Haddad. It was a small group, but its members were highly capable and well trained; it participated in joint operations with other terrorist organizations. The aircraft had landed in Benghazi, Libya, for refueling, and the hijackers had presented the Libyan authorities with a list of terrorists they wanted released.

During the ministerial meeting, Rabin stressed that the passengers' safety was the direct responsibility of the French government, as the airline was state-owned. Peres said that Israel's policy had always been to act against hijackers.[1]

After the meeting, Peres returned to the defense ministry and summoned Motta Gur. They agreed that if the hijackers asked to land in Israel, they would be allowed to do so, but the final goal would be to take over the aircraft and rescue the hostages.

At midnight, the plane was reported to be approaching the Middle East. Peres set out for Ben-Gurion Airport, but was informed that the plane was circling over Khartoum, in Sudan; it couldn't reach Israel for two or three more hours.

At the airport Peres met General Yekutiel (Kuti) Adam, the IDF chief of operations. Adam, a bold and coolheaded soldier, was highly respected for his original thinking, his confidence, and his sharp instincts. Peres and Adam jumped in an army jeep and set off for the base of Sayeret Matkal, the IDF's elite commando unit. Peres and Adam expected to meet there the new Sayeret commander, Yoni Netanyahu. He was one of the three Netanyahu brothers, Peres wrote, "who had almost become a legend already—three brothers, fighting like lions, excelling both in their deeds and in their learning."[2]

Netanyahu shared Peres's great weakness—a deep love of literature and in particular of Nathan Alterman's poetry. But tonight he was away, and Peres was briefed by one of the Sayeret's most glorious fighters, Major Muki Betzer. Under Betzer's command, the soldiers were already rehearsing an attack on a large Airbus aircraft, in case the Air France plane landed in Israel. Peres observed the young soldiers around him. "Most of them," he wrote, "have tousled hair, sunburned faces, silent lips. . . . In this unit one is not allowed to be a dresser (not one of their shirts looks as if it has ever tasted the touch of an iron), one is not allowed to boast. About the future one may say that everything is possible. About the past one is allowed to mention his own mistakes only."[3]

The projected operation was canceled, however, as a new report reached Peres: the Airbus had turned south toward Uganda, in the heart of Africa. Shortly afterward, another report arrived: the Airbus had landed in Entebbe, at the airport of Uganda's capital, Kampala.

Peres got home in the early morning. He tiptoed into his apartment, dragging in the morning newspapers. He thought of Uganda's ruler, Idi Amin, who had trained and equipped his army with Israel's help before changing his policy. Peres remembered having dinner with Amin and his wife, Pamela, in Moshe Dayan's garden before the Yom Kippur War. The dinner had taken place in a very decorative setting—among Dayan's archeological finds, which populated the pleasant garden. They had sat around a table surrounded by ancient columns, engraved stelae, pieces of old pottery, and blocks of chiseled stone. Peres and Sonya sat beside Idi Amin, a huge black man. There was something both attractive and scary in his looks, Shimon thought, "like a jungle landscape, like an indecipherable secret of Nature."[4]

That cruel and ruthless giant now held in his hands the lives of 250 hostages in his African realm, 2,500 miles away from the Land of Israel.

BACK IN HIS OFFICE, Peres perused the reports about the hijacking. Some of the terrorists were German. During their stopover in Benghazi the terrorists had tried to separate the Israeli and Jewish passengers from the others, but the Air France crew courageously rejected that attempt. But at Entebbe the "selection" took place, as it had in Nazi-occupied Europe. "Once again, armed Germans and Arabs were facing innocent people," Peres wrote, "and they separated the passengers, not by age, or by sex, but by their origin; everybody else on one side, and the Israelis on the other."

Peres was shaken in particular by the story of one of the hostages, a Holocaust survivor whose arm bore the tattoo of a concentration camp inmate. "When she saw the German she went into a bout of hysterics. The German tried to talk to her, in vain. The passengers reported later that one of the terrorists, a German woman, was especially mean."[5]

Amin had warmly received the terrorists and had called them

"welcomed guests." He had sent his private plane to Somalia, to bring back the Popular Front leader, Wadi Haddad. Haddad's people handed Amin a list of terrorists held in Israel and other countries, and asked to exchange them for the hostages.

Peres assumed that a negotiation would start under the terrorist threat of assassinating hostages if a quick agreement wasn't achieved. He was determined that in no case should Israel release terrorists. He feared the terrible consequences of such a decision on Israel's image and in particular on the fight against terrorism.

The following day, June 29, the Ministerial Committee was convened on his request. Motta Gur arrived, too. Rabin seemed utterly tense to Peres. "Children will be killed," he kept saying. "They'll throw them out of the plane." He declared that, "as we have no other option, we will have to negotiate with the terrorists. Still, our official position is: 'France is responsible, we shall not give up.' "[6]

The prime minister asked Gur if Israel had "a military option." To both his and Peres's surprise, the chief of staff declared that "there was a military option," and it was being assessed. He had instructed his assistants to check out the possibility of parachuting a squad of soldiers near Entebbe, either into nearby Lake Victoria or on the ground. The soldiers would kill the terrorists and protect the hostages until they could be brought home.

Peres wasn't excited by Gur's idea. "We don't have a solid plan yet," he said. "We'll be able to present a plan only after discussing it."[7]

Rabin congratulated Gur for his fast thinking, but later rejected his plan and called it "the Bay of Pigs," after the botched invasion of Cuba by U.S.-backed Cuban exiles in April 1961.

Gur was troubled by the tension between Peres and Rabin. "The tone of the Prime Minister's question," he wrote, "and the Defense Minister's remarks reminded me again how cautious I should be in my relations with them, in view of the permanent tension and suspicions between them .... By our matter-of-fact approach to the subjects at hand, following our common military past, I was closer to the Prime Minister than to the Defense Minister, who had operated for years in a civilian political setup. On the other hand, in many subjects, like the military industries or general defense issues, I appreciated the Defense Minister's open-mindedness and creativity."[8]

In the evening, Peres summoned the chief of staff and several senior army officers to discuss a military action. He well knew that a military operation in a location thousands of miles from home, in a foreign country, against armed terrorists and perhaps the Ugandan Army as well, was a risky and complicated task. He was aware of the IDF commanders' feeling that this was a challenge that no nation had ever confronted; no army had been asked to deal with such a problem. "We have to use our imagination," Peres said to the generals, "and examine any idea, as crazy as it may seem."

He added, "I want to hear what plans you have."

"We have no plans," Kuti Adam said.

"Then I want to hear what you don't have," Peres retorted.[9]

In the following discussion, some ideas emerged. The only concrete plan was Motta Gur's—to land or parachute a squad of twelve soldiers in the vicinity of Lake Victoria, to reach the Entebbe airport, on the lake's shore, by boat, kill the terrorists, and rescue the hostages. The main flaw with this plan was the inability to take the hostages out of Uganda. If they stayed there, even under the protection of the paratroopers, they would be exposed to attacks and various other dangers.

Some officers presented sketchy ideas; the "craziest" plan was the one suggested by General Beni Peled, commander of the air force. Peled, a courageous and calm pilot gifted with a fertile imagination, conceived a proposal that answered all the questions. We have to take over Uganda, he said. Conquer Entebbe, kill the terrorists, and free the hostages. The air force had enough planes to fly the combat units to Uganda. Later the same planes would take the soldiers and the rescued hostages back to Israel.

The air force chief suggested using large Hercules aircraft for this operation. They could fly from Israel to Entebbe, and then back.

Peres recalled his visit to Georgia a few years before, and his meeting with Governor Jimmy Carter. He had brought Carter his book *David's Sling*. Carter had leafed through the book and said to him, "All David needed then was a sling, but today's David needs more than a sling, he needs a Hercules!" He had invited Peres to visit the Hercules plant outside Atlanta; Shimon and Sonia, who had joined him for the trip, were deeply impressed by the aircraft and felt "like Jonah in the big fish's belly." On his return, Peres had convinced the air force to buy several of the planes, which it called Rhinos.

Peres listened carefully to Beni Peled's words. At first, his plan seemed like a castle in the sky; but on second thought he deemed it "quite realistic." But the other participants in the meeting didn't share his assessment. Motta Gur, in particular, was negative. The plan, he said, "was unrealistic, nothing but a fantasy," and would be better forgotten.

HAIM ISRAELI WALKED into Peres's office. Israeli had been Peres's close friend since his first days in the defense ministry. "You should keep a diary on all that is said and done," Israeli advised Peres, and suggested that he keep copies of all the documents and transcripts concerning the hijacking.[10] With his sharp instincts, Israeli foresaw the development of the crisis, and thought that Peres should document every stage of his initiative. Peres agreed, and started a Minister's Journal on the hijacking.

That morning, he received a list of the jailed terrorists whose release the hijackers were demanding in exchange for the hostages. The list was complicated: forty of the prisoners were held in Israel, six in Kenya, five in Germany (including the leaders of the Baader-Meinhof gang), one in France, and one in Switzerland. One glance was enough for Peres to realize it contained an impossible demand. How could one organize the release of terrorists held in so many countries, according to different laws, and because of different crimes? And what if one of those countries refused to release the terrorists held in its prisons?

Peres knew, for example, that Kenya claimed the six terrorists it had arrested after an attack on an El Al plane were not in the country anymore; Germany would certainly refuse to release the deadly Baader-Meinhof terrorists; France claimed that the terrorist in its territory had been released long ago; the one jailed in Switzerland was a Jewish woman who had fallen in love with a Palestinian terrorist and joined his organization. It was anybody's guess how Switzerland would react to the demand to free the woman.

At the Ministerial Committee meeting, Peres got the impression that the prime minister wanted Israel "to hurry and declare that she is willing to release the prisoners."[11] Yitzhak Rabin produced examples from the past, proving that Israel had released terrorists on several occasions. Peres objected that Israel had never released terrorists "with blood on their hands" like those on Wadi Haddad's list. "Rabin was utterly impatient," Peres wrote. "He didn't let anybody speak and express his views. He interrupted all the participants. He stressed repeatedly, while staring at me, that there was no other option, and we have to negotiate, right away."[12]

On Wednesday, June 30, Peres decided to check another angle.

He summoned three IDF officers who had served in Uganda and had worked with Idi Amin. He asked them to describe Amin's character, his behavior, his attitude toward foreigners. From the conversation emerged the profile of a vain man seeking glory and the world's attention; he therefore might want to protract the affair. He seemed to be a distrustful, cruel man, but also a coward, nurturing feelings of deprivation. The officers didn't believe he would dare to massacre the hostages, but he wouldn't confront the terrorists either. The Ugandan Army wouldn't be "a real obstacle" to an Israeli operation. If Israel used force, though, and harmed the Ugandans, while leaving the hostages in Entebbe, the Ugandans would massacre them.[13] This conclusion ruled out Motta Gur's plan of killing the terrorists but leaving the hostages in Uganda. Peres charged Colonel "Borka" Bar-Lev, who had been very friendly with Amin, with telephoning the Ugandan ruler.[14]

The IDF commanders met again in the morning, under the shadow of the approaching deadline set by the terrorists. Peres didn't believe in the terrorists' ultimatum and thought it would be postponed over and over again. At the officers' meeting he received intelligence reports about the Entebbe airport and especially about a squadron of Soviet-made MiG fighter jets that might intervene in the fighting. Motta Gur again presented his plan about parachuting into Lake Victoria, but it turned out that the previous night's rehearsal of the operation had failed. Gur proposed a new plan—that the soldiers be flown to Kenya, which was Israel's friend, where they would set off on speedboats to Entebbe. But the Mossad director rejected any possibility of launching an operation from Kenyan territory.

Beni Peled's plan was discussed again. Now it was more focused and realistic. It didn't mention conquering Uganda anymore, but only achieving control over the airport at Entebbe, releasing the hostages, and flying them back. Beni Peled spoke now of conquering Entebbe with a thousand paratroopers, dropped from ten Hercules (Rhino) aircraft; Colonel Ehud Barak suggested a more limited operation, and Peres agreed with him.[15]

Generals Dan Shomron and Yanosh Ben-Gal didn't support a grandiose parachuting. They estimated that the operation could be carried out by two hundred soldiers and three Rhinos. Shomron, the chief paratrooper and infantry officer, was already preparing a plan for landing the soldiers at Entebbe using aircraft; he was opposed to any parachuting. He told Beni Peled, "By the time your first paratrooper hits the ground, you won't have anybody left to rescue anymore." When the terrorists saw paratroopers descending on the airfield, he said, they would massacre the hostages in cold blood.

The chief of intelligence, General Shlomo Gazit, warned his colleagues that the African countries might see the confrontation with Uganda as "an African-Israeli War." But Peres stressed that if the Ugandans resisted the IDF operation, Israel would retaliate with force. "A la guerre comme à la guerre," Peres said.

He liked Beni Peled's idea and the plan that Shomron and some other officers were working on. He turned to the generals: "From Israel's point of view, the situation is clear: if we yield to the hijackers' demands and release the jailed terrorists, everybody will understand us, but nobody will respect us. But if we launch a military operation, perhaps nobody will understand us, but everybody will respect us. Everything depends on the result, of course, but one cannot achieve a good result without taking a big risk."[16]

In the meantime, Borka Bar-Lev succeeded in establishing a telephone connection with Amin. Uganda's ruler advised Bar-Lev that Israel should accept the hijackers' demands without delay. Shortly afterward, Amin conveyed a message to Israel "from the number one of the freedom fighters"—meaning Haddad—repeating the demand for an immediate release of the terrorists jailed in Israel.

At the Ministerial Committee meeting, Rabin again said that a military option didn't exist, while Peres appealed to world figures and organizations able to pressure Uganda, thus giving Israel more time to prepare.

"I STARTED THE MORNING in a dark mood," Peres wrote on July 1.[17] In a couple of hours, the original ultimatum set by the hijackers would expire. A few minutes before the Ministerial Committee meeting, Peres and Gur discussed a possible military operation. Gur wouldn't budge from his position that Israel had no military option and Beni Peled's plan was unacceptable. "I, as chief of staff," he said to Peres, "cannot present a plan for the rescue of the hostages. My duty is to inform you that at the last moment I'll have to recommend the release of the terrorists."[18]

When the meeting started, the ministers were informed that

the hijackers had released the non-Israeli hostages, who had been flown to Paris and debriefed there. They had provided valuable information about the Old Terminal, where the hostages were being held, guarded by terrorists and Ugandan soldiers. A few minutes later, news arrived about the hijackers' decision to postpone the ultimatum deadline, as Peres had anticipated. But the atmosphere at the meeting remained tense; Rabin and Peres exchanged hostile and acrid remarks. Peres suggested a combined operation with the French, but Rabin discarded it. He was right; further inquiry proved that there was no chance of a joint French-Israeli action.

Still, Peres insisted that "there is a chance, even if slight, of a military operation"; Rabin countered that "there is not much of a chance." Gur admitted that "the IDF is not built for operating in Entebbe."

"I have no complaints," Rabin summed up. "I just think that we don't have the operational ability of rescuing the hostages."[19]

The confrontation between Rabin and Peres continued at the cabinet meeting. Rabin informed the government that Israel had no operational plan. "If by tomorrow," he said, "nothing happens, the plane will be blown up at 2 P.M. . . . We can't escape the problem, and it is simple: I don't see a military operation, because I don't see how it can be executed. Tomorrow there may be an explosion or a killing, or a postponement by a few hours, but nobody can tell for sure that some Israelis won't be hurt tomorrow. We must decide without delay."

Rabin's wife, Leah, wrote, "Shimon Peres adopted a firm stand at the government meeting, and demanded to try and rescue the hostages in Entebbe."[20] But Rabin didn't spare Peres in his memoirs, and harshly criticized him for his words at the meeting. "The Defense Minister made a flowery speech on the meanings of surrendering to the terrorists' demands. I needed a lot of self-restraint not to interrupt him. Afterwards I said: 'Do you have a concrete proposal? Go ahead. What do you propose?' The Defense Minister's silence was impressive."[21]

Rabin asked the government to accept the terrorists' demands in order to free the hostages. The government unanimously agreed. Peres said that he was against negotiations with the terrorists, but he would support the decision "only as a trick" in order to gain time.[22] A short while later, Rabin told the ministers that the opposition leader, Menachem Begin, agreed to the decision to negotiate with the terrorists. "Peres's face showed his surprise," Rabin wrote. "The responsible behavior of Begin fell on the Defense Minister's head like a cold shower and neutralized his demagogy."[23] He later added that Peres used "demagogical lightnings ... and ornate phrases that sounded totally ridiculous."[24] That was how Rabin regarded Peres's arguments all through the crisis—as pure demagogy. He didn't believe that Peres meant what he said when he demanded that Israel not surrender to the terrorists.

When they left the government meeting, Peres said to Gur, as if there had been no vote, "Let's assemble the officers and examine again their plans, even the craziest."

Gur was amazed. "But you voted for surrendering to the terrorists!"

"That doesn't matter," Peres said. "I am still convinced that it is of vital importance to rescue the hostages, and we have to find a way."

Gur felt "disagreement with that kind of political maneuver, but at the same time respect for Peres's consistency in understanding the importance of a military operation, and his caring for the image of Israel, the IDF and the Jewish people."[25]

The prime minister kept demanding, very nervously, that France be immediately informed of Israel's acceptance of the terrorists' conditions, so that the French foreign ministry could quickly establish contact with Entebbe. The defense minister and the chief of staff tried in vain to make him delay the message by a few hours. Like Gur, Rabin called the military plans that Peres presented to him "fantasies."[26] Gur realized that the prime minister's doubts about the possibility of a military operation had influenced many of the ministers. After all, Rabin was the glorious chief of staff of the Six Day War!

"It was impossible," Gur wrote, "not to notice the basic disbelief of the Prime Minister in any military operation to rescue the hostages. Perhaps because of the great tension between him and the Defense Minister, it seemed that he welcomed almost with pleasure any negative assessment of the operational plans—without trying, in spite of his rich military experience, to delve into their professional details. That behavior was the opposite of the Prime Minister's way of dealing with the army—because he had the habit of summoning officers of all ranks to thorough debates of subjects that seemed important to him."[27]

Yet Gur still objected to any military operation. And Peres, once again, felt he was completely alone. The only good news of the day was a message from Entebbe: the terrorists had postponed their deadline to Sunday, at 11 A.M. Their decision resulted from Amin's departure to an African nations' conference in Mauritius. He was going to be back in a couple of days. The delay gave Peres a little more time.

He decided to freeze all efforts to reach a compromise with the terrorists. Arthur Ben-Nathan had just arrived in Paris to talk with the French about a joint initiative. Peres telephoned him and conveyed a veiled hint, "in typical Parisian prose," to delay his talks with the French. "If you meet the French girl tonight," Peres advised, "please don't get too excited. At most, content yourself with a vague flirtation. As a friend, and not only as a friend, I am telling you: don't take your clothes off." Arthur understood the message, and nothing came out of that flirtation.[28]

Peres tried to persuade the Mossad director, Yitzhak Hofi, to secure the cooperation of Kenya, but Hofi was reserved and skeptical. "Hofi is a nice guy," Peres wrote, "but he moves with a slowness that sometimes looks like indifference."[29] On the military level, Gur refused to change his mind, and rejected the idea of taking over Entebbe. "I won't be a part of this," he said to Peres. "If you want to get immersed in delusions, in fantasies, go ahead."

Gur also conceived the appropriate nickname for the group of generals who kept meeting with Peres to discuss a military operation. The Fantasy Council, the chief of staff called it.

THE FANTASY COUNCIL convened in Shimon Peres's office in the afternoon hours of Thursday, July 1. Kuti Adam and Dan Shomron had already drafted a plan for a direct landing at the Entebbe airport and its takeover by Israeli troops.

Peres remarked, "I understand that the Chief of Staff hasn't yet reached a decision about this program. I understand his concerns and his professional hesitations. But I'm afraid that Israel may come out of this affair defeated and broken if we don't find a solution that doesn't imply surrender."[30]

Peres called another meeting, to which he summoned, besides the members of the Fantasy Council, several other senior officers. Kuti Adam and Dan Shomron presented their plan: the operation would be carried out at night. The Rhinos would land at Entebbe airport; the IDF soldiers would acquire control of the airport, kill the terrorists, and rescue the hostages.

The operation, Dan Shomron went on, wouldn't last for more than an hour, making use of surprise and speed. The first plane to land wouldn't ask permission from the control tower. Shomron wanted to land the plane at 11 P.M., right after a British airliner that was scheduled to arrive at the same time. If the Rhino landed in the shadow of the British aircraft, the airport radar wouldn't be able to detect it. Out of the Rhino would emerge two vehicles laden with IDF commandos. They would move toward the buildings where the hostages were kept. Five or ten minutes later another Rhino would land. Two armored cars, carrying soldiers, would come out of it. Their task would be to gain control over the New Terminal, the main runway, and the fuel reservoirs—for the refueling of the Israeli planes in case of need.

After the soldiers in the two first planes achieved their assignments, two more Israeli aircraft would land, take the hostages on board, and return home.

Peres asked the Mossad director for his thoughts, but Hofi kept voicing reservations. He started counting the risks: What if the Ugandan soldiers fired an RPG (rocket-propelled grenade) at a Rhino and set it on fire? What if they fired machine guns into the aircraft? In such a case some planes might have to be abandoned on the ground. What if soldiers and hostages were hurt? What about the danger that the terrorists might blow up the building? . . . It seemed he wasn't enthusiastic about the plan; he finally said that "our only chance, both from political and military points of view, would be to have a base in Kenya."[31]

A lively discussion followed, with Peres getting down to the smallest details and asking all the upsetting questions: What were the snags that might happen? Would the other planes be able to return if something went wrong during the landing of the first Rhino? What was the capacity of the antiaircraft-defense system at the airport? How dangerous could the Ugandan MiG aircraft be? Would there be enough fuel for the takeoff from Entebbe? "The last deadline for us to carry out the operation is Saturday night," Peres said. "Can we prepare everything by Saturday night?"

The officers' answer was positive.

"What is most problematic in this operation?" Peres asked one of the air force commanders.

"The uncertainty," was the answer. "We don't know everything."

Peres didn't let go: "Elaborate!"

And so, step by step, Peres examined all the details of the plan. But Gur again said that he couldn't approve the plan, mostly because Israel didn't have sufficient intelligence on Entebbe, and because of the tortuous and risky flight itinerary. Peres knew that without Gur's support he couldn't present the plan to the government.

Most of the participants left, and only four people remained behind: Motta Gur, Kuti Adam, Beni Peled, and Shimon Peres. Peres tried to calm Gur down; he had asked the Mossad, he said, to use its agents for obtaining precise information on the Entebbe airport.

Even though Gur hadn't authorized the operation, he now agreed to assemble the task force in a training facility to prepare for the Entebbe assault; the facility would be hermetically sealed, and none of the soldiers would be allowed to leave to prevent any information leaks.

At that meeting, it was also decided to appoint Dan Shomron as the operation's commander. An advanced command post was to be established in an air force Boeing aircraft that would accompany the Rhinos and control the operation from the air.

"What do you say, Motta?" Peres asked.

"There was a decision of the government to surrender," Gur said. "You voted for it. A military operation can be carried out in certain conditions. This is not kindergarten or a game of prestige." He added: "The plan you saw this morning is a very nice plan on the professional side. But to carry it out on Saturday night without enough intelligence, that would be charlatanism!"

Peres insisted, "Motta, would you give this another thought?"

"Without intelligence there is no chance that I'd recommend such an operation. Some of the things I heard here aren't worthy of an army's General Staff. If you want Goldfinger—that's a different story. If [you want] James Bond—not with me!"[32]

AT THE END of the meeting, Peres was assailed by agonizing doubts.

He well knew that the chief of staff's arguments were logical. His objection deeply disturbed Peres; he asked himself whether he hadn't become overenthusiastic about the project, to the point that he failed to see "the formidable, real obstacles."[33] He decided, therefore, to turn to the friend whose opinion he valued more than anybody else's: Moshe Dayan.

Peres found Dayan with some friends at the Capriccio restaurant in Tel Aviv, gulping a bowl of soup. Peres apologized to the guests and dragged Dayan to a nearby table. Over a glass of red wine he told his friend about the projected operation. Dayan's eye sparkled, and he didn't conceal his excitement. That's a great plan, he told Peres, and he supported it one hundred percent.[34] He then returned to his soup, and Peres left the place, strongly encouraged.

Before the next Ministerial Committee meeting at 11 P.M., he met Transportation Minister Gad Yaacobi and described the operational plan to him. Yaacobi promised Peres his support.

The meeting of the Ministerial Committee seemed to Peres absolutely surrealistic. He defined Rabin's behavior as "impatient to the point of surprising some of the participants." The meeting dealt with the details of the projected negotiation with the terrorists, the place where it would be held, the degree of the involvement of the French government in the talks. Peres participated almost not at all in the debate, which ended after midnight. But his workday didn't end yet. At 12:30 A.M. he met with Gur. He spoke with him for several hours, using patriotic and Zionist arguments to persuade him to support the operation. "I spoke," Peres wrote, "with all the persuasive powers I could muster, with all the weight of the responsibility that we carry, with all the fervor of the conviction burning inside me."[35] But Gur refused to change his mind and support "irresponsible operational attempts."[36]

When the two men parted at dawn, Peres could only hope that his long monologue into the night had not been in vain.

AFTER TWO HOURS of restless sleep, Peres woke on the morning of Friday, July 2, to face the attack of a new enemy—a terrible toothache that made him rush to his dentist's clinic. When he finally came back to his office he found two important reports: one came from the Mossad director, informing him that Kenya, Uganda's neighbor, had agreed to authorize a stopover for the Israeli planes on their way to or from their target. The Kenyans were ready to cooperate on two conditions: that Israel would keep the affair in absolute secrecy, and that it would agree to give military assistance to Kenya if Uganda attacked it after the operation. Peres instructed Hofi to promise the Kenyans all the help they might need. The second encouraging report was from the intelligence experts, informing him that several sources had provided them with updated facts about Entebbe. Peres immediately went to Gur's office and presented him with the new information.

"His eyes lit up," he wrote.

Indeed, Gur had changed his position.

The quality intelligence he had so much wanted arrived almost by chance. A senior officer, Amiram Levin, had been sent to Paris to debrief the non-Israeli hostages who had been recently liberated, but most of them were still confused and unfocused. Suddenly, an older Frenchman approached him and introduced himself as a former French Army colonel. "I know what you need," he said. He sat down and gave Levin a succinct description of the Old Terminal—where the hostages were kept—the various halls, and the positioning of the terrorists. He also drew for the Israeli detailed sketches of the building. There were thirteen terrorists, he said, including two Germans and a South American, who apparently was the hijackers' commander. The other terrorists were Palestinians. Some of them had participated in the hijacking, others had been waiting for the plane in Entebbe. Their interactions with the Ugandans were cordial. They were armed with small submachine guns, revolvers, and hand grenades. The hostages were held in the main hall of the Old Terminal. The French crew of the Air France plane was held in the women's restrooms. The plane itself had been parked in a distant area, apparently not booby-trapped.

The report gave full details about the terrorists who mounted guard over the hostages, the size of the Ugandan military unit—about sixty soldiers—and their part in guarding the prisoners. Some soldiers had also been seen on the roof of the building, but they numbered only a few score, and not a battalion, as earlier reports had specified. A wall of empty crates had been erected in the Old Terminal, and the terrorists claimed that they were full of explosives, but they were not connected with wires and no sign of preparation for blowing them up could be seen.

Another intelligence report arrived from Entebbe; it included good-quality photographs. The Mossad had sent to Entebbe a foreign aircraft that allegedly had mechanical problems. The plane circled over the airport, photographing its structures, runways, and equipment.

Now it was time to bring the plan to the prime minister. Some of Rabin's aides claimed that Peres hadn't presented the plan to him earlier because he wanted to reap all the glory. According to Peres, he feared that presenting the plan before getting the support of the IDF might have made Rabin dismiss it the same way he had dismissed Gur's earlier plan.

Peres walked into Rabin's office and told him, "At this moment—and I'm telling you this personally, informally—I believe we have a real military option." Peres described Gur's earlier objections, his turnabout, and then presented the plan to the prime minister.

Rabin's first reaction was skeptical. "If this operation doesn't succeed," he said, "it might do harm to Israel more than anything else. It would harm the army. There is a flaw in the plan, in its very first stage: the landing of the first plane. Anyway, I am bound by the government's decision [to accept the hijackers' demands]." What would happen, Rabin asked, if the Ugandans identified the plane as it landed and shot at it?

The air force chief, Peres said, was certain that the plane could be landed without a response from the ground. The Mossad director, who had joined the meeting, now expressed cautious support for the operation.

Peres left Rabin's office with the feeling that he hadn't succeeded in getting his full support, so he decided to try winning the support of another minister. He drove to the office of Justice Minister Haim Zadok, and described the rescue plan to him. In the debate about the Entebbe hostages Zadok had backed Rabin's position. But after his conversation with Peres he expressed his full support for the rescue operation.

Peres summoned the Fantasy Council and the Mossad director to his office, and Gur announced that he was now ready to present the operational plan before the civilian authorities.

One of the participants suggested preparing a "double" of Idi Amin. When the operation took place, Amin apparently would still be at the African nations' conference. Therefore, it would be helpful to have a black Mercedes, similar to Amin's car, move at the head of the Israeli troops at Entebbe. Inside it there would be a disguised Israeli soldier with his face painted black. At night the Ugandans wouldn't clearly notice the figures inside the "presidential" car, and they'd clear its path out of respect for their leader. On the spot, Gur gave his people the order to find a large black Mercedes that could be used for the deception.

The planners informed Peres that the four Rhinos' approach pattern would be over Lake Victoria. The first Rhino would unload the black Mercedes and two Land Rovers that would head for the Old Terminal. The Sayeret Matkal commandos, under the orders of Yoni Netanyahu, would attack the building and kill the terrorists; the other Rhinos would land at intervals a few minutes apart, and the soldiers they carried would take over the New Terminal building, the runway, and the fueling pumps; they would also destroy the MiG aircraft stationed at the airport. A detachment of soldiers, transported by armored cars, would set up roadblocks on the neighboring highway to prevent Ugandan reinforcements from reaching the airport. The hostages would be led to a Rhino that would take off less than an hour after landing and head for Nairobi, Kenya, for refueling and care of any wounded. The other planes would follow, and from Nairobi they'd fly to Israel and land on the morning of July 4.

Gur reported that the elite units chosen to participate in the operation were practicing without respite. The commanders were counting every minute in the operational plan and measuring every distance, every soldier's task, and every vehicle's course. Peres wrote down the planning for the critical moment—the landing of the first plane: "From the moment of turning on the landing lights of the plane and until it stops—two minutes. Two minutes more are needed to get the forces out of the plane. Five minutes to reach the target. Five more minutes to complete the operation."[37]

Peres went to the prime minister's office, escorted by the chief of staff and the Mossad director. Gur presented the plan in detail and received a cautious approval from Yitzhak Rabin.

The Ministerial Committee was convened at once. Rabin still hesitated. "First of all, I want to say that I still am not certain about this operation," he said. "This would be the most risky operation I ever knew."[38] Yet there seemed to be a change in his position. He decided that the operation would be brought for a final approval to an extraordinary government meeting on Saturday, shortly before the planes took off for Entebbe.

The final plans of the IDF General Staff were to be presented on Saturday, at 11 A.M. But first Peres had to overcome the problem of Friday night: Professor Zbigniew Brzezinski, who was visiting Israel, was to be a guest at his home. Brzezinski was expected to be a future major official at the White House if Jimmy Carter was elected president of the United States.

Sonia had cooked her specialty—honey chicken—and Peres had also invited the *Haaretz* editor in chief, Gershom Shocken, as well as Generals Kuti Adam and Shlomo Gazit.

Brzezinski surprised his hosts by throwing a direct question at Peres: "Why don't you send the IDF to rescue the hostages at Entebbe?"

The confused defense minister started explaining the reasons against such an operation—the distance from Entebbe, the lack of sufficient intelligence, the presence of a Ugandan battalion and Soviet MiG fighters . . .

Brzezinski was not convinced.

IN THE EARLY HOURS of Saturday, Peres returned to his office. He was haunted by fears that some malfunction, no matter how marginal, could cause the operation's failure. "Who can guarantee," he wrote, "that one of these tens of thousands of items of which are built the planes, the armored cars, the weapons, wouldn't fail to function at the most critical moment, or at the most critical place?" He finally summoned the air force chief. He reminded him that during these last weeks a few technical mishaps had occurred in some air force flights. "What if," he began, but Beni Peled had anticipated the question. "Sir," he said, "I ordered them to strengthen every screw, in every aircraft. I took care that there would be zero malfunctions."[39]

Peres was also very worried about his relationship with Rabin. "What would happen if the terrorists opened fire at the hostages? In the present mood, when the Prime Minister wants to negotiate and I am pulling the other way, it isn't hard to imagine what would happen to this country and this government. But this is a decisive hour and one cannot escape it."[40]

In an effort to alleviate the atmosphere, he sent a note to Rabin during a Ministerial Committee meeting. "Yitzhak," he wrote, "here is the last refinement in the planning: instead of a ground service vehicle—a large Mercedes plus flags will descend. Idi Amin is coming home from Mauritius. I don't know if it is possible, but it is interesting."[41]

In all of Israel, the operation's planners couldn't find a black Mercedes similar to Amin's, but they found in Gaza a white one of the same size. It was brought right away to the staging area and painted black. Amin's double was also ready, and the Sayeret got black paint to dye his face.

The Fantasy Council met in Peres's office for a last discussion before the presentation of the plan to the government. Peres could feel the tension, but also the confidence of the officers. "There is no reason why not to carry out the operation," said Gur, who was now a sworn supporter of the project. "The chances of success are great."

The participants asked the defense minister some last-minute questions. "If the control tower asks our aircraft to identify themselves, should we answer?" Peres and Gur decided that the pilots shouldn't reply to any questions. And what to do with the French crew?

"Bring them home," Peres said. "We should treat them as Israelis in every way."

The government meeting approached, and Peres asked Gur, "When should the planes take off?" The chief of staff answered: "From Ben-Gurion Airport to Sharm al-Sheikh—at 1 P.M.; from Sharm al-Sheikh—between 4 and 5 P.M."

Peres authorized the planes to leave for Sharm al-Sheikh. If the government decided otherwise, the planes could be turned around and brought back. He drove with Gur to Ben-Gurion Airport to bid the soldiers farewell. He watched the Rhinos standing on the runways, ready to take off. The soldiers gathered around them, already in combat gear. Some of the commanders rushed to Peres, eager to know if the operation would be approved. Many doubted that the government would be that brave. Dan Shomron, the operation's commander, approached Peres. "Don't worry," he said in his confident, slightly husky voice. "Everything is going to be okay."

The order was given to board the planes. Peres noted, "We saw them climbing the gangway into the giant bird, turn back, wave their hands and disappear in her huge belly, as if they were leaving for some merry adventure. Now, all depended on them. Israel's fate took off with them."

At 2:30 P.M., the government meeting started. Peres made an impassioned speech on the importance of the operation. "I was very careful," he wrote, "not to give my colleagues the impression that I was presenting them with an ultimatum, because at such moments that could have an opposite effect. That's why I said that if the government decided on negotiation [instead of a military operation] I shall support the government's decision."[42]

When Peres finished speaking, Rabin asked him, "When do we have to give the planes the order to take off?" From that question Peres deduced that Rabin had decided to support the operation.[43]

After a long debate, the prime minister spoke: "I am for the operation. I am not idealizing. On the contrary, I know what we are in for—casualties, losses in human lives . . . . The government must know that it decides to launch an operation where there would be a large number of casualties. Nevertheless, I ask the government to approve the operation."[44]

The government unanimously approved Operation Entebbe.

LATE IN THE EVENING, Peres returned to his office. He was joined by the Mossad director, Minister Gad Yaacobi, the prime minister, and some of their closest aides. They sat down and waited in silence. Rabin was withdrawn, crushing an unlit cigarette between his fingers; Peres sat in an armchair, his feet on the table. The office transceiver was tuned to the wavelength of the operation.

At 11:03 P.M., they heard the first voices. The first Rhino had landed at Entebbe, closely following the British airliner that had landed before it.

At 11:10 P.M., Dan Shomron's voice echoed in the loudspeakers: "Everything is fine. I'll report later." Cracking noises were heard in the receivers. Were those gunshots or engine noises?

At 11:18 P.M., the code words "Low Tide" burst out of the receiver. That meant that all the planes had landed safely.

Two minutes later, the small group heard Dan Shomron's voice again: "Everything is perfectly all right. You'll get a report soon."

The code words chased one another over the wireless: "Palestine" announced the beginning of the attack on the Old Terminal. After it, at 11:32, came "Jefferson"—the beginning of the evacuation of the hostages.

And a minute later: "Move everything to 'Galila.'" That was the code word for the movement of the hostages to the Rhino awaiting them.

But at 11:50 they heard a call for medics to "Almond Grove," the force under the command of Yoni Netanyahu. The laconic message mentioned "Two Ekaterina"—meaning two wounded. But nothing was said about their identities.

One minute later came the words everyone was praying for: "Mount Carmel." That meant the end of the evacuation. The operation was over and all the planes had taken off.

"The heart jumps with joy," Peres wrote in jubilation.[45]

The high tension in the room evaporated at once, while the messages kept coming. Ninety-three rescued hostages and the French crew were in the Rhino. The ninety-fourth passenger, Dora Bloch, had been rushed two days earlier to a hospital in Kampala, after getting violently ill. Several days later, news came that she had been murdered at the hospital.

At midnight, Gur called Peres from his office and informed him of the successful denouement. The operation had taken fifty-five minutes; the plane with the hostages had been the first to take off. All the terrorists had been killed. It had been decided to refuel the planes and tend to the wounded in Kenya. At a later stage it was established that during the rescue operation, when the commandos had stormed the Old Terminal and engaged the terrorists in a firefight, some of the hostages had stood up in spite of the orders to lie down. Three of them had been killed and six wounded in the cross fire.

At the end of the operation, Rabin returned to his office, while Peres went to the chief of staff's headquarters, where he met the army generals. He saw Minister Haim Bar-Lev, as calm and confident as ever. Peres knew that his son, Omer, was one of the soldiers at Entebbe; but Bar-Lev, a former IDF chief of staff, kept his cool even when he voted for the operation. Another general Peres noticed was Rafael Vardi, his childhood friend. Rafael had lost one of his sons in the Yom Kippur War; his second son, a combat paratrooper, also participated in the Entebbe operation. "I saw those two fathers," Peres wrote in wonder, "when their sons were taking part in such a daring operation, and I felt that if they could pray at that moment, they would have asked to be at the place of their sons, a kind of upside-down Isaac sacrifice. But they don't show any sign of what is gripping their hearts."[46]

As in a surrealistic finale, Borka Bar-Lev telephoned Idi Amin. Peres instructed him to say one sentence to the Ugandan president: "Thank you for your cooperation." Peres wanted to frame Amin and destroy his credibility with his terrorist friends.

"President Amin speaking," echoed on the telephone speaker.

"Thank you, sir," Bar-Lev said. "I want to thank you for your cooperation and I thank you very much, sir."

"You know you didn't succeed . . ." Amin said.

"Thank you so much for your cooperation," Bar-Lev continued. "What? The cooperation didn't succeed? Why?"

"Did I do anything at all?" Amin asked.

"I just want to thank you for your cooperation."

Bar-Lev continued, "I was asked by my friends, who have good connections with the government, to tell you how grateful they are for your cooperation. I don't know what they mean, but I think that you do."

"I don't know a thing," Amin said, "because I arrived just now. I hurried back from Mauritius in order to solve this problem, before the ultimatum expires tomorrow morning."[47]

The people present couldn't believe their ears: Uganda's president didn't know yet what had happened at Entebbe!

Excitement and elation spread through Motta Gur's office. Young soldiers walked in carrying trays of food—chicken drumsticks, pita bread, peppers, pies. The officers filled glasses with Israeli-made champagne. Gur made a short speech: "We can sum up the operation as a very impressive and successful achievement of the IDF. But I cannot sum up the operation even in this early stage without stressing the drive and the influence on its execution that were centered in one man. I don't know if we can allocate percentages to each of those who had a crucial part in the decision to execute this operation; but if there would be such an allocation of percentages, their bulk would go to one man who pressed on and pushed in every direction, both up and down, for this operation."

"And this is the Defense Minister, who deserves all the credit."[48]

PERES AND RABIN drafted a short press release: "IDF forces tonight rescued the hostages from the Entebbe airport, including the Air France crew."

At 3 A.M., Peres returned to his office to get some sleep before the planes landed. Suddenly, Gur knocked on his door. He looked distressed.

"Yoni is dead," he said. "He was hit by a bullet in the back. Apparently he was shot from the old control tower. The bullet pierced his heart."

Peres was stunned, and the two parted without another word.[49] "For the first time that week," Peres wrote, "I burst out crying."

A few hours later, when Yoni Netanyahu's Rhino landed, Peres rushed to Netanyahu's deputy. "How did it happen?" he asked.

One of the soldiers answered: "He led the attack; he was the first to fall."

A few days later, while the Israeli nation was celebrating the successful operation, Peres eulogized Yoni Netanyahu.

"What burdens didn't we load on Yoni's and his comrades' shoulders? The most dangerous of the IDF's tasks and the most daring of its operations; the actions that were the farthest from home and the closest to the enemy; the darkness of night and the solitude of the fighter; the taking of risks, over and over again, in times of peace and in times of war. There are times when the nation's fate depends on a handful of volunteers . . . . Yonatan was a commander of valor. He overcame his enemies by his courage. He conquered his friends' hearts by the wisdom of his heart. He didn't fear danger and victories didn't make him vain. By falling he caused an entire nation to raise her head high."

Peres quoted the biblical verses of David, where he mourned his friend Jonathan: "I am distressed for thee, my brother

Jonathan; very pleasant hast thou been unto me: thy love to me was wonderful" (2 Samuel 1:26).

Yoni's father, professor Ben-Zion Netanyahu, sent an emotional letter of thanks to the defense minister. Peres's speech created a special bond between him and the Netanyahu family. One of Yoni's brothers, Binyamin, Peres's rival in the 1996 elections, was very cautious not to hurt Peres in any way and remained faithful to the unwritten alliance between the Netanyahu family and Shimon Peres.[50]

ONE OF THE less inspiring results of the Entebbe victory was the ugly dispute that erupted between the sympathizers of Peres and Rabin about credit for the operation. In his memoirs, which appeared three years later, Rabin lashed out at Peres, totally denied his part in the hostages' rescue, and tried to attribute to himself the major role in the operation. The defense minister was mentioned only as someone who made "demagogic" speeches, who didn't do his job properly, and who undermined the prime minister.

Justice Minister Zadok, even though he was a Rabin supporter, was utterly upset by Rabin's description of the Entebbe operation. "I remember," he said in a 1980 television interview, "that Shimon Peres was the man who all the time pressed for such an operation. Yitzhak Rabin was the one who braked and asked questions and had doubts; at the time I was with him all the way. Only after Shimon and the military proved that there was a fair chance for the operation to succeed did I change my mind."[51]

Rabin sent his former minister an angry letter, again trying to prove that he was the one who had chosen the military option, while Peres indulged in "ornate rhetoric."[52] But Zadok stuck to his guns and dismissed Rabin's arguments. "In this case," he said, "the personal hostility had driven Rabin out of his mind."[53]

Several other witnesses, among them Generals Motta Gur and Rafael Eitan, expressed the same opinion.[54]

THE WORLD REACTED to the Entebbe operation with an outburst of admiration. The IDF inspired in the Israelis confidence and pride; foreign nations covered the Israeli commandos with praise. Some even attached a symbolic meaning to the date of the operation's conclusion: July 4, 1976, the two hundredth anniversary of the American Declaration of Independence.

"The Entebbe operation," Menachem Begin proudly said, "will heal the nation of the trauma of the Yom Kippur War."[55]

CHAPTER 24.

THE LONG DUEL (2)

ON FRIDAY, DECEMBER 10, 1976, the first three F-15 jets purchased in the United States arrived in Israel. At the air force base a short ceremony took place. The aircraft arrived at 3:25 P.M. and performed some aerobatics before landing. After some speeches the public dispersed, but night fell before some reached their homes, and according to the Jewish faith that was a desecration of the Sabbath.

In the Knesset, the ultraorthodox Agudat Israel Party presented a motion of no confidence. Even though the National Religious Party (NRP) belonged to the government coalition, its Knesset members abstained from voting. Surprising everybody, Yitzhak Rabin fired the NRP ministers from the cabinet, then resigned himself and called early elections for May 1977. Rabin's supporters called his initiative "the brilliant maneuver." But it turned out that the brilliant maneuver brought a disaster upon the Labor Party.

Soon after the government resigned, Shimon Peres announced his intention to run for the leadership of the Labor Party. He felt a lot of self-confidence when challenging Rabin again. As a defense minister he had accomplished several achievements during the previous three years. He had rebuilt the IDF after the Yom Kippur War. Israel had received Lance missiles, tanks, fighter jets, and armored personal carriers from the United States. The

Israeli military industries had borne quality fruit: the first Kfir fighter jets had been delivered to the air force; the Merkava tank went into production; and according to French documents, Israel was building medium-range missiles. Israel also developed air-to-air and surface-to-surface missiles, laser-guided smart bombs, and other sophisticated equipment. Israel exported military equipment to several countries, including two shady clients—Iran and South Africa. Most of these activities were secret, but triumphs like Entebbe, the Good Fence, and the continuation of the Open Bridges policy with Jordan had been widely publicized.

In addition, Rabin's performance as prime minister was unsatisfactory. Peres was ahead of him in the popularity polls. As the election approached, two more disasters shook the Labor Party: Rabin's nominee for governor of the Bank of Israel, Asher Yadlin, was arrested on corruption charges; and Housing Minister Avraham Ofer, also a Rabin supporter, committed suicide after being accused of corruption as well. Labor's position was shaken; many deserted it and joined a new party, the Democratic Movement for Change, led by Yigael Yadin.

Peres launched his campaign by reviving his alliance with Abba Eban, who had supported him in 1974. The old guard once again rejected Peres's candidacy, maintaining that Rabin's leadership shouldn't be questioned. Rabin himself reacted with great anger. He said to Dov Goldstein, "This 'service dodger' runs against me for prime minister? Me, the Palmach man? The Six Day War chief of staff? This wimp, who is he? A petty politician? He dares challenge me?"[1]

The election was held at the party convention. Three thousand delegates were asked to choose between Peres and Rabin. At the opening of the convention, fearing Peres might get more applause than Rabin, the party apparatus thought of a trick: while Shimon Peres got on the podium alone, Yitzhak Rabin came in as one of "a trio," escorted by Golda Meir and the guest of honor from abroad, former German chancellor Willy Brandt. The expected effect was achieved and the applause was great.

On February 23,1977, the vote took place. Peres got 1,404 votes; Rabin 1,445. The difference between them was minimal—41 votes, 1.4 percent.

The prime minister gave his victory speech, then said a final good-bye to Peres: "And all the best to you, Shimon."

BUT THINGS TOOK a different course.

On April 7, the Israelis watched the European basketball championship on their television sets. The game ended with a victory for the flagship Israeli team—Maccabi Tel Aviv, which became champion of Europe. Israel was euphoric. But after the game ended, Yitzhak Rabin suddenly appeared on the television screens. His face was drawn and he looked distraught. His statement stunned the nation: he was resigning from his position as prime minister and leader of the Labor Party!

Rabin's decision was caused by the revelations of an Israeli journalist, Dan Margalit, in the *Haaretz* newspaper. Margalit had found out that Yitzhak and Leah Rabin kept a bank account in Washington, D.C. That was an infraction of the foreign currency laws; Israeli citizens were not allowed to have bank accounts abroad.

The violation of the law was purely technical; the account dated from the time when Rabin had served as ambassador to the United States, and if he had asked for a permit from the Bank of Israel he would have gotten it within hours. But he and his wife hadn't done so; Rabin, an utterly honest man, realized he had to pay the price. He didn't look for crafty ways to evade his responsibility, but decided to resign.

In another surprising move, Rabin recommended to the party that Shimon Peres, his sworn rival, become the new Labor leader and its candidate for prime minister. So it was decided, and Peres became acting prime minister until the elections.

Peres had apparently reached his goal: he was now the party's candidate for prime minister. But the game was already lost. The poet Haim Gouri said to one of his friends, "We are going to lose the election. The Governor of the Bank of Israel is in jail, the Housing Minister is in his grave, the Prime Minister is standing trial—how can we win?"[2]

Labor's hegemony was threatened for other reasons, too. One was the delayed reaction to the Yom Kippur mishap. Another was a profound demographic change: for the first time, Sephardic Jews were now equal in numbers to the Ashkenazim. Coming mostly from North Africa and the Middle East, the Sephardim nurtured deep feelings of frustration toward the Labor Party, which they deemed vain, haughty, and insensitive to their problems. They hated the word "socialism" and were much more hawkish than the Ashkenazim.

Israel also had changed. The great achievements of the Labor movement in building the country, the kibbutz, the moshav, the Histadrut, didn't seem to be relevant anymore. Labor's charismatic leaders were gone. As long as Ben-Gurion or Golda was prime minister, Menachem Begin's theatricals made him look grotesque in comparison. But compared to Rabin he emerged as a charismatic leader, rooted in the Jewish tradition, a patriot and a gifted orator. To the younger generation he seemed to be the last of the Founding Fathers; furthermore, he was surrounded by a team of promising young leaders like Arik Sharon and Ezer Weizman.

On May 17, 1977, the general election took place. It was an earthquake. The Labor alignment lost nineteen seats and shrunk to thirty-two. The Likud won forty-five seats. The Democratic Movement for Change got fifteen seats—most of what Labor had lost.

The president invited Menachem Begin to form the new cabinet.

YITZHAK RABIN FURIOUSLY ATTACKED Shimon Peres, accusing him of losing the election, even though he had resigned barely a month before. He claimed that the defense minister's activity against him "destroyed the Labor Party, debased the government in the eyes of the public, and finally crowned Shimon Peres with the title of 'leader of the opposition.' "[3]

But the "leader of the opposition" was already immersed in a tremendous effort to rebuild the Labor Party. With a handful of assistants he moved into Labor's deserted headquarters on Hayarkon Street and launched a Sisyphean campaign to get Labor back on its feet. He visited the remotest party branches, spoke at hundreds of rallies, raised money, wrote newspaper articles, and persuaded concerned citizens to join Labor. Once again he displayed his relentless working capacity. "Sleep is a waste of time," he said to his son Yoni. To his younger son, Hemi, he confided, "If you want to achieve great things, you must cross deserts. When you cross deserts you suffer from the heat, the sun is blazing, there's no food, no drink, but if you keep walking—finally you'll make it."

During the crossing of the desert he suffered more blows. His close companion Moshe Dayan crossed the lines and joined Begin's cabinet as foreign minister. Dayan didn't want his career to end with the grim chapter of the Yom Kippur War. He was determined to add another to his life story, to fulfill a dream that would restore his image.

The dream was peace with Egypt. When Begin invited him to join his new government, Dayan agreed, on several conditions. The major one was initiating a peace negotiation with Egypt.

Begin agreed. It was a wise and inspiring move, and Peres supported it wholeheartedly. But the sudden desertion of Dayan, who didn't even consult him beforehand, left a deep scar in Peres's heart.[4] "Moshe did something that is not done," he said to a friend.

Dayan steered the negotiation by secret and tortuous moves, but the results were soon to come. On November 19, 1977, President Sadat, who had succeeded Nasser in 1970, landed in Israel. The arrival of this former foe at Ben-Gurion Airport seemed to the Israeli people like a dream come true. Sadat was warmly welcomed by Begin and his ministers; he spoke at the Knesset and started peace talks with the Israeli leaders. At the Knesset, he said to Golda Meir that he had wanted to meet her when she still was prime minister. "Why didn't you come then?" she said sadly.

But the peacemaking was no longer in Labor's hands. The Likud was in charge of the negotiations now. Peres and his friends watched with envy and frustration the various stages of the negotiations. Peres met Sadat several times in Europe; he asked for Begin's authorization before each of the meetings, and reported to him afterward. But his talks with Sadat had no practical meaning. Menachem Begin and Moshe Dayan were Sadat's interlocutors and the negotiation's success depended on them.

Peres didn't understand a basic rule of politics—the public didn't like people other than the elected government to intervene in matters of state. Peres regarded his meetings with Sadat as important achievements, but the Israeli public was rather upset by them.

Peres also tried to establish secret ties with Morocco's King Has-san and met him twice in Morocco, in deep secrecy. His first trip was kept secret indeed. He flew to Morocco with his assistant Dr. Yossi Beilin and his friend Jean Frydman. Late that night, after a fascinating conversation with the king, Peres decided to tell Frydman about it. Frydman sneaked into his room, but Peres was reluctant to raise his voice, for fear that the Moroccan intelligence services might be listening. Having no choice, he moved to one side of the bed, and Jean lay down beside him. Peres, whispering, described the meeting. "Try to imagine the picture," Frydman later recalled with a smile. "At night, in bed, in the moonlight, facing the palm trees swaying in the window, and me in Shimon's arms."[5]

Peres again flew to Morocco with Yossi Beilin, a few months before the election for the Tenth Knesset. Strangely, the news about Peres's meeting with King Hassan in Morocco leaked as soon as they landed in Paris, on their way back to Israel. Both Peres and Beilin denied being the source of the leak. But the public reaction back home was far from what the anonymous source presumably wanted to achieve: many Israelis severely criticized the opposition leader who once again was carrying out his own diplomacy.[6]

A DEEP CHANGE gradually took place in Peres's political thinking. He had been a prominent hawk in Rabin's cabinet, but now he adopted moderate positions toward the Arab world and the Palestinians in particular; his new positions were different from, and even opposed to, his former views.[7] Peres claimed that the change in his views was a result of Israel's becoming a powerful country. After the Dimona reactor was completed, and Israel's existence secured, she could afford to offer a compromise to her neighbors. But there were also other reasons for Peres's change of views. For the first time in his life, he was no longer subjected to the crushing influence of Ben-Gurion and Dayan. In the past his views had mirrored those of the two leaders. He moved away from Ben-Gurion's shadow after 1967, even if their close relations continued until the Old Man's death in 1973. The close rapport with Dayan, though, continued even when Peres was defense minister. But after Dayan left the Labor Party their alliance came to an end. Now Peres was his own man.

His new policy was influenced by the members of the team that he assembled in Hayarkon Street; most of them were doves, and their views seeped into his own thinking. Another factor that dispelled Peres's hawkish views was the Socialist International, the world organization of socialist parties that Labor belonged to. European leaders such as Germany's Willy Brandt, Austria's Bruno Kreisky, France's François Mitterrand, Sweden's Olof Palme, and Spain's Felipe Gonzales were the major figures in that organization. Many of them held pro-Palestinian views and even wanted to open the gates of the Socialist International to PLO representatives. Peres struggled against that trend, but at the same time he adopted more liberal views on a territorial compromise and Palestinian autonomy, even though he didn't want to hear of a Palestinian state.

But at home, new storms were brewing. Various groups in the

Labor Party, in particular members of the Ahdut Ha'avoda faction and Rabin supporters, refused to accept Peres's leadership. Even when his efforts to revive the Labor Party started bearing fruit, his foes kept sniping at him.

At their head, again, was Yitzhak Rabin. The publication of his *Memoirs* in August 1979 caused a sensation, and portions of the book were read that night during the television news broadcasts. The book was imbued with a violent hatred for Shimon Peres. Rabin furiously attacked him, maintaining that Peres was unreliable, that he had undermined Rabin's position, that he had leaked secret information, that he was not worthy to be defense minister and certainly not prime minister. He accused him of causing the Sebastia fiasco, of botching several arms-purchase deals, of immature political views, of harmful behavior during the Entebbe affair. In the entire book there was not one positive word for Shimon Peres; the worst expression Rabin used against him was "relentless underminer," which would become the battle cry for Peres haters in future generations.[8] The term was coined by Dov Goldstein, the book's coauthor, and Rabin was ecstatic. "After he read the phrase," Goldstein said, "Rabin asked me, Dovaleh, what is your military rank? I said, I am a sergeant. Rabin said, This is the first time that a chief of staff salutes a sergeant."[9]

The book caused indignation in the Labor Party. Peres, after all, was the party chairman. Many suggested that the party expel Rabin from its ranks. At a party bureau meeting, the major leaders angrily criticized Rabin and drafted a resolution severely condemning him. The resolution would have certainly been supported by a great majority of the bureau members, and it turned into a show of strength for Shimon Peres.

At the very last moment, though, Peres recoiled and adjourned the meeting without putting the motion to vote. For many, it was a sign of weakness and indecision. Peres displayed one of his characteristic traits—he was ready to take blows, attacks, and insults but backed away from hitting back. "Shimon doesn't have a politician's poisoned tooth," said his friend Moshe Shalit. "He deserves a mention in the *Guinness Book of Records* as the champion of absorbing blows and insults," political analyst Nahum Barnea added.

Peres's weak response had an impact on the public: Rabin's book was accepted as a true and sincere account of a former prime minister who was the innocent victim of a "relentless underminer." The book was to cause Peres tremendous damage over the years.

For a while, though, it seemed that the book marked the end of Rabin's political career. His place was taken by his former commander in the Palmach, Yigal Allon, who decided to run against Peres at the next party convention. But in February 1980, Allon died of a heart attack. By his open grave, on a day of storm and rain, his widow, Ruth, turned to Rabin, like some biblical figure. "Bear the flag that Yigal raised!" she called to him.

And Rabin did. He returned to politics and announced he was going to run against Peres at the convention. After a campaign strewn with dirty blows on both sides, three thousand convention delegates voted on December 17,1980. Peres won an unprecedented victory; he received 71 percent of the vote, while Rabin was routed with 28.8 percent. After the vote, on the dais of the convention hall, Peres walked to where Rabin sat and stretched out his hand. The public cheered and applauded. Rabin, flushed and embarrassed, reluctantly shook his rival's hand.

Now, after that obstacle had been removed from Peres's path, he felt ready to lead his party to an electoral victory over the Likud.

IN SPITE OF HIS VICTORY, Peres had not recovered his credibility in the eyes of the Israeli public. Rabin kept attacking him; at the Knesset Begin ridiculed him; Likud supporters spread rumors about him, and they stuck. In spite of his modest way of life, many accused him of living in a penthouse (he never had one), of owning a factory (he never did), of holding stock in the Tadiran Electronics company (he never had any). During a political debate in one of the provincial towns, a Labor politician asked his Likud rival why he hated Peres so much. The answer was, "Because his mother is an Arab." The crowd cheered.[10]

All through his career, Peres was haunted by a severe credibility problem. It was partly caused by his fertile imagination, which produced an endless string of ideas. Many doubted his sincerity because of his restraint and self-control, which seemed inhuman. When he was attacked, sometimes viciously, people would have liked to see him slam his fist on the table and shout back at his critics. But Peres always managed to control himself, avoiding any exposure of his feelings. "I am a self-restrained man," he said once. "Culture also means restraint. Why does one walk around dressed and not naked? Culture also means to appear covered. It's better to be restrained."[11]

In politics, Peres was accused of wooing his enemies and neglecting his friends. He always seemed ready to invest considerable efforts in winning the support of his rivals, even if that meant hurting his loyal friends.[12] Party leaders claimed that he didn't keep many of his promises, and that was true.[13] When Abba Eban was asked why Peres didn't fulfill his promise to make him a minister, he quipped cynically, "He didn't want to set a precedent."[14]

Others accused him of not telling the truth. Ben-Gurion used to say that "Shimon isn't always accurate with facts."[15] Golda Meir and Pinhas Sapir complained about that to Ben-Gurion, and he would discuss their complaints with Peres.[16] Peres indeed presented inexact accounts, more than once, and was severely criticized for that flaw.[17] But so did Ariel Sharon, whom Ben-Gurion accused in his diary of not telling the truth;[18] so did Yitzhak Rabin in his account of the Entebbe operation; and so did Menachem Begin in his wild accusations against his political rivals. But the accusations stuck to Peres, while other politicians who did the same had an image of integrity in the public eye.

President Chaim Herzog liked Peres, but didn't spare him his criticism. He wrote, "Peres has unfortunately developed something of a Nixonian image. Because he is so brilliant and so adept at behind-the-scenes maneuvering, he is perceived by some as not reflecting integrity; but, of course, reflection is not reality. Peres does what he has to do to achieve his goals which are lofty. But his methods, like those of any true politician, cannot possibly be. Peres often quoted François Mitterrand, who said it best: 'A politician who doesn't promise before an election is not a politician. A politician who keeps his promises after an election is not a statesman.' "[19]

The writer Amos Oz, who believed in Peres's greatness as a statesman, saw his weakness from another angle. "His most important weakness," he said, "is his unquenchable thirst for love. If he is about to meet a group of right-wing settlers, he wants them to love him. If he meets a group of left-wing radicals--he needs their love, too. Sometimes both meetings take place on the same day. When one reads this in the paper, one would say the man is a chameleon, evasive, lacking credibility. That hurts his image terribly. Don't look for love in the street, look for it at home! That model of a leader looking for love is somewhat neurotic."

"This is Peres's major problem; without it he would have reached lofty heights. His grasp of events, his endless creativity, his talent to open a window in a wall where there are no windows, to find a crack where others see only a concrete wall, to tie things together that others believe could never be tied together, all the things because of which people ridiculed him and called him a man of fantasy—that's his greatness. He has more vision and imagination than Ben-Gurion or any other Israeli politician had."

"He is not a relentless underminer," Oz stressed. "He is a mediocre politician. He hasn't learned what any third-grade politician knows. If he had started his career via the party organization and not at Ben-Gurion's side, he wouldn't have gone far. Love makes him blind; he sees it where it doesn't exist. He is unable to generate real anger, great anger—neither toward those who besmirch him and criticize him, nor toward his rivals. He generates instead stilted explanations, sometimes even contortions, all not to lose the love he seeks."

Oz summed up: "A statesman must be able to clench his teeth and press his lips and walk between two lines of people who spit at him and throw rotten eggs in his face. But Shimon couldn't, all his life, restrain himself from turning to those who spit and throw eggs at him and telling them: 'Actually, you had to love me—if you understood me, you would have loved me.'"[20]

THE PERSON WHO won the public's love without really trying was Yitzhak Rabin. He had stumbled in the bank-account affair, but his expressions of regret convinced the Israeli people, and they forgave him. His unsophisticated appearance, his embarrassment in front of the cameras, his simple and direct way of speaking won the public's trust, while Peres's polished and refined formulas sowed doubts. In the polls his popularity soared and left Peres's behind. Peres realized that he couldn't ignore Rabin's rising star; he finally announced that Rabin would be his defense minister if he won the next election. Rabin, too, announced that he would cooperate with Peres in spite of his book.

Labor's leaders now felt that they would win the 1981 election. After negotiating with Sadat at Camp David, Begin had signed a peace treaty with Egypt and that undoubtedly was a historic achievement; Begin and Sadat were jointly awarded the Nobel Peace Prize. But after the signing of the peace treaty, Begin's government started sliding downhill. In spite of the Camp David accords, Begin didn't establish autonomy in the West Bank and Gaza. One after another, Foreign Minister Moshe Dayan, Defense Minister Ezer Weizman, and Finance Minister Yigal Horowitz resigned from the cabinet. The economic situation worsened, and inflation reached 133 percent a year. The political analysts were almost unanimous—Likud was on its way back to the opposition, and Labor back to power.

DURING THESE YEARS a close friendship developed

between Shimon Peres and François Mitterrand, the French Socialist Party leader. The two men had been introduced in the mid-fifties by former prime minister Pierre Mendès-France at his Paris house. "This man Mitterrand," Mendès-France said to Peres, "is the best pianist in the French parliament. He knows every note on the score, and every key on the keyboard. He is a man you can rely on."[21] Peres was impressed by Mitterrand's character; he found in him some of the qualities he himself yearned to possess: "He was a man capable of absorbing harsh blows without flinching, and equally capable of enjoying heady success without losing his iron self-discipline."[22]

Peres and Mitterrand maintained a close relationship before and after Mitterrand's election as France's president in 1981. Like Peres, Mitterrand loved books. When Peres was invited to the French president's country house, in Latche, in the Pyrenees Mountains, he was overwhelmed. Mitterrand's house was simple and Spartan, and reminded him of Ben-Gurion's hut in Sde Boker. On a wooden table in Mitterrand's room Peres saw an open Bible, and he had long conversations with the French leader about Israel's prophets. Mitterrand deeply admired Moses, but regarded Jeremiah as "an unpleasant man who had created an apocalyptic tone" that he found as intolerable in prophecy as in politics. He also had something to say about Joshua, who "conquered the country and settled down to live on the land, but he died a lonely man and no one came to his funeral."[23]

In François Mitterrand Peres found a reflection of his own convictions: a socialist, but not a doctrinarian; a man trying to adapt egalitarian ideas to the realities of the present; a man of culture who believed that it was his duty as president to develop and spread his country's culture; a political leader who had known many a defeat, but kept rising again and didn't give up till he achieved his goal; a nonconformist, open to new ideas, daring in his initiatives, soaring in his splendid vision.

Mitterrand wasn't as good a friend to Israel as Peres thought. He used harsh, sometimes revolting expressions to condemn

Israel's policy in the occupied territories; he called the Israeli Army's activities in the West Bank "the hunting season." But only years later did Peres discover the real flaw in Mitterrand's personality, on learning that during World War II Mitterrand had been a senior official in the Vichy regime and had even been decorated with the most prestigious medal of collaborationist France. "This chapter is a cloud that will always hang over his biography," Peres wrote.[24]

THE FRIENDSHIP WITH Mitterrand was to cost Peres dearly at a crucial stage of his political life. In the years 1980 and 1981, Israel watched with growing anxiety the completion of the nuclear reactor at Osirak, which France was building for Saddam Hussein close to Baghdad. The construction of that reactor was a threat to Israel's very existence; one day it could produce nuclear weapons that might be used against the Jewish state.

Shortly before the 1981 election Peres told Mitterrand about Israel's concern over the Iraqi reactor. France had undertaken to supply the Iraqis with twenty-four kilograms of enriched uranium. That uranium would enable Iraq to build an atomic bomb right away. The uranium was to be delivered to Iraq in two shipments; the first was already in the Iraqis' hands. "If I am elected president," Mitterrand said, "France will not deliver the second shipment."[25]

Peres briefed Prime Minister Begin about that conversation. But a short time later, he learned that Begin intended to bomb the reactor shortly before the Israeli election. The operation was to take place on the day Mitterrand was to be sworn in as president. Peres asked Begin not to carry out the bombing on that day, as France might interpret it as a provocation. For the same reason he decided not to fly to Paris for the swearing-in ceremony.

The bombing was finally delayed for other reasons. Mitterrand later asked Peres why he hadn't come to his swearing in, and Peres revealed the truth to him. Mitterrand turned to some of his friends and said, "How many people like Shimon do you know, who would stay at home so as not to embarrass a friend?"[26]

But the matter was much more serious. Peres firmly objected to Begin's plan of bombing the reactor. He secretly sent Begin a letter demanding that he not bomb Osirak. "I feel this is my duty to advise you, with all due seriousness and consideration of the national interest, to refrain from that action. I speak out of experience."

Peres hinted that the entire world would ostracize Israel for her operation. "Israel would be like a lone tree in the desert," he added in a poetic tone, "and she also has enough to worry about."

"I join my voice—and this is not my voice only—to those who tell you not to do this, and certainly not at the present time and conditions."[27]

Menachem Begin ignored the letter. On June 6, 1981, a few weeks before the Israeli elections, eight Israeli F-16 aircraft flew low over Eilat, crossed the airspace of Jordan and Saudi Arabia, penetrated into Iraq, and dived toward the nuclear reactor. In an eighty-second bombing run they completely destroyed the reactor and safely returned home.

When the news was published, the Israeli people reacted with a tremendous outburst of enthusiasm. As far as the world reaction went, Peres's forecast turned out to be totally mistaken. The world reacted to the Israeli feat with restraint; many let out a sigh of relief.

In a cynical but smart political maneuver, Begin published Peres's letter even though it was personal and secret. The public reaction was indignant. But Peres didn't back off, and issued several statements that harshly criticized the bombing. By doing so he caused considerable damage to Labor's chances to win the election. All the polls showed that Peres's criticism of the operation caused a large number of votes to shift to Likud. It was not the bombing but Labor's reaction to it that tipped the scales in Likud's favor.[28]

Peres's main arguments against the bombing were rather lame. Furthermore, he had been given the wrong information by Mitterrand. It turned out that the first shipment of uranium delivered to Iraq amounted to 27.8 kilograms. That was enough for the fabrication of one atomic bomb. Besides, Osirak was capable of extracting plutonium from nonenriched uranium that Iraq had already purchased in large quantities. Osirak would have been able to produce enough plutonium for the fabrication of one bomb a year after its activation. By the time of the Gulf War, Iraq would have been able to produce fifteen bombs.

All these facts were included in a secret report that had been delivered to François Mitterrand a few days after his swearing in.[29] France's president was aware, therefore, of the threat that the Iraqi reactor represented, but he didn't take any action. In retrospect, it appeared that Begin did the right thing by destroying Saddam Hussein's reactor.

IN SPITE OF the reactor affair, the Labor Party leaders believed that they had a serious chance to win the election. On the night of June 30, the party leadership met at the campaign headquarters at the Deborah Hotel in Tel Aviv. Many senior journalists, foreign reporters, and television crews rubbed shoulders with the politicians. The atmosphere was tense, everybody expecting the television forecast of the election results.

On the screen appeared Hanoch Smith, the best pollster in the country. He announced that the Labor alignment had won a decisive victory over Likud. Peres was going to form the next government.

The crowd rose to its feet, cheering, shouting, clapping hands. Campaign activists hugged one another and burst into song. Israel Peleg, Labor's spokesman, got up and announced, "Ladies and gentlemen, the next prime minister of Israel!"

Shimon Peres, in an open-collared white shirt, smiling broadly, walked in and the cheers turned into a roar.

"Again! Again!" the reporters shouted. They hadn't managed to get the historic moment on tape. Israel Peleg obediently got up again. "Ladies and gentlemen," he repeated in English, "the next prime minister of Israel!"

Shimon Peres made his way across the hall, stopping to shake hands and exchange hugs with Labor leaders. Yitzhak Rabin rose to face him. They hesitated a second, then embraced, and Peres planted a ringing kiss on Rabin's cheek.

Some Labor leaders were already being interviewed live on national television, explaining why the Labor alignment had won. Then, all of a sudden, Smith's face filled the screen again. He seemed embarrassed. "There has been a dramatic change," the pollster said. "We are receiving results that contradict my previous findings."

The singing and the cheering died abruptly as new projections were flashed on the screen. Soon after, it became clear: Labor had lost again, by one or two seats. It had achieved, indeed, a tremendous feat by leaping from thirty-two seats in the Knesset to forty-seven; but the joy was premature. Likud had won again.

At 3 A.M., Menachem Begin appeared on the screen, in front of cheering Likud members. He had freshened up and was wearing an elegant suit. He acknowledged his victory and announced he was going to form the next government. Then he sarcastically addressed Shimon Peres, mocking his premature victory announcement. "What about the kiss, Shimon?" he said, turning theatrically to the camera. "The kiss you gave your friend Rabin. Now you have to take back the kiss!"

CHAPTER 25.

PRIME MINISTER

ON THE EVENING OF June 3, 1982, four Palestinian terrorists shot the Israeli ambassador to Great Britain, Shlomo Argov, outside the Dorchester Hotel in London. He collapsed, hit in the temple. He was rushed to the hospital in critical condition.

The following morning, Prime Minister Begin ordered the air force to attack several PLO targets in Beirut, even though he had been informed that Argov's assailants were members of another terrorist organization, Abu Nidal. But Begin didn't care about Abu Nidal; what he wanted was to start a war against the PLO in Lebanon.

Begin well knew that the PLO would inevitably react to the air raids by a massive shelling of Galilee. Following the shelling, Begin intended to ask his government to authorize a military operation in Lebanon aimed at destroying the terrorists' artillery. It was a re: quest they couldn't refuse.

This was exactly what happened. The Israelis bombed, the PLO shelled in return, and on Saturday night, June 5, the government approved the invasion of Lebanon in an operation named Peace for Galilee. The next morning, Israel was at war.

In the Knesset, Begin declared that the IDF would advance only up to twenty-five miles inside Lebanon, which was the maximum range of the PLO's artillery. "As soon as we reach the forty-kilometer line, the fighting will stop." Begin also turned to

President Hafez al-Assad of Syria, whose army occupied some portions of Lebanon, and asked him not to intervene in the fighting. "No Syrian soldier will be hurt," he said.

Peres and Rabin decided to support the operation, and the Labor Party voted for the government. Yet insistent rumors maintained that the twenty-five-mile line was only a deception; the true goals of the operation were much more ambitious. They involved an Israeli advance to Beirut, a junction with the Christian militias, and the expulsion of the PLO and the Syrian Army from the country.

After a few days, indeed, the fighting spread over a larger area; in a huge air battle, the air force destroyed about one hundred Syrian fighter aircraft and the antiaircraft missile batteries in the Bekáa Valley. The IDF also engaged Syrian armored units in several battles and defeated them. It became clear that the Israeli goal was not Sidon, within the twenty-five-mile line, but Beirut.

The IDF encircled Beirut and joined the Christian forces to the north of the Lebanese capital. It placed Beirut under a tight siege; thousands of PLO terrorists and Syrian soldiers were trapped in the city.

The leaders of the Labor Party still supported the war; Yitzhak Rabin toured the areas overlooking Beirut with Defense Minister Arik Sharon and even advised him to tighten the siege on the city. Shimon Peres flew to Lebanon with the Foreign Affairs and Defense Committee of the Knesset and was briefed by Chief of Staff Rafael Eitan. He spent a few emotional moments with his son Hemi, now a helicopter pilot, who had participated in the heavy fighting in Damour, one of the main terrorist bases in Lebanon.[1]

At the request of the Socialist International, Shimon Peres flew to the Shuf Mountains, where he met with Walid Junblatt, the leader of the Druze in Lebanon. He promised Junblatt protection and immunity in the name of Sharon and Eitan, and analyzed the military situation in terms that would have pleased both of them. "Syria has been dealt a terrible blow," he said. "She has no capacity to defend herself anymore. The IDF could have destroyed the entire Syrian Army in a day or two, or even in a few hours. Syria's missile air defenses were destroyed in two hours. She lost about a hundred planes without shooting down even one of ours. She lost four hundred tanks, and our Merkava tank, made in Israel, is better than the Russian T-72."

That conversation revealed a basic trait of Shimon Peres, one that was not always visible to others. Peres had indeed become a man of peace, but deep down, he remained Mr. Security, dedicated to Israel's defense. When he spoke with Junblatt, Peres presented the case of the Israeli government and staunchly defended Peace for Galilee, because he viewed it as vital for the security of Galilee's towns and villages. That concern would stay embedded in his character even when he devoted all his energy to achieving peace with the Palestinians; he would recoil from any step that could harm Israel's security. After all, the defense ministry had for many years been Shimon Peres's world.

Yet his position was always based on strong moral and humane principles. When he visited the ruins of Tyre, in South Lebanon, he wrote in his diary, "The heart bleeds, out of shame and sorrow." In the eyes of the Lebanese he saw "the suffering and the pain of refugees," and summed up the description of the painful sights on his route: "Was all this inevitable?"[2] In a meeting with Sharon he objected to the planned invasion of Beirut. "The siege," he told the defense minister, "is more harmful to the civilians than to the terrorists. It would backfire on us and make us look inhuman; and all this after we already went too far by our bombings and artillery fire."[3] He disagreed with Rabin, who supported the tightening of the siege.

During one of the heaviest bombardments of Beirut, Peres telephoned Begin to urge restraint, and found out that the prime minister didn't know what was happening on the battlefield. Begin wasn't aware that somebody had ordered a bombardment, or that it was in progress. "Begin was not in control of the army's actions during the Lebanon War," Peres wrote. "He did not master the flow of material, written and oral, that streamed across his desk. I do not attribute this to any problem of health or advancing age. He would not, in my opinion, have functioned any differently had he been ten years younger. Begin was too often more dramatic than realistic, influenced more by the resonance of events than by their substance .... He was so captivated by the aura of battle-hardened generals like Sharon that he effectively lost or abdicated all responsibility for political decision-making."[4]

WHILE THE FIGHTING in Lebanon was at its peak, the American secretary of state, Alexander Haig, resigned from office. "I never admired his intellectual capacities," Peres wrote, "and these last weeks he acted in a very determined way to support Begin and Sharon. In the short run, that helped the government considerably. In the long run, that will be harmful for us. We shall be intoxicated with victories and we'll go too far."[5]

The public opinion in Europe and the United States started shifting against Israel. Inside Israel the criticism mounted, too. The IDF's losses in Lebanon were on the rise; many Israelis were revolted by the daily bombings of Beirut. In Lebanon the Israeli soldiers were no longer received with flowers, and the Shiites started carrying out terrorist acts against the IDF.

Peres's friends in the Socialist International severely criticized Israel and didn't spare Peres himself. He was painfully affected by Willy Brandt's criticism, and defended his positions in front of a socialist delegation, headed by former Portuguese prime minister Mário Soares, that came to Israel during the fighting.

Soares asked Sharon to receive the delegation and Sharon agreed, and asked Peres to join them. "You have never been to my farm," Sharon complained. Peres therefore went with the delegation to Sycamore Farm, where they were warmly received by Sharon. The defense minister made quite an impression on his guests. His main theory was that Jordan is Palestine, and the Palestinians should make Jordan their homeland. Peres was impressed by Sharon's delivery, but not by the contents of his exposé. "How tragic it is," he noted, "that two generals, both of them sons of the Labor movement, have led Begin: Dayan to peace with Egypt (including the Palestinian autonomy), and Sharon to war with Lebanon (including the destruction of the PLO)."[6]

In the following years, Peres's criticism of Sharon increased, and he maintained that Sharon had tried to apply to the Lebanon War the strategy Dayan had conceived for the Sinai Campaign. "It was like drawing an analogy between a snake and a sausage, on the grounds that both are long and round."[7]

And yet, on August 21, 1982, it seemed that Sharon's scheme had succeeded.

THAT DAY THE FIGHTING in West Beirut came to an end. Yasser Arafat and the PLO terrorists were exiled to Tunisia. The Syrian Army units retreated from Beirut as well. The Lebanese parliament elected Israel's closest ally, the Christian leader Bashir Gemayel, president of Lebanon. An international peacekeeping force of American Marines, French Legionnaires, and Italian commandos landed in the port of Beirut.

That was Sharon's finest hour. But from that moment on, the avalanche rolled downhill. On September 14, president-elect Gemayel was killed in a bombing and Israel lost her staunchest ally. The following day, the IDF entered West Beirut, in spite of Sharon's earlier promises. That night, the IDF authorized the Christian Phalange to enter into the Sabra and Shatila camps, where Palestinian refugees lived in poverty.

The Phalangists claimed they wanted to search the camps for terrorists, but their real goal was to avenge Bashir Gemayel's death. In the dark, they slaughtered hundreds of Palestinians—men, women, and children. The following day between eight hundred and twelve hundred corpses were discovered in the camps' alleys. The world was shaken, and so was Israel. The largest protest in the history of Israel was held in Tel Aviv's main square.

Begin was forced to establish a board of inquiry about the

Sabra and Shatila events; three months later, the Kahan commit-tee, led by Supreme Court president Yitzhak Kahan, published its findings. Sharon was forced to resign as defense minister, but remained a member of the government.

For Begin, the Lebanese tragedy, coupled with a personal tragedy—his wife's death—was too heavy, and in September 1983 he resigned from office.

Likud elected Yitzhak Shamir as his successor.

SMALL, SHORT-LIMBED, with gray curly hair, bushy eye-brows, and a moth-eaten mustache, Shamir was a former leader of the Stern group (Lehi), the most extreme underground orga-nization that had fought against the British before 1948. Shamir was a sworn supporter of the idea of a Greater Israel. After a career in the Mossad, he had entered the world of politics. He held extremist views and had voted against the Camp David accords. He was a bad speaker, and his vocabulary was limited; the words came out of his mouth hacked and with difficulty, as though he regretted them. Yet he was an honest and a truthful man, who wouldn't use sly political maneuvers or double-talk to achieve his goals.

Begin had anointed him as his heir not because Shamir was a leader but because he was not one. He was a candidate of com-promise between the warring factions of Likud. But very soon Israel found out that he was poorly qualified for his job. Shamir was unable to cope with Israel's major problems: the Lebanon War, the Palestinian problem, the galloping inflation that threat-ened to destroy Israel's economy. He faced the crises without budging. He had turned immobility into a religion; under his reign the government sank into complete torpor.

Peres's patience was put to a test. He couldn't wait for the elections, scheduled for November 1985. He began feverishly maneuvering in the Knesset and succeeded in advancing the election date to July 1984. When the election took place, it turned out that Labor lost three seats, falling from forty-seven to forty-four. Yet Likud lost seven seats, winning only forty-one.

For the first and only time in his life, Peres had won a national election. He was charged by President Herzog to form the new government.

"Peres seemed stunned," Herzog wrote in his memoirs. "He asked Shamir to join him in creating a new government, and embraced me. He went to the Wailing Wall and inserted a small note with the prayer 'Put our hearts together.' "[8]

VERY SOON, THOUGH, Peres realized that a formidable obstacle blocked his way to the prime minister's office. He had won the election—but couldn't form a coalition. Likud, together with the religious parties and the extreme right wing, had succeeded in forming a block of sixty members of parliament; Labor couldn't gather more than sixty seats, either. The result was a deadlock.

Some analysts and politicians started speaking about new elections. But Peres and Shamir, with the help of Sharon, were able to break the deadlock. They invented a unique formula—a national unity government, based on a rotation agreement. In the first two years Peres would be prime minister, and Shamir his deputy and minister of foreign affairs; in the last two years of the term they would switch positions. Likud and Labor would have the same number of ministers in the government.

Peres had insisted that he be the first to serve as prime minister. This was not the result of a caprice or of his impatience to reach the coveted position. "In the Labor Party councils, I argued in favor of our being first," Peres wrote. "I couldn't see Shamir, if he were now to continue as Prime Minister, carrying out any of the main planks of our platform: withdrawing from Lebanon; beating inflation; reaching agreement with Egypt over Taba"—the last area in the Sinai still in dispute between the two countries—"or launching negotiations with Jordan and the Palestinians." Peres feared that in twenty-five months the country would be mired in even deeper trouble.[9]

In the new government, Rabin received the defense portfolio. Yitzhak Navon, the former president, was appointed minister of education and culture; Sharon was minister of commerce and industry.

Shimon Peres was sworn in as Israel's eighth prime minister.

A FEW DAYS LATER, Peres went to the modest house in the Kirya—the government complex—where Prime Minister Ben-Gurion's office used to be. He entered the house alone. The obscure hallway, the stairs to the second floor, the windows offering a view of the serene Kirya garden—every step brought with it a surge of memories. Deeply moved, he entered Ben-Gurion's office. Everything in the room looked as he remembered it from the times they used to work together. "The same chair, the same desk, the same books. Nobody had touched a thing. I walked around the desk, and sat down in the chair. All the excitement of being sworn in as prime minister, the official cars, the entourage, the bodyguards, and the police officers jumping to attention—all those had no meaning for me. For the first time I felt I was the prime minister, when I sat down on the Old Man's chair."[10]

CHAPTER 26.

1984

WHEN THE SIXTY-ONE-YEAR-OLD Shimon Peres assumed power, on September 13, 1984, peace became his major goal. He was determined to revive the peace process with Israel's neighbors. However, there were more urgent matters on the government agenda. The economy was crumbling under an inflation rate approaching 500 percent. The banking system was in a shambles after the crash of its artificially inflated stock; the IDF was mired in Lebanon; Israel's image abroad was tarnished by the Phalange's massacres in the Palestinian camps.

Peres got off to a slow start. Because he didn't achieve any dramatic results in his first months in office, the press labeled him a lame duck and a chronic loser.[1] But in utmost secrecy, the chronic loser was engaged in some of the most ambitious operations of his career.

The first goal was the pullback from Lebanon. Operation Peace for Galilee had so far cost Israel 660 human lives—plus thousands of wounded—and hundreds of millions of dollars. It had shattered the national consensus on the sacrosanct issue of security. It had brought severe destruction upon Lebanon, caused many casualties among the civilian population, and engendered a new terrorist organization—Hezbollah—that was supported by Iran.

A few days after his swearing in, Peres told *Haaretz* reporter

Dan Margalit that in nine months the IDF would be out of Lebanon.[2] Four months later, Defense Minister Rabin presented a withdrawal plan to the cabinet. In order to break the impasse between the Likud and Labor ministers, Peres quietly maneuvered and persuaded Likud ministers David Levi and Gideon Pat to vote for the pullback, in spite of Shamir's angry objections. On January 14, 1985, Israel's government decided to withdraw from Lebanon. At the end of the pullback, in June, Israel controlled only a security zone of 340 square miles, adjacent to its northern border.

SIMULTANEOUSLY, PERES LAUNCHED an effort to check the stampeding inflation that had turned into a nightmare. In the supermarkets, harried employees daily worked their way along the aisles, sticking new price tags on every product. By the end of 1984, the inflation had reached a yearly rate of 445 percent. The foreign currency reserves hit rock bottom.

Peres feared that inflation would cross the 1,000 percent mark. Some advised him to order a series of draconian measures: cut the defense budget by half; cut the budgets of the other ministries, almost immobilizing their activities; decree a 30 percent devaluation of the shekel, causing mammoth unemployment; freeze prices; bring down wages; and other painful steps. Peres admitted that these were logical economic solutions, but he believed that politically and socially they were inapplicable. He realized that without wide public support he couldn't carry out the painful surgery needed in Israel's economy.

Into the battle Peres launched his private army, a small group of young men who called themselves the Hundred-Day Team. They were better known as the Blazers because of the dress code some of them had adopted—elegant blue jackets with gilded buttons.

The group had been created by Peres's longtime assistant, Dr. Yossi Beilin, a baby-faced, bespectacled young man with a perpetually timid expression. Beilin, a former spokesman for the Labor Party, had become Peres's closest assistant, thanks to his sparkling intelligence, his orderly mind, and his utter loyalty to his boss. His devotion to Peres was so overwhelming that Rabin had called him Peres's poodle.

On the eve of the 1984 election, Beilin quietly recruited a group of scholars and economists—the Hundred-Day Team. Their purpose was to set up the goals of the new government, plan the measures to be taken in different fields, and define each minister's tasks.

A major adviser for economic affairs, Professor Haim Ben-Shachar, who was not a member of the team, was one of Israel's leading economists. About six weeks before the elections, Ben-Shachar had suggested that Peres establish a small group of experts to prepare an economic plan, "for you to have handy when you win." The group Ben-Shachar established included three other professors—Yoram Ben-Porat, Michael Bruno, and Eitan Berglas—the former finance ministry director Emanuel Sharon (no relation to Ariel Sharon), a couple of renowned economists, and Amnon Neubach, a former finance ministry employee. This group prepared an economic plan, but Peres wasn't too interested. On Election Day, the group faded away.

When the Peres government was formed, Beilin was appointed government secretary and Amnon Neubach economic adviser to the prime minister. Emanuel Sharon was reappointed as the Ministry of Finance's director general by the new finance minister, Yitzhak Modai. Emanuel Sharon and Neubach relentlessly urged Peres to launch a comprehensive economic plan. Peres was reluctant, fearing that such a plan would trigger a confrontation with the powerful Histadrut. Instead, he tried several "package deals" between the employers association, the trade unions, and the government; their success, however, was limited. "You've produced a pretty package," Ben-Shachar told him ironically. "You've packed a handful of burning embers in beautiful wrapping paper, but it will finally catch fire and burn to ashes."[3]

Two package deals were made, one after the other, prolonging the agony for a short while. All kinds of quacks came to Peres, suggesting miracle cures for the inflation: to establish a weekly lottery in dollars, stop imports of whiskey and cars, or lower interest rates. Peres, who was not an economist, called his economic team and asked them why these cures wouldn't work. When he insisted on knowing why lowering the interest rate wouldn't lower inflation, former Bank of Israel governor Moshe Zanbar told him: "Shimon, there are questions that you shouldn't be asking; it's embarrassing."

Finally, Peres realized that there was no other way out of the mire but adopting a tough, comprehensive economic plan.

Emanuel Sharon brought Peres and Modai a handwritten plan that was mostly based on the plan established by the small advisory group before the election. Its main points were a 20 percent devaluation of the shekel; a steep increase in prices immediately followed by a price freeze; a cut in government subsidies by a billion shekels; a reduction of the government's deficit by drastic cuts across the board of all the ministries' budgets; and, finally, a sharp erosion of wages.

Peres approved the plan. He flew to Washington for his first visit as prime minister, and the Reagan administration promised to help Israel's economic recovery by providing a "safety net" of $1.5 billion for the next two years. An American-Israeli joint economic and development group was established. Under-Secretary of the Treasury Allen Wallis was appointed chairman of the group, and the American representatives in it were Herbert Stein and Stanley Fischer. (Fischer immigrated to Israel in 2004 and was the governor of the Bank of Israel for several years.) An intensive exchange of letters between Secretary of State George Shultz and Peres followed. Shultz, an economist, supported Peres's request for a safety net, but pressured him to carry out some far-reaching economic measures, which he detailed in his letters. One of Peres's aides angrily said that Shultz didn't have the right to tell Israel what to do. "Believe me," Peres quipped, "he earned that right."[4]

Months passed and the plan was still waiting. Peres decided to wait until the Histadrut elections, which took place on May 13; Labor won a decisive victory.

On Election Day, Peres summoned the economists' team to his home, and they decided to launch the plan. Henceforth, the project looked like a military operation: a task force was created that held meetings in utmost secrecy, sometimes at the Science Academy in Jerusalem, sometimes at Emanuel Sharon's private apartment or even in a secret service safe house. The plan was prepared to the smallest detail; every second evening Neubach reported to Peres. Once a week, Peres met the entire group. Most of the time Peres just listened, without saying a word, until he was ready to go ahead. "He listened and he listened," said Eli Horowitz, Teva's president, "and all of a sudden he roared forward like a bulldozer and didn't let go."[5]

Finance Minister Modai was not active in the preparation of the plan, but he didn't interfere. Peres decided to present the plan to the government on Sunday, June 30. On Friday he held a final meeting of the group.

Emanuel Sharon presented the detailed plan. Fearing a leak that could cause a general assault on the banks, he ordered that they be closed on Sunday.

And on Sunday morning, Peres brought the plan to the government meeting. He declared that he would resign if the plan was defeated.[6] He called the directors of the electronic media and told them, "Gentlemen, either we'll have an economic plan tomorrow morning—or there will be no government."[7]

It turned out that most Likud ministers were utterly opposed to the plan. Only Shamir and Modai sided with Peres. Arik Sharon, Moshe Nissim, Moshe Arens, Moshe Katzav, David Levi—they all objected, and voiced prophecies of doom and gloom. Peres let all of them speak, but he fought stubbornly to make them accept the drastic cuts in their budgets, which was in his eyes the only way to convince the employers' association and the Histadrut to go along with the plan. "I personally brandished the 'knife,' " he wrote, "meticulously reviewing item after item, slashing remorselessly. Every expenditure of more than $100,000 was a legitimate subject of discussion." The meeting lasted for hours, but Peres rejected the demands of some ministers to stop the discussion and meet again the following day. "Morning turned to afternoon, and then to night, but still I sat there while the speech making continued. I knew that, when it came to hanging in, I was as strong as any of them—indeed, as all of them together."[8]

Monday dawned and still the debate continued, but some of the ministers were getting tired. Rabin declared he was against the plan, because Peres wanted to cut $500 million from the defense budget. Some ministers protested against the long debate, claiming that they were exhausted, some others napped in their chairs. Peres brushed off the complaints. "An Israeli minister shouldn't sleep," he said. "During the war we debated for entire nights, and a minister's duty is to stay awake."[9]

At 9:30 A.M. Peres suddenly said: "We still need to cut another eighty-two million dollars." The debate flared again, but Peres agreed with Minister Moshe Shachal's suggestion that all government budgets be cut again in a proportional mode. He finally brought the plan to the vote. Fifteen ministers supported him, seven voted against; three, including Rabin, abstained.

After twenty-five hours of marathon debate, the ministers walked out, exhausted and red-eyed. The economic plan was adopted.

The next battle was with the mighty Histadrut. Secretary General Israel Kessar and his deputy, Haim Haberfeld, did everything they could to sabotage the plan. They threatened some of its authors ("I'll take care that you won't live in Israel anymore," Haberfeld yelled at Professor Michael Bruno. "Wherever you go, we'll get you expelled"), and when the prime minister decided to explain his plan on national television, they ordered the studio technicians to walk out. The television screens turned black that night.

Peres also had to face the ire of some rebellious Labor Knesset members, and of quite a few economists and economic editors who ferociously attacked the plan. "What we have here," a leading editorialist wrote, "is not an economic plan but a declaration of war of the government against the Israeli people."[10]

But the plan was already on its way. The shekel was devalued by 20 percent. The harsh measures were implemented to the letter. In August 1985, the month after the plan was put in motion, inflation dropped from 20 percent in June and 28 percent in July to a mere 2.5 percent. By the end of the year, inflation stabilized around a monthly rate of 1.5 percent, and kept dropping in the following years. The plan turned out to be a tremendous success. Peres's popularity soared to 70 percent, a higher rate than any of his predecessors.

Today, the Israeli plan is taught in universities around the world. "This was a most successful recovery plan," President Reagan said when Peres came to visit him in October.[11] The resilience and leadership that Peres displayed at the crucial moments surprised many. But once the decision was made, he lost interest in the plan's technical details.

Besides, a new crisis had broken out, shaking the nation to its very core.

ON OCTOBER 29, 1985, Peres had an unusual visitor: Reuven Hazak, the deputy director of the General Security Service (the Shabak). Peres knew that Hazak wanted to talk to him about an embarrassing affair that had occurred in the service during Shamir's term of office. He had heard about it from Avraham Shalom, the Shabak director. But Shalom had also warned him that Hazak and two other senior Shabak officers, Rafi Malka and Reuven Radai, wanted to use the incident against him, bringing his downfall so that they could take his place.[12]

Peres fully trusted Shalom, a short, stout man exuding intelligence and authority. Shalom respected Peres, too, and regarded him as a man with a vision, unlike his predecessors, Begin and Shamir.[13] Peres believed Shalom's account about the affair and the plot against him. He thought that he should "give backing to the Shabak Director. There always are intrigues against the Director .... This is an internal attempt of three officials who want to seize power and i cannot allow it."[14]

During the meeting with Peres, Reuven Hazak described the astounding episode, which was only partially known to the prime minister. Eighteen months before, on April 12, 1984, four terrorists had hijacked a bus with forty passengers on board. They ordered the driver to head to the Gaza Strip. Israeli security forces chased the bus; close to the town of Dir el Balah, in the Gaza Strip, the bus was forced to stop after Israeli soldiers riddled its tires with bullets.

At dawn, an elite commando unit broke into the bus, killing two of the terrorists and rescuing the passengers. The other two terrorists were seen and photographed while being taken away by Shabak agents. A few hours later, however, an IDF spokesman released a puzzling statement, saying that two of the terrorists had been killed during the assault on the bus, and the other two had died "on their way to the hospital." Yet the world press had published photographs showing the two terrorists alive and apparently unharmed; that triggered a storm in Israel and in world opinion. Israel was accused of killing the two terrorists after their capture.

Somebody, indeed, had killed the two terrorists. Two successive boards of inquiry pointed an accusing finger at General Yitzhak Mordechai, the chief paratrooper and infantry officer. Mordechai, fearing that explosive charges had been placed on the bus, had repeatedly hit the two terrorists with his handgun during their interrogation, hoping to extract information. Mordechai became the prime suspect, but the medical findings proved that he had not killed the Palestinians. The five Shabak agents who had interrogated the Palestinians and taken them away were also cleared. The autopsy revealed that the terrorists had died because of blows to the back of their heads with blunt objects. The boards of inquiry concluded that the terrorists had belatedly succumbed to blows with rifle stocks, dealt by the soldiers during the assault on the bus.

These facts were known to Peres. But now he heard from Hazak the whole truth: the Shabak agents *had* killed the terrorists after capturing them, on the explicit orders of the Shabak director, Avraham Shalom. When the first board of inquiry was established, it included a Shabak representative, Yossi Ginossar. Ginossar was actually the Shabak's Trojan horse. He reported to Shalom after each board meeting, and the Shabak people fabricated evidence and coordinated their testimony in order to cover up their actions and deceive the board of inquiry.

Shalom had told Hazak that all those actions, including the fabrication of false evidence, had been approved by Yitzhak Shamir, the prime minister at that time. The government, Shalom said, had decided that the truth of the affair would never be made public. Hazak therefore cooperated with Shalom and even took part in the cover-up, until he found out that this was the Shabak director's private initiative, and there had not been any order by the prime minister to do so. He confronted the Shabak director and demanded his resignation.

"Why are you doing that?" Shalom said. His term of office was almost over. "In a few months you'll be the Shabak director."

Hazak answered: "I am through with that. I don't want to be the Shabak director. We have to resign, all of us. I don't want your job."[15]

"I asked him," Peres later reported, "Why did you come to me today? A year and a half have passed since the bus affair. Why didn't you stop this before? Why didn't you come to me—or to Shamir a year and a half ago? You're coming to me after three successive judicial procedures. I am not a judge, I am the prime minister. I cannot reopen a judicial case. This is not my business."[16]

A few days later, Peres called Hazak to a second meeting. "I considered the matter," he told the Shabak official. "I am not a judicial authority. I believe the Shabak director's account. I understand there is a dispute between the two of you. The Shabak cannot function in a dispute. There must be discipline, so you have to step aside."

"Are you throwing me out?" Reuven Hazak asked, deeply disturbed and on the verge of tears.

"No, I am not judging you—God forbid. I am only stating that in this organization, when the director and his deputy quarrel, one of the two should go, and I see no reason to make this director go."[17]

Hazak left, deeply frustrated. That meeting ended the first stage of the affair.

But beneath the ashes, the embers were smoldering. Three months later, Hazak disclosed some of the details of the incident to the deputy state's attorney, Dorit Beinish; on her advice he also spoke with the attorney general, Professor Yitzhak Zamir.

And Pandora's box burst wide open.

ON FEBRUARY 13, 1986, Zamir announced to the press his decision to quit the job of attorney general, which he had held for seven and a half years. But the following day, Beinish came to his office and revealed to him the details of the bus affair. Zamir was stunned. He asked the prime minister for permission to interview Hazak, Malka, and Radai. Peres procrastinated for a while under different pretexts. It was not until early April that the three Shabak rebels testified before Zamir.

Zamir now asked Peres for an investigation of Shabak procedures. Peres refused. He sought the support of "the prime ministers' club"—which included, besides him, former prime ministers Shamir and Rabin. The trio used to meet often and discuss subjects of crucial importance. Shamir and Rabin fully agreed with Peres's position. "My duty as prime minister," Peres said, "was to defend an organization dealing with secret and complicated matters, which needed protection more than others. Its members are not wearing uniforms and are not fighting on the front lines. They operate in a twilight zone and I had to protect them."[18] Peres feared that a judicial procedure might result in the revelation of state secrets, with "batteries of lawyers" quoting precedents and bringing to light "matters that the entire nation agrees should remain secret."[19]

The prime minister's position utterly upset the attorney general. "Until this very day," he said later, "I don't really understand Peres's position. I don't understand why he went all out to defend what looked like the [personal] interest of Shamir, who was his rival . . . . Peres and Shamir exerted tremendous pressures on me. Peres all the time tried to thwart my handling of this affair."[20]

Shamir, who was implicated in the affair, became a loyal supporter of Peres in this case. "I was adamant that Zamir should drop this matter. Perhaps somebody helped [the Palestinians] die, I don't know. But I didn't know that somebody ordered to kill them. I couldn't imagine that somebody wanted to lead astray a board of inquiry." He thought that Zamir was politically motivated, and that "he wasn't that smart." Shamir was angered by Zamir's daring to stand up to the prime minister and the ministers of defense and foreign affairs. "He's being stubborn," he said.[21]

The prime ministers' club rejected any idea of a compromise, but the snowball kept rolling. Zamir filed a complaint with the chief of police. Rafi Malka, one of the three Shabak whistleblowers, who had been brutally dismissed from his functions, appealed to the Supreme Court and asked to be reinstated.

Finally, on May 24, the first item about the affair was broadcast on the television news. Even though it was formulated in vague terms, it triggered a wave of comments and rumors. Six days later, Shimon Peres invited some of the leading ministers of his party and Avraham Shalom to his house.

Shalom maintained that he had acted "on the authority and with the permission" of Prime Minister Yitzhak Shamir. Now he felt that the ministers were forsaking him. He suddenly broke down and started to cry. "It was a terrible moment," Minister Shachal recalled. "I also had tears in my eyes."[22] "It was a hard and unforgettable moment," Peres noted.[23]

On Sunday morning, ten minutes before the beginning of the weekly government meeting, Zamir was called to the prime minister's office. "I got in and Peres told me, Today you're being replaced, we are going to appoint a new attorney general. For me this was a total surprise."[24]

At noon the government was asked to approve the appointment of Justice Yossef Harish as attorney general to replace Yitzhak Zamir. The formal reason given was that Zamir had asked to resign some time before, but everyone understood that Peres had fired him. The prime minister and the justice minister wanted to replace Zamir with Harish right away, but Minister Yossef Burg intervened. "Even when I fire my housemaid," he protested, "I give her a two-week notice." Finally the ministers agreed that Harish would assume his functions the following Wednesday.

YOSSEF HARISH WAS viewed by the media and the body politic as the prime minister's docile servant, who would do what he was told and wouldn't take an independent stand, as his predecessor had. That certainly was the intention of those who had appointed him, but things took a different turn.

On June 22, at a ministerial meeting, Shamir asked Harish to cancel Zamir's complaint to the police. But Harish said that the police investigation should continue.

Shamir exploded in anger. "Why don't you stop this investigation? Why do you need it?" Harish stuck to his guns. If the government rejected his opinion, he said, "then it should discuss the appointment of a new attorney general."[25]

To find a way out of the impasse, Peres's lawyer friends turned to President Herzog and asked for a presidential pardon for the Shabak officials who had participated in the cover-up, even before they had been indicted and tried. Herzog agreed, in spite of the doubtful procedure. His pardon put an end to the affair.

SHIMON PERES ERRED in his dealing with the bus affair. If he had listened to Hazak, he could have solved the crisis long before it reached such monstrous dimensions. The attorney general would have been satisfied with the firing of the officials involved in the cover-up; the affair wouldn't have returned to the headlines and the Shabak's image wouldn't have been tarnished. The public wouldn't have witnessed the efforts of the prime minister and the ministers of defense and foreign affairs to impose a political decision on the judiciary. Peres himself realized he had gone too far. "Perhaps I did not have all the facts at my disposal," he later wrote; "perhaps my judgment of the persons involved was wrong."[26]

His mistakes resulted first and foremost from his true nature as Mr. Security. He sincerely believed he had to save the Shabak from the nightmare of a disastrous exposure in the courts and the media. He fully supported the Shabak and its director, and proved, once again, that deep in his soul he remained rooted in the world of security.

Another reason for his behavior was his memory of the Lavon affair. "I could hear the voice of Ben-Gurion," he wrote, "in different but not altogether unsimilar circumstances. For he had fought—and sacrificed—for the principle of separation of powers, for the fundamental democratic tenet that government ministers cannot double as judges."[27] But this comparison was fallacious. Nobody had asked him to be a judge, to condemn or to clear someone, as in the Lavon affair. He was asked to make sure that justice was done. If he had really followed Ben-Gurion's legacy, he would have established a judicial board of inquiry.

Peres possibly didn't want to make any move that could be regarded as a maneuver for toppling Yitzhak Shamir. Shamir was the one accused of having instructed the Shabak to kill the two terrorists. If Peres had ordered an inquiry, it might have produced grave accusations against Shamir and perhaps even prevented the rotation. But Peres feared that such a move would be viewed by the public as a sly political maneuver and damage his credibility. He therefore recoiled. His fear of losing his credibility muddled his judgment.

And yet, even though clumsy and lame, the pardon of the

Shabak people served Israel's security by preventing the washing of dirty laundry in public. Perhaps that was the reason why the affair didn't leave a strong impact on the public, and didn't blemish Peres's image as an excellent prime minister.

"Prime Minister Peres was solving problems at an almost superhuman rate," President Herzog wrote. "Shamir resented the positive reception greeting the prime minister as he made his dynamic changes."[28]

THE PUBLIC IMAGE of Shimon Peres underwent a deep change. He settled down in his official residence in Jerusalem and quickly adapted himself to the way of life of a prime minister. Gone were the short-sleeved shirts and the light-colored pants; he now came to the Knesset in custom-made suits and exquisite ties. As in the past, he was always tanned and vigorous; in the spring and summer he spent long hours reading in the sun. In his daily life he stuck to a strict routine: ten minutes of gymnastics every morning, carefully planned meals of fruits for breakfast, fish for lunch, cheeses and vegetables for dinner. When invited to receptions and cocktail parties, he would nibble only the edges of cookies and croissants; at dinner, he would mix the food items on his plate so it would look as if he had eaten more than he had. He developed a gourmet's taste for world cuisine, but chained his gastronomic longings in a steel discipline; when he decided that he should stop smoking, he eradicated cigarettes from his life. He would enjoy a drink only once in a while. His hair acquired a silver hue, and his appearance exuded respectability and self-confidence.

Peres also succeeded in improving his country's image abroad. Israel had lost much of the world's sympathy after the Lebanon War and the stalemate with Jordan and the Palestinians. Peres, however, stressed his resolve to achieve peace and offered a territorial compromise in the West Bank and Gaza. In Europe in particular he achieved tremendous popularity. He was imbued with European culture, was at home in the intellectual circles in France, knew statesmen and cultural gurus throughout the continent, and was the most eminent leader in the Socialist International.

Even when Israel used tough measures against her enemies, Peres knew how to convince his colleagues of her righteousness. Soon after he ordered the bombing of the PLO headquarters in Tunis in October 1985, he flew to the Socialist International meeting in Italy. "Austria's Chancellor Bruno Kreisky was furious," recalled Uzi Baram, the Labor Party secretary, "and wanted to throw Peres out of the International. Peres appeared before the other leaders, explained his reasons, and the following day they almost threw Kreisky out of the International."[29]

PERES ALSO IMPROVED Israel's relations with the United States, in spite of some embarrassing episodes that took place during his term of office. One of them was the Jonathan Pollard affair. Pollard, an American Jew, was employed by an American intelligence agency in Washington, and for a few years stole and delivered to Israel precious intelligence material. After his arrest by FBI agents it turned out that he had been spying for a little-known Israeli agency, the Bureau for Scientific Relations (Lakam). This was a secret unit of the defense ministry headed by Rafi Eitan, who later became the leader of the Pensioners Party and a minister in the Israeli government.

The arrest of the Jewish spy deeply distressed the Israeli leaders. There was an unwritten agreement with the Americans that Israel would never spy on them, as the United States was Israel's closest ally. When Pollard was unmasked, Israel apologized, closed the Lakam, and returned the stolen documents to the United States. Pollard's activities had taken place under Peres's predecessors, but he was the one who restored the relations with the United States and renewed the ties of trust and confidence between the two nations.

Another deplorable affair that erupted during Peres's tenure as prime minister was the Iran-contra scandal.

AT THE END of May 1985, an American journalist, Michael Ledeen, arrived in Israel. Ledeen, formerly connected with the

CIA, met with Peres on the recommendation of Robert MacFarlane, President Reagan's national security adviser.[30] He revealed to Peres that he had come on a top-secret mission, outside the normal operating channels. He wanted to find out if Israel could help the United States in establishing contact with opposition circles in Tehran and in seeking ways to obtain the release of American hostages held in Lebanon by Iranian-backed terrorists.

Peres gave an affirmative answer. His experts had discerned three main political trends in Iran: the fanatical followers of Ayatollah Khomeini; a more moderate faction; and a group that was basically pro-Western, anti-Soviet, and favoring a free economy. Peres believed that Israel should go along with the United States in this matter. The Americans had hostages in the hands of Hezbollah, and Israel, too, was on the quest for some missing soldiers possibly held by the same organization. Israel held several Shiite prisoners and was ready to exchange them for Israeli and American hostages.

Peres briefed Shamir and Rabin. On Shamir's instructions, the foreign ministry's director, David Kimche, discussed the matter during a visit to the United States in July. He met with MacFarlane, who confirmed that he had been the author of the request to Peres, on President Reagan's authority. In August, Kimche visited Washington again. Peres and Shamir instructed him to make sure that Secretary of State Shultz had been informed of MacFarlane's request. At first, MacFarlane hesitated, but finally told Kimche that the president had decided to bring Shultz in.[31] MacFarlane informed Shultz that Peres had insisted he should be briefed about the matter.[32]

But MacFarlane apparently hadn't presented a full report to the secretary of state. In June, the U.S. ambassador to Israel, Samuel Lewis, reported Michael Ledeen's visit to Secretary Shultz. Shultz was furious and rushed an angry letter to MacFarlane, who distanced himself from Ledeen and claimed that it had been an Israeli initiative. He said the same to President Reagan.[33]

In the meantime, a channel with Iran was conceived. It was an effort to establish connections with the Tehran regime, by using Iran's interest in acquiring weapons.[34] The Iranians were at war with Iraq; they desperately needed TOW and Hawk missiles. In their hour of need, they turned to Israel as well, using the services of various intermediaries.

Peres approved their request and charged his trusted friend Al Schwimmer with the management of the top-secret operation. Schwimmer brought with him Colonel (res.) Yaakov Nimrodi, a businessman and a former Israeli military attaché in Tehran. The two operated through a Saudi millionaire, Adnan Khashoggi, and an Iranian arms dealer, Manuchehr Ghorbanifar.

General Shlomo Gazit, a former IDF chief of intelligence who was involved in the operation, didn't like the foreign partners, whom he called "dark figures." He also disliked the sloppy and manipulative methods of Nimrodi and Schwimmer, and decided to step aside.[35]

Thus began an entangled and harrowing venture, strewn with dubious deals, discreet deposits in Swiss banks, intrigues in the White House, and hollow promises. Some White House and CIA officials encouraged the Israelis to negotiate with the Iranians on a weapons sale in exchange for the liberation of the hostages. Israel was a vital link in that enterprise, as the Americans refused to be involved in an arms deal with Iran in any way. Finally, Israel supplied the Iranians with antitank and antiaircraft missiles, and the Americans sent Israel replacements for those arms.

The Iranians paid considerable sums of money for the weapons; the payments were deposited in Swiss banks and later transferred to the United States; but some White House employees, Colonel Oliver North and his colleagues, channeled the money to the financing of the rebellion by the "Contras" against the left-wing government in Nicaragua. That was to trigger one of the ugliest political scandals in America in the post-Vietnam years.

The terrorists released one hostage, the Reverend Benjamin Weir, in September 1985; Peres maintained that Reverend

Lawrence Jenco and David Jacobsen, released in 1986, were also a part of the weapons deal,[36] even though other sources denied it. In the meantime, a secret crisis shook the Israeli side of the operation. Amiram Nir, Peres's gifted and ambitious antiterrorism adviser, gradually gained control of the Iranian operation and muscled out Schwimmer and Nimrodi. Peres was unable to appease the warring factions and his indecisiveness caused repeated confrontations and angry quarrels. But Amiram Nir established an excellent rapport with his American colleagues and even flew secretly to Tehran in their company. Using a false name and a false ID, on board a camouflaged plane, he flew to the Iranian capital with Robert MacFarlane and a CIA official, hoping to establish contact with some moderate Iranians. But all the Iranians wanted from the delegation were additional arms shipments and the release of some Shiite prisoners held by the West. "That visit was not a success," Peres wrote.[37]

President Reagan was grateful to Israel for her efforts on behalf of the hostages. When Peres visited the White House in September 1986, Reagan warmly thanked him for Israel's efforts to obtain the hostages' release. He also sent to Peres a letter of thanks for Amiram Nir's actions.[38]

And yet the entire endeavor left the aftertaste of a reckless adventure that wasn't to Israel's credit. In November 1986, the affair exploded in banner headlines in the American media and turned into a major scandal, the so-called Irangate. The public indignation targeted, in particular, the illegal transfer of money to the Contras. When the shady deals with the Iranians became known, the White House staff scurried for cover; they instigated an all-out effort to cast the blame on Israel. Oliver North even accused Israel of conceiving the idea of transferring the money from Iran to the Contras. He claimed that the idea had been suggested by Amiram Nir to Vice President Bush during a visit to Jerusalem. Peres and Nir denied the charges and Bush even made public the minutes of his meeting with Nir, proving that the Iran-Contra deal had never been mentioned.

Yet the Irangate affair had been an erroneous venture. Most of the American hostages were not released, while the Israelis appeared in the eyes of the world as arms dealers, involved in murky deals and suspicious money transfers.

The main casualty on the Israeli side was Peres himself, who suffered a scalding attack by George Shultz for allegedly having refrained from informing him about the affair. This charge was unfair.

Shultz's fury erupted when he found out that some of the Irangate aspects hadn't been divulged to him. In all his meetings and contacts with Peres throughout the operation, he said, the Israeli prime minister never mentioned the Iranian connection.[39] Peres, on the other hand, claimed he was certain that Shultz had been fully briefed by the president and the White House staff, according to standing rules of government procedure.[40] Peres was baffled by discovering "the extent of the disunity" between some major administration figures—MacFarlane; Shultz; Admiral John Poindexter, MacFarlane's successor as national security adviser; and Defense Secretary Casper Weinberger. "I couldn't have conceived such a situation in my worst nightmares," Peres confessed. "My admiration for the United States was such that I was naturally convinced that they could always rely on the most thorough and coordinated staff work in reaching policy decisions."[41]

The affair had an eerie epilogue. After leaving government service, Amiram Nir started a business venture in South America. In November 1988, his light plane crashed in Mexico, and Nir perished. Insistent rumors claimed that the plane crash had not been an accident—that Nir had been assassinated because of his part in the Iran-Contra affair. No evidence has ever been found to support that allegation, but it refuses to go away, like all those political mysteries that linger for years in sensation-hungry magazines.

PART 5.

THE MAN WHO WON'T DESPAIR

CHAPTER 27.

THE FATAL MISTAKE

PERES SENT OUT his first feelers for peace in the spring of 1984, before the Knesset elections. From the Labor Party head-quarters he dispatched several secret messages to King Hussein of Jordan. He offered Hussein a renewal of their relations "as in the good old days" when he had served as defense minister in Yitzhak Rabin's government.

"I want to bring Israel to a crossroads," Peres said to the Hundred Days' Team. "I want her to choose between her present course and the road leading to the Jordanian option. If Hussein wants to go along with us, we should take that road. If not, I want Israel to face the mirror and ask herself what we should do with one and a half million Palestinians."[1]

Peres was convinced that the Jordanian option still existed because Hussein's basic interests hadn't changed. Peres objected to the creation of a Palestinian state because of the danger it would represent for Israel. Such a state would become a danger for Jordan as well.

Peres always saw the solution of the Palestinian problem in a tripartite framework—Jordanian, Israeli, and Palestinian. In 1974, during his first meeting with Hussein, together with Allon and Rabin, Peres presented his idea of a tripartite framework. He put forward the idea of a demilitarized Palestinian entity that would be jointly governed by Jordan and Israel. An economic union would be created between the three components of the framework; the sovereignty of that Palestinian "entity" would be shared by Israel and Jordan.

Hussein didn't reject the idea, and labeled it "interesting."

The basic interests of Hussein, Peres said to his team, have not changed. For the king, the question was who would give orders to whom: Jordan to the Palestinians or the Palestinians to Jordan?[2] It was of the utmost importance, Peres continued, to lure Hussein to the negotiating table. But he had no intention of entrusting his foreign minister, Yitzhak Shamir, with that task. Shamir objected to any initiative that could lead to a territorial compromise; Peres had no doubt that the Likud leader would sabotage the process. He preferred to bypass the routine channels and use members of his inner circle to carry out his initiative.

As he settled into the prime minister's office, he assigned two of his closest aides to that task: Dr. Beilin, the government secretary, and Dr. Nimrod Novik, his foreign-policy adviser. Beilin was also unofficially put in charge of improving living conditions in the West Bank and Gaza. Novik was assigned the Great Powers, mainly the Americans and the Russians.

To protect the secret of the Jordanian negotiation, Peres and Beilin decided not to show the relevant documents even to a typist. Beilin would spend long nights writing memos and position papers, and personally photocopying documents; he kept all the files locked in his own cabinets.

Peres realized that no progress could be made without Egypt's help. Egypt could play a crucial part in bringing Israel and Jordan together. But Egypt's president, Hosni Mubarak, wouldn't even talk to Peres before the Taba issue was resolved. Taba was a tiny piece of beach on the Israeli-Egyptian border that both sides claimed.

President Mubarak publicly declared that as long as the Taba dispute wasn't settled, he wouldn't meet with Israel's prime minister. Peres tried to convey to Mubarak his sense of urgency, but Mubarak wouldn't budge. A long negotiation followed that would result, eighteen months later, in an agreement on international arbitration. Only then would Mubarak agree to receive Peres in Cairo. Israel and Jordan were to pay dearly for those eighteen months wasted because of Mubarak's stubbornness.

PERES COULDN'T WAIT for Mubarak, and started the first stage of his peace offensive in October 1984. But he faced a major obstacle. Hussein announced that he would negotiate with Israel only in the framework of an international conference. That conference was to include the five permanent members of the U.N. Security Council.

Peres flatly refused. He knew that an international conference, by definition, would try to impose its resolutions on the parties in dispute.[3] No Israeli leader could let foreign powers draw his country's boundaries and decide how to guarantee its security. "The idea of an international conference," he said at the Knesset, "has been rejected by everybody in Israel. Its real aim is to deprive Israel of the possibility of negotiating on equal terms."[4]

To find a way out, Peres offered Hussein a choice of other options: direct negotiations; negotiations by proxy; simultaneous bilateral talks with a few Arab countries; a meeting in Cairo chaired by U.S. representatives; a regional peace conference with Egypt and Saudi Arabia; talks at Camp David; at Williamsburg, Virginia; in San Francisco . . .

But Hussein wouldn't soften. An international conference, he said, and nothing else.

The talks stalled.

But the Americans and the Israelis didn't despair. Hussein wanted to equip his army with American weapons. He regarded an arms deal with Washington as a test case of American and Israeli goodwill. The State Department decided to use Hussein's demand as leverage for prodding him toward the negotiating table. The U.S. Congress would approve your demand, U.S. diplomats told Hussein, if you proclaim the end of belligerence with Israel.

Hussein decided to visit the United States. He spoke at the

United Nations in New York, then headed for Washington to meet with President Reagan. It was arranged that on the White House lawn, he would utter the magic formula. "He would say 'end of belligerence,'" one of Peres's advisers chuckled, "and in Washington it would sound like 'open sesame!' The American arsenals would open before him like Ali Baba's cavern."

But when he stood with President Reagan on the White House lawn, Hussein backed off. Instead of saying that the conflict with Israel would be solved only by "nonbelligerent means," he said "in a nonbelligerent environment."

Washington and Jerusalem were deeply disappointed. "The man was asked to give a commitment," Peres cracked, "and instead he gives us a weather forecast."

The United States refused to give weapons to Hussein, and he returned to Amman frustrated and bitter. "The Zionists are in control in Washington," he said to a friend, "and the U.S. Congress is a branch of the Knesset."

Yet Peres wouldn't let go. He now realized that there would be no negotiation with Hussein without an international conference. He therefore decided to square the circle; in the words of one of his aides, he suggested that they "castrate" the conference. Let's remove from the conference all the elements that worry us, Peres said to his aides. Let's keep only the "international umbrella" that Hussein wants.

Some of his men disagreed. "This man is stalling you, Shimon," one of them said. "He has been making a living out of saying no." But Peres believed in Hussein's sincerity. "The king wants to reach an agreement," he said. "And if he can't go along with us without a conference, let's give him one."

And he gave it to him in October 1985, from the podium of the U.N. General Assembly.

PERES'S AIDES METICULOUSLY prepared the prime minister's speech for the General Assembly. That speech had a secret goal: to launch several terms and formulas connected with the international conference, and to test the response in Israel and throughout the world. Peres kept repeating to his aides, "When you negotiate with the other side, remember that you're also negotiating with your own people. You must be sure that your people will go with you."[5] Peres decided not to go as far as saying the dangerous words "international conference," but he would agree to an international "opening" and international "support" of the negotiation.

On October 11, 1985, Peres addressed the General Assembly. He offered direct negotiations to Jordan, then added: "Those negotiations may be initiated with the support of an international forum, as agreed upon by the negotiating states .... The permanent members of the Security Council may be invited to support the initiation of these negotiations. This forum, while not being a substitute for direct negotiations, can offer support for them."[6]

The international reactions to the speech were excellent; and in Israel the protests of right-wing leaders didn't generate any storm; not even when Peres made the same speech at the Knesset. The government coalition meekly voted to enter the prime minister's address in the Knesset record.

Peres had survived this first test in his own home. But he misinterpreted Likud's moderation. He believed that Likud was ready to resign itself to his peace initiative, while the truth was that Shamir's party was firmly opposed to his policy. But fearing that Peres might refuse to carry out the rotation in October 1986, they were ready to keep their heads down temporarily. Shamir's goal was to make sure that Peres would respect the rotation agreement; he therefore decided to let him go ahead with his plan.

Peres now felt that he could speed the peace process, and he entered the second stage of his undertaking.

RICHARD MURPHY, GEORGE SHULTZ'S special envoy, became the permanent liaison between Peres and Hussein. In January he prepared the first draft of an agreement, a ten-point document that was kept secret for many years. The draft agreement, later called the "first London document," proved that the two nations had moved closer to each other; its first paragraph was a personal triumph for Shimon Peres. The paragraph said, in so many words, that both sides agreed to convene "a pro forma international conference." This was a major breakthrough; Hussein had accepted Peres's "castrated conference" concept.

Yet three main points remained in dispute. Hussein wanted the Soviets to participate in the "international umbrella"; Peres agreed, on two conditions—that the Soviet Union restore its diplomatic relations with Israel, which had been broken off in 1967, and that it allow free Jewish immigration to Israel. The answer of the Soviets was long in coming, and more precious time was lost.

A second disagreement concerned the PLO. The winter of 1985 had turned into a brief honeymoon between Hussein and Arafat, and the Jordanian king insisted that the PLO participate in the conference. Peres refused. Arafat still refused to renounce terrorism and recognize Israel; therefore he wasn't a partner.

The third disagreement was the most important. This was the "Referral Clause" formulated in Paragraph 7 of the draft agreement. The plenary opening session was to be only ceremonial, as the two sides had agreed. Afterward the conference would split into bilateral committees—Israel-Jordan, Israel-Syria, and Israel-Lebanon, with no third parties participating.

But at this point, Hussein introduced the Referral Clause. In case of a deadlock in the bilateral negotiations, he said, the issue would be referred to the plenum of the international conference.

No way, Peres said. If Hussein's clause was accepted, he explained, then it wouldn't be a pro forma conference anymore. A referral to the plenum meant his worst nightmares coming true; the conference would decide on all the major issues and impose a solution on Israel.

Once again the talks reached a stalemate. The "first London document" was stillborn.

STILL, ALL WAS NOT LOST. In February 1986, a fierce dispute erupted between Hussein and Arafat, and the Jordanian king canceled his demand that the PLO participate in the peace conference. One of the three stumbling blocks had been removed.

The second obstacle, the Soviet hard-line policy toward Israel, was also about to change, after a dramatic meeting of Shimon Peres with the new Soviet foreign minister, Eduard Shevardnadze. The existence of millions of Jews behind the Iron Curtain, and the possibility that the meeting might influence their fate, made it a moving encounter for Peres. The meeting took place at the U.N. General Assembly. Novik saw it as an event of historic importance. "This was the only time," he said, "when I saw Shimon preparing for a meeting internally. We had a room at the U.N. Shimon asked everybody to leave the room. And for half an hour he sat in his place, bent down, withdrawn into himself, and one could feel that his shoulders carried the weight of the Jewish people's history. Shimon believed he could create a crack in Shevardnadze's position, to stir in him even a hint of curiosity for this meeting to have a sequel." It turned out to be, Novik said, "an amazing conversation of intellectual uplifting, and Shimon played Shevardnadze like a violin."[7]

The chink in the Soviet minister's armor had indeed appeared. The Israelis were at the airport, on their way back to Israel, when Novik received a message that the Soviets wanted to see him at their Washington embassy. The meeting was the first of several; the Soviet obstacle was considerably softened. In November 1986, at a meeting with a young Russian diplomat, Novik received the promise that starting in March 1987, Soviet Jews would be permitted to immigrate to Israel at the rate of five hundred a month. The Russian also promised that diplomatic relations would be restored. There was no doubt that a new wind was blowing from Moscow.[8]

The second obstacle to the peace negotiation had now been removed. The Referral Clause remained the last point of discord between Peres and Hussein.

As a confidence-building measure, Peres and Beilin made a big effort to improve the life of the Palestinians in the West Bank. Rabin was very cooperative in that endeavor. They prepared a comprehensive plan of electing new mayors, creating an Arab bank, launching projects in agriculture, irrigation, and industry, free transfers of funds from Jordan, and direct exports of agricultural produce from Gaza to Egypt. Peres also established direct international dialing from the occupied territories to the outside world.

But King Hussein watched the Israeli initiatives with growing suspicion, fearing that their true goal was to improve the image of the occupation in the world media. He also didn't understand the urgency in restarting the peace process before the rotation in Israel took place.

Only seven months remained until Peres had to step down and leave Shamir at the helm. It was the time to act. The PLO was out of the game; Hussein was worried about the changing atmosphere in the West Bank, where many viewed him with growing hostility; the British and the Americans were ready to help; and Gorbachev was molding a new Soviet Union.

But nothing happened. Peres believed he had time; strangely enough, he was convinced that the rotation wouldn't take place. Hussein also made a mistake, by interpreting the Likud's silence as an approval of Peres's peace initiative. Thus, the peace process flowed quietly, irreversibly, toward a dismal failure.

Peres's last effort to revive his initiative was an official visit to Morocco. Peres wanted to enlist King Hassan's help in the negotiations. But the visit failed, because Hassan expected Peres to recognize the PLO, which Peres refused to do.

––––––

AS THE ROTATION DATE approached, a growing number of Labor Party leaders started urging Peres not to transfer power to Shamir. Many maintained that he was the best prime minister Israel had had since David Ben-Gurion. He had started a spectacular economic recovery and a peace process; it was clear that the conservative Shamir wouldn't follow in his footsteps. Some Labor activists suggested disbanding the national unity government and calling new elections.

The issue was included in the agenda of the party convention in April 1986. But even before the convention, several crises shook the Peres-Shamir government. Each of them offered Peres a good reason to break up the coalition with Likud.

The first erupted in August 1985, when Sharon brutally pounced on Peres in public speeches. "They can jump as much as they want, Peres and his cronies," he shouted.[9] "Peres and Rabin are hypocrites and liars!"[10] Peres immediately threatened to fire Sharon. It was clear that if he did, the government would collapse. But Peres reconsidered at the last moment, and the crisis was over.

Less than three months passed, and Sharon insulted Peres again. He called his position "feeble and lacking dignity" and accused Peres of "leading the government down a tortuous path without its members knowing what's going on."[11] Peres sent him a formal letter: "I am hereby relieving you of your functions as a minister in Israel's government."[12] That same day, Peres rushed firm letters to the other government ministers, informing them of Sharon's dismissal.[13]

The news spread throughout the country; the national unity government was on the verge of collapse. In a Labor Party meeting, Peres made a firm and determined speech. The party activists cheered. But Peres was unable to go all the way. He backed away at the last moment, after Sharon scribbled a few words of apology on a sheet of paper. "I never said those things," Sharon wrote, "I didn't mean . . . I am sorry . . ."[14] Peres immediately accepted the apology and the government was saved.

In January 1986, the third crisis broke out. The government met to discuss the Taba issue, which had poisoned Israel's relations with Egypt. The Likud ministers strongly objected to Peres's proposal to transfer the Taba dispute to international arbitration. Peres announced that he would resign if Likud rejected arbitration.

On the eve of the meeting Peres summoned his close aides to his home; Sonia, too, took part in the meeting. Peres asked his people how to deal with the situation. His aides were unanimous; "That's the moment, and that's the issue, to break apart the government if our proposal doesn't pass."[15] Peres said, "How would I look my grandchildren in the eyes if I didn't keep my word?"

They answered, "How would you look your grandchildren in the eyes if you abandon the nation to Shamir's hands?"

Sonia, though, firmly objected to the idea of dissolving the government. Her main argument was Shimon's credibility issue. "How long will they still accuse you of lacking credibility?" she asked, and demanded that Shimon honor his agreement with Shamir.[16] Some of the participants felt that she had a decisive influence on Shimon's decision.

Still, Peres's advisers insisted that if Likud foiled his Taba initiative he should resign and call new elections. "You're at the peak of your popularity now," they said.

Peres summed up the meeting. "I heard you," he said.

"My popularity ratings were topping 80 percent," he wrote, "and there was plainly a broad popular support of what I had been able to achieve in the short time allotted to me. Rather, then, these advisers suggested, end the National Unity coalition and bring about early elections. I dismissed such advice. As far as I was concerned, I had given my word and now I must keep it."[17]

The cabinet met for a final debate on the Taba issue on January 12, 1986, in the early evening. That was to be one of its longest meetings—thirteen hours, till dawn broke. During the debate, some of the Likud ministers attacked Peres personally and kept placing new obstacles in his way. One of the most active among them was Arik Sharon.

During the breaks in the debate, Peres's advisers kept trying to make him change his mind: "That's enough, Shimon, how long should you stand them? Go to the president and resign." He flatly refused. That night, in spite of the jabs, the insults, the maneuvers, he didn't lose his patience. Finally, early in the morning, he succeeded in passing a resolution accepting arbitration.

One after another the exhausted ministers left. Novik entered Peres's office. The prime minister raised his bleary eyes. Novik didn't say a word, but Peres got the message: Novik felt he had missed the chance to resign. Peres looked back at him and said, "I still have time, Nimrod."[18]

THUS, THE GOVERNMENT swayed and staggered and limped from one crisis to the next, but remained in power until the Labor convention in April 1986.

Shimon Peres was at the peak of his career and the Labor Party was stronger and more confident than ever. Its unity was in sharp contrast with the recent Likud convention, which had turned into a violent confrontation between rival factions. Hotheaded delegates had jumped on the dais and overturned the chairman's desk. The convention had been interrupted while fistfights were raging in the convention hall.

On the day of the Labor convention it seemed, once again, that the unity government was on its deathbed. Another crisis erupted, after another Likud minister launched an attack on Peres. This time it was Finance Minister Yitzhak Modai who insulted Peres and called him "a flying prime minister," implying that Peres spent his time in overseas trips instead of taking care of matters at home. Peres announced that he wouldn't take it anymore. He wrote a letter to the foul-mouthed minister and informed him: "I relieve you of your functions."[19] But at the last moment he decided not to send the letter. Still, the press heralded the imminent collapse of the government.

Against this agitated backdrop, the Labor convention was asked to vote on the motion to break up the government and call for new elections.

ON THE DAY the vote, Peres spoke with M. Haver (his name has been changed), the party activist who had presented the motion to the convention. "Why don't you remove your motion from the agenda tonight?" he asked.[20]

Haver was surprised. He knew that his motion had been discreetly encouraged by the prime minister. Peres's faithful assistant Elhanan Yishai had called Haver almost daily, encouraging him to proceed with his initiative. Now Peres had decided to back off.

"Shimon," Haver said, "in six months you're going to hand the keys of the country to Shamir. That's going to be a catastrophe for the nation, for the party, and for you. We shouldn't allow this to happen. I have a feeling that the majority of the delegates will vote with me if you don't interfere. So don't."

Peres said: "Do you really believe that I am going to give the premiership to Shamir? Do you think I am out of my mind? Don't you worry. I'll take care that the government collapses before the rotation date. David Levi will attack Shamir from one side and Sharon from the other. They are at each other's throats anyway. I'll take such initiatives that will force the Likud out of the government."

"Shimon," Haver said, "you are not a 'relentless underminer,' as Rabin called you, but you're a relentless optimist. Good God, what are you talking about? Do you really believe that they'll leave the government of their own free will? For almost two years your Likud partners have been enduring the worst humiliations, with only one goal in mind: to reach October 20, when you'll transfer your power to them. They'll crawl on their bellies, they'll swallow all the insults you'll feed them, just to reach the rotation date."

"Don't you trust me?" Peres said.

"No," Haver answered. "Shimon, if you don't want Likud to return to power, don't fight me tonight. Just go up on the podium and say that you'll accept the convention's verdict. They'll understand."

"No," Peres said. "We don't need this. I'll oppose your motion."

At that moment Haver realized that the battle was lost.

That evening, when Haver presented his motion to the convention, Peres and several leaders of the Labor Party opposed it vigorously. When the vote was finally taken, only a few hands were raised in support of Haver's motion. The overwhelming majority of the delegates voted against it.

Peres stuck to the rotation agreement and carried it out when the time came.

He acted that way in order to prove his credibility. But he didn't prove a thing. Peres didn't realize that his opponents wouldn't change their opinion about him even if he proved he was the most trustworthy man in the country. Yitzhak Shamir's reaction was the best proof. During the years 1984 through 1986, when Shamir was foreign minister and Peres prime minister, Shamir kept telling his aides, "You'll see—this liar and cheat, Shimon Peres, will never give me the prime minister's job." But on October 20, the transfer of power took place according to the agreement; Peres fulfilled his commitment. Now Shamir said to his aides: "Did you see? This liar and cheat, Shimon Peres, gave me the prime minister's job."[21]

Shortly after the rotation took place, M. Haver went to Peres's new office at the foreign ministry. Haver reminded Peres of their talk at the convention, and his assessment that there would be no rotation.

"So I made a mistake," Peres curtly said.[22]

THAT WAS SHIMON PERES'S greatest political mistake. "He made a historic mistake by not canceling the rotation," said his office director, General Avraham Tamir. "He would have won the support of the people. He was Israel's leader."[23] Many others thought the same. In 1986 he was at the apex of his power, a popular and admired prime minister. If he had broken up the unity government and called new elections, he would have had an excellent chance of beating Yitzhak Shamir.

Peres certainly understood that the breakup of the unity government was the right step to take for the nation's good. But he backed off and didn't dare go all the way. He carried out the rotation because he was determined to prove his credibility. But his image didn't change and his credibility wasn't restored. He made one of the greatest mistakes in his life because he wanted to prove that he was a man of his word.

Peres gave up the chance to lead Israel to new horizons. He hoped—in vain—that at the next election the people would remember his great days as prime minister.

CHAPTER 28.

THE LONDON DOCUMENT

ON APRIL 11, 1987, at dawn, Foreign Minister Peres climbed into an executive jet that immediately took off. He wore an elegant blue suit, and a brown wig to conceal his identity.[1] With him was Yossi Beilin, now director of the Ministry of Foreign Affairs. Peres and Beilin were on their way to London for a secret meeting with King Hussein of Jordan.

Hussein still dreamed of recovering the lands he had lost in 1967. One spring night in 1984, when hosting an American Hadassah delegation, he invited the women to his palace's terrace and pointed at the scintillating lights of Jerusalem, some fifty miles away: "My heart is there," he said sadly. For years, Jordan had paid the salaries of teachers and municipal employees in the West Bank even though they were under Israeli occupation. Many mayors and prominent Palestinians openly declared their allegiance to King Hussein. But Hussein realized that the only way to recover his lands was by negotiating with Israel.

The two-year term of Peres as prime minister had passed in sterile negotiations between them. Only after Peres had handed the premiership to Shamir and assumed the position of foreign minister did Hussein wake up to the new reality. Yitzhak Shamir had no intention whatsoever of reaching a territorial compromise. Hussein's only hope for peace was to forge an agreement with Peres and let the foreign minister try to convince the Israeli cabinet to accept it.

Now, finally, the king of Jordan was ready to talk. When approached by a close friend, the London attorney Victor Mishcon (later Lord Mishcon de Reya), Hussein agreed to a secret meeting with Peres on April 11.

Prime Minister Shamir was well aware of Peres's contacts with Hussein but didn't take them seriously. "Why is Shimon doing this?" he would sigh morosely when Beilin came to brief him. "Nothing will come out of this."[2] Yet on the eve of Peres's flight to London, Shamir couldn't contain his seething anger. "An international conference is madness," he declared at a public meeting, "and one has to be mad to act for such an idea .... There is no danger that an international conference will ever be held, in spite of the relentless efforts of the foreign minister."[3] Shamir grumbled that Peres had decided to support the "madness" after "a night of nightmares." In a speech before the Liberal Party, he turned to his partner in the bizarre coalition government: "I call upon Peres to leave alone that silly idea, stop this nonsense!" Still, Shamir did not dare thwart Peres's initiative,[4] as this could bring down the unity government.

DURING THE FLIGHT, Peres said to Beilin: "Why don't you put on paper the main points of our position vis-à-vis the Jordanians? This may be helpful." Beilin promptly prepared a handwritten draft.

At the airport in London, another Israeli was waiting for them—Efraim Halevy, a senior Mossad official.[5] In a fierce rainstorm, he drove them to Victor Mishcon's home. Mishcon, a Jew, was a former chairman of London's City Council. His daughter Jane had gone to Oxford with Hussein's sister Basma, and the two families had become friendly. Mishcon had already hosted several meetings between Peres and Hussein. Today, the two men met at Mishcon's London home, off Hyde Park. Hussein was accompanied by his prime minister, Zeid al-Rifai.

To preserve secrecy, the Mishcons had given their house staff the day off, and Mrs. Mishcon cooked and served lunch to her guests. When it was over, Hussein offered to help her clean; Peres and the king joined Mrs. Mishcon in the kitchen and dutifully washed the dishes.

The talks started in a very congenial atmosphere. Short, slim, and aristocratic, Hussein sported a stylish mustache and his lively eyes often lit up in laughter. His English was impeccable, spiced with an Oxford accent. He described a hilarious conversation with President Reagan, who had asked him about the prospects of "fishing in the Dead Sea."[6] He then spoke about his son, a Cobra helicopter pilot in the Jordanian Air Force. "My son is a Cobra pilot too!" Peres exclaimed.[7]

Zeid al-Rifai contributed an anecdote about his recent visit to Cairo. Late at night, he said, he had failed to gain access to the government guesthouse, as the guards on duty didn't recognize him. Suddenly remembering how popular Peres was with the Egyptian authorities, he then introduced himself as Shimon Peres and was immediately admitted to the building.

When their talks moved to more serious issues, Peres was in for a surprise. He described his position on the international conference, and waited to hear Hussein's diverging view. To his amazement, however, the king did not object. He understood Israel's worries about an international conference, he said, "but the goal is peace, not a conference." Jordan, he added, wasn't interested in a conference "where Israel would feel isolated or victimized."[8]

A second surprise—Hussein did not mention the Referral Clause. And a third surprise—the Jordanian king didn't demand a simultaneous Israeli-Syrian negotiation. That meant he was ready to accept the idea of a separate peace! Moreover, Zeid al-Rifai, who in the past had adopted a tougher position in the negotiations, voiced his full support.

Peres felt that he and the king were "on the same wavelength."[9] That feeling intensified when they spoke of the PLO. Hussein sharply criticized the PLO leadership and agreed with Peres's objection to Arafat as a partner for peace. He also agreed that the peace talks should be held between an Israeli and a Jordanian-Palestinian delegation that would not include PLO representatives.

Step by step, the two men reached agreement on most of the subjects discussed. Hussein defined his commitment to the goal of peace as "a holy challenge" and as his personal "religious duty."[10]

As the conversation progressed, it dawned on Peres that the seemingly insurmountable obstacles to a negotiation with Jordan were crumbling, one after another. He could hardly control his emotions. For the second time that day, he asked, "Why don't we put this on paper?"

"Good idea," said the king. He and Rifai had another engagement in town, he said, but they would be back in an hour. He suggested that Peres and his aides draft two documents, one setting up the principles and modus operandi of the international conference, and the other describing the agreements between Israel and Jordan about the negotiation procedure.[11]

Peres and Beilin prepared the papers with Halevy's help, while Victor Mishcon contributed the legal formulas. Finally, Mishcon drafted the two documents in his neat handwriting.[12]

An hour later, the king and his prime minister were back. They carefully read the two documents. Rifai wanted to propose a few changes, but the king refused. He agreed that the documents fully reflected the agreements he and Peres had reached.[13]

"THE U.N. SECRETARY GENERAL," Paragraph A of the agreement read, "will issue invitations to the five permanent members of the Security Council and the parties involved in the Arab-Israeli conflict in order to negotiate a peaceful settlement based on Resolutions 242 and 338, with the object of bringing a comprehensive peace to the area, security to its states, and to respond to the legitimate rights of the Palestinian people." Paragraph B invited the parties to form "geographical bilateral committees" to negotiate mutual issues.

The real bombshell was in Paragraph C.

Jordan and Israel had agreed, the document stated, that "the international conference will not impose any solution or veto any agreement arrived at between the parties." The conference would break down into bilateral committees that would negotiate directly and "independently."

By agreeing to this paragraph Hussein betrayed an earlier commitment to Syria. The meaning of the word "independently" was far-reaching. The king was now agreeing to make peace with Israel even if her negotiations with Syria failed.

Peres and Hussein agreed that the Jordanian-Palestinian delegation would include only people who accepted the U.N. resolutions and renounced violence and terrorism. By that definition, no PLO members would be allowed to join the delegation.

Finally, to remove any doubt about the passive role of the international conference, the document stated that "other issues will be decided by mutual agreement between Jordan and Israel."

The second document was an appendix specifying some secret agreements between the two parties.

The agreement was short—barely one page. But it represented a tremendous victory for Peres and his colleagues. They had achieved all their objectives: a toothless international conference, direct negotiations leading to a separate peace, no intervention by any other power in the negotiations, and exclusion of the PLO from the talks.

The king approved of the document. Peres felt that they had achieved "a momentous breakthrough."[14] The king, too, seemed happy, confident, and deeply moved. Peres promised the king to do all in his power to get the agreement adopted by the Israeli cabinet. If he failed, he said, he would bring down the government.[15]

The grim battle looming at home prompted Peres to suggest to Hussein an unorthodox maneuver to ensure success. He proposed that the London document be communicated secretly to the United States. Both the Jordanians and the Israelis would ask

Washington to present the agreement officially as an American proposal.[16] This, Peres argued, would make it easier for Hussein to formally accept the draft. After all, he could hardly admit to his people that he himself had met Peres, his enemy, and reached a secret agreement.

The idea of an "American proposal" was not new. It had been discussed before between Peres and the American assistant secretary of state, Richard Murphy, and Thomas Pickering, the U.S. ambassador to Israel.

Peres hoped that the endorsement of the document by the United States would make its rejection very difficult for Shamir. American pressure was the only way to force Shamir's hand and make him agree to the international conference he so doggedly rejected. Shamir might discard a Peres initiative, but if the United States assumed authorship of the document—at least formally—he could not dismiss it outright.

Therefore, Peres and Hussein added a last paragraph to the London document: "The above document is subject to approval of the respective governments of Israel and Jordan. The text of this paper will be shown and suggested to the USA."[17]

THAT NIGHT, PERES, Beilin, and Halevy flew back to Israel. Peres was elated. In the plane he spoke to his companions about the historic breakthrough and repeated his commitment to bring down the government if Shamir refused to cooperate. In his own words, Peres felt "deeply gratified . . . with a sense of eager anticipation."

The aircraft landed in Israel on Sunday morning and Peres called Shamir right away. The two men agreed to meet after the weekly cabinet session.

Now that he was so close to achieving his goal, Peres should have moved with extreme caution, as he had done on the Lebanese withdrawal, the inflation issue, and the Taba settlement when he was prime minister. He should have prepared the ground meticulously by secretly gaining the support of at least one Likud cabinet member. Shamir had opposed him both on the withdrawal from Lebanon and on the Taba settlement with Egypt, but the support of other Likud ministers had helped Peres prevail. Today it was more important than ever for Peres to repeat this maneuver.

He did not. He was so excited by his achievement in London that he assumed the agreement with Hussein would do the job of persuasion for him. That was a mistake.

His relationship with Shamir was at a record low. Peres despised Shamir, whom he saw as a dour, inflexible politician, unable and unwilling to undertake any political initiative. He regarded him as the master of immobility. "If Shamir had a gun with only one bullet," Peres said, "he would have shot Galileo because Galileo believed that the planets move around the sun."[18]

But now Shamir was prime minister. He did not trust Peres, either. Shamir was a very severe judge of people, because of his tough background. As a leader of the underground Stern group, he had lived an undercover life in which nobody trusted anybody. Caught by the British and brought to trial, he had spent years as a prisoner in a British camp in Eritrea. The limelight of the political arena apparently hadn't affected his secretive character. This taciturn man was openly suspicious of the extroverted and energetic Peres. Shamir held Rabin in high esteem, while he found Peres exasperating. Staunchly devoted to the idea of a Greater Israel, Shamir would not give up one grain of sand from the historic land. At a public rally, when asked why Israel should not give land for peace, he answered, "Why? Because." This, of course, was a difficult argument to beat.

Shamir regarded many of Peres's ideas, especially his dream of a territorial compromise, as dangerous or fantastic or both, and suspected him of every possible manipulation behind his back.

He was in for a shock when Peres placed the London document on his desk, on April 12, 1987. Frowning, he perused the agreement between Hussein and his foreign minister. Peres described the meeting with Hussein and Rifai, and outlined the next stage agreed on by the two parties. "Shamir was stunned," one of Peres's aides recalled.[19] "Until that morning he had thought nothing would come of Peres's initiative. Now, all of a sudden, he found out that this was a serious matter."

Shamir read the document in silence, without expressing any objections, although his angry face betrayed his thoughts. A tense moment ensued when he picked it up to have it photocopied, but Peres refused. "That's the only copy," he said, "and the handwriting in the margins is Zaid al-Rifai's. I have to protect him."

"You don't trust me?" the prime minister asked.

"I trust you, but I am afraid one of your aides may leak the information," Peres said.[20] "Anyway," he added, "the idea is that the Americans would put these agreements forward as their proposal; it would be better, therefore, if you received the document from the Americans."[21]

Shamir seethed with anger. "He felt hurt and humiliated," one of his aides recalled. Peres's boys had the right to handle the document, but he, the prime minister, was denied the right to keep it in his files. Some of Peres's friends, including Lord Mishcon, strongly believed that Peres should have behaved differently.

Actually, the document that Peres showed Shamir was not "the only copy." While they were meeting in Jerusalem, Yossi Beilin was talking on the telephone with the U.S. ambassador, Thomas Pickering. Pickering immediately grasped the tremendous importance of the agreement. "If you've got a story of such magnitude," he told Beilin, "you must get to Secretary Shultz right away and brief him about it." Shultz was on his way to Moscow, he said, and Beilin should intercept him in Helsinki.[22]

It was 10 A.M.; the next flight was leaving in an hour. Beilin rushed to Ben-Gurion Airport. He had no passport, and no flight ticket. On the way he telephoned Peres, and Peres said: "Go!"

Pickering was already at the airport. He informed Beilin that Shultz had just arrived in Helsinki. The secretary of state was going to spend the night there before continuing to Moscow to meet with President Gorbachev. With the help of Efraim Halevy, the flights and connections were arranged.

As the aircraft soared over the Mediterranean, Beilin thought, "We've done it! I'll bring the document to Shultz, he'll show it to Gorbachev, the Great Powers will support us and we'll put an end to the conflict." He thought briefly of the internal Israeli scene. The Likud could not reject such a proposal. It meant peace![23]

IN HELSINKI, BEILIN RUSHED to the Kalastajatorppa government guesthouse, situated on the bank of a frozen lake. He met there with Ambassador Charles Hill, a close aide to Secretary Shultz, and handed him a copy of the document.[24] The meeting of Hussein and Peres was a breakthrough, Beilin told Hill. "It is an agreement, the first ever. Peres and Hussein didn't sign. They wrote the paper and then shook hands. This handshake had the feeling of an historic event."

King Hussein and Shimon Peres, Beilin went on, requested that the international conference proposal be presented to the parties as a United States initiative. Therefore, a visit of Secretary Shultz to Israel was needed. "Don't let it evaporate," Beilin concluded. "It's in your hands now."[25]

Charlie Hill reported Beilin's words to George Shultz, who reacted with enthusiasm. "We've got a touchdown!" he exclaimed.

The secretary of state, however, apparently did not understand Beilin's message and acted erratically and inconsistently during the following days. "[Peres's] urgent request," he wrote in his memoirs, "was extraordinary: the Foreign Minister of Israel's government of National Unity was asking me to sell to Israel's Prime Minister, the head of a rival party, the substance of an agreement made with a foreign head of state—an agreement revealed to *me* before it had been revealed to the Israeli government itself! Peres was informing me, and wanting me to collaborate with him, before going to his Prime Minister."[26]

This was utterly false. When Beilin landed in Helsinki, Peres had already met with Shamir and briefed him. What he was asking Shultz to do was facilitate the acceptance of the agreement by both parties by attributing it to the United States.

Shultz apparently doubted Beilin's report as well; he abstained from informing Gorbachev of the breakthrough, and on his return to California he advised President Reagan "to find out King Hussein's views directly."[27] American diplomats in Amman got in touch with the royal palace and the Jordanians, indeed, "fully confirmed" Beilin's description of the agreement.[28]

Both the secretary's actions and recollections about the London document are puzzling. On April 20, Shultz returned to Washington and was informed by Richard Murphy that Peres had indeed briefed Shamir about the London agreement. Murphy's report should have set the record straight. Still, eleven years later Shultz repeated that "in 1987 Peres tried to use me in order to deceive Shamir . . . and wanted me to say that it was an American initiative. I said: 'No . . . this is not true. [Presenting the agreement as an American document] would be cheating.' "[29]

And yet, on April 22, 1987, on Shultz's instructions, Pickering met with Prime Minister Shamir and brought him the London document!

Arye Mekel, Shamir's political adviser, was the only other person who participated at the meeting with Pickering. Pickering behaved as if he assumed that Shamir didn't know about the agreement, and Shamir behaved as if he was hearing the story for the first time. Pickering read the entire document and the secret appendix, then discussed some points of the agreement.[30]

Shamir was furious. He didn't say a word, but he became red in the face, as if he were on the verge of an outburst. Arye Mekel feared for him, and several times he offered to bring him a glass of water but Shamir refused. Afterward he told Mekel: "I was driven crazy by that situation—this goy [Gentile], Ambassador Pickering, is telling me that my foreign minister has reached an agreement with an Arab country in London. That will never happen!"

"That day, Shamir declared war on Peres and on the London document."[31]

Later that day, Shultz called the prime minister. There was

a lot of empathy between the two men, and Shamir regarded Shultz "as a great friend of Israel."[32] Shultz told Shamir that Peres and Hussein had informed him about the London document, and he was ready to come to the Middle East "to work with him, seizing upon this very positive moment to go forward in the peace process."[33]

Shamir answered that he wanted to think about the idea for a couple of days, but Shultz sensed that he was "dead set against it." That same evening, Elyakim Rubinstein, the Israeli government's secretary, called Shultz. Shamir didn't approve of the London document, Rubinstein said. He was against an international conference; he feared that the PLO would certainly become involved in the negotiation, and therefore Shamir didn't welcome a visit from Shultz at the present moment. "Shamir is very upset," Rubinstein said. "This international conference has become a passion. He is utterly against it . . . . Nothing personal toward the Secretary, but an international conference? 'A healthy head into a sick bed,' that's the Prime Minister's view."[34]

Peres, on the other hand, was delighted by Shultz's call to Shamir. On April 23, he called Shultz and thanked him. He stressed that he would risk breaking the government over this issue. "In London," he said, "Israel and Jordan have been in direct negotiations and have achieved agreement. Would the Israeli Prime Minister now turn away from this opportunity?"[35]

The following morning, however, an unexpected visitor appeared in Shultz's office in Washington. It was Moshe Arens, a minister in Shamir's cabinet and a hawkish leader of the Likud Party.[36] Arens had been urgently dispatched to Washington by Shamir.[37] His official cover was a lecture tour for Israel Bonds. Actually, his mission was to dissuade Shultz from going to Israel. He regarded Peres as a man "whose daring was on the verge of fantasy," and feared that his initiative would result in a real international conference. "We were suspicious," he said to a friend. "Perhaps the international conference in the London agreement was only an opening conference indeed, but who could know

what would happen later? [Besides], Peres did something unfor-
givable. There is a prime minister ... who didn't give him the
authority; he concludes some agreement that he isn't even ready
to leave with Shamir .... There is nothing sacred for him, the
goal justifies the means."[38]

At his meeting with Shultz, Arens said, "On this subject there
is a political debate between Likud and Labor. Do you want to be
involved and become a part in it?"

Shultz agreed that this was not what he wanted.

Arens pointed at the "impropriety" of what Peres had done by
negotiating an agreement, even *ad referendum* (until approved by
the cabinet). "This has never happened in Israel's history before,"
Arens said.[39] To this argument, Peres was to respond later, "Isn't
negotiating *ad referendum* what every Foreign Minister does?"[40]

Shultz, in his own words, tried to convince Arens that "the
Prime Minister arguments" were wrong, and that the London
agreement "represents a possibility that never existed before. My
instinct is to work on it." Arens, however, "would not budge."

Shultz bowed to Arens's pressure. He was ready to come to
the Middle East at any moment, he said, "but since Shamir is
opposed, I'm filling up my calendar. But it's too bad."[41] To his
aides he said, "I cannot force myself upon him. If the Prime Minister doesn't want me to come, I shall not come."[42]

ONE CANNOT HELP wondering whether a more energetic
secretary of state would have bowed to such pressure. "If it had
been Henry Kissinger," a U.S. diplomat mournfully remarked, "he
would have brushed aside Arens's arguments and said, 'Sorry, but
I'm coming in the name of the president.' "[43]

"But Shultz wasn't Kissinger, he was not even James Baker,"
remarked Shamir's confidant Yossi Ben-Aharon.[44] An affable
man, very elegant and moderate in his pronouncements, Shultz
held America's allies in high esteem. The prospect of Soviet participation in an international conference made him rather luke-
warm to that aspect of the London agreement. True, he had been
ready to go to the Middle East, but Arens had had little difficulty

in dissuading him. Shultz also feared that by coming to the Middle East he might precipitate a political crisis in Israel.[45]

Shultz backed down, and by doing so he condemned the London agreement to a dusty death in some forgotten archive. "[In] my opinion," Shultz summed up later, "this was a very promising initiative. The Foreign Minister took this initiative . . . . [But] how could I respond positively to something that the Prime Minister objected to?"[46]

Arens won the battle, leaving behind him a most promising but dead initiative that could have changed the face of the Middle East. "Peres will never forgive me for that," Arens said sixteen years later.[47]

The rest was like a bad dream. From that moment on, nothing could help; neither the frantic letters and telegrams from Washington to Shamir trying to quell his fears about PLO participation in the conference, nor the marathon talks between Ambassador Pickering and the prime minister, nor Peres's aides' psychological warfare—they leaked the London document to the press—nor even Hussein's bold declarations to the *Boston Globe* that it wouldn't be realistic to expect an Israeli withdrawal from *all* the occupied territories, and that Jerusalem shouldn't be a divided city again.

On May 13, 1987, at a cabinet meeting, Shamir succeeded in killing Peres's initiative. He saw one of his greatest achievements in the thwarting of the London agreement.[48] After the cabinet meeting, Peres told Shamir, "I am through with you. It's over."[49]

Many of Peres's colleagues, among them Beilin and Ministers Rafael Edri and Moshe Shachal, urged Peres to resign.[50] Hadn't he promised the king to do so if he failed?

But Peres didn't resign. He claimed that he could not do so, as he had promised King Hussein to keep the agreement secret and did not want to embarrass him.[51] The king, however, expected Peres to fulfill his promise; he was deeply disappointed with Peres when nothing happened. After that their relationship became cold and distant for a long time.

"That's Shimon," one of his close friends said. "He never goes all the way."

A FEW MONTHS LATER, Hussein disengaged from the Palestinians and the West Bank. The failure of the peace initiative deepened the despair of the Palestinian people, and the growing pressure in the West Bank and Gaza soon exploded in the rocks and the firebombs of the intifada.

The collapse of the London agreement and King Hussein's ensuing disengagement prompted Peres to direct his relentless efforts for peace elsewhere. Since King Hussein was no longer a partner, the only possible interlocutor left was the PLO. And so, in the late eighties, Peres started sending feelers toward yesterday's vilest enemy, the Palestine Liberation Organization.[52]

Shamir's success in blocking the peace process with Hussein paved the way for the 1993 Oslo agreements with Yasser Arafat.

CHAPTER 29.

THE LONG DUEL (3)

FOR SHIMON PERES, 1987 was a year of painful awakening. His friends noticed that he was bitter and frustrated. The media maintained that he was depressed because of being relegated to the rank of number two. The relations between Peres and Shamir worsened. Peres claimed that Shamir didn't want peace. "This man, Shamir, cannot head the unity government," he said to his party colleagues. During his last flight to the United States as prime minister, he said to the journalist Akiva Eldar, "What did you think, that I would work for Shamir as foreign minister? I'll make him swallow toads and snakes and scorpions. I'll continue my efforts with Hussein and my contacts with the Arab leaders!"[1]

Shamir, too, used a brutal and offensive language toward Peres. He spoke of his foreign minister as "a man with a puzzling hobby called international conference."[2] When Peres left for a visit in Egypt, Prime Minister Shamir declared that "he doesn't represent the government." When Peres set out on a visit to Spain and Italy, Shamir sent him some strange wishes: "I hope he will not succeed," he said.[3]

Shamir defined Peres's political moves as "forsaking the country and weakening it"; he accused him of "harming Israel's interests" and declared that he was acting out of "a lust for power." Peres angrily retorted to Shamir's accusations, "What is his right to be arrogant? To be contemptuous? We got from Shamir a government with 500 percent inflation, mired in Lebanon, what's his authority to be so demeaning? This is a government based on incitement, hatred, and character assassination against me."[4] Soon the two stopped talking to each other.

THE ELECTIONS TOOK PLACE on November 1,1988. Peres hoped to cash in on his success as prime minister, but that was wishful thinking. In the two years that had passed, his achievements were forgotten. Many analyzed the situation in simplistic terms: Shamir was now prime minister, and Peres fought him out of frustration.

Moreover, Peres adopted a policy that clearly turned to the left, leaving the center to Shamir. The Labor Party under his leadership slid to the left, and Likud hurried to fill that void. "We are the center!" Shamir declared at a party meeting.

At the eleventh hour, bad luck struck Shimon Peres again. On October 30, forty-eight hours before the elections, terrorists threw Molotov cocktails onto an Israeli bus as it crossed Jericho; the bus burst into flames and became a death trap. A woman, Rachel Weiss, and her three little children were burned alive. A brave soldier, David Delarosa, who tried to save them, succumbed to his wounds as well.

The terrible murder shook the nation. Apparently it had an impact on some voters, who shifted their votes to the hard-liners. The right-wing bloc that included Likud won a few more seats.

As always before the elections, the polls predicted a great victory for Peres, and, as always, were wrong once again. Likud won forty seats, one less than at the 1984 election; Labor, on the other hand, lost five seats, winning only thirty-nine seats in the Knesset. The results were a heavy blow to Peres. "The Israelis," Peres cynically said, "are the only people in the world who say the truth to the pollsters and lie at the polling stations."[5]

A unity government was established again, but this time without the rotation. Peres accused Rabin of preventing a rotation government by reaching an agreement with Shamir that he would be prime minister for the entire term.[6] Under the pressure of the kibbutz movement, Peres agreed to help it, and took the portfolio of finance minister, a job that didn't suit him.

Rabin was defense minister again. And once again voices were heard in the Labor Party, demanding that Peres be replaced as its chairman. Rabin started preparing to run against his old rival.

FOR SHIMON PERES, these were painful days of political decline. The feeling of urgency that motivated him shattered against a worsening reality. In the West Bank and Gaza the first intifada raged; Peres regarded it as a result of the Shamir government's inaction.

Rabin and Shamir got along very well. "Their relations were very good," said Dan Meridor, Shamir's confidant. "Both Rabin and Shamir didn't believe in *grands actes* [great deeds]. Rabin was a man of small and cautious steps, trial and error. Shamir, too, was very cautious. They both were birds of a feather, security minded . . . . There were no differences of opinion between them."[7]

Peres felt the ground burning under his feet. Shamir defeated any attempt to start a peace negotiation and confronted the United States on this issue. Reagan's successor, George H. W. Bush, and his secretary of state, James Baker, were determined to promote the peace process, but Shamir blocked any attempt to move ahead. The secretary of state presented Shamir with a question and bluntly demanded his answer. Will Israel be ready, he asked, to enter into a negotiation with the Palestinians in the West Bank, including the inhabitants of East Jerusalem? Shamir stammered and twisted, delayed and postponed, but didn't answer, fearing a revolt in Likud.

Baker couldn't rein in his fury at Shamir's behavior. President Herzog wrote, "Despite sensible advice to go easy with the United States and particularly with Secretary of State Baker, he had made every possible mistake. He had opened every front at once—with the United States, with Labor, within his own party."[8]

Peres decided to bring down the immobilized unity government. He concocted a political maneuver with Knesset members Yossi Beilin and Haim Ramon that involved a joint action with the ultraorthodox parties, and a vote of no confidence in Shamir's government. Rabin opposed the move.

Peres's friend Giora Eini didn't believe in the Ramon-Beilin maneuver and tried to thwart it. "Shimon," he said to Peres, "you're going to make the mistake of your life. You won't be prime minister, certainly not when Ramon is in charge of the negotiation." Eini suspected that Ramon cared more about his own interests than about Peres. But Peres was confident he would succeed. He presented to Eini his plan to establish an alternative government, explained to him why the three ultraorthodox parties and the National Religious Party would join him, and concluded that his government would be supported by seventy Knesset members. This was Peres's wishful thinking at its best. Eini was stunned, and tried to explain to Peres why his plan couldn't work. Minister Shachal, too, warned Peres that if his plan failed, his head could be on the block.

But Peres was already storming ahead.

A rumor reached Shamir that the ultraorthodox Agudat Israel Party would present to the Knesset a motion of no confidence, and the Labor Party would support it, bringing his downfall. He therefore decided to fire Peres. At the March 13, 1990, government meeting, Shamir read a letter dismissing Peres from the functions of deputy prime minister and finance minister. "Mr. Peres," Shamir stated, "acted and is still acting for the breakup of the unity government, and is undermining its existence. He unjustly accuses the government of not promoting the peace. I have no other choice but [to] put an end to Mr. Peres's service in the government."[9] Shamir handed the letter to Peres, but he repelled it, disdain painted all over his face. "Your documents are good for the archives," Peres fumed. "You're not a prime minister for me, you chronic agreement violator, you untrustworthy man .... You'll never be a prime minister for me again."[10]

The Labor ministers signed a collective letter of resignation from the government. Rabin didn't support the move and tried to reach a compromise, but he signed the letter like everybody else.

On March 15, the Knesset voted on the no-confidence motion. Peres and his allies succeeded in defeating Shamir's government by sixty votes to fifty-five. That was the first time in Israel's history that a government fell in a no-confidence vote.

President Herzog charged Peres with forming a new government. But when Peres started counting his potential partners, he realized that he could rely only on the support of the left-wing and Arab parties. The cooperation of the ultraorthodox parties was not guaranteed. From faraway Brooklyn, the famous Lubavitcher Rebbe sent to his disciples—two of the Agudat Israel Knesset members—the order not to vote for Peres's government. The resourceful Peres called his friend General Shlomo Gazit, who was on sabbatical in Washington, and asked him to go to the Rebbe's residence and try to get him to change his mind. Gazit did as asked, but failed.

In Israel, the Labor leaders stormed the yeshivas of the ultraorthodox rabbis, trying to obtain their support. After realizing that the Labor activists enthusiastically supported Peres's maneuver, Rabin joined the effort. He bluntly attacked Likud at the Labor Central Committee, then donned a black skullcap and went to visit some famous rabbis, trying to persuade them to join Peres's government.[11] Yossi Beilin and other Peres aides allegedly promised the ultraorthodox leaders funds and grants for their institutions, and the public saw that as a despicable effort to buy the religious vote. A Labor Knesset member who revolted against the ugly horse trading was furiously attacked by Peres.

The secret negotiation had its up and downs. Shas, the ultraorthodox Sephardic party, discreetly informed Peres that it wouldn't vote for his government. Another effort of Peres's people to tempt a Likud Knesset member to cross the lines failed. And yet Peres announced that he had put together a government coalition; he asked the Knesset speaker to convene an extraordinary meeting of the Knesset on April 11, the day after Passover, for presenting his new government.

But it turned out that all the frantic activity, the promises, the nightly visits at the rabbis' courts had not helped. On April 9, Passover's eve, Knesset member Avraham Verdiger of Agudat Israel called Peres at 5 A.M. and informed him that he wouldn't vote for his government. Another Agudat Israel Knesset member, Eliezer Mizrahi, simply vanished from the face of the earth. It was later established that he had been hidden by Minister Ariel Sharon. Two days before presenting his government to the Knesset, Peres realized that he had no coalition.

That morning turned into a weird, surrealistic experience. While Israel was getting ready for the holiday, Peres's office teemed with delegations of party members who had come to demand ministerial jobs for their leaders in Peres's future cabinet. The leaders of the left-wing parties, also an integral component of the coalition, waited outside. The newspapers announced in banner headlines that in forty-eight hours Peres would be prime minister. But Peres knew the truth.

Peres turned on the radio. A newscaster announced that Knesset members Verdiger and Mizrahi wouldn't vote for Shimon Peres. And Peres, the symbol of self-control, the man with nerves of steel, broke down and burst into tears.

"That was terrible," recalled Shulamit Aloni, the leader of the Meretz Party. "He suddenly realized that Verdiger had cheated him. He burst into tears; it was really sad."[12]

Aloni hastily drove everybody out of the room. "He cried in my arms," Moshe Shachal added. "Shimon wouldn't admit it, it was very short, but at that moment I saw the steel breaking."[13]

Peres returned home dejected and depressed. He instructed his aides not to tell anybody that his coalition was falling apart; he still hoped to convince a couple of Knesset members to vote for his government.

Peres's nightmare continued at the meeting of the Labor Central Committee on the night after Passover. Merry and enthusiastic party activists came from all over the country and turned the Labor meeting into a victory celebration. The only killjoy was the Knesset member M. Haver, who spoke against the shameful courting of the ultraorthodox parties and the sacrifice of Labor's values and honor in exchange for power. He was angrily booed, and Peres got on the podium and attacked him fiercely.[14] Only later would the truth surface: Peres knew what his rejoicing supporters didn't know. He had no government.

The festive meeting ended in an atmosphere of euphoria. The following morning, at ten o'clock, the Knesset convened for a vote of confidence in the new government.

AS THE PLENUM MEETING began, the Knesset members saw Sonia Peres in the visitors' gallery, waiting for her husband's swearing in. This was one of the rare occasions when Sonia participated in a political event. Nobody knew that at 6 A.M., Peres had visited Rabbi Ovadia Yossef, the spiritual leader of Shas, and asked him for the votes of two Shas Knesset members in order to achieve a majority at the plenum session. Ovadia Yossef had agreed, and Peres calmed down, but not for long. At 10 A.M., one of Shas's leaders called him. In spite of what Ovadia Yosef promised, he said, no Shas member would vote for his government. Peres didn't have a majority.

He had to swallow the bitter pill and ask the speaker to cancel the Knesset vote. The Labor Party suffered a terrible humiliation.

Peres reached the president's residence, "looking the worse for wear"; he was on the verge of collapse, as he hadn't eaten or drunk anything so far that day. Herzog's wife prepared a meal for him, as "he was physically, and perhaps mentally, at the end of his tether."[15]

Herzog gave Peres fifteen more days to assemble a coalition. Peres tried almost everything, but his efforts kept failing. The president realized that politicians, aides, and apparatchiks were misleading Peres; he spoke to him "a bit harshly" and tried to make Peres understand what the real situation was. But Peres kept stubbornly repeating that he would put a coalition together.

He even tried to gain the support of the extreme right-wing Moledet Party. He was pathetically clutching at straws, but to no avail. Chaim Herzog realized that "he was going to make any deal he could to regain the position of Prime Minister."[16]

Finally, Peres gave up.

A few weeks later, Shamir formed a right-wing government with the support of the religious parties. Labor was no longer a member of the government coalition.

Rabin, who had actively supported Peres since the unity government's collapse, now dissociated himself from his endeavor and named it "the stinking maneuver."

Peres was beaten and sore. The party was disappointed and furious. From all over, voices were raised, calling for new leadership. Rabin announced that he was going to run for the leadership of the Labor Party.

RABIN HAD TO WAIT for more than two years for the Labor primaries. Together with Peres he sat on the opposition benches during Desert Storm, the Scud-missile attacks on Israel, and the American victory over Saddam Hussein. They watched from afar the conference in Madrid that the United States convened after the Gulf War in an attempt to achieve peace in the Middle East. They both witnessed the peace process launched at Madrid getting mired in bilateral and multilateral committees that didn't yield any results.

Peres resented the status as leader of the opposition that he had brought upon himself. Only rarely did he find time to relax and take a short vacation. In December 1990, he went on a cruise in the Mediterranean on a sumptuous cruise ship with hundreds of the best American economists, politicians, and academics. He was one of several personalities invited to speak before the passengers about their countries or their professions. Shimon Peres spoke of the Middle East and was impressed in particular by two of his fellow-lecturers: one was Simeon of Saxe-Coburg-Gotha, the Bulgarian king-in-exile, who was later elected prime minister of Bulgaria. The other lecturer was a charming Texan who told his audience how he had bought and managed a baseball team. His name was George W. Bush.[17]

The ship sailed through smooth seas, but it didn't take long before Peres was back, fighting the turbulent waves of Israeli politics. As the primaries approached, Peres felt betrayed; many of his friends, who had supported him for years, decided to vote for Rabin. Yitzhak Navon, Peres's soul mate, told him that Rabin should head the Labor Party list.

"Why Rabin?" Peres asked. "The Arabs won't vote for him."

Navon said, "He is the only candidate who has a chance to win the election. Maybe some of the Arabs won't vote, but a large number of Jews will vote for us if Rabin is at the head of Labor."

"Why not somebody else?" Peres asked. He was ready to accept even an outsider, as long as it was not Rabin.

"Who?" Navon asked.

"Why not a writer?"

"Who?"

"Amos Oz."

"Why him, out of all our writers?"

"He is a great writer."

"Why not A. B. Yehoshua?" Navon asked. "He is a great writer, too."

"So why in Czechoslovakia did they elect Vaclav Havel president?"

"Because he isn't only a writer," Navon answered. "He spent five years in jail. He is a political leader. He has become a symbol."

Peres mentioned the name of an IDF senior officer. He seemed ready to step aside in favor of any candidate, if only to prevent Rabin's return.

"Shimon," Navon said. "Rabin is the only chance of the party to win."[18]

It wasn't easy for Navon to transfer his support from Peres to Rabin. They had come a long way, and in spite of occasional friction, Navon still held Peres in high esteem and regarded him as "a unique and special man."

On February 19, 1992, the Labor primaries took place. The Histadrut secretary, Israel Kessar, who also ran, received 18.77 percent of the vote. Shimon Peres got 35 percent and Rabin 40.59 percent. According to party regulations, if only one of the candidates received more than 40 percent, he was the winner.

Rabin was the new chairman of the Labor Party. The following day he moved into Peres's office on HaYarkon Street.

"And then," said Nissim Zvili, Peres's confidant, "the worst period in Shimon's life began."[19]

ON JUNE 2.3, 1992, Yitzhak Rabin won the general election and was elected prime minister. Shimon Peres was elected to the second place in Labor's Knesset list.

CHAPTER 30.

OSLO

"IF YOU PROMOTE the peace process," Peres said to Rabin after the Rabin government was sworn in, "I'll be your most loyal supporter. If you thwart the peace process—I'll be your staunchest rival."[1]

The relations between the two men were tense and hostile. After Peres's failure at the primaries, many of Rabin's supporters wanted to settle their accounts with him. Some of them mocked him and joked that he would be appointed "minister of pepper and coriander" in Rabin's cabinet.[2] Peres himself was bitter and distressed. "This was an especially painful defeat for me. . . . I was bitter in my heart for what had happened. I had been unfairly removed from the leadership just when global and regional developments brought peace into prospect." However, he tried to overcome his disappointment. "Bitterness is not statesmanship," he wrote. "It was my duty now to prove that I had the strength to accept tough and unpleasant decisions, when these were part of the democratic process."[3]

The "pepper and coriander" declarations turned out to be nothing but hot air. Rabin couldn't ignore Peres, who had received the votes of more than a third of the party members. Under pressure from the party, he appointed Peres foreign minister, but significantly curtailed his functions.

"Rabin made Shimon foreign minister in charge of cocktails," said Minister Haim Ramon, who was close to Rabin. "He took away from him the relations with the United States and the peace negotiations. Peres accepted that, because this is Peres: between being out and being in—even humiliated—he'll always be in."[4] The worst humiliation was that Rabin summed up his meeting with Peres in a written document, stating that Peres wouldn't be involved in the peace negotiations with Syria, Jordan, Lebanon, or the Palestinians.[5] He allowed Peres to deal only with the multilateral talks that the Madrid conference had initiated; Rabin didn't attach too much importance to them.

"During that first year, Rabin kept humiliating Shimon," Ramon recalled. "Shimon had no idea what was happening with the Jordanians; talks were held in Washington, but he didn't know a thing. One day he heard that Rabin was going to visit the United States. He burst out shouting and I went to Yitzhak. I said to him, Yitzhak, you can't behave like this. Why do you do this to him? Tell him you are going to America. What could happen if he knows?" But Rabin's suspicions and alienation didn't fade away. More than once, he furiously attacked Peres when he suspected that he was negotiating with the Palestinians behind his back.[6]

And yet, only a few months later, Peres would be conducting a groundbreaking negotiation with the Palestinians that would produce the Oslo agreements!

The process developed in a tortuous way. After the failure of the London agreement, Peres decided to turn to the only other possible partner—the PLO. Rabin didn't agree at first; he still saw a terrible danger in the creation of "an Arafat state," and described Yasser Arafat as a bloody and vile enemy. But being a realist, he accepted the inevitable conclusion. Both Rabin and Peres realized that they would have to negotiate with the PLO. Yet they differed in their approach.

At first, Rabin stuck to the Madrid conference resolution to initiate negotiations between Israel and the Palestinians on establishing autonomy in the West Bank and Gaza. The negotiations took place in Washington; for a while, Rabin insisted that the Palestinian delegation not include PLO representatives. Yet everybody knew that the Palestinians negotiating with Israel in the American capital were receiving their instructions from the PLO headquarters in Tunis.

Peres, on the other hand, believed that nothing would come out of the Washington channel. For years he and his deputy Yossi Beilin had been maintaining secret contacts with Palestinian leaders like Faisal Husseini and Hanan Ashrawi. Their main go-between was Professor Yair Hirschfeld of Haifa University, a hefty, warm man who knew how to charm his Arab interlocutors and win their trust.

By July 1992, the negotiations with the Palestinian delegation in Washington were all but stalled. Rabin considered freezing the Palestinian option and concentrating on secret talks with Syria. That had been his main reason for appointing Professor Itamar Rabinowitz, one of Israel's leading experts on Syria, ambassador to Washington. But at that point, Hirschfeld received a discreet signal from one of the PLO leaders, Abu Ala'a, Arafat's "finance minister." They met in London in December; Hirschfeld was accompanied by his colleague Dr. Ron Pundak. The meeting took place in the utmost secrecy with Yossi Beilin subtly pulling the strings.

The Israelis and the Palestinian leader decided to continue their meetings. Yossi Beilin gave Hirschfeld the green light to proceed, without even asking for Rabin's and Peres's permission. The Norwegian diplomat Terje Larsen, a friend of Beilin and the director of a Norwegian research organization, FAFO (Forskningsstiftelsen for Studier av Arbeidsliv, Fagbevegelse og Offentlig Politikk), offered to host the talks in Norway.

In January 1993, an unusual "manpower seminar" began meeting in a secluded villa in Sarpsborg, near Oslo. The atmosphere was almost pastoral—a house in the snowbound forest, friendly Norwegians, exchanges of niceties—a place very distant from the turbulent, violent reality of the Middle East. Only five people participated in the "seminar"—Hirschfeld and Pundak on the

Israeli side, and Abu Ala'a, Maher el-Kurd, and Hassan Asfur on the Palestinian side. At the first meeting the Israelis realized the talks could be very important, and that Yasser Arafat and Abu Mazen were involved in the endeavor. Pundak regarded Abu Mazen (also known as Mahmoud Abbas) as a key figure. "In 1988, he transformed the PLO and led them to accept U.N. Security Council Resolution 242; in 1993 he led them to Oslo," he said later.[7]

The secret meetings lasted two days. Beilin decided to inform Peres, who was trying to promote two major ideas: a negotiation with Arafat, and the transfer of the Gaza Strip to his control, according to the formula "Gaza first."

Peres believed that a breakthrough with the Palestinians would be achieved only when Arafat returned to Gaza. He knew that nobody really wanted Gaza. He had visited the strip scores of times, and every time came back "ashamed anew of the slums and shantytowns, the desperate poverty, the sprawling, dusty refugee camps." He believed that the only way to solve the Gaza problem was to hand it to its inhabitants, under Arafat's leadership.

Peres had been promoting the "Gaza first" idea since the eighties, but had met with strong objections. The Israeli right wing was virulently opposed to the idea, but the Palestinians, too, were reluctant—first, because it came from an Israeli, and they suspected that all Israelis were concocting devious plans against them; second, because they feared that "Gaza first" might turn into "Gaza last." They suspected that in the end they would remain with only Gaza in their hands, while the Israelis would take over the West Bank and Jerusalem. To dispel their suspicions, Peres wanted to offer the Palestinians some tangible asset.[8] He thought that Jericho, the sleepy resort town by the Jordan River, might be a possible addition to Gaza.

He tried to revive the idea in talks with Rabin, who didn't like it; and he wasn't the only one. "Are you out of your political mind?" Avi Gil, Peres's chief of staff, threw at him. "All right, so you want to talk with the PLO, but bring Arafat to Gaza? You're out of touch with the Israelis. This demon, this terrorist, will be sitting at spitting distance from Ashdod, Ashkelon, Tel Aviv . . . . No Israeli will support you in this."[9]

Peres went back to Rabin on February 9, 1993. A few days earlier, the "two professors," Hirschfeld and Pundak, had brought Yossi Beilin a three-point proposal submitted by Abu Ala'a.

The first point was a PLO version of "Gaza first." Israel, Abu Ala'a wrote, would retreat from Gaza in two or three years, and a trusteeship regime would be established under the management of Egypt or an international authority.

The second point dealt with the launching of a "mini-Marshall Plan for the West Bank and Gaza," for the development of the Palestinian economy.

And the third point spoke of establishing economic cooperation between Israel and the provisional Palestinian authorities.

Following the lines of the London agreement, both Israelis and Palestinians suggested that the Abu Ala'a document should be officially presented to the sides as an "American initiative."[10]

That document indicated a revolutionary change in the PLO position. For the first time, the PLO accepted the "Gaza first" offer, and the idea of an interim agreement in the West Bank and Gaza; the PLO also embraced with surprising fervor the idea of tight economic cooperation with Israel. That was more than Israel could expect from the Palestinian delegation at the Washington talks, which were going nowhere.

Yossi Beilin brought the document to Shimon Peres with several other papers regarding foreign ministry issues. "I told him, you should know that Yair Hirschfeld is meeting with Abu Ala'a in Oslo. Shimon had no idea who Abu Ala'a was. I told him—he is a PLO man." Their meeting was as routine as can be. "I didn't define it as a turning point in the Arab-Israeli conflict," Beilin wrote, "and not as a historic milestone."[11]

"All right," Peres said. "I'll read it and I'll see if it is of any interest. Anything else?" He didn't display any emotion.

"I went down the steps," Beilin wrote, "thinking that at that moment the Palestinian and the Norwegian leaders are biting their nails, eager to know if Israel would agree to the paper that might—perhaps—put an end to the Israeli-Palestinian conflict. I submit a paper to Peres, one out of many, I don't urge him and he doesn't even ask me why didn't I report to him about this before."[12]

In a word—fireworks didn't illuminate the skies that night and nobody heard the wings of History flapping overhead.

Peres wasn't excited by the document that Beilin brought him, both because it mentioned the right of the East Jerusalem Arabs to vote for autonomy and because of the idea of international trusteeship. He was very reluctant "to negotiate with the entire United Nations," which was supposed to supervise the trusteeship.[13] He also wasn't overly excited by the meeting itself. "At that time," he said, "meetings were taking place all over the world. Quite a few people were talking with PLO envoys. Ezer Weizman had met them before, and now Efraim Sneh, Shlomo Gazit, and others were also talking .... The question was not if one met PLO people and wrote a paper with them. I had a lot of papers. The goal was to find someone of the PLO people who could deliver the goods! Someone with whom we could progress toward peace."[14]

He nevertheless decided to brief Rabin on the Oslo talks. He brought him Abu Ala'a's paper and presented him with a draft reply, supporting the retreat from Gaza and the economic ideas of Abu Ala'a. He decided, however, to ignore the idea of international trusteeship.

Peres actually intended to offer Abu Ala'a much more than a trusteeship and a three-year interim period. He wanted to transfer Gaza to the Palestinians with the shortest delay. He suggested to Rabin that the Oslo talks continue in secret, and that the official Palestinian delegation in Washington not be informed.

Rabin didn't object to the talks, perhaps because he didn't take them seriously. The main reason for his mild response, however, was Peres's way of presenting them—as marginal discussions on the academic level. By adopting that tactic he succeeded in preventing Rabin from vetoing the talks.[15] "When Peres came back from Rabin," Yossi Beilin wrote, "he said, That's okay, you can go ahead."

On February 11 and 12, the participants of the "manpower seminar" met at Sarpsborg again. They progressed with surprising speed, mostly because of the PLO people's readiness to compromise on essential issues. Apparently, the PLO badly needed an agreement with Israel because of its shaky political and financial situation. The PLO hadn't recovered yet from Arafat's silly gamble on Saddam Hussein during the 1991 Gulf War.

The participants in the Sarpsborg meetings drafted a common declaration of principles, a plan for Israeli-Palestinian economic cooperation, and guidelines for a regional Marshall Plan. The main goal of the talks was to lay the foundations for an Israeli-Palestinian interim agreement and, subsequently, to start a negotiation for a final peace agreement.

On their return, the professors briefed Peres, who reacted very fast. He met with Rabin at once; the same day he established an "Oslo team" with Beilin; Gil, Beilin's assistant; and the two professors; he then spent a long time meeting with Pundak and Hirschfeld in preparation for the third seminar scheduled for March.

At the end of their talk, Peres instructed the professors to ask Abu Ala'a a pertinent question, which was of overwhelming importance: "If we reach an agreement, when would Chairman Arafat want to return to Gaza?"[16]

THAT QUESTION HERALDED the beginning of a basic change in Israel's policy. It acknowledged Arafat's status, and recognized him as the legitimate leader of the Palestinian people.

The Palestinians who arrived at Sarpsborg for the next session, to be held March 20 through 22, also had news for the Israelis. They said that they had revealed the secret of the Norwegian connection to President Mubarak; his reaction was "enthusiastic."[17]

The results of the talks, at this stage, were encouraging. On the eve of the meeting the entire team met in Peres's office for a last briefing. Everybody noticed the deep change in Peres's behavior. At their previous meeting Peres had been reluctant, and had behaved as if he were going to back off from the negotiation. His conduct toward the team members was angry, impatient, and so aggressive that Pundak asked Yossi Beilin if he could send him as an attaché to some very distant embassy, like Uzbekistan, to escape Peres's wrath. Perhaps Peres thought that the talks had gone too far and too fast. After all, he was leading Israel to a move of historic significance, but one that involved tremendous risks.

But the foreign minister quickly adjusted to the new reality. The Oslo team members noticed that Peres now took the talks very seriously. "It was clear that the man had become 'addicted' to the idea," Beilin wrote. "He was well versed in the material, and was interested in a rapid success of that channel. In his mind he was already there, taking part in the talks. Henceforth, the success of the talks was his own, personally and ideologically. Instead of being a Foreign Minister of multilateral talks and cocktails, he was at the head of what he considered as the best chance for a breakthrough in the stalled negotiations."[18]

Rabin, on the other hand, still regarded the talks as something marginal. He still thought that they might serve as a background or a support to the negotiation with the Palestinian delegation in Washington. His attitude changed in April when the Washington talks were interrupted by the Palestinian delegation because of a dispute with the Israelis. Surprisingly, the Palestinians resumed the talks after receiving a PLO order, issued after a request by Hirschfeld and Pundak. That was a significant move that proved to Rabin and Peres the importance of the Oslo channel.

In Jerusalem, the U.S. State Department official Dan Kurtzer was secretly briefed by Hirschfeld and Pundak. He was deeply impressed; the documents drafted in Norway, he said, indicated that the PLO had adopted more moderate positions than the Palestinian delegation in Washington! He suggested that these negotiations be turned into an alternative strategy to the Washington talks.[19]

The most important development came from the PLO delegation in Oslo, which signaled it was ready for further concessions. It accepted the idea of a federation between the West Bank and Jordan and agreed to a tripartite federation including Israel as well. The PLO representatives also asked to raise the level of the talks, with Shimon Peres representing Israel. The PLO leaders seemed eager to reach a written agreement with Israel in the near future.[20]

Peres was impressed in particular by one of Abu Ala'a's confidence-building measures. In the Palestinian delegation to the multilateral talks scheduled for May in Rome, Peres singled out two PLO members who were known by Israel to be terrorists. When Abu Ala'a was informed of Peres's discontent, he immediately canceled their participation. That convinced Peres to concentrate on the Oslo channel from then on. "Finally I had found in Abu Ala'a a man who could deliver the goods."[21]

The time had come for another meeting between Peres and Rabin.

ON FRIDAY, MAY 14, 1993, Shimon Peres summoned Uri Savir, the director general of the foreign ministry, to his Jerusalem residence. The foreign minister, looking relaxed, waited for Savir with Avi Gil. Peres served a glass of wine to his guest, and asked him casually, "What do you think of spending a weekend in Oslo?"[22]

Uri was very excited. Only a few days before he had heard from Yossi Beilin about the Oslo channel. "He was flabbergasted," Beilin recalled.[23]

On May 13, the day before he spoke with Savir, Peres had met with Rabin. Peres told Rabin that the PLO people in Oslo were "more flexible, more creative, and more dependable" than the Palestinian delegation in Washington.[24] Peres spoke of the "Gaza first" idea as a move that would be supported by most Israelis, who dreamed of getting rid of the terror hothouse thriving in Gaza.

Peres also knew that the PLO was in dire financial and political straits; therefore, this was the moment to close a deal with it.[25] A few days before, his friend Amos Oz had called him and said, "Shimon, Arafat is in trouble. We must save him!"[26]

"Saving Arafat," of course, was a formula meaning that it was the moment to reach an agreement with the weakened PLO, and also to avoid chaos in the organization by helping keep its leader in control.

Peres told Rabin, "It is time to seize the bull by the horns and carry out a formal negotiation in order to finalize the declaration of principles and get it signed."[27] Peres was ready to fly immediately to Norway, to proceed with the talks with the Palestinians.

Rabin cooled his enthusiasm. Peres's involvement in the talks, he pointed out, would commit the government, which still ignored the Oslo negotiation. We can't upgrade our representation to ministerial level, the prime minister said. He agreed, though, to raise the level of the talks and accepted Peres's suggestion to put Uri Savir in charge.

That decision was of primary significance. Israel's foreign ministry director—a top-level government official—was going to meet PLO leaders. His appointment turned the talks into an official and binding negotiation.[28] Henceforth, Israel couldn't pretend anymore that the talks were "a private initiative of two professors." Now she was negotiating directly with the PLO, in spite of her official objection to any such contacts.

The upgrading of the talks had another far-reaching meaning, and it is unclear whether Rabin and Peres understood it right then. From that moment on, the issue was no more the establishment of autonomy in the West Bank and Gaza. After thirty years of bloody struggle, the PLO wouldn't be satisfied with running an autonomous administration in the West Bank under Israeli sovereignty The PLO's goal was to create a Palestinian state, and it certainly wouldn't accept any other solution. Peres and Rabin didn't seem to realize that by agreeing to negotiate with the PLO, they had actually abandoned the position that rejected an independent Palestinian state.

Uri Savir secretly flew to Oslo; there he was welcomed by the two professors, and Terje Larsen and his wife, Mona Juul, who were involved in the secret talks.

A few days later, Savir was joined by the legal expert Yoel Singer, who was held in high esteem by both Peres and Rabin. Singer, who had earned his stripes during the Taba negotiation, now worked for a Washington law firm. He agreed, however, to fly to Israel—and to Oslo—every weekend to participate in the secret negotiations.

Rabin now established a team of four to supervise the negotiations—Peres, Beilin, Singer, and himself. The team met secretly every week in Rabin's office or in the foreign ministry, and more than once in Rabin's Tel Aviv apartment. Amos Oz was privy to the secret. Peres believed that he had to hear once in a while some wise words of advice from the great writer. Oz was the one who drew Peres's attention to the danger of strengthening the terrorist organization Hamas at the expense of the PLO. "That advice alone was worth my trust in him," Peres said.[29]

ON JUNE 6, 1993, on the eve of the next round of talks, Peres and Rabin met alone to discuss the Oslo channel. Peres returned to his office, his face drawn. "There is no one whose face betrays him more than Shimon," Yossi Beilin said.[30] Peres told his confidants that Rabin was "not so happy" with some paragraphs in the documents the Israelis had presented in Oslo; he had ordered a delay in the Oslo talks until the resumption of the Washington negotiations on June 15.

This was a much understated description of the harsh confrontation that had erupted between the two; Rabin was irritated and furious. His anger had been triggered by an internal ten-point memorandum drafted by Uri Savir, and by several paragraphs in the proposed declaration of principles.

But he went much further than that; he wrathfully repudiated the Oslo talks. "He accused the Tunis-based PLO," Peres recalled, "of sabotaging the Washington talks on purpose, and accused me, personally, of fostering the Oslo channel in order to thwart the Washington talks and take over the negotiation."[31]

The letter that Rabin rushed to Peres the following day was brutal and grave. The Oslo talks, Rabin wrote, were "a danger to the peace negotiations" and an attempt by "the Tunis people"—meaning Arafat and the PLO veterans—to sabotage the Washington talks and to weaken "the positive element there, the West Bank inhabitants included in the Palestinian delegation." Rabin claimed that the PLO was dispatching extremist instructions to the Palestinian delegation in Washington. In a rather apocalyptic prophecy, Rabin wrote that the same "Tunis people" were about to endanger the peace processes with Syria, Lebanon, and Jordan as well. He called the proposals of the PLO representatives "a catastrophe"; he lashed out at the draft of the declaration of principles, and maintained that it hadn't been coordinated with him. He also rejected two of the declaration's paragraphs. He finally ordered a stop to the Oslo talks, until after the resumption of the Washington negotiations or a further discussion with Peres.

Rabin's strange outburst had no logical explanation. Peres surmised that Rabin might have received an intelligence report that attacked the Tunis PLO, or expressed anxiety about the settlers' security—all that, of course, without the report's authors knowing a thing about the Oslo negotiation. In any case, Rabin apparently became alarmed and ordered the talks to halt.[32]

Knesset member Ephraim Sneh, a close aide to Rabin, later suggested a different explanation for Rabin's erratic behavior. Sneh had been trying for a long time to convince Rabin that he had to open a direct negotiation channel with the PLO, bypassing any other contacts. In May 1993, Sneh said, Rabin finally agreed; and on June 7, he sent Sneh to a secret meeting with Nabil Shaath, Arafat's envoy, in London.[33] Sneh met with Shaath and tried to check out the possibility of establishing a direct channel between Rabin and the PLO leadership; he and Shaath even drafted a joint document. But an intelligence report that Rabin received soon after made it clear that Arafat objected to another channel. [34]

When Rabin's letter of June 7 arrived at Peres's office, some of his men sank into despair; the letter, they thought, meant the end of the Oslo negotiation. Others were less distressed. "I didn't despair," Avi Gil recalled, "because from the 'no' in Rabin's letter one could deduce the 'yes.' Rabin actually had trapped himself. He said, Because of a, b, c, stop the talks! And I realized that if we brought him a, b, and c he would change his mind." Gil explained to his colleagues the method to adopt when dealing with Rabin. "In many ways, Oslo was based on the idea of 'taking Rabin to the details.' He loved getting into details—a point here, and a phrase there." (And yet, when the talks finally yielded the famous agreement of September 1993, Avi Gil revolted.[35] "To present Rabin as the hero of Oslo is pure nonsense. You read the letter he wrote on June 7, and you ask yourself—is this the man responsible for Oslo?")

Peres sent an answer to Rabin, pointing out that the Washington talks were restarting on June 15, because of some steps taken in Oslo. The Oslo channel, he added, was meant only as a support to the Washington talks and not as an alternative to them. Peres stressed that the declaration of principles submitted to Israel in Oslo was more moderate than the one drafted by the Palestinians in Washington. He agreed with Rabin's criticism on the two paragraphs "that were unacceptable" in the declaration of principles, and made it clear that "the ten points" in Uri Savir's document had never been submitted to the Palestinians. He suggested discussing all the issues with the legal adviser Yoel Singer, whom Rabin fully trusted.

And so the crisis dissolved quietly. Sneh maintained that at that moment, Rabin realized that Arafat wouldn't go for any other agreement, and that "Oslo was the only game in town." Rabin realized that if he rejected the Oslo agreement, he wouldn't reach a settlement with the Palestinians in the first nine months of his term, as he had pledged during the 1992 electoral campaign.

When Rabin met with Peres and his team, they steered him to the details of the written paragraphs. Rabin, as was his custom, got into the fine points and obtained clarifications and assurances on some of the paragraphs. At the end it was Yoel Singer who pointed at the heart of the problem: he proposed a mutual recognition between Israel and the PLO.

Rabin looked at Peres, who said, "I don't think we should recognize the PLO now."

Singer insisted: "And if I propose this in Oslo as a private suggestion, in my name only?"

Rabin shrugged. "In your name, propose whatever you want." And so, without giving it too much thought, Rabin went much further down the road than the position he had furiously blasted in his June 7 letter. He gave the green light to a move that was about to produce mutual recognition between Israel and the Palestine Liberation Organization.[36]

"MY STRATEGIC GOAL," Peres wrote, "was to obtain, in return for the 'return' [of the PLO and Arafat to Gaza and Jericho], an undertaking from the PLO to recognize Israel, to forswear terrorism finally and irrevocably, and to abrogate those provisions of its charter which committed the organization to fight for the destruction of the Jewish State. Tactically, my purpose was to defer this aspect of the negotiation until as late as possible, knowing how important it was to the other side. And indeed, the talks on mutual recognition between Israel and the PLO reached their climax only after the Declaration of Principles had been initialed."[37]

The goal was to secretly draft in Oslo a document about an interim agreement that would be approved later in the Washington negotiations. The interim agreement was to give limited powers to the Palestinians; it would be followed by talks on the final settlement. Five years after the signing of the interim agreement, the sides would reach a comprehensive settlement.

The Oslo negotiations focused now on detailed provisions for local elections and a Palestinian representative council; the establishment of an armed police force in the West Bank and Gaza; and issues of water, finance, taxes, and common economic endeavors. Yossi Beilin and Yair Hirschfeld were somewhat worried about the effort and the concessions invested in the interim agreement; they would have preferred that most of Israel's concessions be a part of the final settlement.[38]

On June 23, Peres was suddenly given the opportunity of meeting Arafat when the journalist Mira Avrech visited Tunis. Mira was a close friend of Shimon and Sonia Peres, and Arafat's adviser Bassam Abu Sharif entrusted her with a handwritten letter to Shimon Peres. Abu Sharif covered Peres with praise for his vision of a new Middle East and offered to set up a meeting between him and Arafat.[39]

Peres realized that the handwriting was Abu Sharif's but the message had been dictated by Arafat. He gently eluded the offer; the time for a summit meeting with Arafat hadn't come yet. That was a prize that shouldn't be awarded to Arafat before the end of the negotiations. Peres also doubted if such a meeting could be kept secret. Besides, any meeting with Arafat was going to reignite Rabin's suspicions.

Rabin, indeed, suspected Peres of acting behind his back, and often lashed out at him during the supervising team's meetings, claiming things were being done without his knowledge. Rabin disliked having to rely on the information brought to him by Peres and his young aides; therefore he was secretly checking it out. He instructed Haim Ramon to establish contact with Dr. Ahmad Tibi, a Palestinian close to Abu Mazen and Arafat. Ramon was charged with determining whether Peres's reports were accurate, and whether the Palestinian delegation in Oslo represented both Arafat and Abu Mazen. Arafat, on the other hand, wanted to make sure that not only Peres, but also Rabin, supported the Oslo talks. Ramon followed Rabin's instructions and met with Tibi several times. "This was the only channel Peres didn't know about," Ramon said. "One day it leaked to the media, on the Palestinians' initiative, and Peres went berserk."[40]

Ramon and Ephraim Sneh were not the only ones who were sent by Rabin to Palestinian personalities unbeknownst to Peres. He also used the services of the Knesset member Yossi Sarid and the former Shabak official Yossi Ginossar. Even at that advanced stage Rabin still hesitated, and preferred the Syrian option. In a letter to President Bill Clinton at the end of July, Rabin still mentioned the "Syria first" scheme.[41]

Moreover, on August 4 Rabin took a step that could have terminated the Oslo talks once and for all. He delivered to President Clinton and Secretary of State Warren Christopher a top-secret political "deposit." That was a commitment by Rabin that in exchange for peace with Syria he would be ready to pull back from the entire Golan Heights. He didn't say a word to Peres about it. Itamar Rabinowitz, Israel's ambassador in Washington, believed that if the Americans had used Rabin's "deposit" more wisely, "Oslo would never have happened. Rabin hesitated about Oslo."[42] But the Americans did not use Rabin's commitment for a vigorous initiative, and Oslo became a political reality; Rabin was drawn into it, and resigned himself to it. Rabinowitz said, "He could have told Peres in August, 'I won't do a thing by the Oslo channel.' He could have stuck to 'Syria first.' But he realized that if he didn't do anything, his term as prime minister might end without any tangible progress."[43]

In July, Peres started losing patience. He felt the need to instill an element of urgency into the negotiations. When Terje Larsen and Mona Juul visited Jerusalem, he warned them, "Don't let the Oslo track become like chewing gum, like the Washington track has become."[44] When the negotiation was over, he said, the Oslo agreement should be revealed and signed in Washington. "The only problem is how to reveal it," he said, and once again mentioned the doubts haunting him since the London document's fiasco. "We want the Americans to get all the credit, but we fear that if we give this to them too early, they'll manage it badly, as they ruined the agreement with Hussein."

An issue that really obsessed Peres was Arafat's credibility. He stressed that many warned Israel against conducting a dialogue with Arafat. "He can't be trusted," he bluntly said. "He must build up his credibility. He's got very little of that. We want him here, but as a part of the interim agreement."

Peres and his team sent many feelers toward Arafat, using the good services of Terje Larsen, of Norway's foreign minister, Jørgen Holst, and of President Mubarak. Arafat, they learned, was tremendously excited by the prospects of returning to Gaza soon. Savir surprised the Palestinians by suggesting that the Gaza Strip be handed over to the PLO in a few months, after the signing of the declaration of principles.[45] The astonished Palestinians told the Israelis that "Arafat is fascinated by the idea of returning to Gaza and would be willing, in exchange, to compromise on many other issues."[46] It doesn't seem, however, that the Israelis made full use of Arafat's readiness for concessions; they didn't try to make him compromise on the main issues at hand.

ON AUGUST 16, 1993, Peres's close friends threw a surprise party at his office for his seventieth birthday. Peres, embarrassed at first, made a short speech. "Soon," he said, "perhaps in a very short time, we shall witness an historic breakthrough in our contacts with the Palestinians." Most of the people present, who were not aware of the Oslo talks, thought that Peres was again letting his imagination soar. His conclusion summed up his credo. "I have devoted most of my life to defense. What is left for me now, after we built a strong Israel, is to bring peace to our young generation."[47]

The agreements with the Palestinians had almost been completed. Peres couldn't wait any longer. This was the moment to conclude the negotiations, he told his aides, lest "we succeed to achieve a peace treaty, but there would be no government left to sign it." On the internal scene, indeed, a new crisis threatened the coalition: Shas's leader, Minister Arie Deri, had been indicted on grave financial charges, and his party considered pulling out of the government. Peres had to act fast and reach an agreement.

By a happy coincidence, he was about to set off on an official visit to several Scandinavian countries including Norway. His first stop was Stockholm, the capital of Sweden. Yossi Beilin alerted Jørgen Holst, the Norwegian foreign minister, who was on a visit to Iceland, and asked him to fly urgently to Stockholm and meet Peres. A few hours later, Holst knocked on the door of the royal guesthouse in the Swedish capital. To the puzzled Swedes Peres and Holst told a cover story about an old dispute between their two countries that they wanted to settle before Peres arrived in Norway.

Holst was accompanied by Terje Larsen and Mona Juul; Peres waited for him, flanked by Avi Gil and Yoel Singer. That was the beginning of the "night of the long telephones."

It had been meticulously organized. The negotiating teams were waiting, each at its base. The PLO delegation, with Abu Ala'a at its head, was in Tunis; Yossi Beilin and Uri Savir were in Jerusalem. Late at night, contact was established between the guesthouse in Stockholm and the PLO headquarters, and a marathon sequence of telephone conversations followed. Nine phone conversations took place that night, lasting seven long hours. Holst and Larsen spoke from Peres's room with Arafat's headquarters. Peres didn't participate in the conversations; he listened to them and kept briefing and advising his Scandinavian friends.

Larsen spoke with Abu Ala'a in an improvised code. "I have with me the two fathers," he said. "My father would like to talk to you." The fathers were, of course, the foreign ministers, and "Larsen's father" was Minister Holst. Holst picked up the phone and started reading the problematic paragraphs that still hadn't been agreed upon. Whenever he wanted to mention Israel, he uttered in the receiver the code word "blurp." The repeated "blurps" triggered explosions of laughter in Peres's room.[48]

But the laughter soon was replaced by intensive discussions.

The talks stopped and resumed several times during the night. In the wee hours Peres went to sleep, but Singer and Gil kept waking him up to get his approval for another formula that had been agreed upon between the sides.

When the last obstacle was removed, a tremendous emotion swept the PLO leaders in Tunis. Peres and his friends listened to the excited shouts that echoed in the receivers. At the other end of the line Peres could hear the voices of Arafat and his aides. "We could hear them cheering and weeping and we knew that they were hugging one another."[49]

AVI GIL URGENTLY summoned Uri Savir and the professors to Oslo; the Palestinian delegation also landed in the Norwegian capital. On August 19, Peres arrived in Norway on an official visit and was lodged in the government guesthouse, a three-story building on the outskirts of Oslo. At 10:30 P.M., the state dinner was over, Holst made a routine speech in the name of the Norwegian government, and Peres followed suit with a routine speech in the name of Israel. After the speeches, Peres announced that he was exhausted and was going to sleep. He even went to bed, but couldn't close his eyes. He knew that in two hours, under the cover of the utmost secrecy, he would participate in the signing of the first peace agreement with the Palestinians.

A few hours before, Peres had spoken with Rabin and informed him that all the obstacles had been removed and "tonight we'll sign the agreement." Rabin made no comment.

The lights in the guesthouse went out. The members of Peres's delegation, who were not privy to the Oslo secret, fell asleep in their rooms. Israel's ambassador to Norway, pleased with the successful visit of his minister, went home. The only one still awake was Avi Gil, who was busy putting the last touches on the forthcoming event. Only Fellini, he thought, could have dreamed up a set like this.

At midnight, Peres got up from bed, dressed, and tiptoed up the stairs to the top floor, where the Norwegians had prepared three rooms: one for the Israeli delegation, one for the Palestinians, and one for the Norwegians. Secret-service cars picked up the Israeli and Palestinian delegations at the Oslo Plaza Hotel and drove them separately to the guesthouse. It was vital to get everybody on the top floor without waking up the Israeli diplomats, who slept the sleep of the just on the ground floor. The members of the two delegations sneaked surreptitiously through kitchens, storerooms, and back corridors, and climbed to the top floor. The desk on which the agreement was to be signed, in the Norwegian delegation's room, was the historic desk on which Norway's agreement of secession from Sweden had been signed in 1905. The hosts had prepared champagne bottles to celebrate the event, but Peres asked them to remove the champagne; a few hours before, seven Israeli soldiers had been killed in South Lebanon, and this was not the time for champagne.

At 2:30 A.M., a receiving line was formed by the door: Foreign Minister Holst, his wife, and Shimon Peres. The two delegations walked in and shook hands. For the first time, Peres shook Abu Ala'a's hand. Peres abstained from participating in the signing, and from any public statement. The agreement with the Palestinians had yet to be debated and approved by the government, and until then Peres refrained from any formal move.

Uri Savir and Abu Ala'a signed the agreement, and Jorgen Holst signed as a witness and a host. The moment, when only the scribbling of pens on paper was heard, stirred deep emotions.

After the signing, Holst, Abu Ala'a, and Uri Savir made short speeches. Abu Ala'a burst into tears. At the end of the ceremony, he asked to speak with Peres, alone, and told him: "This agreement is a present for your birthday."[50] He thanked Peres in the name of Arafat and assured him that all the PLO leaders would support the agreement. Abu Ala'a also thanked Peres for his effort to raise funds for the development of the Palestinian economy. Peres answered him by describing one of his less realistic visions. "The fate of Gaza," he said, "can be like that of Singapore. From poverty to prosperity in one sustained leap."

Yet Peres still wouldn't admit that the meaning of the agreement was the creation of a Palestinian state in the future. "How strange it is," he thought, "that we Israelis are now granting the Palestinians what the British had granted us more than seventy years ago, 'a homeland in Palestine,' in the words of the Balfour Declaration of November 1917."[51] He wouldn't acknowledge that the real issue wasn't "a homeland" for the Palestinians, but an entity that might one day become a sovereign and independent state.

Yet Peres could be satisfied with his personal achievement. The Oslo agreement would never have been reached without his relentless efforts.

From his room, Peres called Amos Oz. He described to him the signing ceremony, and the Palestinians' emotional outbursts. "That was a once-in-a-lifetime experience," Oz thought. "There are no two 'virginity nights' in one's life."[52]

Peres went to bed, but didn't even try to sleep. "I lay waiting for the dawn of a new day," he wrote.

And added: "What a night!"[53]

TEN DAYS LATER, the Norwegian foreign minister's plane landed at a U.S. Navy base in California. A small group of passengers disembarked from the aircraft—Holst, Peres, Gil, Singer, and the Larsen couple. They were received by the Secretary of State Warren Christopher and a senior official of the State Department, Dennis Ross. The two of them had interrupted their vacations in California to meet with Peres and Holst, who had secretly flown over.

Now, as they faced the Americans, Peres and Holst described the negotiations with the PLO and their results. Christopher was enthusiastic. "You've done a tremendous job," he said. "My initial response to these developments is very, very positive."[54]

Yet Christopher rejected Peres's request that the agreement between Israel and the PLO be presented to both sides as an American proposal. His refusal meant that there was no chance that the Palestinian delegation in Washington would sign the agreement reached with PLO-Tunis. It was also clear that the

PLO wouldn't accept, at this advanced stage, giving up the authority to sign the agreement.

Peres told Christopher that the Palestinians and Israelis were negotiating a seven-point document dealing with a mutual recognition of Israel and the PLO. He said wistfully, "I learned my lesson from the London agreement. Shultz got cold feet at the last moment. Shamir sent Moshe Arens to Shultz to stop him from coming out to the region—and everything was destroyed."

"There are two ways of dealing with the PLO: by force or by political wisdom. And I'm frankly not sure that force is a workable option."[55]

Peres quoted Winston Churchill: "He who wants to leap over an abyss, he'd better do it not in two steps but in one."[56]

It was Dennis Ross who asked the key question: "Are you sure that Arafat would honor his engagements?"

"Yes," Peres said.[57]

EVEN THEN, AFTER THE signing of the agreements, Rabin kept suspecting Peres and doubting the Oslo channel. Without Peres's knowledge, Rabin again sent Sneh to London, to a meeting with Nabil Shaath. Rabin gave Sneh a detailed list of questions dealing with several paragraphs and terms in the signed agreements, to make sure that Arafat and his people agreed with his own interpretation of the documents. Sneh flew to London on August 29, met with Shaath, and got satisfying answers to most of his questions. Yet on the eve of his departure, Rabin shared with him his reservations about Peres and his aides. "Wait," he said to Sneh, "let's see first what Peres's people are blabbing there in Oslo."[58]

On August 30, the Oslo agreement was finally submitted to the stunned government ministers. The most astounded of all was the government secretary, Elyakim Rubinstein, who had headed the Israeli delegation to the sterile and inept negotiations in Washington. At the government meeting, all the ministers but one approved the agreement. Eitan Haber, Rabin's chief of staff, heard of the agreement while on a trip to Italy. He hadn't known anything about the negotiation, and therefore he returned to Israel and wanted to resign, but Rabin calmed him down: "Eitan, believe me. I didn't suppose anything would come out of this."[59]

The news exploded in the world headlines, stirring tremendous emotions.

THE FORMAL SIGNING was set for September 13, 1993, at the White House, in the presence of hundreds of guests from all over the world. The media hailed and praised the historic reconciliation between Jews and Arabs and predicted a new era in the Middle East. Peres's formula, "a new Middle East," became immensely popular. In Israel, a wave of unprecedented enthusiasm swept large portions of the public; in spontaneous left-wing rallies, young people danced in the streets. The reaction of the right wing and the settlers was sporadic and limited. This created the impression that Israel overwhelmingly supported the agreement.

But the road to the signing was still strewn with obstacles. The first was the bitter confrontation between Peres and Rabin. The prime minister decided not to participate in the signing ceremony. He preferred that Peres head the Israeli delegation. In a television interview, he announced that he was not going to Washington.

Peres was pleased. After all, it was only natural that he would represent Israel at the historic event in Washington. He meticulously prepared the list of guests he would take with him to the signing. In a display of misguided pettiness, he decided not to include in the delegation the two professors, Yair Hirschfeld and Ron Pundak (the two finally went to Washington as members of the Norwegian delegation). In the same vein, he later avoided mentioning Yossi Beilin in his book about the Oslo agreement, which hurt his confidant needlessly, as Beilin was the one who had initiated the entire process. Some claimed that Peres didn't want to share with Beilin the Oslo glory.[60]

Peres didn't know, however, that Rabin's close aides had not given up on the prime minister's participation in the signing ceremony the following Monday. Shimon Sheves, the director general of the prime minister's office, called Haim Ramon on Friday night. "Haim, what shall we do?" Sheves asked. "He must be there."

"Let me check that out," Ramon answered. He called Ahmed Tibi, Arafat's confidant, and asked him: "What about the Palestinian delegation? Who is going to head it?"

"Arafat is dying to go," Tibi said, "but he can't go if Rabin doesn't."

Ramon and Sheves concocted a new idea: the invitation for Rabin should allegedly come from the Americans, and he wouldn't be able to reject it.

Their efforts started to bear fruit. Late at night, Warren Christopher called Rabin; the president, he said, wanted very much for him to come to the ceremony. "If Arafat isn't coming, I cannot come either," Rabin said.

"Arafat is coming," Christopher announced.

At midnight, Sheves called Rabin and informed him that Arafat had received an invitation from President Clinton and was going to Washington. The last assault in the persuasion campaign took place on Saturday, at 5 A.M., when Ambassador Rabinowitz called from Washington and informed Rabin that he had just received an official invitation for the prime minister to participate in the signing ceremony. Rabin made up his mind and answered that he was coming.[61]

At 8:20 A.M., Eitan Haber, Rabin's chief of staff, called his colleague Avi Gil to update him about the prime minister's decision. Immediately afterward, he alerted the national radio. It was an important piece of news, and the reporters broke into the morning program to announce Rabin's departure to Washington. Peres heard the news on the radio; he was stunned.

Rabin himself called Peres to inform him of his change of plans, and invited him to join him. Peres ended the call and exploded in rage and frustration. He summoned Beilin, Savir, and Gil—and in their presence gave vent to his fury. He told them he was not going to Washington. They tried to convince him to swallow the bitter pill and go anyway.

But Peres was terribly upset. "After Peres had made tremendous efforts for the process to succeed," Yossi Beilin wrote, "it would be now the Prime Minister, who almost thwarted the process, who would shake Arafat's hand."[62] Peres called Amos Oz and told him that he was going to resign from the government.[63] He also failed to conceal his wrath from two senior reporters, Nahum Barnea and Shimon Shiffer of *Yediot Abaronot*, who came to interview him that morning.

During the interview, Peres received a phone call. It was Giora Eini. The two reporters didn't know him; for many he was a mystery man, whom they met once in a while, surreptitiously leaving Peres's or Rabin's home or office. Eini was a skinny young man with long, rather unkempt hair, a mustache, and glasses, and always dressed in a light-gray suit and a colorful tie. A Histadrut official, Eini was gifted with a quick, creative mind and unusual discretion. A few years before, he had volunteered to mediate between Peres and Rabin. He never asked for anything for himself; all he wanted was to reconcile Peres and Rabin. As the years passed, he became indispensable to the two warring partners. Whenever their never-ending duel flared up, Eini miraculously materialized beside them, offering a satisfying solution to their new confrontation.

When Eini called that morning, Peres asked the two reporters to excuse him for a few minutes. They left the room, but their voice-activated tape recorder remained on the table, recording Peres's outburst.[64] Peres yelled into the receiver, pouring out all his bitterness. "This man, Rabin," he shouted, "has ruined my life."

"Rabin has misgivings, too," Eini said, and suggested that the two meet later that same day.

"I am sick and tired of hearing that Rabin does trust me, or doesn't trust me! I treated him with the respect that becomes a king! He paid me back with insults!" Peres used some harsh expressions and his loud shouts echoed in the room. Finally, though, he agreed that Eini should come to see him.

Shortly after, Eini arrived. From Peres's home he called Rabin and set up a meeting between the two. Leah Rabin called Sonia Peres and tried to calm her down.[65] Rabin drove to Jerusalem and received Peres at his residence. Finally, the storm abated, and the following day they flew to Washington together.

At the last minute, though, a crisis broke out between Israel and the PLO. A couple of hours before the signing, Dr. Tibi came to Peres's hotel room. If Israel didn't agree to a last-minute change in the Declaration of Principles, he said, Arafat would leave. Arafat demanded now that the term "PLO" would replace the formula "the Palestinian team" in the declaration.

Peres agreed to the demand; after all, he said, Israel had recognized the PLO, why not call it by name? But Arafat now insisted that the letters PLO be printed in the document, and not added by hand. A hectic search for a printer followed, and the entire document was reprinted. "Sometimes," Peres remarked, "the fate of a momentous historic event depends on the difference between a pen's ink and a laser printer."[66]

The signing ceremony took place on the White House lawn, in the presence of a select crowd of guests and the world media. On the chairs, lined up in front of the podium, sat presidents, prime ministers, foreign ministers, parliamentarians, senators and congressmen, Arab and Palestinian leaders, Jewish personalities, senior journalists. On the dais, President Clinton's tall figure hovered over all the others. He was flanked by Yasser Arafat in his military uniform, Abu Mazen in an elegant suit, Yitzhak Rabin, tense and ill at ease, and Shimon Peres, smiling and happy, the eternal optimist who was already thinking, during the ceremony, about "how to build the New Middle East."[67]

Clinton good-humoredly conducted the ceremony and the handshake of Rabin and Arafat. That was going to become the most famous image of the signing—the PLO leader, in uniform and peaked keffiyeh, offering his hand, and Rabin, his face expressing revulsion and embarrassment, reluctantly shaking it. "Now it's your turn," he whispered to Peres as he stepped back, letting the foreign minister shake Arafat's hand.

Peres and Abu Mazen signed the documents.

A year later, on December 10, 1994, Rabin, Peres, and Arafat received the Nobel Peace Prize in Oslo.

THE OSLO AGREEMENTS stand for a splendid dream—and a painful failure.

The agreements led to a breakthrough in the relations between Israelis and Palestinians. But they also turned into a setback in the quest for peace.

In the first place, they were supposed to be an interim stage in the peace process. This didn't happen. The Israeli leaders refused to admit the obvious—that after the first interim agreement a negotiation should start, paving the road to a comprehensive settlement. Peres and Rabin refrained from defining their political goals; they recoiled from any serious negotiation about the comprehensive settlement.

That strange reluctance stemmed mainly from the hesitant attitude of both Peres and Rabin toward the issue of a Palestinian state. In 1995, two years after Oslo, they were still talking in vague terms about the West Bank's future. Rabin objected to a Palestinian state, and Peres spoke about a solution that would transcend national sovereignty and emulate the European Union. But no new Middle East modeled after Europe could ever be created without first establishing a Palestinian state.

Instead of declaring that the Oslo agreements were the prelude to a Palestinian state, Israel preferred to embark on a series of interim agreements with the Palestinians, by which she gave away tracts of land without getting in return anything but promises. The interim agreements, finally, led nowhere.

The second mistake of the Israeli leaders was to agree that the PLO was not responsible for fighting terrorism in the areas under its control. Israel should have made the PLO's antiterrorist struggle a condition to the implementation of the Oslo accords.

But the PLO didn't liquidate Hamas, the Islamic Jihad, or other terrorist groups. The Israeli people gradually moved away from Oslo, realizing that the return of the former PLO terrorists to the West Bank and Gaza hadn't improved their personal security in any way.

The third error was the choice of a partner. The Israeli leaders naively believed that Arafat would metamorphose into a historic, world-class leader like Egypt's Sadat before him and Jordan's King Hussein after him. They didn't understand that he hadn't changed. Arafat remained a typical terrorist leader who didn't care about the sophisticated documents that learned Palestinians and Israelis had drafted with such devotion. The Israelis mistakenly treated Arafat as a responsible and peace-loving leader—their own mirror image—without realizing that he thought and acted differently.

There could be no doubt that Arafat was the only one who could make the PLO change its policy and accept the Oslo agreements. But the change in policy didn't herald a change in Arafat; even after returning from exile, he kept using terror as an alternative strategy. His very return to Gaza symbolized the forthcoming disaster. In his own car, beneath his seat, he smuggled into Gaza weapons and wanted terrorists.[68]

"Without Arafat," Shimon Peres sadly said, "the Oslo accords wouldn't have been signed. With Arafat, they couldn't be implemented."[69]

CHAPTER 31.

REMEMBER NOVEMBER THE SECOND!

ON OCTOBER 19, 1993, Rabin met with King Hussein in Aqaba and asked him to sign a peace agreement. Hussein refused. According to one of Rabin's close advisers, "Hussein told Rabin, I cannot sign a peace treaty, only some interim agreements. Rabin said, All or nothing. That was the end of it."[1] IDF intelligence and the American State Department agreed—Hussein wouldn't budge before Israel signed a peace treaty with Syria.[2]

The Jordanians wouldn't go along, Rabin said to Peres. They demanded four things: some territory in the Arava Desert, which lies between Jordan and Israel; water; the solution of the Palestinian refugees' problem; and Jerusalem.

Peres answered, "I believe we can make a deal with them on land and water. All the rest is lip service."[3] Rabin allowed Peres to try reaching an agreement with Hussein.

Peres called his aides. "We must storm Jordan," he said.[4] On November 1, Peres and Avi Gil traveled to Amman to meet the king. The Jordanians kept the visit secret because of the approaching elections. After all, Israel and Jordan were still formally in a state of war. Mossad experts disguised Peres, put a hat and a wig on his head, and stuck a mustache on his face. The Mossad official Efraim Halevy joined Peres and Gil on their journey. Halevy had participated, six years before, in the meeting between Peres and Hussein in London. Halevy enjoyed the trust of the royal family in Amman; he was also close to Rabin.

The following morning, Peres and his aides met with Hussein at the royal palace. Hussein came with Prince Hassan and Prime Minister Abdelsalam al-Majali. Peres did indeed storm the Jordanians. He spoke for a long time and described to the king his splendid vision of a flourishing Middle East. "His idea," Efraim Halevy said, "was to bypass the political issues by launching a large-scale economic project for the Middle East."[5] Peres spoke of a world economic conference that would convene in Amman, with the participation of the economic and financial leaders of America, Europe, and Asia. He painted before the king a picture of the new Middle East where large investments from all over the world would pour into the area; the economic prosperity would overcome poverty and help establish a durable peace between Israelis, Jordanians, and Palestinians.

For Gil, who listened with wonder, this was a "master class in diplomacy." Peres concluded his proclamation, went to another room with his two companions, and "in one breath" dictated an agreement between Israel and Jordan. "He said to Efraim, 'Take your pen and write.' There was no drafting committee. Peres just fired the entire agreement from his head into Efraim's pen."[6] When Halevy brought the paper to the Jordanians, they made some minor changes, but otherwise accepted the Israeli draft as it was.

The agreement was titled a "Non-Paper." Its first paragraph defined its purpose: to establish a comprehensive peace in the Middle East. The other paragraphs described in detail the agreements between the two sides on economic and financial questions; the convening of an economic conference in Amman; the establishment of several committees with the participation of the United States, Egypt, and the Palestinians, to deal with the issue of refugees; and the development of the Palestinian, Jordanian, and Israeli economies. Another committee was to offer solutions to the political, strategic, economic, and territorial issues, so that the sides could sign a full-fledged peace treaty. As for Jerusalem, Paragraph 8 stated that Israel wouldn't agree to any change in Jordan's special status in the Holy Places. That was the "lip service" Peres had mentioned to Rabin.

This was a far-reaching document; King Hussein had actually abandoned his former position and affirmed his willingness to sign a peace agreement with Israel. The name of the game wasn't "interim agreements" anymore, but an official peace treaty. Peres and Hussein initialed the document and shook hands[7] In one conversation, Peres had convinced King Hussein to draw out his pen and sign an agreement.[8]

Hussein asked his guests to keep the agreement completely secret. Elections to the Jordanian parliament were due in five days, and the strength of the fanatical Muslim Brotherhood was on the rise. Therefore the agreement had to be kept secret until the election was over.

But Peres was so eager to get the credit for his success that he made a rash, thoughtless mistake. While still in Jordan, he removed his false mustache and when crossing the bridge over the Jordan River he spoke loudly, probably trying to attract attention. Peres later claimed that he had removed the mustache because it bothered him.[9] But others say that he wanted the news of his visit to leak to the media. Yet that didn't happen.

Back in Israel, he was scheduled to be interviewed on television, on a different subject. But before entering the studio, he announced: "Remember November the second!"[10] He repeated that phrase several times; finally, his words were reported by the media. The reporters deduced that he had visited Jordan and reached some agreement there. "He has not changed," Rabin angrily snapped in a conversation with a friend.[11]

"That was the first time," Gil said, "that I spoke to him with anger. He acted recklessly. I assumed that would cause him tremendous damage. That phrase severely hurt Peres's status."[12]

When the story was leaked to the Israeli media, King Hussein erupted in terrible anger. "Why did he do this to me?" he grumbled.[13] Hussein refused to meet Peres anymore. Only after a long time and considerable effort did Israeli envoys succeed in calming the king down. But their relations never fully recovered. For Rabin's aides, that episode was an excellent reason to exclude Peres from the peace talks with Jordan.

During the subsequent negotiation, Rabin's aides maltreated Peres and humiliated him, with the full knowledge of the prime minister. During a trip to Jordan to put the final touches on the agreement, Rabin met with King Hussein, but Peres was not allowed to participate in the meeting; he was sent to talk with Prince Hassan.

"Rabin decided that he would be in charge of making peace with Jordan," said Ambassador Itamar Rabinowitz, who was involved in the process. "There was an embarrassing episode in the White House, when the Declaration of Principles with Jordan was signed in July 1994. Rabin showed the document to Peres minutes before the signing; he took it out of his pocket in front of King Hussein, so that the king would see that he was showing it to Peres at the last moment. At the dinner in my house after the signing, Rabin said that Efraim Halevy was the man who achieved peace with Jordan. He added that there were people who acted and people who talked. It was a very upsetting moment. I got up and sat down beside Shimon. I felt very awkward."[14]

Peres had his revenge on Efraim Halevy, whom he suspected of inciting King Hussein against him. When Rabin put up his name as his candidate for the post of ambassador in Jordan, Peres vetoed it. Halevy asked to meet him and Peres told him frankly, "If you are the ambassador in Jordan, you'll be Yitzhak's ambassador in Jordan."[15] Halevy had to give up all hope.

The Jordanian chapter was over.

Peres, however, was already engaged in a new, exciting project.

IN ENCHANTING SAMARQAND, at the foot of the Turkestan Mountains of Uzbekistan, stand the breathtakingly beautiful "blue madrassas." Behind them wind the tortuous alleys of the bird market and the bread and food market. That morning, like every day, local babushkas displayed their goods—fragrant, artfully ornamented bread, spices, vegetables, slain chickens.

"I am going in," Peres announced, stunning his security guards. The foreign minister stepped into the bustling market and started shaking hands and exchanging greetings, while his traumatized guards tried to follow. "Shimon, this is not the Tel Aviv market," his aide Avraham Katz-Oz said to him. "These people are not voting for you!" But Peres was delighted. "The babushkas," Katz-Oz recalled later, "didn't understand what he wanted, who this man was. That was an astonishing sight."[16]

Peres hadn't come to Samarqand as a tourist. He was on a journey that took him to Uzbekistan, Kazakhstan, and Turkmenistan. The goal of his trip was to further Turkey's interests. The Soviet empire had crumbled down, while in Iran rising Islamic fanaticism threatened to spill over into the Muslim republics of the former Soviet Union. It was also a danger to Turkey, whose regime was secular and pro-Western. Peres wanted to brake the surge of Islamic fanaticism and stir those Muslim nations toward Turkey, which was Israel's ally. Peres conceived the idea of an Israeli-Turkish-American project for the development of those countries' agriculture. America and Turkey were to invest the funds, while Israel contributed the know-how. They hoped to defeat the poverty and hunger threatening to drive those nations into the ayatollahs' arms.

Peres's journey, in the private plane of his American friend Danny Abraham, was crowned with success. Many Israeli training stations were established and Peres obtained large American grants for local development.

During his visit in Ashkhabad, the capital of Turkmenistan, the Turkmenis organized a horse race in Peres's honor. The race was impressive, and Peres cheered "as if he knew about horses."[17] His enthusiasm paid off: his hosts presented him with a fine horse. Unfortunately, there was no way to get the horse into Danny

Abraham's plane. Peres's horse is still waiting for him in Turkmenistan.

Peres lost a great horse, indeed, but strengthened Israel's ties with Turkey. He described one of his motives to Katz-Oz: "There are two rising forces in our area. One of them is Egypt, but she is strong only in words, she is not a power. The other one is Turkey: she is a power, and she also controls the water of Iraq and Syria. If you hold Turkey in your hand, you're holding Iraq and Syria by the [here Peres mentioned a male body part]. Iraq and Syria are Israel's enemies. He who controls their water—if he wishes, they live, and if he wishes, they don't. That's why we have to maintain tight relations with Turkey."[18]

Peres laid the foundations for an informal alliance between Turkey, Jordan, and Israel. He also helped Turkey in her efforts to join the European Union. "Most of Europe was governed by socialist regimes," recalled Zvi Alpeleg, Israel's former ambassador in Ankara. "Shimon knew personally almost all the leaders. As the vote at the European Parliament approached, Shimon picked up the phone and spoke with almost all of Turkey's opponents. 'What do you want?' he asked them, 'a neighboring country located mostly in Asia and a member of the European Union or a pro-Khomeini nation on your borders? That's the choice.' By his actions in that matter, Shimon achieved a place in Turkish history. Turkey's prime minister, Tansu Çiller, called me and said, 'It's good to know that we have a friend like Peres.' I don't think that today there is any foreign leader as popular in Turkey as Shimon."[19]

IN SPITE OF HIS many friends throughout the world, Peres projected the image of a lonely man. That impression largely resulted from the fact that his wife, Sonia, was not at his side. Everywhere he went—to state functions, receptions, public appearances, meetings, and conferences in Israel and abroad—he went alone.

Things had not always been like that. In the past, when Shimon was director general of the defense ministry or Rafi's secretary general, Sonia was always at his side. But things changed over the years, and in the early eighties Sonia disappeared from the public's eye. To her friends she would say that as long as Shimon worked with Ben-Gurion or was in the defense ministry, she saw his occupation as vital, even sacred. But after Ben-Gurion was gone and Shimon was no more involved in security matters, she didn't want to take part in his public life anymore. Politics disgusted her. After Labor's defeat in the 1981 elections, Sonia was seen in public very rarely. The second time she turned her back on politics was in 1992, when Shimon was beaten by Rabin at the party primaries. She told him: "That's enough, Shimon." After the primaries Tziki burst out crying at the breakfast table. Sonia turned to Shimon. "You see?" she said. "Do you think there is anything in the world worth making your daughter cry?"[20]

Sonia couldn't forgive Shimon for giving up, disregarding the insults and the humiliations, looking for a compromise instead of fighting back. Sonia held strong and lucid opinions, and in the past used to take part in her husband's meetings with his confidants; she expressed her views clearly and firmly. Justice was also very important to her, and she examined each of her husband's moves in the light of the principles of justice and morality. "My mother belongs to the 'justice coalition,' " her son Hemi said.[21]

Sonia contributed to society in her own way—by discreetly volunteering in institutions for sick and handicapped people and homes for mentally handicapped children. She never sat on boards or public committees, like the wives of other politicians, but spent her time cleaning, sweeping floors, and personally tending to the sick; she didn't recoil before any kind of work but did it with lots of love and devotion.[22]

Still, her absence at Peres's side hurt his political career. Her captivating personality could have added another dimension to her husband's image—and instead of the lonely, sad man, many would have seen a couple bound by love and understanding. Many politicians believed that the very presence of Sonia at Shimon's side would have brought him many votes and perhaps some victories.[23] But that was not Sonia's character; she was a stubborn, direct, and mostly honest woman. If it had been up to her, she would have returned to Kibbutz Alumot right away.[24] In Alumot, Sonia experienced the best years of her life, and her dream was to return to the simple and modest life of the kibbutz and the breathtaking landscapes of Lake Kinnereth and the Galilee Mountains.

Yet her bond with Shimon was very deep; she didn't conceal her admiration for his talents and her pride in his achievements. Shimon, too, showed respect for Sonia's decision and was never heard complaining about her refusal to share his public life. He also avoided steps that could trigger gossip about his private life. When Colette Avital, a smart and pretty diplomat, was a candidate for the position of media adviser to the prime minister in 1984, Peres chose somebody else. He explained his decision to her: "You're a woman and you're pretty. They'll gossip about us."

"Is it that bad that I'm pretty?" Colette protested. "Don't I have any other qualifications, no professional capacities?"

Peres answered, "What would they say if a lock of blond hair fluttered in the prime minister's car window?" A few years later, the gossip columns mentioned a romantic connection between Colette Avital and Shimon Peres; they both firmly denied the rumors.[25]

And yet, in later years, Peres slipped some hints about his private life into newspaper interviews. "I definitely like pretty women," he said. "I will not say anything beyond that, because I don't look for sensations."[26] He didn't explain what kind of sensations he had in mind.

"THIS MORNING I DROVE with Sonia and Tziki to the ceremony ending Yoni's boot camp training," Peres wrote in his diary on April 8, 1971. "He is in the Sappers, in a camp at the Bloc of Etzion. 120 soldiers finished their training course . . . . Yoni is tanned and seems quite happy, in spite of being so introverted. The army has done him good. He looks older, more serious, and independent. I let the tears flow under my dark glasses. A father is a father, there are no tricks. What awaits these young boys? Another war? It is so cruel thinking about this."[27]

For Yoni, a bitter experience was in store. A bullet was discharged from his rifle by accident, killing another soldier, Haim Ashtibekar. Yoni was sentenced to three months in prison and was sent to an army jail.[28] Peres often went to visit him. He tried to be calm and self-possessed, but the blow suffered by his son caused him profound pain and many tears.[29] Yoni overcame his predicament, and after his discharge from the IDF he returned to his old love—taking care of animals. The younger Hemi made his father proud when he graduated from the Air Force Academy, in spite of his asthma, and became a helicopter pilot before entering the business world. Tziki got a Ph.D. in children's linguistics. She was the most involved of the three in her father's political life, and assisted him in his political campaigns with amazing energy.

Peres continued his passionate affair with the world of books. He enthusiastically welcomed every book written by one of his favorite authors—and wrote long and detailed letters to Amos Oz, A. B. Yehoshua, and many others. He translated a chapter of Vladimir Nabokov's *Speak, Memory*. "His English language is very difficult," he admitted. "The translation work is like moving to another apartment; you need porters in order to climb and descend all these floors, and you have to decide what comes first .... But Nabokov gives you a special pleasure, as if you were listening to Beethoven (from the point of view of authenticity) and to Paganini (from the point of view of the wit)."[30] The translated chapter was published in the prestigious literary magazine *Keshet*.

A few weeks before Rabin was assassinated, he visited New York, and was walking down the street with Colette Avital, who at that time was Israel's consul general. Suddenly it started raining and they found refuge in a bookstore on Madison Avenue. Avital noticed Mikhail Gorbachev's biography and asked Rabin, "Have you read this?"

"I am reading it now," the prime minister answered. "Shimon

gave it to me. Don't you know? Shimon gives me all these books and tells me what to read."[31]

"DURING THIS PERIOD," Leah Rabin wrote, "the relations between Yitzhak and Shimon Peres developed and deepened. The two of them had never before assessed what a tremendous contribution their cooperation could produce .... Their relations never turned into friendship, but they were now partners for peace. Fate had brought them together."[32]

Leah Rabin's somewhat idyllic description was only partly true. Rabin and Peres worked together, indeed, although there was still no love lost between them. Ambassador Rabinowitz described the way the two leaders completed each other: "Peres and Rabin are traveling in a car in a hilly area. Peres already looks four hills ahead, while Rabin has an X-ray machine that analyzes exactly what happens to the car during the trip. That was why they were so good when they worked together; but it was not always so."[33]

Yet the picture that remained in the collective memory of the Israelis and the world, that night of November 4, 1995, was of the two men hugging each other, singing the song of peace, yearning to lead Israel, together, to new horizons, to a new world.

CHAPTER 32

1996

ONE DAY, SHIMON PERES wrote a poem about himself:

Shimon, Shimon
A man without a watch
The poorest of Israel's tribes
And the richest in the world's dreams
Innocently, feverishly dreaming
Dream after dream.
He'll bring the dawn to morn
He'll cast the yesterday into tomorrow
And when he falls, he'll rise again
And will soar to great heights
And he'll return to the lake of poetry
And a silver wave will wake him up
Your light, Shimon, will shine.
For God has heard my words.

When he read the completed poem, Peres apparently backed away, for it seemed pretentious and even arrogant. "Your light, Shimon, will shine / For God has heard my words . . . ." Peres didn't speak of himself that way, and God, too, didn't always play an active role in his forecasts. Therefore he rewrote the poem, and instilled in it a few drops of humor.

Shimon, listen Shimon
You live without a watch . . .

And you are burning in a fever
Dream after dream . . .
And even when you fall you'll rise
Refusing to stop before a blank wall . . .
Shimon, look Shimon
Go and buy yourself a watch
And with the change purchase a calendar,
Time speeds by, spirit is not enough.

The poem's ending carried good advice for Peres when he replaced the assassinated Rabin as prime minister. He should have looked at his watch and checked the calendar; as a skilled politician he should have advanced the date of the election and won with a comfortable margin. At that time there was a large popularity gap between Prime Minister Peres and Binyamin (Bibi) Netanyahu, the new Likud leader. Rabin's assassination had shaken the Israeli people, who closed ranks around Shimon Peres.

But Peres stubbornly stuck to the original date of the election, which was still several months away. To some he said that he wanted to complete the second stage of the Oslo negotiations.[1] To others he explained that he hoped to make peace with Syria, now that Savir was negotiating with the Syrian foreign minister at the Wye Plantation, in Maryland. But it was neither the negotiation with the Palestinians nor those with the Syrians that blocked the way to early elections. It was Peres's unwillingness to return to the premiership on the coattails of the dead Rabin.

To his confidant Nissim Zvili, the Labor Party secretary, Peres said, "I don't want to be seen as someone who has been elected on Rabin's blood."[2] He wanted to return to the prime minister's office as a leader sent there by the people, not as a politician who had cynically taken advantage of his partner's death.

Peres's motives were moral and dignified, but politics had their own rules. "Shimon made his greatest mistake," his friend Arthur Ben-Nathan said, "because of his ego. He refused to win because of Rabin; he wanted to be elected because of himself."[3] His opponent, Netanyahu, added, "If he had called an election right after the assassination, he would have won an easy victory. When he didn't do it, I said to my wife, he lost the elections."[4]

Rabin's death was for Peres a more painful blow than his friends could imagine; he couldn't shake off the harrowing thought that he could have been assassinated together with Rabin, or in his stead. To his aides he seemed detached and pre-occupied.[5] He also felt a terrible loneliness. In spite of his constant bickering with Rabin, the two were partners who acted and decided together.[6] Now he remained all alone.

Peres's advisers concocted the myth of the great reconciliation between him and Rabin in the hours before the assassination. Over and over again the television screened the footage from the November 4 peace rally. Over and over again Peres and Rabin appeared on the screens, hugging each other, smiling at each other. Peres stressed this friendship in his emotional eulogy of Rabin, when he called him "my older brother."

The truth was different. The tension and the mutual suspicion between the two leaders continued until the last moments of Rabin's life. During the peace rally, Giora Eini kept going back and forth on the podium, trying to reconcile the two men, for a new crisis had broken out. It had to do with the Nativ organization, which was in charge of immigration from the former Soviet Union. Rabin was supposed to transfer Nativ's management to Peres, but the two disagreed on several points. Eini brought to Rabin a compromise draft before the rally began; during the speeches he conferred with Peres and got his approval.[7] Shortly before the assassination, Rabin angrily said to Binyamin (Fuad) Ben-Eliezer: "Shimon will haunt me till my last day!"[8]

But the last proof of Rabin's alienation was brought to Peres by President Bill Clinton. The American president attended Rabin's funeral in Jerusalem. He met with Peres and revealed to him the existence of the "deposit," the secret commitment Rabin had made to give back the Golan Heights to Assad in exchange for peace. Peres was stunned. He knew nothing about Rabin's commitment. Rabin's "deposit" contradicted his party platform, which stated that Israel would stay in the Golan even after a peace treaty with Syria.[9]

Nevertheless, Peres promised Clinton that he would honor the late prime minister's pledge.[10]

IN EARLY 1996, a cruel fate befell Shimon Peres. Five bloody terrorist attacks struck Israel—three in Jerusalem, one in Tel Aviv, one in Ashkelon. The first explosion struck Jerusalem on February 25. From the charred remains of a bus serving City Line 18, the rescuers carried 26 dead bodies and 44 wounded. After the explosion, one of Peres's advisers predicted, "Three more bombings like this, and Peres will lose the election." The three, and a fourth, too, arrived in succession. February 25, suicide bombing at Ashkelon crossroads, 1 dead, 34 wounded; February 26, the French Hill in Jerusalem, 2 dead and 23 wounded; March 3, a second bombing on Line 18 in Jerusalem, 18 dead, 7 wounded. March 4—the Festival of Purim—suicide bombing in Tel Aviv, 14 dead, 157 wounded.

Peres said that the first week of the bombings was the worst week in his life. By the smoldering carcass of the bombed bus, the crowd booed him, shouting "Peres—murderer" and "Peres is next." He insisted on visiting the bombing sites in spite of the angry shouts. He rejected the suggestion to hit Hamas and Islamic Jihad hard. Peres also rejected the idea of appointing General Ehud Barak defense minister. Barak, a former IDF chief of staff, had been an outstanding officer, and his appointment could have raised the nation's morale.[11] Peres apparently wanted to be both Israel's prime minister and minister of defense like Ben-Gurion and Rabin before him.

The only practical initiative Peres put forth was to organize an international conference at Sharm al-Sheikh, where world leaders flocked to express their determination to fight terrorism. The summit was a very impressive enterprise that only Peres could have carried out; but its impact on Israel's public opinion was nil. Peres still hadn't understood that international conferences had no influence on Israelis; a single military operation against the terrorists would have been much more effective.

Peres finally unleashed the IDF—but against Hezbollah, not against Hamas. After a massive rocket attack on Galilee, Peres ordered Operation Grapes of Wrath—an incursion against Hezbollah in South Lebanon. But his bad luck didn't let go. On April 18, an Israeli artillery salvo hit the wrong target and killed 102 Lebanese civilians near the village of Kafr Kana. Israel admitted her error, and Grapes of Wrath ended in confusion and embarrassment. It didn't achieve its goals, and Peres suffered heavy personal damage—on Election Day, many Israeli Arabs would stay away from the polling stations as a protest against the bloody fiasco.

Peres finally gave in and advanced the elections to May 28. But it was too late. When the results started arriving, the Labor leaders were dismayed. Following a reform in the electoral system, Israelis now elected the prime minister by direct vote. Netanyahu got 50.5 percent of the vote, and Peres 49.5 percent.

The young Netanyahu had defeated the experienced Peres by a thirty-thousand-vote margin.

ON THE DAY after the election, Nissim Zvili came to Peres's office. Peres looked at him and said, "How did this happen to us, Nissim, what happened?"[12]

But on Friday morning, Peres was at work at 7 A.M., as usual. He reacted to the painful blow with stoical calm, but his body betrayed him. His media adviser, Aliza Goren, found him alone in his office, breathing heavily.

Aliza alerted Peres's daughter and asked a paramedic to examine Peres.

The results were alarming: the paramedic found that the heartbeat was irregular. The situation was not critical, however, and no hospitalization was necessary. That short crisis became the greatest family secret. But Peres, like a phoenix, recovered completely.

And like a phoenix, he launched a new effort to find a way

out of his quandary. He tried to persuade his colleagues to establish a unity government with Netanyahu. But Netanyahu rejected the idea. "I heard all the stories about him acting behind Rabin's back. I feared he'd do the same [to me]. A few months later I found out that that was not true; basically he is a loyal man. You can clinch a deal with him, and he makes good on his promises. In retrospect I regret that I didn't establish a unity government with him. That was a mistake, my mistake, because of my inexperience and misunderstanding."[13]

If some Jerusalem resident had identified the car that often appeared at the prime minister's residence in the black of night, or had recognized its passenger, he would have been flabbergasted. The prime minister's secret guest was none other than the leader of the opposition. A secret and very special connection had been established between Peres and Netanyahu, and very few people knew about it.

More than once, the new prime minister needed the advice and the experience of Shimon Peres. And the same Peres who led the opposition's fiery attacks on the government during the day kept visiting the head of that government at night. Peres would come with one of his aides, most frequently Yona Bartal, and a few times with Uri Savir. "We put on disguises, and coordinated our trips with the secret service," Yona Bartal recalled. "Sometimes we spent the entire night with Bibi Netanyahu, and Shimon would advise him how to approach the Palestinians, and how to exchange messages with them."[14] Netanyahu considered those nightly meetings to be very important. "When Shimon came, my wife would host him, and prepare a bottle of whiskey." At Netanyahu's request, Peres met with Arafat and discussed various issues with him.[15] "Shimon did that for the good of the nation," Bartal said. "For him it always came first. But if that had become known they would have expelled him from the Labor Party."

AFTER PERES'S DEFEAT in the elections it was clear that he couldn't lead the party anymore. His successor was Ehud Barak, a kibbutznik, a general, a former interior minister in Rabin's cabinet, and the foreign minister in Peres's last government. Both Peres and Rabin had groomed him for the position of party leader.

Peres announced that he was resigning from the post of party chairman. His supporters wanted him elected party president, but Barak suddenly launched a maneuver that thwarted that proposal. On May 13, 1997, Peres spoke to the three thousand delegates of the Labor Party convention. "I don't want powers," he declared. "I don't want honors, but I also don't want insults. I announced my decision to resign from the position of party chairman. Did somebody push me into doing that? Am I trying to stick to my job?"

"Yes! Yes!" some of the delegates shouted.

Peres reminded them that in 1977 he had undertaken to restore the party's power. "At the 1981 elections I brought the party from thirty-two to fifty seats [actually Labor had won only forty-seven seats]. Afterwards they came and said, 'Peres is a loser.' " He turned to the public and asked angrily, "Did I lose the elections? Am I a loser?"

"Yes! Yes!" the crowd shouted.

"If I were such a loser, where were you all? Why didn't you run [for the party leadership]?"

At the end of his tumultuous speech, Peres mentioned his age—seventy-four. "I apologize for being healthy, for not getting old according to plan, for having energies. Even without being president I won't stop working for peace."[16]

Peres sat beside the party secretary and muttered, "Scoundrels!"[17]

But his rhetoric didn't help. The convention decided not to put Peres's candidacy for president to the vote. For him, it was a painful failure.

The papers announced, somewhat hastily, "the end of Peres's era."

PERES'S ADMIRERS HECTICALLY tried to find a new job

for their hero. Some wanted him to run for U.N. secretary general. Others thought he should be president of the Socialist International. Finally they all joined together to create a new organization where he could contribute to his most precious goal: "the Peres Center for Peace." The center was to promote peace between the Middle Eastern peoples by bringing together Jews and Arabs, encouraging cooperation between them, and raising the Palestinians' living standards. Peres turned to world leaders and they enthusiastically agreed to join the center's board. The list of board members reads like the World Figures' Hall of Fame: presidents, past and present, prime ministers, heads of international organizations, world-famous writers and artists, Nobel Prize winners, producers and actors, leading businessmen. Uri Savir, who became the center's chairman, called it "Peres's dream factory."

Peres started traveling intensively to raise funds for his center. He met with political leaders and business tycoons, and spoke to select audiences. Israelis gradually realized that Peres had become one of the most admired world leaders because of his stubborn struggle for peace. He was received everywhere with respect and high regard, and many saw him as one of the world's greatest statesmen.

But Peres was not a prophet in his own country.

In mid-1999, Netanyahu's government collapsed, and Israelis went back to the polls. Ehud Barak led Labor's list and won by a landslide. He formed a new government, but refrained from giving Peres a major position. He entrusted him with the unimportant portfolio of regional cooperation. Peres didn't protest and didn't take offense—at least not publicly.

But less than a year later, a splendid opportunity suddenly emerged: becoming Israel's president. President Weizman resigned before the end of his term, and Peres seemed the ideal candidate. Peres could be the best president Israel ever had. Nobody had any doubt that when the 120 Knesset members voted for the next president, Peres would win. The votes of the

Labor Party, the Arabs, and the left-wing Meretz were guaranteed; he only needed a few more votes to achieve the needed majority. Very few gave any chance to the Likud candidate, former minister Moshe Katzav.

True, some rumors maintained that Prime Minister Barak wasn't happy with the prospect of President Peres interfering in the country's policies. But nobody ever assumed that Barak's reservations might find their way into the ballot box. Others warned Peres not to trust the promises of Shas's leaders when they said that they would vote for him.

Still, Peres's election seemed assured. The day before the vote, Peres's staff was busy preparing the guest lists for the inauguration party.

On July 31, 2000, the vote in the Knesset took place, by secret ballot. When the ballot boxes were opened, after two rounds of voting, it turned out that Peres had received fifty-seven votes. Moshe Katzav was elected president with sixty-three votes.

Peres had lost again.

"There was in him something tragic," the author S. Izhar said. "Blow after blow, a man who makes you think of Job, but without Job's mentality."[18] Some, indeed, described Peres as a tragic figure, because of all the defeats that had befallen him; others, however, saw him as an incurable optimist, the man who would never give in. But at the end of that bitter day, he felt the scorching failure branding his flesh. "A curse hovers over me," he sadly said to his friends.

Amos Oz stood up. "No curse can haunt a man who has left such an impact!"

ON SEPTEMBER 21, 2003, Shimon Peres attended a party to celebrate his eightieth birthday. A myriad of world leaders took part in the festive event held at the Mann Auditorium in Tel Aviv. The guest list included ex-presidents Clinton, Gorbachev, and De Klerk; the presidents of Germany, Slovakia, and Malta; prime ministers; actors and artists; businessmen; and Nobel Prize winners. Everybody spoke of Peres's amazing accomplishments, and stressed that he owed his world stature to his relentless struggle for peace.

Israeli and Palestinian children sang moving songs to Peres; immigrants from Ethiopia and Russia, artists and statesmen, terrorism survivors, teenagers and army officers encouraged him to continue his efforts for peace. President Katzav thanked him in the name of the nation. President Clinton told him, "You are a light unto the nations and unto your people. . . . I thank you for your vision of a New Middle East. You're the most stubborn man I've ever met." He described Peres's efforts to achieve peace: "That seed sowed by Shimon Peres came to life as the first flower after a long cold winter." Clinton added, on a lighter note, "At such an occasion it is customary to slap the eighty-year-old on the back and thank him for what he has done—but you're only halfway there!"

Prime Minister Sharon stuck to the same trend: "Perhaps, Shimon, we could still go forward together, for one common goal—the strengthening of the State of Israel, in security and peace."

These were not only niceties; Peres was back in the saddle. After his defeat in the presidential election, it seemed for a short while that he had stepped down, but this was an illusion. In 2000, Ehud Barak's government fell after his failure to reach a comprehensive peace agreement with Yasser Arafat. The negotiations had been held at Camp David, under President Clinton's auspices. When they collapsed, the intifada erupted again in the West Bank and Gaza, more murderous than ever.

Barak ran for prime minister again, this time against Ariel Sharon. When the polls showed that Barak had no chance of winning, Peres declared he was ready to run against him and Sharon. As Barak was the Labor candidate, Peres didn't hesitate to look for another political base. He turned to the left-wing Meretz Party and asked to be its candidate for prime minister.

This time he didn't get any support. The party leader, Yossi Sarid, rejected his request, and even Amos Oz opposed him. But

Oz well knew what made Peres run: "My friend Shimon," he said, "runs and stumbles, runs and falls, because his eyes are in the stars."

At the elections, Sharon crushed Barak. Sharon established a unity government, and Peres surfaced again, as the eternal phoenix, and was appointed foreign minister. The government fell two years later and the new Labor chairman, Amram Mitzna, led his party to another defeat.

In the chaos that ensued, the Labor Party remained a flock without a shepherd. After a stormy period it found the solution. The same party that had thrown out Peres four years before reelected him now as its provisional chairman.

Shimon Peres, back at the helm, made true Clinton's amused prophecy at his eightieth birthday: "When I read in the Israeli press about a new generation of leaders, I know that when this new generation comes to power, Shimon will stand at the head of the line."[19]

PART 6.

_____

... AS IF ALL HIS LIFE LIES AHEAD OF HIM

_____

CHAPTER 33.

THE LITTLE DUTCH BOY

ON DECEMBER 21, 1959, in the ninth Israeli cabinet, Shimon Peres was appointed deputy defense minister. Forty-seven years later, on May 4, 2006, Peres became deputy prime minister in the thirty-first Israeli cabinet.

In the Labor primaries of November 2005, the party members elected their chairman and candidate for prime minister. Shimon Peres, who was eighty-two years old, ran in the primaries and was beaten by the energetic Histadrut chairman, Amir Peretz.

The failure made Peres utterly bitter, both toward Peretz, whom he had supported in his bid to join the Labor Party, and toward the party that had forsaken him. Amir Peretz focused on social issues, while Peres believed that the major issue in the forthcoming years should be the peace process. In a dramatic move, Peres quit the Labor Party, which had been his ideological home since his early youth.

"This is a very painful day for me," Peres declared to the press on November 30, 2005. "I found a contradiction between the party I am a member of and the political situation; and without playing down the spiritual bond that I feel to the party's ideology, I must prefer the immediate and most important consideration." Peres believed that Sharon was the man who could bring peace and security to Israel. He therefore joined Sharon, who seceded from Likud and founded a new party, Kadima. The greatest victory of his political philosophy, Peres said, was Sharon's support of the partition of Eretz-Israel into an Israeli and a Palestinian state. "I didn't join Sharon," he said, "Sharon joined me."[1]

Many ridiculed Peres and accused him of pursuing status and honor. He didn't know how to quit and retreat in dignity, they said. He didn't understand that he was too old.

He answered, "Age is not a crime."

His supporters pointed out that Ben-Gurion had been an active politician till the age of eighty-four. Others quoted Moshe Dayan's words, in the twilight of his life, to his daughter Yael. Why do you still remain in politics as the head of a tiny party, Yael asked, in spite of being sick with cancer, losing your sight, and feeling your forces wane? Dayan answered, "As long as I can still raise my hand in the Knesset and have an impact on what is happening, I won't leave."[2]

Yossi Beilin said, "How many Shimon Pereses are there in the world? Even if you sometimes feel anger toward this man, you have to ask yourself—how many people can speak like that, read like that, understand so fast, how many people are so young at the age of eighty?"[3]

"Shimon really believes in the chance to make peace," Arik Sharon said with wonder. "He tried and didn't let go and he is trying over and over again and his efforts would not stop. He is the man who never despairs."

Even when Sharon suffered a terrible stroke and vanished from the political arena, Peres didn't give up. He became deputy prime minister in Ehud Olmert's government and continued his relentless quest for peace.

Yet deep down he remained Mr. Security. When the war against Hezbollah in Lebanon erupted in the summer of 2006, Peres loyally and eloquently defended Israel's policy in various international forums and in the world media. But in the secret discussions in Israel's cabinet, he adopted a different view. He had serious misgivings about the military's plans to carry out the offensive mainly by air attack. "You have to decide," he told Prime

Minister Olmert. "You can either launch an all-out war, in the air and on the ground, with all its consequences and the heavy price it would exact—or you don't go to war at all. There are no half measures. If you are not ready to go to a full-scale war against Hezbollah, you shouldn't go to war at all, and should seek other solutions." His advice was not heeded, and the war ended inconclusively.

In 2006 Peres conceived a new idea: establishing "a corridor of peace" all along the Jordan Valley, where Israelis, Palestinians, and Jordanians would work together to offer an economic solution to the Middle East conflict. With the enthusiastic support of Mahmoud Abbas, King Abdullah of Jordan, President Clinton, and other world leaders, Peres dreamed of launching several ambitious economic projects intended to prove that peace can be achieved through cooperation, mutual trust, and prosperity.

Later that year, Israel's President Moshe Katzav was urged to resign after being accused of sexual offenses; Peres emerged again as a most likely candidate to succeed him as Head of State.

The truth about Peres is simple: he could not stop. Like a swimmer, who would sink and drown if he didn't keep moving; like a bird, which would fall and crash if it stopped flapping its wings—like them, Peres could not stop either. His eyes, as always, looked far into the future. At the age of eighty he was captivated by nanotechnology, the new miniaturization science, and assailed scientists, government ministers, and potential donors with plans for developing it in Israel and making the nation again a symbol of excellence.

Peres didn't suffer from his advanced age. But his age instilled in him a sense of urgency. He admitted to not having enough time for all he wanted to do. Among other things, he became more critical and impatient about the books he read. "Like life," he wrote, "books too are a matter of age. Taste changes with age, and we cannot return to the innocent and sweet taste of youth. The only way for us to stay connected with our youth is by nurturing our curiosity for the future; as I grew older, this curiosity remained my real bond with my lost youth."[4]

Amos Oz said, "People see in Shimon traits that he doesn't have. They say he has a huge lust for power. He has just a normal lust for power. But he has a deep feeling of urgency and personal commitment; he feels that he is the little Dutch boy with his finger in the dike."

"I know two kinds of adults. One carries inside himself the dead child that he once was. The other is a very rare kind of adult, who carries inside himself a living child—curious, thirsty for love, thirsty for knowledge .... This is Shimon. I am watching him, and all the time I see the curious, restless, active child who behaves as if all his life lies ahead of him. He is over eighty, but what interests him—and this is not a pretense—is what will happen forty years from now."

"He lives as if all that has happened so far is only a prelude."

"People attack him for this, and I am telling you that this is his greatness."[5]

CHAPTER 34

PRESIDENT OF ISRAEL

On June 13, 2007, at a plenary session of the Knesset, Speaker Dalia Itzik announced that three Knesset Members were running for the presidency: Reuven (Ruvi) Rivlin, a veteran Likud representative, a warm, friendly man and a former Knesset speaker, very popular among his peers; Colette Avital, a blond, pretty Labor member and a former Consul General in New York, who wanted to "break the glass ceiling" and prove that a woman could be elected President; and Shimon Peres. The one hundred and twenty Knesset members were going to elect the next President of Israel by secret ballot.

Peres's candidacy triggered various reactions. Many supported it; but large sectors of the body politic and in particular the mass media reacted with mockery and vicious jabs at the candidate. Major newspapers, as well as radio and television networks reminded their audience that Peres was the eternal loser, describing again the pathetic 1997 Labor Party convention when he rhetorically had launched at the assembly the question: "Am I a loser?" And the crowd had yelled back: "Yes!"

That loser now wants to be a president? the media asked.

The press pundits maintained that the other candidates had much better chances than he had, that anyway he was too old, almost eighty-four. They predicted another stinging defeat for the eternal Israeli politician. "Shimon Peres," a reporter for TV

Channel 10 declared, "should have retired from political life as early as 1977 (when Labor had been defeated by the Likud). He already had caused enough damage back then, but we had to live with the empty shell of his lust for honors, which is all that remained of him during the last thirty years."[1] One paper gleefully published the last joke about Peres: when a group of Israeli tourists traveled to the Cairo pyramids, the Sphinx opened its mouth and asked: "Is Shimon Peres still a Knesset Member?"

The irony even reached the foreign press. A great New York newspaper snickered at Peres: "The man who would be President – if not for these pesky elections..."[2] The media seemed to attach no importance to the polls, indicating that more than 70% of the Israelis supported Peres's candidacy.

Peres himself hesitated a long time before deciding to run. He remembered the former presidential election, on July 31, 2000, when many Knesset Members promised to vote for him and betrayed him at the polling booth. That day it looked as if his election was a sure thing. His friends and admirers, happy, proud and festively dressed, filled the Knesset, expecting to share his triumph. His family watched the proceedings from the Knesset gallery, waiting for the election results that would finally make their man the Head of State; but it was Moshe Katzav, a pedestrian Likud member, whom nobody expected to win, that got the absolute majority of the vote, including at least three members of Peres' s Labor party.

Katzav's presidency ended in scandal, when he had to resign from office because of shocking accusations of rape and sexual harassment. He was tried and sentenced to serve seven years in prison. Katzav became the first president in the history of Israel and of the Western world in many years to be thrown from the President's mansion into a jail cell.

In 2007 Katzav didn't threaten Peres anymore, but the public believed that another Likud member, the immensely popular Ruvi Rivlin, had the best chances; while the third candidate, Colette Avital, who insisted on running although she didn't have a chance, was certain to get many of the Labor Party votes that Peres counted on. Only the Kadima faction in the Knesset stood behind Peres, as well as a few other Knesset members who had promised to support him – but they had made the same promise seven years before. Peres feared another debacle that would ridicule him; besides, his wife Sonia didn't stand by him, and warned him that she would not join him in his new duties. Peres dismissed the warning, but wavered a lot before throwing his hat in the ring.

That June 13, the first round of vote was carried out in an atmosphere of intense tension. The result was stunning: Peres got fifty-eight votes, leaving the two other contenders so far behind, that a few minutes later both Rivlin and Avital conceded defeat and asked their supporters to vote for Peres. In a rare display of national unity, the Knesset elected Peres in the second round as the ninth President of Israel.

Peres's victory stirred a wave of enthusiasm throughout the country. The same media that only hours before had ridiculed the "loser" Shimon Peres, now heaped on him praise and glory. The polls that followed the election gave him an approval rate of more than 80 percent. Political leaders of both the right and left declared they were happy to have Peres as Head of State, even though the function of President in Israel is considered a purely ceremonial position.

But since the moment he stepped in the President's office, Peres was to prove that he had no intention to become a figurehead. Ceremonies were not what he looked for and he was determined to leave his mark on Israel's future.

Peres walked into the President's office in Jerusalem surrounded by a team composed mostly of women – a director general, a deputy-director general, a chief of staff, a spokeswoman, and several senior aides. "For most of my life," Peres said, "I was surrounded by generals, and today all my senior staff is female. The women's management reduces frictions and fosters the individual. Man is spoiled and in need of hierarchy, territory, assistants, credit, while a woman simply gets devoted to her functions."[3]

Since his election, Peres plunged again into his hectic work style, crossing the country, meeting with communities, women groups, teenagers, soldiers, students, academics, Jews and Arabs. Very quickly he earned the people's trust and his popularity soared. Nobody was more surprised by this change than Peres. He was used to confront, almost daily, bitter enemies who attacked him relentlessly. He had to defend himself and fight back. That was a part of his life. Now, all of a sudden, he became the most admired leader in Israel and his rivals vanished from his sights. He was not used to that. "In the public eye he ceased being a politician," later wrote journalist Nahum Barnea, "He became a living statue, a historic figure, a walking reminder of what we wanted to be, of what we could be."[4]

Peres, totally devoted to the idea of peace, launched again his initiatives – creating a "Valley of Peace", an industrial and agricultural park by the Jordan river where Jordanians, Palestinians and Israelis would work together; the "Two Seas Canal" that would establish a waterway between the Red Sea and the Dead Sea; the restarting of the peace negotiations with the Palestinians. In his weekly meetings with Prime Minister Netanyahu he didn't stop assailing him with his ideas. He was delighted when, on June 14 2009, Netanyahu made a speech at Bar-Ilan University and accepted the "Two State solution" to the Israeli-Palestinian conflict. This solution, supported by Peres and the international community, was based on the creation of a Palestinian State beside Israel, a State that would include most of the West Bank and the Gaza strip.

But the idyll was short-lived. The gap between Peres's drive for a negotiation and Netanyahu's reluctance kept growing. Peres, the eternal optimist, claimed that peace could be rapidly achieved; Netanyahu didn't share his enthusiasm. Peres considered the Chairman of the Palestinian Authority, Mahmoud Abbas, a suitable partner for peace negotiations; Netanyahu apparently was very skeptical about it. At the 2011 Herzliya yearly conference Peres declared: "History has lost her patience, she moves forward at a galloping speed; we'd either gallop with her or she would gallop away without us." A few days later he told the Presidents' Conference of the major American Jewish organizations that the gaps between Israel and the Palestinians had shrunk considerably and it was possible to complete the peace process with them.[5] He kept defending the Oslo agreements in spite of the criticisms by some of his partners and friends; he also kept repeating that the "New Middle East"—as he had titled his book after the signature of the agreements – was a reality; but he sadly ignored the bloody wars in Iraq and Syria, the rise of ISIS, the collapse of Arab nations and the massacre of hundreds of thousands during the terrible conflicts that raged in the Middle East.

Another point of discord between him and Netanyahu was the policy toward Iran. Peres didn't underestimate the Iranian nuclear project and regarded Iran as the greatest danger to Israel and the free world. "The Iranian people is not our enemy," he said in a speech to the UN General Assembly in August 2009. "Its problem is the Iranian fanatic leadership. Iran combines long range missiles with short range brains."[6] Yet, Netanyahu seriously considered an attack of Iran's nuclear centers by the Israeli army alone, in order to thwart her attempt to build a nuclear weapon. Peres, on the other hand, firmly believed in President Barak Obama, asserting that if the sanctions and the diplomatic efforts to stop Iran's nuclear project failed – then the United States would attack Iran. The boundless trust of Peres in President Obama was not shared by many Israelis, but he kept saying that Israel shouldn't act alone and must rely on the United States.

A special bond between Peres and Obama had emerged out of their meetings. When they first met, Obama was a junior senator, and Peres seemed to be in the twilight of his career. Obama asked Peres for advice and Peres insisted that the future was not only for the young. "Leave the future to me," Peres said, "I have time."[7]

"I think of him sitting in the Oval Office," Obama would recall later, "this final member of Israel's founding generation, under the portrait of George Washington, telling me stories from the past, but more often talking with enthusiasm of the present – his most recent lecture, his next project, his plans for the future, the wonders of his grandchildren."[8]

Obama presented Peres with the Presidential Medal of Freedom; Peres reciprocated the following year, during Obama's visit to Israel, by bestowing upon him the Presidential Medal of Distinction. "An international odd couple with seemingly little in common," the Jerusalem Post commented, "a 40-something African -American born in Hawaii and an octogenarian Zionist born in a shtetl in Poland. But somehow Barack Obama and Shimon Peres hit it off."[9]

CHAPTER 35.

A SKULLCAP IN THE REICHSTAG

January 27, 2010, International Holocaust Remembrance Day. Berlin, Germany.

In the late morning Shimon Peres entered the magnificent Reichstag building, once Hitler's lair, today the seat of the Bundestag, Germany's Parliament. As he walked in, Peres remembered that among these walls used to strut, drunk with triumphs and violence, the Nazi party leaders in their brown shirts; here was paved the way to the humiliation, imprisonment and mass murder of millions of Jews; here Hitler made his lunatic speeches that hypnotized an entire nation.

In front of a full Bundestag, watched by scores of visitors from the gallery, Peres got to the podium, put a skullcap on his head, and started by saying "Kadish" the ancient prayer for the dead, in memory of the Nazis' six million victims. "Yitgadal Veyitkadash Shmeh Raba..." he recited, and the ageless Arameic words echoed in the hushed chamber. His adviser, Yoram Dori, watching from the Visitors' Gallery, rose on his feet in tears; most of his mother's family, who lived in Germany, had perished in the Holocaust. After Dori a group of Holocaust survivors, who had joined the President on his trip, got on their feet as well, followed by all the members of the Bundestag. All of them stood in front of Peres, somber, still, their heads bowed. Thus all of Germany's leaders, the Parliament members, the ministers, the

Prime minister and the President, stood in silence in that building that had been the holy of holies of Naziism, and listened to the antique words that the President of Israel pronounced, commemorating the victims of their ancestors.

Gripped by profound emotion, Peres spoke of his grandfather and his family, who all had been burned to death in their synagogue by the Nazis. He demanded of Germany to arrest and punish the Nazi criminals who still walked free. Yet, he also described the close relations of Israel with the new Germany and stressed the desire of Israel to live in peace with her neighbors. He concluded his speech with the words of the national anthem, "Hatikva", The Hope.[1]

Peres' speech in the Bundestag was the highlight of his official visit to Germany. During his presidency he didn't stop traveling abroad, in order to improve Israel's relations with the outside world. Everywhere he was received with respect and admiration, as a man of peace and the last world leader of his generation. More than once he was accompanied by businessmen, scientists and experts who could establish useful connections with their counterparts. In Vietnam, he promoted the Israeli initiative to build huge dairy farms that would supply milk to the country's children. In China, he agreed to send Israeli agriculture experts to a huge farming project. In Brussels and Strasbourg he met with several heads of European states and spoke to the European parliament about the prospects of peace. In South America, he spoke with Presidents and Prime Ministers, faced a tumultuous protest in Buenos Aires, yet found the time to exchange soccer mementos with the legendary player Ronaldo. He was among the first leaders to be invited to the Vatican in Rome and meet with Pope Francis; the Holy See awarded him the Medal of Peace in the Basilica of Assisi.

Peres became very popular as a speaker on the world stage, because he didn't only convey the peace message of Israel, but addressed global problems and suggested original solutions. He spoke about the technological revolutions, the changing world, the hunger, the poverty, and his ideas to deal with them. He mostly focused on the Far East countries, China, India and others, and predicted that in the future they would overshadow the economic and political power of the West.

In every visit abroad, after all the official functions, the men and women of Peres's team would collapse on their hotel beds. Not Peres. He would always find the energy to visit a a café or a bar, where philosophers, writers and other men of letters would hang out. The author of this book spoke with Peres about these nocturnal habits. "I think," he said, 'that we were exiled from Paradise because the serpent taught us to distinguish between good and evil. But he who can't distinguish between good and evil can be neither a statesman nor a scientist. The scientists gave us the nuclear bomb and we don't know what to do with it. Therefore I am interested in human ethics, in human thought, in human poetry. This is the balancing element that every man needs."[2]

He later added, at a meeting with high school students: "In ten years you won't recognize the world, because an unprecedented scientific outburst is going to occur. Science is the war against blindness. That's why history is not important. Moses, who took the Jewish people out of Egypt, had a tremendous brain – but he didn't have glasses, a microscope or a telescope, and his sight range was as long as the staff he was holding in his hand. It was not his fault. We have glasses, binoculars… We are in the process of researching the most brilliant instrument that God created – the human brain."

And his testament to the young people was: "Each of you can be as small as his ego or as great as the goal he aspires to achieve."[3]

*

In May 2008, while Israel was celebrating its sixtieth birthday, Peres inaugurated the President's conference, that had been named "Tomorrow." Peres hosted many of the world greatest statesmen, men of letters, scientists and Nobel Prize winners in an impressive congress in Jerusalem. The event was dedicated to the future of the planet. At the podium Peres unveiled his dream – to harness Israel's capacities in science, technology and agriculture to a world scale effort to improve the lives of billions of people throughout the planet. The conference became a tradition of Peres's presidency and was repeated every year in Jerusalem. Yet, the conference organizers didn't know how to translate the mind-boggling brainstorming during its sessions – into action. Scientists, intellectuals, great statesmen came to Jerusalem, spoke to excited crowds – and flew back home. The President's conference did not have any results, except for meetings, speeches and debates.

The real action was taking place elsewhere – in the Presidential residence. In his vision Peres regarded Zionism entering the third stage in its development. He believed that the father of Political Zionism, Theodore Herzl, dreamt of the Land of Israel as a territorial center for the Jewish people; the writer and philosopher Achad Haam wanted to turn the Land of Israel into his people's spiritual center; but today Zionism was entering the third stage – making Israel a world scientific center.

And here Peres's initiatives were successful. His dream of developing nano-technology, that at first stirred mockery and disdain—another fantasy of Peres, many said—became a reality. Peres succeeded to arouse enthusiasm among scientists and businessmen who joined his initiative, and launched an unprecedented research effort. In a few years Israel climbed to the top of the nano-technological research and became one of the world's leading nations in developing and implementing nano.

Peres also launched an effort to boost the research of the human brain. He was determined to devote the next decade to solving the mystery of the brain, "the most enigmatic and amazing organ" of the human body.

Another of his campaigns was to introduce computers to every school and community center in the Middle East. He firmly believed that science and technology can be the keys for a peaceful solution. In the past, he said, nations went to war in order to conquer lands for survival, as agriculture was the main source of food. But today land had lost its importance as science had become the new food source. Land conquest had lost much of its importance; armies could not conquer science and one of the main reason for warfare was disappearing.

*

In June 2013, shortly before the President's conference, Peres celebrated his ninetieth birthday. The event took place in Jerusalem. The three thousand guests included all the political, social and scientific elite of Israel, beside the illustrious guests who had arrived from all over the world —Presidents Clinton and Gorbachev, former Britain's Prime Minister Tony Blair, Prince Albert of Monaco, the presidents of Albania and Ruanda, the Hollywood stars Barbara Streisand, Robert de Niro and Sharon Stone. The presidents of the US, France and Russia and other statesmen sent televised greetings. The celebration was most elaborate. Yet, the lavish and expensive event triggered a lot of criticism in Israel as it took place while painful austerity measures were being imposed, because of the dire economic crisis. The fact that both the birthday celebration and the conference that followed had been funded exclusively by private contributions, did not dispel the angry reactions, Another cause for protest was that some of the items in the festive program left an aftertaste of personality worship. A less showy celebration would have been much more appropriate. But Peres loved the attention and the honors, and turned a deaf ear to his critics.

The conference was soon over and ninety-year-old Peres was back in his office, his agenda more hectic than ever.

CHAPTER 36.

ALONE

Peres's life as President was not always as intense. In his free evenings, when no formal event or official dinner was scheduled, he again felt lonely. The staff would leave the residence in the early evening, and Peres would be left alone, with two body-guards. Even the kitchen staff would go home. "They leave me a few things in the kitchen," Peres told me, "and I fix something to eat." These were lonely dinners, of a lonely man in a big house, who sat by himself in front of the television, switching channels. On Sabbath or a holiday, Peres often was all alone in the res-idence, and friends and family members would visit him for a while, trying to dispel his solitude. But his friends died one after another, and he grimly watched the emptiness they had left, from the height of his advanced age.

Indeed, with all the fame and glory of his political and inter-national position Peres badly needed friends – friends, in whose presence he could discard his official attire, have a drink or two and relax in his armchair in slippers and an old pair of jeans. He yearned for the wonders of free speech, without restraints, with-out political correctness, without fearing that his words might be leaked to the media or the ears of some conniving politician.

That was not only a dream. For more than twenty years Peres kept very close ties with a group of 7-8 younger friends, who loved and admired him. The group was called "the Haim Cohen team", after its founder. The author of this book was a member of that team. Peres used to secretly meet with his friends every couple of weeks, and thoroughly enjoy their warmth and esteem. Only in their company did he allow himself to boast about his achievements in Israel and abroad, and quote with delight the words of praise that world leaders had bestowed upon him. He also had frank – at times harsh, quite unpresidential – words for his rivals, and for political leaders, including those at the country's helm. Often he would plunge in his memories, and find excuses for each of his political failures. These would always be a treacherous politician, an unexpected event, a sudden crisis, that he would accuse of this or that fiasco. Perhaps that capacity to find other culprits than himself instilled in him the force to rise and try again, the hope that next time he will make it. In the company of the Haim Cohen team he also would praise his own successes as a politician and a statesman. He would often exaggerate in his descriptions but most of his guests preferred enjoying him to contradicting him.

 Not a word of these conversations ever leaked to the media; nor did the country hear about the yearly dinner the Haim Cohen team organized for Peres's birthday. The dinner was always held in a team member's home. The team would choose an evening in August, and come with their wives and a few chosen members of Peres's senior staff. Each team member had a part: some would don starched aprons and cook, others would bring bread and fruit, cheeses, wine and desserts. A couple would lead the party in singing vintage pioneer songs and Peres would join with enthusiasm. Often he would dance with some of the ladies. He enjoyed these dinners thoroughly, but then he would go back home alone.

*

All his life Shimon had been a loner. But his loneliness became utterly painful when Sonia left him.

During the last few years Sonia got far away from the political world; she hated the public life and told her husband: "Shimon, enough!" She hated political maneuvering and politicians' hypocrisy and wanted to tear her husband away from anything that had to do with politics.

Shimon was always alone at political events and public meetings. Sonia joined him at a few trips abroad but that ended as well. The last time she had joined him was when he flew to Oslo to receive the Nobel Peace Prize, together with Yitzhak Rabin and Yasser Arafat. The rift reached its peak when she refused to join him at the huge party for his eightieth birthday. It was held in the Culture Palace in Tel Aviv for two thousand five-hundred guests, including friends, ministers, prime ministers and presidents from all over the world. Sonia stayed home and watched it on television. According to some family members, one of them was so shocked by her behavior that he refused to speak with her for several months. The only voice that defended her was Shimon's. That's her right, he claimed, she must act as she feels she should.

Shortly before Shimon was elected President, Sonia told me: "Tell Shimon that I won't join him in Jerusalem, at the President's house." I told Peres, but he said: "Don't worry, she'll come." But she didn't. He hoped to convince her, but failed. On Election day Sonia didn't appear at the Knesset Gallery. After Shimon was elected, he told her over the phone: "You married a shepherd – and you got a president." She fired back: "I prefer a shepherd." She was always utterly truthful and sincere – and when she said something, she meant it.

Even before the election, Sonia placed an impossible choice before Shimon: he should either resign from all his public duties (including the presidency that was yet to come) and join her in an old-age home—or each of them would go their own ways. "She thought that I had done enough," Shimon said, "and wanted that we grew old together, quietly. I felt that as long as I still had the force to contribute to the country I couldn't stay home."[1]

And when he rejected her request, Sonia left him, and left him in anger. She demanded that he immediately take his books and stuff from their home, and made sure to be out of the house when he came. She changed her name to Sonia Gal (the Hebrew version of her maiden name, Gelman) and replaced the sign on the house intercom, that read now Sonia Gal instead of Sonia Peres. There could be no doubt that she wanted to cut all ties to Shimon.

How painful it was for Shimon and Sonia's friends to witness that separation between two people who loved each other passionately; how painful it was to see him alone in his lofty mansion in Jerusalem—and her, in her long, embroidered gallabiyah dress, shopping in the neighborhood supermarket or driving her old ramshackle car to one of her volunteering missions – as if she lived on another planet.

And yet, with all her anger, Sonia still loved Shimon and Shimon missed her badly; and in some of his interviews the President frankly spoke of his love for her. "I miss Sonia" he admitted in a press interview. "Sometimes I am lonely. She remains the love of my life, but it is not enough anymore. Women feel hurt by things that men do not even understand."[2] That seemed to be a veiled hint – perhaps she would change her mind and come back to him. Deep in his heart he hoped that one day—during his presidency or perhaps after he completed his term—the two of them would get back together.

But fate had other plans. On January 20, 2011, Sonia died in her sleep at the age of 87. It seemed that somewhere in heaven a decision was taken that a woman like her was worthy of leaving us quietly, modestly, in a painless death.

Tidy and orderly as she was, she had decided long ago where she would be laid to rest. Her wish was not to be buried in The Great Leaders of the Nation's plot on Mount Herzl, as a President's wife. She was buried in Ben Shemen where she had grown up and where she had fallen in love with Shimon. Shimon added his own phrase to the inscription on her tombstone: "I loved you at first sight, I will love you till my last. Shimon."

Sonia's memory kept on haunting Shimon. On Israel's sixty-third Independence Day he said in a press interview: "Sonia lives inside me and with me to this very day and my love is with her, I can feel it. There was not a moment in my life that I did not respect and love her. This love was mutual."[3]

Yet, with Sonia's death Shimon remained lonelier than ever.

On July 24 2014, after seven years of presidency, Shimon Peres completed his term, and Reuven Rivlin was elected President after him.

Shimon came back to Tel Aviv, but not to his old home. "I don't see in this [apartment] a home", he said, as he walked into his new lodging by the sea. "I see walls, and I see loneliness between them. Children – that's a home. Sonia was home. She was the center of my life. I saw in our old apartment my home, but I didn't want to stay there. I didn't want to live there with the memories."[4]

CHAPTER 37.

GONE

He returned to his old love – making peace with the Palestinians -and moved his headquarters to the Peres Center for Peace. Its new home was a concrete and glass structure, perched on top of a hill in Jaffa, overlooking the sea and flanked by an old Muslim cemetery and a park gently descending to a golden beach. Shimon's office overlooked the sea. He brought over most of his female staff and immediately plunged into intense activity – organizing Jewish-Arab encounters, technology courses for Arab women, medical assistance to the Palestinians, an ambitious project to absorb 10,000 Arab engineers in Israel's high-tech industry, creating bonds between Jewish and Palestinian children by social networks, organizing soccer games between Arab and Jewish kids...

His agenda filled again with meetings and speeches, his opinions and statements reappeared on the front pages; again he traveled abroad, meeting heads of state and dignitaries, raising money for his projects and speaking to huge audiences. An American TV network found out that he was getting the highest fees in the world for his lectures – 300,000 dollars, which he transferred directly to the Center.

I asked him what was the secret of his vitality, and Peres answered: "Three things: First – don't look back. The past has no importance, only the future. Always look forward to the future.

Second – don't bother with small, trivial things, always deal with great projects, visions, programs and dreams. And third – never retire. You retire – you die!"

*

On January 14 2016 Peres suffered a mild heart attack and underwent a cardiac angioplasty that opened a blocked artery. He was hospitalized again with heart fibrillation and finally received a pacemaker. He announced several times that after being "refurbished" he would go back to his intensive agenda, speeches and travels. But deep inside he was worried. He always was proud of his stunning health, of his unusual physical capacity, and many saw his presence and tremendous activity as something eternal. But for the first time he discovered that even his health had its limits and he felt forced to adopt a slower rhythm. He realized that time was running short.

And yet, on July 21 2016, in a moving ceremony, he inaugurated the transformation of the Peres Center for Peace into the Peres Center for Peace and Innovation. An audience including the leaders of Israel's hi-tech watched with wonder Jewish and Arab youths, alongside successful young man and women, display their inventions and applications that had rightly crowned Israel with the title "start-up nation". President Rivlin, Prime Minister Netanyahu and their host, Peres, made enthusiastic speeches about development, research and the unique Israeli quality of thinking out of the box, that had turned Israel into a scientific Mecca. There was no doubt that the Center would soon become a hothouse for talent and creativity in technology, industry and agriculture.

The name change of the Peres Center, however, contained a hint of defeat. The Center for Peace had been active for twenty years now, and hundreds of millions of dollars had been invested in its initiatives. But it could claim no significant success in its pursuit of peace. True, the Center's staff had launched intensive dialogues, moving encounters, computer courses, medical assistance and soccer games – but except for the isolated cases of a few bold Palestinians who spoke a few words in support of peace, nothing had changed; and peacemaking between the two peoples had not progressed. Many of those who came on that sunny July morning to the glass building facing the Jaffa beach, hoped that the new direction the Center was taking would produce more tangible results.

So the Center for Innovation, with the hopes it embodied for more understanding and cooperation with the Israeli Arabs and the Palestinians, was to become the personal and Zionist testament of Shimon Peres.

*

A couple of weeks after the pacemaker was planted inside him, after speaking for two hours before hundreds of hi-tech researchers and foreign investors, Peres felt unwell and was rushed to the hospital where he lost consciousness. He had suffered a severe stroke with bleeding in the brain. He immediately was sedated and intubated; his family and his personal doctor, who also was his son in law—Professor Rafi Walden, hurried to the hospital. Media reporters arrived immediately, while Israeli and world leaders, the Pope, and thousands of admirers throughout the world dispatched wishes of recovery and prayed for his life. The President of Israel, the Prime Minister and hundreds of citizens came to the hospital where he was fighting for his life.

Peres did not regain consciousness. He died two weeks later, on September 28. His death was a shock for the people of Israel, both his supporters and opponents. For many his death was also the death of their dream for peace. One of the first to react was President Obama who called Peres's children with condolences and published an unusually long statement. "I will always be grateful that I was able to call Shimon my friend," Obama wrote, "Shimon was the essence of Israel itself."

Ninety delegations from seventy countries brought to Peres's funeral hundreds of statesmen, presidents, prime ministers and ministers, kings and princes. But the Arab nations boycotted the funeral of this man who had restlessly fought for achieving peace with them. Except for Mahmud Abbas, the Chairman of the Palestinian Authority, no Arab dignitary came to Mount Herzl. Angry Palestinian crowds, and many of their leaders, screamed insults to Abbas for his "treachery". The Arab-Israeli Knesset members also boycotted the funeral, spewing vicious verbal attacks on Peres. It was sad to see the Arab leaders turning their backs to this man, who had offered them an olive branch.

In a poignant ceremony, the world bade farewell to Peres. One after the other, a few men and a woman, standing beside the coffin and framed by Israeli flags waving in the wind, pronounced their eulogies to Shimon. Israel's President Rivlin turned to Peres. "You were our heart," he said," a heart that loved the state, the country and the people. You were the fountain of youth of all of us, the man whom we thought time could never stop... Your death is the sealing of an era, the end of the age of the giants." Prime Minister Netanyahu recalled the moving speech of Shimon on the open grave of his brother, Yoni Netanyahu, the fallen hero of the Entebbe raid. "You cried then, Shimon," Netanyahu said: "and today I am crying for you. I loved you, dear man, outstanding leader."

President Clinton said he "always was in awe of Shimon's endless capacity to move beyond even those crushing setbacks in order to seize the possibilities of any new day." Writer Amos Oz stressed Peres's unswerving effort to reach peace, that was inevitable as both the Israelis and the Palestinians have nowhere else to go. The three children of Peres, the sons Chemi and Yoni and the daughter Zvia (Tziki) paid a moving tribute to their father. Yoni recalled that when he asked Shimon what inscription should be engraved on his tombstone, his 93-year old father answered: "Died Prematurely."

The last to speak was President Obama. "I would be the tenth US President since John F. Kennedy to sit down with Shimon", he said, "the tenth to fall prey to his charms." In a sweeping narration he described Peres's life from his birth in the Polish shtetl, then moved to his own. "As an American, a Christian, a person partly of African descent, born in Hawaii – a place that could not be further than where Shimon spent his youth – I took great pleasure in my friendship with this older, wiser man… I think our friendship was rooted in the fact that I could somehow see myself in his story, and maybe he could see himself in mine. Because for all our differences, both of us had lived such unlikely lives. It was so surprising to see the two of us where we had started, talking together in the White House, meeting here in Israel. And I think both of us understood that we were here only because in some way we reflected the magnificent story of our nations."

Obama concluded his speech by the Hebrew words "Todah Rabah Chaver Yakar " – Thank you very much, dear friend.[1]

.

After the funeral many said that one person was missing from this dramatic gathering – Shimon Peres himself.

And what would he have said – if he only could – when departing?

Here is what he wrote probably about himself, in his poem: "A prayer for the road":

"No, I am not a bloodthirsty hunter
  Nor a desperate and naïve man –
  Didn't I swear – you won't break, man!
  For this who falls is he who rises.
  And when, abyss, on your edge I'll stand –
  From my heart won't virtue be undone."[2]

ACKNOWLEDGMENTS

IT IS A PLEASANT TASK to thank those who have supported and assisted me in the writing of this book. First I should thank the devoted team that worked with me, headed by Nilly Lurie-Ovnat, my research assistant for many years, who directed the research project with savvy, devotion, and personal involvement; I also thank her colleagues Limor Vidas-Yuran and Etty Abramov. Many people and institutions helped me in my work at various archives and documentation centers: Mr. Yehiel Horev of the Israel Defense Ministry; Aviva Karton, Avi Zadok, and Doron Avi-Ad in the Army Archives, under the efficient direction of Michal Tzur; Malka Liff and Hani Harmolin at Ben-Gurion's House; Dr. Tuvia Freiling, the state's archivist; and the directors and the employees of the following archives: the Labor Party Archives, in Beth Berl; the Lavon Institute, the Labor movement's archives, in Tel Aviv; Yad Tabenkin, the kibbutz movement's archives, in Ramat Ef'al; the United Kibbutz Movement's archives, in Hulda; the State Archives, in Jerusalem; the Ben-Gurion Heritage Center Archives, in Sde Boker; the Levi Eshkol Archives, in Jerusalem; the Knesset Archives, in Jerusalem; the Yediot Aharonot Archives, in Tel Aviv; the Jabotinsky Institute Archives, in Tel Aviv; the Hagana Archives, in Tel Aviv; the Mordechai Ben-Porat (private) Archives, in Or Yehuda.

I obtained important documents in foreign archives and appreciate the assistance of their employees: Archives du Ministère des Affaires Etrangères, Quai d'Orsay, Paris; Archives du

Service Historique de l'Armée de Terre and Archives du Service Historique de l'Armée de l'Air, Château de Vincennes, Paris; Public Record Office, Kew, London; National Archives, College Park, Maryland (including materials from several presidential libraries); President Jimmy Carter's archives, the Carter Center, Atlanta, Georgia.

I interviewed Shimon Peres himself more than a hundred times. His sons and especially his daughter, Dr. Zvia Valdan, willingly cooperated. I also received the assistance of Peres's office: Hannah Kohavi, who was in charge of Peres's archives; the secretaries' team; and the senior officials Yona Bartal, Yoram Dori, and the Peres Center director, Efrat Duvdevani.

The late Moshe Shalit, Peres's friend and lawyer, and Minister Yitzhak Herzog were of great assistance. My son the lawyer, Gil Bar-Zohar, gave me fine legal advice.

NOTES AND REFERENCES

Almost 90 percent of the bibliographical material for this book is in Hebrew. Therefore I decided not to append a bibliography to this English-language edition. Those who would like to research the books, articles, and documents I used should refer to the Hebrew version of the book, *Shimon Peres*, published by Yediot Aharonot, Tel Aviv. For the same reason, I didn't include here a list of the hundreds of people I interviewed. The list appears, in detail, in the Hebrew version of the book.As for the books and articles quoted in the notes, I translated the titles of both books and articles into English, for the reader to understand what the book or the article was about. I saw no reason to quote the hundreds of books and articles in Hebrew, except to exasperate the foreign reader. Books, articles, and documents are marked with the letter (E) for English, (F) for French, and (S) for Spanish. All the others are in Hebrew.

A final remark about the interviews: most of them were done for this book. Some, however, had been done for my former books, and I used them if they happened to be relevant for this book. People such as David Ben-Gurion, Moshe Dayan, Yitzhak Rabin, Guy Mollet, Christian Pineau, Maurice Bourgès-Maunoury, Abel Thomas, General Pierre Koenig, Wernher von Braun, and others are long gone; they are still very much alive, however, in my archives and in their historical roles.

ABBREVIATIONS

AA	Army Archives
BGA	Ben-Gurion's Archives
BGA2	Archives of the Institute for Ben-Gurion's Heritage
BGD	Ben-Gurion's Diary
DDF	Documents Diplomatiques Français
DS	Department of State
FRUS	Foreign Relations of the United States
LPA	Labor Party Archives
PRO	Public Record Office, London
SP	Shimon Peres
SPD	Shimon Peres's Diary
USNA	United States National Archives

PROLOGUE NOVEMBER 4, 1995

1. The author was present at the scene,
2. Ibid.
3. Interview with Shimon Peres (henceforth SP).
4. Ibid.
5. Ibid.
6. Ibid.
7. Interview with Dov Goldstein, coauthor of Rabin's autobiography.

PART ONE: BLUE SHIRT AND KHAKI PANTS

CHAPTER 1: A VOYAGE IN A SUBWAY

1. Interview with SP.

2. Shimon Peres and Robert Littell, For the Future of Israel (Baltimore: Johns Hopkins University Press, 1998) (E), p. 9.
3. Shimon Peres, "Youth's Draft," Prosa, a Literary Magazine, 1981.
4. Haim Abramson, ed., The Memorial Book of the Vishneva Community (Tel Aviv: 1972), p. 21.
5. Shimon Peres, "An Autobiographical Note," manuscript, no date, Army Archives (henceforth AA).
6. Ibid.
7. Shimon Peres, with David Landau, Battling for Peace (London: Weidenfeld and Nicolson, Orion edition, 1995) (E), p. 12.
8. Peres, "Youth's Draft."
9. Interview with Gershon Peres.
10. Interview with Shula Lilian, Sarah Persky's niece.
11. Getzel Persky, "Recollections of a Merchant," in Abramson, The Memorial Book, p. 172.
12. Peres, Battling, p. 9.
13. Rafael Bashan, "When I Was Sixteen," Ma'ariv Lanoar, 17 Sept. 1957.
14. Peres, Battling, p. 15.
15. Interview with Gershon Peres.
16. Ibid. Shimon Peres denies his brother's account.
17. Interview with Oded Israeli, Shimon's cousin.
18. Peres, "Autobiographical Note," and Battling, p. 9.
19. Peres and Littell, For the Future, pp. 3-4.
20. Abramson, The Memorial Book, photographs.
21. Interview with Shimon Podverski, who was originally from Vishneva, 22.
22. Abramson, The Memorial Book, p. 173.
23. And not in 1934, as told by Shimon Peres. Interviews with Peres family members; interview with Gershon Peres.
24. Interview with SP.
25. Peres and Littell, For the Future, p. 9.

CHAPTER 2: THE TALL SYCAMORES

1. Peres, "Autobiographical Note."
2. Peres, Battling, p. 18.
3. Interview with SP.
4. Peres, Battling, p. 19.
5. Peres, "Autobiographical Note."
6. Interview with Rafael Vardi.
7. Ibid.
8. Interview with SP's classmate Batya Yogev (Korngold).
9. Shimon Peres, "Misunderstood," manuscript, 1937.
10. Interview with Rafael Vardi.
11. Interview with Hephzibah Cohen (Levy).
12. Interview with SP.
13. Peres, Battling, p. 22.
14. Ibid.
15. Ibid.; interview with SP.
16. Matti Golan, Peres (Tel Aviv: Shocken, 1982), p. 11.
17. Interview with SP; exchange of letters between Peres and Mulla Cohen throughout the years.
18. Interview with Gershon Peres.
19. Golan, Peres, p. 11.
20. Interview with Rafael Vardi.
21. Peres, Battling, p. 24.
22. Ibid.
23. Interview with Moshe Shalit.
24. Shimon Peres, "Remarks," Nativ, April 1938 (stenciled copy).
25. Interview with Moshe Shalit.
26. Interview with Ambassador Moshe Er'el, Shimon's classmate.
27. Interview with Itzhak Shemer, Shimon's classmate.
28. Peres, Battling, p. 26.

CHAPTER 3: A GREEN BOWL IN AN OCEAN OF HATRED

1. Shimon Persky, "Why I Aspire to Study and Live in Ben-Shemen," manuscript, September 1938.
2. Interview with SP.
3. Shimon Peres, interview for a radio program, Unknown Land, for the sixtieth anniversary of Ben-Shemen, 15 Nov. 1987.
4. Interview with David Landau.
5. Unknown Land SP interview.
6. Shimon Peres, "Son of His Generation," autobiographical notes, AA.
7. Interview with Amos Oz.
8. Interview with Aliza Eshed.

9. Shimon Persky, "Harvest," Bamaaleh 10 (199), 2 June 1939.
10. Interview with SP.
11. Peres, "Youth's Draft."
12. Ibid.
13. Peres, "Harvest."
14. Unknown Land SP interview.
15. Peres, "Youth's Draft."
16. Interview with SP; Peres, "Son of His Generation."
17. Peres, "Youth's Draft."
18. Ibid.
19. Ibid.
20. Interview with Avraham Greidinger.
21. Peres, Battling, p. 40; interview with Nachman Raz.
22. Shimon Ben-Amotz (Persky), "As Time Goes By," manuscript, 9 March 1939, AA.
23. Peres, Battling, p. 38.
24. Interview with SP; interview with Nachman Raz.
25. Interview with SP.

CHAPTER 4: A MAN IN LOVE

1. Peres, "Youth's Draft."
2. Interview with SP.
3. Interview with Hannah Yishai.
4. David Ben-Gurion, "An Effort to Establish a Jewish State," 12 Sept. 1939, Bamaaracha (Tel Aviv: Am Oved, 1957), vol. 3, p. 18.
5. Interview with Avrahan Greidinger.
6. Interview with SP.
7. Shimon Persky, draft of a letter to Sonia, manuscript, no date, AA.
8. Shimon Persky, letter to the members of Working Youth, manuscript, no date, AA.
9. Peres, draft letter to Sonia.
10. Interview with SP.
11. Peres, Battling, p. 41.
12. Shimon Persky, letter to his comrades in Geva, 1941.
13. Interview with Nachman Raz, member of Kibbutz Geva.
14. Golan, Peres, p. 17.
15. Interview with Nachman Raz.
16. Interview with SP.
17. Interview with Nachman Raz.
18. Interview with Ben-Ami Rivlin, SP's friend.
19. Shimon Persky "Autobluffography," manuscript, no date (apparently from the years 1940—42). It is not clear if the article was ever published. AA.
20. Ben-Ami Rivlin, "Memorandum on Working Youth's First Journey to Masada," June 1999, Labor Archives, Hulda.
21. Shimon Peres, "Shmaria Gutman," in Hagit Goren, ed., Shmaria (Kibbutz Naan, 1997), pp. 34-38.
22. Avshalom Zoreff, letter to Shimon Persky, manuscript, January 1942, AA. Zoreff worked in the organization department of Working Youth.
23. Rivlin, "Memorandum."
24. Copy of the scroll, signed by the participants, Labor Archives, Hulda.
25. Shimon Persky, "The Moving Stone," manuscript, no date, AA; "The Moving Stone," Bamaaleh 4 (261), 27 Feb. 1942; interviews with SP and Ben-Ami Rivlin; and Rivlin, "Memorandum."
26. Ben-Ami Melamed, "Diary of the Masada Expedition," unpublished, private archive.
27. Ibid.
28. Interview with SP.
29. Interview with Nachman Raz.

CHAPTER 5: FIERCE WINDS

1. Shimon Persky, "At Poriya," Bamaaleh 21 (278), 29 Nov. 1942.
2. Shimon Persky, "A Song to Lake Kinneret," SPA.
3. Shimon Persky, draft letter to Sonia, AA.
4. Persky, "At Poriya."
5. Shimon Persky, handwritten notes, undated, AA; interview with SP.
6. Shimon Persky, "A Few Remarks on the Marriage in the Kibbutz—to Elhanan and Hannah on Their Wedding Day," The Kibbutz Bulletin, Working Youth, Kibbutz Alumot, Poriya, number 18; "The Man's Speech," remarks on the wedding day, undated, AA; "The Bachelor Song," manuscript, undated, AA.
7. Interview with Micha Talmon.
8. Interview with SP.
9. Shimon Persky, draft letter to "The Strange Sonia," manuscript, undated, AA.
10. Shimon Persky, draft letter to "A woman soldier," manuscript, undated, AA.
11. Ibid.

12. Shimon Persky, "The Voyage to Aqaba," lecture, 23 Jan. 1945. The minutes were transcribed by Arye Katz, and served as the basis for SP's articles in Bamaaleh ("Landscapes and Arroyos in the Negev," Bamaaleh 3 [330], 9 Feb. 1945), and in Al Hamedukha, Shevat-Adar, 5705, by the Hebrew calendar.
13. Peres, "Shmaria Gutman," p. 37.
14. Persky, "Voyage to Aqaba."
15. Ibid.
16. Ibid. A similar account is published in Shimon Peres, "We Haven't Been There for Two Thousand Years," Davar, 24 Jan. 1945.
17. Persky, "Voyage to Aqaba."
18. Peres, "We Haven't Been There."
19. Interview with SP; also Golan, Peres, pp. 19-20.
20. Davar, 17 Jan. 1945.
21. Ibid.
22. Interview with SP; and Golan, Peres, p. 21.

CHAPTER 6: HERBS AND LIZARDS

1. The story of the captivity and the actions of Getzel Persky during World War II is based on the interviews of Gershon Peres, Shimon Peres, and Zvia Waldan; and on Orly Azulai-Katz, "The Man Who Didn't Know How to Win," Yediot Akaronot, 1996, pp. 38-40; see also Shimon Peres, "He Knew No Fear," Monitin, September 1983, pp. 51-53, and Peres, Battling, pp. 57-60. The most important source is Getzel Persky's testimony of 14 Jan. 1965, deposited with Aaron Hoter Ishay, attorney at law. See also John Castle, The Password Is Courage (London: Souvenir Press, 1954).
2. Peres, Battling, p. 60.
3. Ibid., p. 58.
4. Peres, "He Knew No Fear."
5. Peres, Battling, p. 57.
6. Interview with Shulamit Aloni.
7. Golan, Peres, p. 21.

CHAPTER 7: THE FIFTH CONGRESS

1. Baruch Eisenstadt, I. Baunberg, and Shimon Persky, "Report on Working Youth," presented to David Ben-Gurion, 27 Oct. 1944.
2. Interviews with Nachman Raz and Amos Degani, members of the Working Youth bureau.
3. Interview with Nachman Raz.
4. Interview with Amos Degani.
5. Interview with Munia Admati, a Working Youth activist.
6. Interview with Saul Bauman.
7. Interview with Amnon Magen.
8. Interview with an Ahdut Ha'avoda activist.
9. Peres, Battling, p. 55.
10. Interview with Amnon Magen.
11. Yitzhak Nishri, at a symposium with Binyamin Hachlili, "Comrades Participate in a Discussion," published by Working Youth, Yad Tabenkin, 31 Jan. 1989, p. 23.
12. Letter from the bureau of the Mapai kibbutz movement to Kibbutz Alumot, 20 Dec. 1945.
13. Shimon Persky, "In a Dove's Coop," 5 Dec. 1946 (SP mistakenly wrote the date of 3 Nov.), AA.
14. Shimon Persky, "The Congress Inaugural Session," manuscript, 9 Dec. 1946, AA.
15. Shimon Persky, "The Congress and the Nation," Mishmeret, 9 Jan. 1947 (written in Basel on 20 Dec. 1946).
16. Shimon Persky, "From a Bee's Mouth" (regular column), Ashmoret 5 (24), 30 Jan. 1947.
17. Peres, Battling, p. 66.
18. Shimon Peres, "The Invalides," Bamaaleh 1-2, 21 Jan. 1947, pp. 377-78.

CHAPTER 8: A NEW WORLD

1. Interview with SP; Davar, 1 Oct. 1965; Golan, Peres, pp. 27-28.
2. Reports from the Haganah envoys, sent to Shimon Peres among others, 11 and 27 Nov. 1948, etc. Yad Tabenkin Archives.
3. Peres, Battling, pp. 71-72.
4. Ibid.
5. Interview with SP.
6. Ben-Gurion's diary (henceforth BGD), 19 Jan. 1948 (without mention of names), 22 Jan. 1948.
7. BGD, 23 Jan. 1948.
8. Shimon Peres, draft papers and plans for the conquest of Eilat, "Summary of a Memorandum for the Conquest of Eilat and the Arava Desert," undated. Ben-Gurion's archives (henceforth BGA).
9. Note from the defense minister to the Navy General Staff, 12 April 1949, AA.
10. Peres, Battling, p. 93.
11. Interview with Uri Avnery.
12. Interview with Tzvi Tzur.
13. Interview with Yossef Nahmias.

14. Ibid., quoted by Yossef Nahmias.
15. Interview with Dov Goldstein.
16. Interview with Izhar Smilansky (the writer S. Izhar).
17. Interview with SP.
18. Shimon Peres, Personal Army File, 678444/M, AA.
19. Peres, Battling, p. 88.
20. Peres and Littell, For the Future, p. 54.
21. Affidavit of the Drafting Center, Army Headquarters, Ministry of Defense. "Subject: Persky Shimon 45546," 25 Aug. 1948. This affidavit with adjoining documents are kept in Shimon Peres's file under the original number, 45546. After his conscription was annulled the file was shelved; when he was drafted in 1952 a new file was established, with a regular military number, 678444/M, AA.
22. Ibid., handwritten note in Peres's personal army file.
23. Peres, personal army file.
24. Interview with SP.
25. Interview with SP; Shimon Peres, "A Language Is Like a Red-Cheeked Apple," university essay (E), 1950, AA.
26. Peres, Battling, p. 96.
27. Peres, "A Language."
28. Interview with Al Schwimmer.
29. Interview with SP.
30. Golan, Peres, p. 30.
31. Interview with SP; also Shimon Peres, David's Sling (Jerusalem: Weidenfeld and Nicolson, 1970), p. 100.
32. Ibid., pp. 100-101.
33. Golan, Peres, pp. 30-32.
34. Interview with SP.
35. Ibid.; also Golan, Peres, pp. 29–30.
36. Shimon Peres and Abba Eban, telegrams to Foreign Minister Moshe Sharett, 25 Nov. 1951; Shimon Peres, telegram to General Mordechai Makleff, 25 Nov. 1951, AA.
37. Shimon Peres, letter to Dr. M. Rosenbluth, Treasury of the State of Israel, New York, 31 Dec. 1951 (E); Fanny Speiser, Jewish Agency, memorandum to Shimon Peres (E), 27 Nov. 1951.
38. Shimon Peres, letter to Samuel Bronfman (E), New York, 1 Jan. 1952.
39. Interview with SP.
40. David Ben-Gurion, letter to Kibbutz Alumot, 1 Feb. 1952.
41. Interview with Tzvia Valdan.
42. Interview with SP.
43. Interview with Sonia Peres for the film Alumot.
44. Shimon Peres, Entebbe journal (Tel Aviv: Idanim, 1991), p. 9.
45. Interview with Tzvi Tzur.

CHAPTER 9: DEATH ON THE NILE

1. Interview with SP.
2. Moshe Sharett, Journal (Tel Aviv: Marriv Editions, 1978), entry for 29 Nov. 1953.
3. For instance, BGD, 3 May 1958.
4. Interview with Meir Amit.
5. Interviews with Haim Israeli and others.
6. Peres, Entebbe, p. 11.
7. Interview with SP.
8. Peres, Entebbe, p. 10.
9. Conversations of the author with Moshe Dayan.
10. Interview with SP.
11. Interview with Tzvi Tzur and others; also see Golan, Feres, p. 35.
12. Peres, Battling, p. 178.
13. Interview with SP.
14. Sharett, Journal, 18 Jan. 1955.
15. Quotes of Ze'ev Sherf and Zvi Maimon in Colonel Nehemia Argov's private diary, 10 Aug. 1954.
16. Golda Meir, My Life (Tel Aviv: Maariv Editions, 1975), p. 210.
17. Interview with Mordechai Makleff; also Shabtai Tevet, Moshe Dayan (Tel Aviv: Shocken, 1971), pp. 416-20.
18. Peres, Battling, p. 99.
19. BGD, 6 Feb. 1954.
20. Peres, Battling, p. 100.
21. Nehemia Argov's diary, 9 June 1954.
22. Pinhas Lavon's remarks at a high-level meeting, 17 Oct. 1960; BGA.
23. Moshe Dayan's diary, 18 June 1954.
24. Nehemia Argov's diary, op. cit.
25. Moshe Dayan's diary, 18 June 1954.
26. Nehemia Argov's diary, 10 Aug. 1954; BGD, 7 Aug. 1954.
27. BGD, 24 Aug. 1954.
28. Hagai Eshed, Who Gave the Order (Tel Aviv: Yediot Aharonot, 1979), p. 45.
29. Nathan Alterman, "The Open Page," Davar, 11 Feb. 1955.
30. Sharett, Journal, 5 Jan. 1955.

31. Epi Evron, Lavon's assistant, letter to Elhanan Yishai; also Elhanan Yishai, letter to Shimon Peres, 20 June 1957.
32. Roni Medzini, The Proud Jewess: A Biography of Golda Meir (Tel Aviv: Yediot Aharonot, 1990), p. 216.
33. Peres, Battling, pp. 104-5.
34. Yitzhak Olshan, Memoirs (Tel Aviv and Jerusalem: Shocken, 1978), pp. 268-69, 285-86.
35. Olshan, Memoirs, pp. 268–69.
36. Justice Yitzhak Olshan, letter to Peres, 9 Oct. 1976.
37. Haim Israeli, Megilat Haim (Tel Aviv: Yediot Aharonot, 2005), p. 119.
38. Sharett, Journal, 11 and 18 Jan. 1955.
39. Argov's diary, 12 Feb. 1955.
40. Pinhas Lavon, letter to Sharett, 2 Feb. 1955.
41. Interview with SP; also Peres, Battling, p. 105.
42. Note of Ben-Gurion, 10 Oct. 1960.
43. Shimon Peres, draft of a letter to Shaul Avigur, 3 March 1955.
44. Argov's diary, 15 Feb. 1955.
45. Sharett, Journal, 7 Feb. 1955.
46. Ibid., 11 Feb. 1955.
47. Ibid.
48. Peres, draft of a letter to Avigur.
49. BGD, 17 Feb. 1955.
50. Peres, draft of a letter to Avigur.

PART TWO: OUR FRIEND AND OUR ALLY

CHAPTER 10: THE MAN IN THE BLUE SUIT

1. Elkana Gali, "Song of Praise for a Young Man," Davar, 18 Jan. 1957.
2. Shimon Peres, "The Night of the Decision, 1956," typed script, p. 15.
3. Ibid., p. 4.
4. Interview with Avraham Ben-Yossef.
5. Defense Committee, 11 July 1955, London, Secret (E), PRO; "Brief for Secretary of State, Centurion Tanks for Israel," 6 July 1955, London (E), PRO.
6. "Aide-Memoire on the Supply of Mystère Aircraft by France to Israel," August 1955, Foreign Office, London (E), PRO.
7. Jack Nicholls, British Embassy, Tel Aviv, letter to C.A.E. Shuckburgh, Foreign Office, London, 6 Aug. 1955, Secret (E), PRO.
8. Peres, "Night of the Decision," p. 29.
9. Pinhas Lavon, letter to Shimon Peres, 29 Jan. 1954.
10. Interview with SP.
11. Interview with Arthur Ben-Nathan.
12. Peres's diary, quoted in "Night of the Decision," pp. 31-32.
13. Interview with Mira Avrech; also Mira Avrech, The Small World of the World's Great Men (Tel Aviv: Idanim, 1990), p. 54.
14. Yossef Levite, "From a Bullet to a Vautour," Bamahane, 2 Dec. 1958.
15. Interview with Diomède Catroux.
16. Report of the Director General to the Israeli Cabinet, 24 Oct. 1954.
17. BGD, 2 May 1955.
18. Interview with General Pierre Koenig.
19. Shimon Peres, letter to General Koenig, 9 May 1955, Archives du Quai d'Orsay, Cabinet du Ministre, Afrique-Levant 34, dossier 97-98 (F); also Shimon Peres, report to the defense minister, 25 May 1955, AA.
20. Peres, report to the defense minister, 25 May 1955, AA.
21. Interview with Aliza Eshed, Peres's chief of staff; personal letters from Maurice Bourgès-Maunoury, Abel Thomas, and others.
22. Shimon Peres, letter to Haim Laskov, 2 March 1955.
23. Shimon Peres, telegram to Yossef Nahmias, 27 Sept. 1955.
24. John Foster Dulles, U.S. Delegation at the Foreign Ministers' Meetings, telegram to the Department of State, Secret, 3 Nov. 1955 (E), Department of State (henceforth DS) Central Files, 396.1-GE/11-355, also at Foreign Relations of the United States (henceforth FRUS), 1955–1957, vol. 14, pp. 705–7 (E).
25. Report of the Director General to the heads of the Defense Ministry, 21 Dec. 1955.
26. Ibid.
27. Ibid.
28. Shimon Peres, telegram to Chief of Staff Moshe Dayan and Colonel Nehemia Argov, 16 Nov. 1955.
29. Shimon Peres, telegram to the Defense Minister and the Chief of Staff, 12 Nov. 1955.
30. Report of the Director General to the heads of the Defense Ministry (restricted), 19 Dec. 1955.
31. Peres, David's Sling, p. 37.
32. Interview with SP.
33. Report of the Director General, 19 Dec. 1955.
34. Interview with SP; also report of the Director General to the heads of the Defense Ministry, 28 Dec. 1955.
35. Ibid.

36. Telegram from the Embassy in France to the Department of State, 17 Dec.1955. Top Secret (E), Department of State, Conference Files, Lot 60, D627, CF638; also in FRUS, 1955-1957, vol. 14, pp. 876-78.
37. Memorandum of a Conversation, Secretary Dulles' Residence, Washington, 30 Dec. 1955, Top Secret (E), DS S/S-NEA files: Lot 61, D417, Alpha Volume 16.
38. For example, telegram from the Embassy of Israel to the Department of State, 21 Dec. 1955 (E), SD Central Files, 684A, 86/12-1955.
39. Telegram from the Department of State to the Embassy in Egypt, Washington, 22 Nov. 1955 (E), SD Central Files, 684A, 86-11-2255.
40. Telegram from John Foster Dulles at the Embassy in France to the Department of State, 17 Dec. 1955 (E).
41. Mordechai Bar-On, Challenge and Quarrel (Beersheba: The Center of Ben-Gurion Heritage, 1991), p. 114.
42. Interview with SP; also Yossef Evron, For a Rainy Day (Tel Aviv: Otpaz, 1968), p. 25. The book is mostly based on Peres's diaries.
43. Interview with Yossef Nahmias.
44. Interview with Abel Thomas.
45. Interview with Yossef Nahmias.
46. Evron, Rainy Day, pp. 38-39.
47. Abel Thomas, Comment Israel Fut Sauvé (Paris: Albin Michel, 1978), pp. 56-58 (F).
48. Interview with Yossef Nahmias.
49. Interview with SP.
50. Interview with Guy Mollet.
51. Interview with Christian Pineau.
52. Evron, Rainy Day, pp. 145-46.
53. Ambassador Yaakov Tzur, letter to the Minister of Foreign Affairs, Christian Pineau, 22 Feb. 1956 (F), Archives du Quai d'Orsay, Cabinet du Ministre, dossier 000092-94.
54. Evron, Rainy Day, p. 28.
55. Interview with Moshe Dayan.
56. Interview with Yaakov Tzur.
57. Moshe Sharett, letter to Ben-Gurion, 3 April 1956; letter from Ben-Gurion to Sharett, 4 April 1956; letter from Sharett to Ben-Gurion, 4 April 1956.
58. Shimon Peres, letter to the National Defense Minister and the Secretary of State for Air, 3 April 1956 (F), Archives du Quay d'Orsay, Cabinet du Ministre, dossier 000088-000090.
59. Report of the Director General to the heads of the Defense Ministry, 30 April 1956.
60. Interview with Yaakov Tzur.
61. Yaakov Tzur, Paris Journal (Tel Aviv: Am Oved, 1968), pp. 242-43.
62. Peres, "Night of the Decision," pp. 35-38.
63. Ibid.
64. Ibid., p. 33.
65. Note de la Direction d'Afrique-Levant, Paris, 19 April 1956 (F), DDF 1956-1, pp. 623-24.
66. Note de la Direction d'Afrique-Levant, Paris, 11 May 1956 (F), DDF 1956-1, PP. 774-76.
67. Note de la Direction d'Afrique-Levant, Paris, 13 June 1956 (F), DDF 1956-1, pp. 985-86.
68. Note de la Direction d'Afrique-Levant, Paris, 19 June 1956 (F), DDF 1956-1, pp. 1011—12.
69. David Ben-Gurion, letter to Guy Mollet, 12 April 1956, BGA; also Peres, "Night of the Decision," pp. 38-39.
70. Shimon Peres, "Report on My Trip Abroad Between 13 April 1956 and 28 April 1956."
71. Shimon Peres, The Next Stage (Tel Aviv: Am Hasefer, 1965), pp. 30-31.
72. Peres, "Report on My Trip Abroad."
73. Interview with SP; also Peres, "Next Stage," p. 30.
74. Interview with SP; also Peres, "Next Stage," p. 32.
75. Report of the Director General to the heads of the Defense Ministry, 30 April 1956; also Peres, "Report on My Trip Abroad."
76. Report of the Director General to the heads of the Defense Ministry, 30 April 1956
77. The author, who was a foreign correspondent in Paris during the years 1959 to 1964, was a witness to Peres's nightly outings and participated in some of them.
78. Interview with Arthur Ben-Nathan.
79. Interview with Mordechai (Moka) Limon.
80. Peres, "Night of the Decision," pp. 41-43.
81. David Ben-Gurion, telegram to Shimon Peres, 24 April 1956, BGA; telegram from Peres to Ben-Gurion, 24 April 1956.
82. Minutes of a phone conversation between the Director General and the Envoy of the Defense Ministry in Europe, 1 May 1956.
83. Sharett, Journal, 13 June 1956.
84. Moshe Dayan, Milestones (Tel Aviv: Yediot Aharonot, 1976), pp. 205-6.
85. Ronen Bergman, "An Interview with Yuval Neeman," Yediot Aharonot, 18 March 2005.
86. Interview with Yossef Nahmias.
87. Yossi Goldstein, Eshkol (Jerusalem: Keter, 2003), p. 396.
88. Dayan, Milestones, p. 207.
89. Ibid., p. 210.
90. Nathan Alterman, "One of Those Nights" (read by David Ben-Gurion at the Knesset, 15 Oct. 1956).

CHAPTER 11: SUEZ

1. Shimon Peres, telegram to David Ben-Gurion and Moshe Dayan, 27 July 1956, BGA.
2. Interview with SP; also Peres, Battling, p. 139.
3. Peres, David's Sling, pp. 155-56; interview with SP.
4. Interview with SP; interview with Yossef Nahmias.
5. Michael Bar-Zohar, Ben-Gurion (Tel Aviv: Am Oved, 1978), vol. 3, pp. 1210-13.
6. Evron, Rainy Day, p. 71.
7. Dayan, Milestones, p. 228.
8. Interview with SP; Evron, Rainy Day, pp. 72-73; also Peres, David's Sling, p. 156.
9. Interview with SP; also Evron, Rainy Day, p. 73.
10. Interview with SP; also Peres, David's Sling, p. 159.
11. Interview with SP.
12. Peres, David's Sling, p. 160; also Peres, Battling, pp. 140—41.
13. BGD, 25 Sept. 1956.
14. Dayan, Milestones, p. 232.
15. Ibid., p. 230; more details about the meeting in BGD, 25 Sept. 1956.
16. BGD, 25 Sept. 1956.
17. David Ben-Gurion, letter to Golda Meir, 27 Sept. 1956, BGA.
18. Medzini, Proud Jewess, p. 239.
19. Meir Barely, From a Movement to an Apparatus (Tel Aviv: Elilev, 1974) pp. 168-69; also interview with Meir Bareli. The Mapai activist was Yitzhak Bareli, Meir's father.
20. Peres, Battling, p. 142.
21. Medzini, Proud Jewess, p. 243; also interview with SP.
22. Peres, Battling, p. 142.
23. Dayan, Milestones, p. 233; also Mordechai Bar-On, "With Golda Meir and Moshe Dayan at the Saint Germain Delegation," Maariv, 8 June 1973.
24. Minutes of the meeting at Louis Mangin's home, 30 Sept. 1956, and Dayan, Milestones, p. 234.
25. Interview with SP.
26. Peres, David's Sling, pp. 162-64.
27. Medzini, Proud Jewess, p. 243.
28. Peres, Battling, p. 142.
29. Ibid., p. 144.
30. Evron, Rainy Day, p. 92; Evron's interview with General Challe.
31. Peres, "Night of the Decision," p. 53.
32. Ibid., pp. 52-53.
33. BGD, 18 Oct. 1956.
34. Dayan's diary, 18 Oct. 1956.
35. Interview with Avraham Ben-Yossef.
36. Peres, "Night of the Decision," pp. 55-57.

CHAPTER 12: THE SECRET CONFERENCE AT SEVRES

1. Peres, "Night of the Decision," pp. 57-58.
2. Ibid., p. 60.
3. Thomas, Comment Israel (F), pp. 172-75.
4. Evron, Rainy Day, p. 127.
5. Peres, "Night of the Decision," p. 66.
6. Moshe Dayan, Story of My Life (New York: Da Capo Press, 1992) (E), p. 218.
7. Interview with Christian Pineau.
8. Peres, "Night of the Decision," p. 73.
9. Ibid., p. 74.
10. Peres, David's Sling, p. 168.
11. Interview with Christian Pineau.
12. Interview with SP.
13. Peres, Next Stage, p. 35.
14. Dayan's diary, 24 Oct. 1956; also Dayan, Story, p. 229.
15. BGD, 24 Oct. 1956.
16. Interview with SP. The author was shown the map that is kept in Peres's house.
17. Protocol (F) and appended letters, Ben-Gurion archives, Institute for Ben-Gurion's Heritage (BGA2).
18. Evron, Rainy Day, p. 144.
19. Peres, "Night of the Decision," (part 2), p. 27.

CHAPTER 13: ONE HUNDRED HOURS

1. Anthony Eden, letter to Guy Mollet, Secret and Personal, 25 Oct. 1956 (E), BGA.
2. Guy Mollet, letter to Ben-Gurion, 25 Oct. 1956; letter from Bourgès-Maunoury, 25 Oct. 1956; letter from Ben-Gurion to Guy Mollet, 26 Oct. 1956 (F), BG A2.
3. Michael Bar-Zohar, Ben-Gurion: The New Millennium Edition (Tel Aviv: Magal, 2003) (E), p. 246.
4. Thomas, Comment Israel, p. 284.

5. Interview with Yossef Nahmias.
6. Shimon Peres, telegram to the defense ministry envoys to Paris and London, 1 Nov. 1956.
7. Peres, David's Sling, p. 175.
8. Report of the Director General before the heads of the Defense Ministry, 9 Nov. 1956.
9. Uri Dan, "What Good Will the Phantoms Do?" Maariv, 6 Aug. 1971.
10. Peres, David's Sling, p. 175.
11. Report of the Director General, 9 Nov. 1956.
12. General de Division Beaufre, Commandant de la Force A, "Rapport sur l'Operation d'Egypte," Secretariat d'Etat aux Forces Armées, Terre, Etat Major de l'Armée, 1er Bureau, 4 Aug. 1956 (F), Service Historique de l'Armée de Terre, IR 23, p. 4
13. Report of the Director General, 9 Nov. 1956.
14. Shimon Peres, speech in the memory of Moshe Dayan, Tel Aviv Museum, 13 Oct. 1982.

CHAPTER 14: NEW HORIZONS

1. Shimon Peres, report of the Director General at the meeting of the IDF General Staff, 10 Feb. 1957; also report of the Director General to the heads of the Defense Ministry, 15 Feb. 1957.
2. Davar, 31 Dec. 1956
3. Report of the Director General after visiting the Aerial Show at Le Bourget, 17 June 1957.
4. Shimon Peres, report about his visit at the missile-testing ground at Colomb-Béchar, 17 June 1957.
5. Golan, Peres, pp. 70-71.
6. Michel Bar-Zohar, Suez Ultra-Secret (Paris: Fayard, 1964) (F), p. 244.
7. Golan, Peres, p. 83.
8. BGD, 6 March 1959.
9. Golan, Peres, p. 83.
10. Interview with SP.
11. Interview with Yossef Nahmias.
12. Report of the Director General before the heads of the Defense Ministry, 21 Aug. 1957.
13. Golan, Peres, p. 79.
14. Shimon Peres, speech before the Newspaper Editors' Commission, 13 March 1958.
15. Shimon Peres, letter to Colonel Somoza, 20 Feb. 1957; also Golan, Peres, pp. 86-89.
16. Bar-Zohar, Suez, p. 233.
17. David Ben-Gurion, letter to the French Embassy in Paris, 18 March 1957.
18. Shimon Peres's diary (henceforth SPD), 17 June 1960.
19. BGD, 28 Oct. 1958; also 13-14 Dec. 1958.
20. John Foster Dulles, letter to David Ben-Gurion, 8 Feb. 1959 (E), BGA.
21. Report on the visit of Shimon Peres to London on 25-27 Aug. 1958; Isser Penn, report on the talks held by the Director General in London, 8-10 Oct. 1958; telegram, Shimon Peres to the Defense Minister, 12 Oct. 1958.

PART THREE: AGAINST ALL ODDS

CHAPTER 15: A BLIZZARD IN GERMANY

1. Interview with Arthur Ben-Nathan; also Arthur Ben-Nathan, The Impudence to Live (Tel Aviv: M.O.D., 2002), p. 118.
2. Interview with SP, also Peres, David's Sling, pp. 54-55.
3. Shimon Peres, report to Ben-Gurion, BGD, 7 June 1957.
4. Interview with SP; interview with Arthur Ben-Nathan; also, Peres, Next Stage, p. 168; Ben-Nathan, Impudence, p. 106.
5. Shimon Peres, "A Debate on Germany and Her People," Maariv, 19 Feb. 1965.
6. Statement of the Deputy Defense Minister at the Knesset, 25 May 1963.
7. Peres, Next Stage, p. 171.
8. Ibid., p. 169.
9. Golan, Peres, p. 76.
10. Ibid.
11. Ibid.
12. BGD, 7 July 1957.
13. Golan, Peres, p. 76.
14. Shimon Peres, report to Ben-Gurion, 7 July 1957.
15. Shimon Peres, telegram to the Defense Minister, 4 July 1957.
16. Shimon Peres, handwritten notes made after the meeting, Munich, 27 Dec. 1957.
17. BGD, 6 March 1958.
18. Ben-Nathan, Impudence, p. 118.
19. BGD, 29 Dec. 1957.
20. Shimon Peres, report of a meeting with Franz Josef Strauss in Bonn, 28 March 1958.
21. Golan, Peres, p. 79.
22. BGD, 6 March 1960.
23. Ibid., 26 Dec. 1959.
24. Interview with SP; also Shimon Peres, letter to Strauss, personal, 31 March 1960.
25. Interview with SP; also Peres, David's Sling, pp. 58-59.

26. Shimon Peres, handwritten text of telegram to the defense ministry envoy in Bonn, April 1963.
27. Peres, David's Sling, p. 60.
28. Shimon Peres, report of a meeting with Franz Josef Strauss at his home in Bonn, 29 Sept. 1960.
29. Ben-Nathan, Impudence, pp. 118-19.
30. Report on the meeting of the Deputy Defense Minister with Chancellor Adenauer, 8 June 1962; also interview with SP; Peres, David's Sling, pp. 59-60.
31. Report on the meeting with Chancellor Adenauer, 8 June 1962.
32. Konrad Adenauer, letter to Ben-Gurion, 15 Oct. 1962, BGA.
33. Shimon Peres, diary of a trip to West Germany, 8—18 Feb. 1962, entry from 9 Feb. 1962.
34. SPD, 9 Feb. 1962.
35. Report of a meeting of Shimon Peres with Franz Josef Strauss at his home in Bonn, 29 Sept. 1960.
36. Ibid., and BGD, 23 Aug. 1960.
37. Draft of talking points for the meeting with the German Chancellor, June 1962 (no precise date).
38. Draft agreement between the Government of Israel and the Government of the Federal Republic of Germany.
39. Briefing by the Deputy Defense Minister to the IDF General Staff, 24 June 1963.
40. Report on the Deputy Defense Minister's visit to Germany, 8 June 1963.
41. Shimon Peres, report before the heads of the Defense Ministry, 17 Jan. 1963.
42. Briefing by the Deputy Defense Minister to the IDF General Staff, 24 June 1963.

CHAPTER 16: THE HOLY ROOM

1. Interview with Zvia Valden.
2. Interview with Haim Carmon.
3. Interview with SP.
4. Nehemia Argov, letter to his friends, 2 Nov. 1957.
5. Shimon Peres, eulogy for Nehemia Argov, a month after his death, 2 Dec. 1957.
6. Interview with Yoni Peres.
7. Peres, "Youth's Draft."
8. Ibid.
9. Levite, "From a Bullet."
10. BGD, 12 Dec. 1958.
11. Like Algemeen Handeljblad, Amsterdam, 23 March 1957.
12. Elhanan Yishai, letter to Shimon Peres, 20 June 1957.
13. Golda Meir, speech at Mapai's Secretariat, 2 Sept. 1960, Labor Party Archives (henceforth LPA).
14. Interview with columnist Shimon Shiffer.
15. Interview with David Landau.
16. Interview with SP.
17. BGD, 3 May 1958.
18. Ibid., 2 May 1958.
19. Medzini, Proud Jewess, p. 260.
20. Golan, Peres, p. 91.
21. BGD, 30 June 1958.
22. Golda Meir, speech at Mapai's Secretariat, 6 Dec. 1958, LPA.
23. BGD, 13 Nov. 1958.
24. Ibid., 26 Nov. 1958.
25. SPD, 17 Dec. 1959.
26. Peres, Battling, pp. 128-33.
27. Medzini, Proud Jewess, p. 235.
28. BGD, 13 May 1957.
29. Interview with SP.
30. BGD, 7 July 1957.
31. Interview with Arthur Ben-Nathan.
32. Ben-Nathan, Impudence, p. 106.
33. BGD, 7 June 1957.
34. Ambassador Eliahu Sasson, report to Foreign Minister Golda Meir and the heads of the Foreign Ministry, 30 Nov. 1957.
35. Interview with economist Moshe Zanbar.
36. Bar-Zohar, Ben-Gurion, vol. 3, p. 1469.
37. Interview with Miriam Eshkol; Miriam Eshkol's diary.
38. Interview with Avraham (Baiga) Shohat, Eshkol's son-in-law.
39. Sharett, Journal, vol. 8, p. 2301.

CHAPTER 17: AGAINST ALL ODDS

1. Peres, "Night of the Decision," p. 83.
2. Ibid., p. 85.
3. Peres, Battling, p. 155.
4. bid.
5. Ibid., pp. 155-56.
6. Coopération Nucléaire Franco-Israélienne. Note du Service des Affaires Atomiques, Ministère des Affaires

Etrangères, Paris, Secret, 25 June 1964, Documents Diplomatiques Français (henceforth DDF) 1964, Tome II, Doc. 279, pp. 649-52 (F).
7. Interview with Abel Thomas.
8. Interview with SP.
9. Pierre Péan, Les Deux Bombes (Paris: Fayard, 1982-91) (F), pp. 109-10.
10. Ronen Bergman, "Interview with Yuval Ne'eman," Yediot Aharonot, 8 March 2003.
11. Péan, Les Deux Bombes, p. 92.
12. Ibid., p. 94.
13. Avner Cohen, Israel and the Bomb (Jerusalem and Tel Aviv: Shocken, 2000), p. 94; also p. 464, notes 43-44.
14. Péan, Les Deux Bombes, pp. 95—97.
15. Ibid., pp. 185-98.
16. Aide-Mémoire, Communication du Ministère des Affaires Etrangères à l'Ambassade d'Israël, nn. 3, 1 Aug. 1960, DDF, 1960, Tome II, Doc. 57, p. 183 (F).
17. Coopération Nucléaire, DDF.
18. Francis Perrin, Haut Commissaire a l'Energie Atomique, Note 2K 128, remise au Président de Gaulle, le 29 Juillet 1959, DDF 1959, Tome II, Doc. 69 et note, PP. 175-78 (F).
19. Interview with SP.
20. Aide-Mémoire, 1 Aug. 1960.
21. Golan, Peres, pp. 71—74.
22. BGD, 6 Oct. 1957.
23. Ibid., 1 Oct. 1957.
24. Golan, Peres, pp. 71-74.
25. Interview with SP.
26. Aide-Mémoire, 1 Aug. 1960.
27. Golan, Peres, pp. 71-74.
28. Coopération Nucléaire, 25 June 1964.
29. Aide-Mémoire, Crédits à long terme à Israël, 16 Dec. 1957, Archives du Quai d'Orsay, Cabinet du Ministre, 000104-000105 (F).
30. Peres, Battling, p. 154.
31. Ibid., pp. 156-57.
32. Ibid.
33. Yossi Melman, "Discreet: Binyamin Bloomberg," Haaretz, 22 April 2005.
34. Shimon Peres, The New Middle East (Tel Aviv: Steimatzky, 1993), p. 13.
35. Shimon Peres, Discourse in Memoriam of Shalhevet Freier: His Legacy and His Political Idea, Dan Marom, ed. (Tel Aviv: Nuclear Energy Commission, 1995), p. 10.
36. Interview with Amos Manor, former director of the General Security Service (Shabak).
37. Cohen, Israel and the Bomb, pp. 291-92; also Efraim Inbar, Rabin and Israel's National Security (Washington: The Woodrow Wilson Center Press, 1999),pp. 114-15.
38. Peres, Battling, p. 157.
39. Zaki Shalom, Between Dimona and Washington (Beer-Sheba: Ben-Gurion University, 2004), pp. 87-89.
40. Cohen, Israel and the Bomb, pp. 196-97, 291-92, 302-3.
41. Dan Margalit, I Saw Them (Tel Aviv: Zmora-Bitan, 1997), p. 54.
42. Peres, Battling, p. 155.
43. Interview with Professor Israel Dostrovski.
44. Interview with SP; interview with Professor Saul Friedlander, Peres's former assistant.
45. Interview with SP; interview with Eli Horowitz.
46. Peres, Battling, p. 157.

CHAPTER 18: DEPUTY

1. Interview with Yitzhak Navon.
2. Interview with SP.
3. Ibid.
4. Topics for Peres's lecture at the Information Bureau in Jerusalem, 31 Jan. 1959.
5. Discourse of Shimon Peres, 6 Sept. 1960.
6. Interview with SP.
7. Yoel Marcus, "Interview with Shimon Peres," Galei Tzahal Radio, 8 Feb. 1960.
8. Interviews with the defense ministry envoys in Paris, 1959-60.
9. DDF 1960, Tome II, Note de la Direction Politique, 30 Nov. 1960, pp. 674-75, nn. et annexe (F).
10. Interview with Jean Frydman.
11. Charles de Gaulle, Mémoires de l'Espoir (Paris: Plon, 1970), vol. 1, p. 336 (F).
12. DDF, Note 2K 128.
13. Péan, Les Deux Bombes, p. 130.
14. DDF, Note 2K 128.
15. Péan, Les Deux Bombes, pp. 138—39..
16. Ibid., pp. 139-40.
17. DDF, Note 2K 128.
18. Ibid.
19. Interview with Jacques Soustelle.
20. DDF, Note 2K 128.

21. DDF, Coopération Nucléaire.
22. Peres, Battling, p. 158.
23. DDF 1960, Tome II, 1 Aug. 1960, p. 183.
24. Ibid.
25. SPD, 16 May 1960; also Golan, Peres, p. 100.
26. Ibid., 7 June 1960.
27. Golan, Peres, 100–101.
28. Ibid., p. 101.
29. DDF, 1960-II, p. 183.
30. Golan, Peres, p. 101.
31. SPD, 13 June 1960.
32. Ibid., 14 June, 1960.
33. DDF, 1960-II, p. 183.
34. Ibid., 1960-II, pp. 183–84.
35. Ibid.
36. Golan, Peres, p. 102.
37. Peres, Battling, p. 163. There are some mistakes in Peres's account, like the date of the meeting.
38. SPD, 8 Nov. 1960; also Golan, Peres, p. 102.
39. Peres, Battling, p. 163.
40. Ibid., p. 164.
41. Ibid.
42. Ibid.
43. Interview with SP.
44. DDF, Coopération Nucléaire.
45. Couve de Murville, draft letter to the Ambassador of Israel, corrected by Minister Guillaumat, DDF, Note de la Direction Politique, 30 Nov. 1960, et Annexe, Tome II, pp. 674-75 (F).
46. Interview with Amos Degani; Amos Degani, Harvest Time (Havazelet, 2005), p. 190; also interview with SP.
47. Deganí, Harvest Time.
48. Peres, Battling, pp. 159–61; also interview with SP.
49. Ibid.
50. Ibid.

CHAPTER 19: LAVON'S REVENGE

1. BGD, 26 Sept. 1960; also Ben-Gurion's letter to his daughter, Geula Ben-Eliezer, 3 Oct. 1960.
2. Pinhas Lavon, press release, 5 Oct. 1960.
3. Bar-Zohar, Ben-Gurion, vol. 3, pp. 1488-89.
4. Discussion by Shimon Peres and defense ministry senior officials, 11 Oct.
5. 1960.
6. Ibid.
7. Peres, Battling, p. 110.
8. Report of the Committee of Seven, 20 Dec. 1960, BGA.
9. Minutes of the government meeting, 25 Dec. 1960, BGA.
10. David Ben-Gurion, draft letter to the party secretariat, BGA.
11. Time Magazine, 13 Dec. 1960, and other publications.
12. David Ben-Gurion, briefing to the press, 8 Jan. 1961, BGA; also telegram from the State Department to the Embassy in Israel, 31 Dec. 1960, USNA (E).
13. Ben-Gurion, briefing to the press.
14. Interview with Saul Friedlander.
15. DDF, Coopération Nucléaire.
16. Note de la Direction Politique, Service des Affaires Atomiques, au Ministre, 15 July 1963, DDF, 1963, Tome II, Document 9, pp. 61-63 (F). David Ben-Gurion, letter to Charles de Gaulle, April 1961, BGA.
17. Charles de Gaulle, letter to Ben-Gurion, 16 May 1961, BGA.
18. Report on the Ben-Gurion–Kennedy conversation, 31 May 1961, BGA.
19. Melman, "Discreet."
20. Embassy of Israel in Washington, minutes of a conversation between Shimon Peres and President Kennedy, 2 April 1963, Levi Eshkol Archives.
21. Telephone conversation with Mr. Feldman of the White House, 5 April 1963, Kennedy Library, National Security files, Countries Series, Israel (E).
22. Entretien du President Kennedy avec M. Couve de Murville, Washington, 6 May 1963, Quai d'Orsay Archives, Entretiens et Messages 1956-1966, vol. 17-18, P11921 (F). See also Memorandum of Conversation, Washington, 25 May 1963, Kennedy Library, National Security files, France, Secret (E).
23. "Chronology of Israel Assurances of Peaceful Uses of Atomic Energy and Related Events," DOSF, NEA files, NEA/IAI, Near East Arms Initiative, National Archives, Washington (E).
24. Entretien entre le President Kennedy et M. Couve de Murville, Washington, 7 Oct. 1963, DDF, 1963, Tome II, Document 133, p. 374 (F). Also Télégramme de M. Herve Alphand, Ambassadeur de France à Washington, suite à un entretien avec M. Dean Rusk, Washington, 10 July 1964, DDF 1964, Tome II, Doc. 19, pp. 57-58 (F).
25. Entretien de M. Couve de Murville avec M. Shimon Peres, Secrétaire d'Etat israélien à la Défense, 15 June 1963, Quai d'Orsay Archives, Entretiens et Messages 1956-1966, vol. 17-18 (F).

26. Lettre de M. Couve de Murville à M. Couture, Administrateur Général délègue du gouvernement auprès du Commissariat à l'Energie Atomique, 4 April 1963, DDF, 1963, Tome I, Doc. 125, p. 352 (F).
27. Note de la Direction Politique, DDF, 1963; also Argentina's Official Gazette, 18 Jan. 1962 (S).
28. Ibid.
29. Report of the SDECE, 2 May 1963 (F). Note de la Direction Politique, DDF, 1963.
30. Lettre de M. Couve de Murville à M. Couture, DDF.
31. Note de la Direction Politique, Service des Affaires Atomiques, au Ministre, 13 July 1963, DDF, 1963, Tome II, Doc. 24, pp. 103-4 (F).
32. Ibid.
33. Melman, "Discreet."
34. Note du Service des Affaires Atomiques pour le Ministre, Paris, 11 Feb. 1964, DDF, 1964, Tome 1, Doc. 86, pp. 185-86 (F).
35. Interview with SP.
36. Note de la Direction des Affaires Politiques, Service des Affaires Atomiques, annotée par le Ministre, Paris, 14 Oct. 1965, DDF, 1965, Tome II, Doc. 191, p. 441 (F).
37. Lettre de M. Lucet, Directeur des Affaires Politiques, à M. Jacques Roux, Ambassadeur de France au Caire, 7 Sept. 1964, DDF, 1964, Tome II, Doc. 92, pp. 219-20 (F).
38. Entretien entre le President John Kennedy et M. Couve de Murville, 7 Oct. 1963.
39. Entretien du President de Gaulle avec le Roi Hussein de Jordanie, Paris, 19 Nov. 1964, DDF, 1964, Tome II, p. 472 (F).
40. Péan, Les Deux Bombes, p. 141.

CHAPTER 20: THE DEATH RAYS

1. IDF General Staff meeting, 30 July 1962.
2. Shimon Peres, telegram to Franz Josef Strauss, 17 Aug. 1962, BGA.
3. Interview with Amos Manor.
4. Testimony of Shimon Peres before the Knesset Committee of Foreign Affairs and Defense, 4 Dec. 1962.
5. Cohen, Israel and the Bomb, pp. 301-2.
6. BGD, i Jan. 1963.
7. BGD, 24 Feb. 1963.
8. Golda Meir's speech at the Knesset, 20 March 1963.
9. Knesset minutes, 20 March 1963.
10. Interview with Meir Amit.
11. Ibid.
12. Interview with Wernher von Braun.
13. Ben-Nathan, Impudence, p. 122.
14. Peres's statement on the television show This Is Your Life, 9 July 2004.
15. Report by Yeshayahu Ben-Porat, Yediot Aharonot.
16. Interview with Teddy Kollek.
17. BGD, 16 June 1963.
18. Interview with SP.
19. Shimon Peres, "Why I Support D.B.G.," Haaretz, 9 July 1965.
20. Shimon Peres, Go with the Men (Jerusalem: Idanim, 1978), pp. 15-17.
21. Interview with SP.
22. Levi Eshkol, handwritten note to Peres, undated.
23. Ephraim Kishon, "Ministerial Defense Committee," Maariv, 15 July 1963.
24. Shimon Peres, notes of a speech at Mapai ministers' forum, 14 July 1963.
25. Shimon Peres, letter to Eshkol, 18 July 1963, Eshkol's archives.
26. David Ben-Gurion, letter to Peres, 19 July 1963, BGA.
27. Golan, Peres, p. 130.
28. Goldstein, Eshkol, p. 482.
29. SPD, 1 June 1964; also Peres, Battling, pp. 303-4.
30. Ben-Nathan, Impudence, p. 120.
31. Ibid., pp. 123-24.

CHAPTER 21: SIX DAYS IN JUNE

1. Goldstein, Eshkol, p. 497.
2. Shimon Peres, handwritten note to Eshkol, undated.
3. Levi Eshkol, letter to Peres, 27 Jan. 1965, Eshkol's archives.
4. Shimon Peres, handwritten note to Eshkol, undated, probably January 1965.
5. BGD, 18 Feb. 1965.
6. Minutes of Mapai's secretariat meeting, 14 May 1965.
7. Shimon Peres, letter to Eshkol, 19 May 1965.
8. Interview with Haim Israeli.
9. The author was present at the meeting.
10. BGD, 29 June 1965.
11. Péan, Les Deux Bombes, p. 120.
12. Peres, Battling, p. 112; also interview with SP.

13. Peres, "Why I Support D.B.G."
14. Interview with SP; interview with Rafael Eitan.
15. Interview with SP.
16. Levi Eshkol, letter to Shimon Peres, 2 Aug. 1965, Eshkol's archives.
17. Shimon Peres, letter to Eshkol, undated.
18. Munia Mardor, Raphael (Tel Aviv: M.O.D., 1981), p. 409.
19. SP, in conversation with the author, summer of 1966.
20. Interview with SP.
21. Interview with Haim Ramon.
22. Interview with David Ben-Gurion.
23. Minutes of Rafi Parliamentary Group meeting, 21 May 1967.
24. Shlomo Nakdimon, Toward H-Hour (Tel Aviv: Ramdor, 1968), p. 126.
25. Interview with SP.
26. The account is based on interviews with SP; Zaki Shalom, Like Fire in His Bones: David Ben-Gurion, (Beer Sheba: Ben-Gurion University, 2004), p. 257; also Peres, Battling, pp. 119-22.
27. Degani, Harvest Time, p. 225; also Peres, David's Sling, p. 199.
28. Peres, Battling, p. 121.
29. Interview with SP.
30. Ibid.
31. Peres, David's Sling, p. 199.
32. Cohen, Israel and the Bomb, p. 354; Peres, Battling, pp.166—67; Margalit, I Saw Them, p. 99.
33. Report of a meeting between the Prime Minister and Minister Shimon Peres, 17 Feb. 1970.
34. SPD, 13 Jan. 1972.
35. Report of a meeting between the Prime Minister and Minister Shimon Peres, 17 Feb. 1970.
36. Interview with Aliza Eshed.

PART FOUR: THE FANTASY COUNCIL

CHAPTER 22: THE LONG DUEL (I)

1. SPD, 16 Oct. 1973.
2. Exchange of notes, quoted in SPD, 18 Oct. 1973.
3. SPD, 19 Oct. 1973.
4. Medzini, Proud Jewess, p. 476.
5. Ibid., p. 473.
6. Golda Meir's remarks at the Labor Parliamentary Group meeting, 10 April 1974.
7. Golan, Peres, p. 151.
8. Yitzhak Rabin, The Rabin Memoirs (Tel Aviv: Maariv, 1979), p. 418; also interview with Yossi Sarid.
9. Interview with Aliza Goren.
10. Rabin, Memoirs, pp. 558-59.
11. Medzini, Proud Jewess, p. 476.
12. Interview with Shlomo Nakdimon.
13. BGD, 11 Jan. 1963.
14. BGD, 25 Nov. 1963.
15. SPD, 4 Dec. 1960.
16. Rabin, Memoirs, pp. 111-12.
17. Interview with Tzvi Tzur.
18. Rabin, Memoirs, pp. 418-19.
19. Interview with Dov Goldstein.
20. Ibid.
21. Interview with SR
22. Rabin, Memoirs, p. 417.
23. Ibid., p. 418.
24. Ibid., p. 420.
25. Peres, Battling, p. 181.
26. Rabin, Memoirs, p. 421.
27. Ibid.
28. Ibid, pp. 480-81.
29. Ibid.
30. Interview with SP.
31. Interview with Rafael Eitan.
32. Interview with SP.
33. Rabin, Memoirs, p. 480.
34. Interview with Dov Goldstein.
35. Hagai Huberman, "Alon Moreh," in Avraham Shvut, The Ascension of the Mountain (Ariel: Judea and Samaria Academic College, 2002), pp. 48-49.
36. Interview with Hanan Porat.
37. Gershon Shafat, Gush Emunim (Beth-El Books, 1994), p. 193.
38. Shimon Peres, speech at the Knesset, 18 May 1975.
39. Interview with Hanan Porat.

40. Interview with Aliza Eshed.
41. Interview with analyst Reuven Pedehzur.
42. Margalit, I Saw Them, p. 51.
43. Avi Bettelheim, interview with Yitzhak Rabin, "Gush Emunim and Its Influence on the Decision Making of Rabin's Government." Research Paper for Bar-Ilan University, 1 Feb. 1979.
44. Interview with Ron Nahman, mayor of Ariel.
45. Margalit, I Saw Them, p. 28.
46. Rabin, Memoirs, p. 498.
47. Haaretz, 12 May 1976.

CHAPTER 23: ENTEBBE

1. Motta Gur, The Chief of Staff (Tel Aviv: Maarakhot, 1998), p. 178.
2. Peres, Go with the Men, p. 162.
3. Operation Entebbe: Journal of the Defense Minister, 27 June 1976.
4. Shimon Peres, Entebbe Diary (Tel Aviv: Yediot Aharonot, 1991), p. 37.
5. Journal, 1 July 1976.
6. Ibid., 29 June 1976.
7. Peres, Entebbe Diary, p. 47.
8. Gur, Chief of Staff, pp. 205-6.
9. Interview with Dan Shomron.
10. Interview with Haim Israeli.
11. Peres, Entebbe Diary, p. 52.
12. Ibid., p. 53.
13. Journal, 30 June 1976.
14. Interview with Avraham Ben-Yossef.
15. Gur, Chief of Staff, p. 217.
16. Peres, Entebbe Diary, p. 59.
17. Journal, 1 July 1976.
18. Peres, Entebbe Diary, p. 63.
19. Gur, Chief of Staff, p. 223.
20. Leah Rabin, Walking in His Path (Tel Aviv: Yediot Aharonot, 1997), p. 176.
21. Rabin, Memoirs, p. 527.
22. Haim Zadok, letter to Yitzhak Rabin, 3 Nov. 1980.
23. Rabin, Memoirs, p. 527.
24. Ibid., p. 533.
25. Gur, Chief of Staff, p. 236.
26. Ibid., pp. 239—40.
27. Ibid., pp. 224-25.
28. Journal, 1 July 1976; also Peres, Entebbe Diary, p. 72.
29. Journal, 1 July 1976.
30. Peres, Entebbe Diary, p. 75.
31. Fantasy Council deliberations, attached to Journal, 1 July 1976.
32. Fantasy Council deliberations and restricted team discussions, attached to Journal, 1 July 1976; also Peres, Entebbe Diary, pp. 82-90, and Gur, Chief of Staff, pp. 236-47.
33. Peres, Entebbe Diary, p. 81.
34. Journal, 1 July 1976.
35. Peres, Entebbe Diary, p. 93.
36. Gur, Chief of Staff, p. 246.
37. Peres, Entebbe Diary, p. 97.
38. Gur, Chief of Staff, p. 255; also, minutes of the meeting, attached to Journal, 2 July 1976.
39. Peres, Entebbe Diary, p. 105.
40. Journal, 3 July 1976.
41. Shimon Peres, handwritten note to Rabin, 2 July 1976.
42. Minutes of the conversation of the Defense Minister and the Chief of Staff with the Prime Minister, the Foreign Minister, and their aides, attached to Journal, 3 July 1976; also Gur, Chief of Staff, p. 270.
43. Peres, Entebbe Diary, p. 110.
44. Gur, Chief of Staff, pp. 272—74.
45. Journal, night of 3-4 July 1976.
46. Peres, Entebbe Diary, p. 114.
47. Ibid., pp. 114—15.
48. Motta Gur, transcript of speech, Chief of Staff's Office, 4 July 1976; also quoted in Haim Zadok, letter to Rabin, 3 Nov. 1980, and mentioned in Gur, Chief of Staff, p. 288.
49. Gur, Chief of Staff, p. 288.
50. Interview with Binyamin Netanyahu.
51. Transcript of national television interview of Haim Zadok, 21 Oct. 1980.
52. Yitzhak Rabin, letter to Zadok, 29 Oct. 1980.
53. Haim Zadok, letter to Rabin, 3 Nov. 1980.
54. Margalit, I Saw Them, pp. 52-53.
55. Journal, 4 July 1976.

CHAPTER 24: THE LONG DUEL (2)

1. Interview with Dov Goldstein.
2. Michael Bar-Zohar, Facing a Cruel Mirror (Tel Aviv: Yediot Aharonot, 1990), p. 86.
3. Rabin, Memoirs, p. 533.
4. Interviews with Haim Israeli and Yossi Chahanover.
5. Interview with Jean Frydman.
6. Bar-Zohar, Facing a Cruel Mirror, p. 112.
7. Debate between Shimon Peres and Pinhas Sapir at Mapai's Secretariat, 9 Nov. 1972, LPA; also interview with Mordechai Ben-Porat.
8. Rabin, Memoirs, p. 534.
9. Interview with Dov Goldstein.
10. The author was present at the debate in April 1981.
11. Interview of Shimon Peres on Channel 2, Israel television, 7 Feb. 2002, transcript.
12. Amira Lam, "Interview with Nissim Zvili," Yediot Aharonot, 23 May 1997.
13. Interviews with Uri Sabbag, Raanan Naim, and others.
14. Bar-Zohar, Facing a Cruel Mirror, p. 109.
15. Ronni Hadar, "Interview with Renana Ben-Gurion—Leshem," Yediot Aharonot, 24 Sept. 2004.
16. Interview with Yitzhak Navon.
17. Shabtai Tevet, "The Illusions in Shimon Peres's Memory," Maariv, 28 Dec. 2001; Shimshon Arad, letter, 10 Nov. 1997, and excerpts from Peres, Battling.
18. BGD, 24 Nov. 1958 and 29 Jan. 1960
19. Chaim Herzog, Living History (New York: Pantheon Books, 1996) (E), p. 254.
20. Interview with Amos Oz.
21. Peres, Battling, p. 244.
22. Ibid.
23. Ibid., pp. 254-55.
24. Ibid., p. 255.
25. Interview with SP.
26. Interview with SP; also Peres, Battling, pp. 245-47, 249-50.
27. Shimon Peres, handwritten letter, photocopy dated 10 May 1981, Yediot Aharonot, 11 June 1981.
28. Bar-Zohar, Facing a Cruel Mirror, pp. 113—14.
29. George Amscl, "Osirak, la bombe et les inspections," Le Monde, 16 Oct. 2002 (F). The report was published in September 1981, in Les Temps Modernes, numéro 422 (F).

CHAPTER 25: PRIME MINISTER

1. SPD, 18 June 1982.
2. Ibid.
3. SPD, 28 June 1982.
4. Peres, Battling, p. 267.
5. SPD, 25 June 1982.
6. SPD, 2 July 1982.
7. Peres, Battling, p. 268.
8. Herzog, Living History, p. 272.
9. Peres, Battling, pp. 272-73.
10. Avrech, Small World, pp. 85-86; also interview with SP.

CHAPTER 26: 1984

1. Yoel Marcus, "100 Days of Grace," Haaretz, 22 May 1983.
2. Margalit, I Saw Them, pp. 64-65.
3. Haaretz, 15 Jan. 1985.
4. Matti Golan, The Road to Peace (New York: Warner Books, 1989) (E), pp. 244-45.
5. Interview with Eli Horowitz.
6. Peres, Battling, p. 278.
7. Gad Becker, "Either We'll Have an Economic Plan Tomorrow Morning, or There Will Be No Government," Yediot Aharonot, 5 July 1985.
8. Peres, Battling, p. 278.
9. Yeshayahu Ben-Porat, "An Interview with the Prime Minister," Yediot Aharonot, 5 July 1985.
10. Dov Gnechovski, "What to Expect After the Economic Measures," Yediot Aharonot, 3 July 1985.
11. Minutes of a conversation between President Reagan and Prime Minister Peres, Ministry of Foreign Affairs, Communications Department, 18 Oct. 1985.
12. Interview with SP; also Charles Enderlin, Paix ou Guerres (Paris: Stock, 2000), p. 488 (F).
13. Interview with Avraham Shalom.
14. Yehiel Guttmann, Crisis at the Shabak (Tel Aviv: Yediot Aharonot, 1995), p. 36.
15. Ibid, pp. 66-67; also interview with Reuven Hazak, Peleg Radai, and Rafi Malka.
16. Remarks of the Prime Minister at the Knesset, 27 May 1986.
17. Ibid.
18. Guttmann, Crisis at the Shabak, p. 49.

19. Remarks of the Prime Minister at the Knesset, 27 May 1986.
20. Interview with Yitzhak Zamir.
21. Guttmann, Crisis at the Shabak, pp. 48-49.
22. Interview with Moshe Shachal.
23. Peres, Battling, p. 299.
24. Interview with Yitzhak Zamir.
25. Interview with Yossef Harish; also the Attorney General's letter to the Prime Minister, 9 July 1986.
26. Peres, Battling, p. 299.
27. Ibid., p. 296.
28. Herzog, Living History, p. 280.
29. Interview with Uzi Baram.
30. Shlomo Gazit, "Memorandum to Michael Bar-Zohar," 30 May 2005.
31. Peres, Battling, pp. 288-89.
32. George P. Shultz, Turmoil and Triumph: My Years as Secretary of State (New York: Scribner's, 1993) (E), p. 796.
33. Ronald Reagan, An American Life (New York: Pocket Books, 1992) (E), pp. 504-6.
34. Interview with Shlomo Gazit.
35. Gazit, Memorandum.
36. Peres, Battling, p. 290.
37. Ibid., p. 291.
38. Ibid.
39. Golan, Road to Peace, p. 277.
40. Interview with SP.
41. Interview with SP; also Peres, Battling, p. 293.

PART FIVE: THE MAN WHO WON'T DESPAIR

CHAPTER 27: THE FATAL MISTAKE

1. Interviews with the Hundred-Day Team members; interview with SP.
2. Peres, Battling, p. 347.
3. Ibid., p. 356.
4. Shimon Peres, Government's statement at the Knesset, 3 Dec. 1984.
5. Interview with SP.
6. Shimon Peres, speech to the U.N., Government's statement to the Knesset, 28 Oct. 1985.
7. Interview with Nimrod Novik.
8. Bar-Zohar, Facing a Cruel Mirror, pp. 186-87.
9. Ariel Sharon, speech, Haaretz, 22 Aug. 1985.
10. Ariel Sharon, speech, Yediot Aharonot, 23 Aug. 1985.
11. Ariel Sharon, speech, Haaretz, 13 Nov. 1985.
12. Shimon Peres, letter to Minister Sharon, 13 Nov. 1985, LPA.
13. Shimon Peres, letter to the ministers, 13 Nov. 1985, LPA.
14. Ariel Sharon's letter to Peres, 14 Nov. 1985, LPA.
15. Interview with Nimrod Novik.
16. Interview with Aliza Eshed and two other participants in the meeting.
17. Peres, Battling, pp. 355-56.
18. Interview with Nimrod Novik.
19. Shimon Peres, letter to Minister Modai, 13 April 1986, LPA.
20. Bar-Zohar, Facing a Cruel Mirror, pp. 181—83.
21. Interviews with two of Shamir's close aides.
22. Bar-Zohar, Facing a Cruel Mirror, p. 183.
23. Interview with Abrasha Tamir; interview with Micha Talmon.

CHAPTER 28: THE LONDON DOCUMENT

1. Interviews with SP and Yossi Beilin; see also Peres, Battling, p. 357.
2. Interview with Yossi Beilin.
3. Yitzhak Shamir, speech, 9 April 1987, "Shamir: The Conference—an Insane Idea. Peres: I'll Keep Working for Peace." YEDIOT AHARONOT, 10 April 1987.
4. Ibid.
5. Interview with Efraim Halevy, former chief of the Mossad.
6. Interview with SP.
7. Ibid.
8. Peres, Battling, p. 360.
9. Interview with SP; also Peres, Battling, p. 358.
10. Peres, Battling, p. 360.
11. Interview with SP; also Peres, Battling, p. 360.
12. Interview with Lord Mishcon.
13. Interview with SP, also Battling, p. 360.
14. Peres, Battling, p. 361.
15. Interviews with the other participants at the talks.

16. The Peres-Hussein London Agreement, 11 April 1987, private archives. Also interview with SP; interview with Yossi Beilin; and Maariv, 1 Jan. 1988.
17. Ibid.
18. Interview with SP.
19. Interview with Nimrod Novik, Peres's adviser. Also interview with Yossi Ben-Aharon, director general of Prime Minister Yitzhak Shamir's office.
20. Interview with SP.
21. Ibid.; also Peres, Battling, p. 361.
22. Interview with Ambassador Thomas Pickering.
23. Interview with Yossi Beilin.
24. In his memoirs, Shultz says that Yossi Beilin briefed him about the London document. He is mistaken. Beilin didn't meet with him, but with Charles Hill, who reported to him later. See George Shultz, Turmoil and Triumph, pp. 937-38; and interview with Yossi Beilin.
25. Shultz, Turmoil and Triumph, p. 938.
26. Ibid., p. 939.
27. Ibid.
28. Ibid., p. 940.
29. Yediot Aharonot, 18 Jan. 1998, transcript of an interview of George Shultz by Israel's Channel 2.
30. The description is supported by the interview with Ambassador Pickering.
31. Interview with one of Shamir's aides.
32. Interview with Yitzhak Shamir.
33. Shultz, Turmoil and Triumph, p. 940.
34. Ibid.
35. Interview with SP; Shultz, Turmoil and Triumph, p. 940.
36. In Turmoil and Triumph, Shultz states that Moshe Arens was Israel's defense minister (p. 941). That's a mistake. In the national unity government, Arens was a minister without portfolio. The defense minister was, of course, Yitzhak Rabin.
37. Interview with Moshe Arens.
38. Ibid.
39. Schultz, Turmoil and Triumph, p. 941.
40. Peres, Battling, p. 364.
41. Shultz, Turmoil and Triumph, p. 941.
42. Interview with a senior American diplomat, on condition of anonymity.
43. Ibid.
44. Interview with Yossi Ben-Aharon.
45. Interview with Ambassador Thomas Pickering.
46. Interview with George Shultz, Yediot Aharonot, 18 Jan. 1998.
47. Interview with Moshe Arens.
48. Interview with one of Shamir's aides.
49. Interview with SP.
50. Interview with Yossi Beilin; interview with Moshe Shachal.
51. Interview with SP; also Peres, Battling, p. 364.
52. Interview with SP.

CHAPTER 29: THE LONG DUEL (3)

1. Interview with Akiva Eldar.
2. Ilan Kfir and Peer-li Shachar, "Report," Hadashot, 13 Feb. 1987.
3. Yoel Marcus, "Run, Shimon, Run," Haaretz, 7 April 1987.
4. Davar, 13 May 1987.
5. Yoel Nir, Arye Deri (Tel Aviv: Yediot Aharonot, 1999), p. 176.
6. Interview with Moshe Shachal; interview with SP.
7. Interview with Dan Meridor.
8. Herzog, Living History, p. 363.
9. Yitzhak Shamir, letter to Shimon Peres, 13 March 1990, Bar-Zohar archives.
10. Amnon Barzilai, Ramon (Tel Aviv: Shocken, 1996), pp. 168-69.
11. Conversation of the author with Yitzhak Rabin, 10 April 1990.
12. Interview with Shulamit Aloni; also interviews with Haim Ramon, Yossi Beilin, and Yossi Sarid.
13. Interview with Moshe Shachal.
14. The author was present at this meeting.
15. Herzog, Living History, p. 366.
16. Ibid., p. 367.
17. Interview with SP.
18. Yitzhak Navon, personal letter to Peres, 25 June 1990; also report of Yitzhak Navon to a group of friends, 8 May 2005.
19. Interview with Nissim Zvili.

CHAPTER 30: OSLO

1. Interview with SP; also Peres, Battling, p. 367.

2. Remarks by several of Rabin's supporters in the presence of the author.
3. Peres, Battling, p. 367.
4. Interview with Haim Ramon.
5. David Makovsky, Making Peace with the PLO: The Rabin Government's Road to the Oslo Accord (Boulder: Washington Institute for Near East Policy/Westview, 1996) (E), pp. 23-24.
6. For example: Yair Hirschfeld, Oslo: Formula for Peace (Tel Aviv: Rabin Center for Israel Research, Am Oved, 2000), p. 90.
7. Interview with Ron Pundak.
8. Peres, New Middle East, p. 27.
9. Interview with Avi Gil.
10. Hirschfeld and Pundak to Shimon Peres, "Report on Two Meetings with the PLO Delegation," 12 March 1993; interview with Yossi Beilin; interview with SP; also Hirschfeld, Oslo, p. 112.
11. Yossi Beilin, Touching Peace (Tel Aviv: Yediot Aharonot, 1997), p. 87.
12. Ibid.
13. Interview with Yair Hirschfeld.
14. Interview with SP.
15. Ibid.
16. Hirschfeld, Oslo, p. 112.
17. Hirschfeld and Pundak, "Summarized Report on the 3rd Sarpsborg Meeting," 23 March 1993 (E).
18. Beilin, Touching Peace, p. 96.
19. Hirschfeld and Pundak, "Report to Yossi Beilin, Meeting with Dan Kurtzer," 14 April 1993.
20. Yair Hirschfeld and Ron Pundak to Shimon Peres, "Proposal for the Continuation of the Dialogue with the PLO by the Norwegian Channel—Points for a Meeting," 22 April 1993; appendixes to that report: Appendix One—An Understanding for Rome (E); Appendix Two—Abu Alaa's Views on Short, Medium and Long-term Arrangements (E); Appendix Three—Major Statements of Abu Alaa (in Oslo, April 30-May 1, 1993) (E); also Hirschfeld and Pundak to Shimon Peres, "Report of a Meeting with the PLO Delegation, 2 May 1993"; and Hirschfeld and Pundak to Yossi Beilin and Shimon Peres, "Report of a Meeting with the PLO Delegation, 11 May 1993."
21. Interview with SP.
22. Uri Savir, The Process (Tel Aviv: Yediot Aharonot, 1998), p. 18; also interview with Uri Savir.
23. Interview with Yossi Beilin.
24. Peres, Battling, p. 385.
25. Ibid.
26. Interview with SP.
27. Beilin, Touching Peace, p. 100.
28. Peres, Battling, p. 385.
29. Interview with SP.
30. Beilin, Touching Peace, pp. 108-9.
31. Interview with SP.
32. Ibid.
33. Ephraim Sneh, Navigation in a Dangerous Zone (Tel Aviv: Yediot Aharonot, 2002), p. 22.
34. Interview with Ephraim Sneh; also Sneh, Navigation, p. 23.
35. Interview with Avi Gil; interview with Yossi Beilin; also Beilin, Touching Peace, pp. 108-9; also Savir, The Process, p. 43.
36. Beilin, Touching Peace, p. 112.
37. Peres, Battling, p. 394.
38. Interview with Yair Hirschfeld.
39. Bassam Abu Shariff, letter to Shimon Peres, manuscript, by Mira Avrech, 23 June 1993 (E).
40. Interview with Haim Ramon.
41. Ben Kaspit, "How the Hope for Peace at Oslo in 1993 Turned into a Reality of War and Desperation in 2001," Maariv, special issue, 17 Sept. 2001.
42. Interview with Itamar Rabinowitz.
43. Ibid.
44. Peres, Battling, p. 400.
45. Ibid., p. 387.
46. Informal report by Uri Savir after an Oslo meeting, 23 July 1993.
47. Savir, The Process, pp. 74-75.
48. Peres, Battling, p. 404.
49. Ibid, pp. 404-5.
50. Peres, New Middle East, p. 11.
51. Peres, Battling, p. 409.
52. Interview with Amos Oz.
53. Peres, Battling, p. 409.
54. Ibid., pp. 412—13.
55. Ibid., p. 411.
56. Peres, New Middle East, p. 33.
57. Peres, Battling, p. 413; also Beilin, Touching Peace, pp. 138-39.
58. Interview with Ephraim Sneh.
59. Kaspit, "How the Hope."
60. Margalit, I Saw Them, p. 75.
61. Leah Rabin, Walking, pp. 264-65.

62. Beilin, Touching Peace, p. 147.
63. Leah Rabin, Walking, p. 265.
64. Interview with Nahum Barnea; interview with Shimon Shiffer; also Nahum Barnea, "A Governess and Two Masters," Yediot Aharonot, 26 Nov. 1993.
65. Interview with SP.
66. Peres, New Middle East, p. 35.
67. Ibid, p. 36.
68. Interview with Yair Hirschfeld.
69. Interview with SP.

CHAPTER 31: REMEMBER NOVEMBER THE SECOND!

1. Interview with one of Rabin's close advisers, on condition of anonymity.
2. Interview with Avi Gil.
3. Interview with SP.
4. Interview with Avi Gil.
5. Interview with Efraim Halevy.
6. Interview with Avi Gil.
7. Non-Paper, notes of a meeting held in Amman, 2 November 1993, attended by: H.M. King Hussein, Crown Prince Hassan, Prime Minister Majali, Foreign Minister Peres, Mr. A. Gil, Mr. E. Halevy.
8. Margalit, I Saw Them, p. 74.
9. Interview with SP.
10. Ibid.
11. Interview with Avraham Baiga Shohat.
12. Interview with Avi Gil.
13. Interview with an Israeli envoy who met with King Hussein.
14. Interview with Itamar Rabinowitz.
15. Interview with Efraim Halevy; interview with SP.
16. Interview with Avraham Katz-Oz.
17. Ibid.; also interview with SP.
18. Interview with Avraham Katz-Oz.
19. Interview with Zvi Alpeleg.
20. Interview with Zvia Valdan.
21. Interview with Nehemia (Hemi) Peres.
22. Sarit Yishai-Levi, "Sonia," Hadashot, 26 July 1985.
23. Lam, "Interview with Nissim Zvili"; also interview with Nissim Zvili.
24. Interview of Sonia Peres for the documentary Alumot, private production, Lea and Zvika Koren.
25. Interview with Colette Avital; also Hila Alroi-De-Beer and Gil Riva, "This Is Evil," Yediot Aharonot, 13 April 1998.
26. Nehama Duek, "Peres: I Love Cottage Cheese, Wine and Pretty Women," Yediot Aharonot, 17 Aug. 2005.
27. SPD, 8 April 1971.
28. Arnira Lam and Avner Hopstein, "Like a Military Secret," Yediot Aharonot, 14 July 2000.
29. Interview with SP.
30. SPD, 15 Feb. 1972.
31. Interview with Colette Avital.
32. Leah Rabin, Walking, pp. 273-74.
33. Interview with Itamar Rabinowitz.

CHAPTER 32: 1996

1. Orly Azulai-Katz, "I Am Not a Loser" (interview with SP), Yediot Aharonot, 5 July 1996.
2. Interview with Nissim Zvili.
3. Interview with Arthur Ben-Nathan.
4. Interview with Binyamin Netanyahu.
5. Interview with David Landau.
6. Interview with Amos Oz; interview with SP.
7. Interview with SP.
8. Interview with Binyamin Ben-Eliezer; interview with Dalia Rabin.
9. "Peace and Security," Labor Party platform, 1992 elections, LPA.
10. Interview with SP; also Azulai-Katz, The Man Who Didn't Know How to Win, p. 18.
11. Interview with Moshe Shachal; interview with Nissim Zvili.
12. Amira Lam, "Scoundrels, Peres Muttered" (interview with Nissim Zvili), Yediot Aharonot, 23 May 1997.
13. Interview with Binyamin Netanyahu.
14. Ibid.; interview with Yona Bartal; interview with SP.
15. Interview with SP.
16. Yossi Verter, "I Am a Loser?" Haaretz, 14 May 1997; also Orly Azulay-Katz, "Peres: Did I Lose? The Audience Roared: Yes!" Yediot Aharonot, 14 May 1997.
17. Lam, "Scoundrels."
18. Interview with S. Izhar.
19. President Bill Clinton, speech at the Mann Auditorium, Tel Aviv, 21 Sept. 2003.

PART SIX: . . . AS IF ALL HIS LIFE LIES AHEAD OF HIM

CHAPTER 33 . . . The Little Dutch boy

1. Public dialogue of Peres and Bar-Zohar, Tmol-Shilshom Cafe, Jerusalem, 11 June 2006.
2. Interview with Yael Dayan.
3. Interview with Yossi Beilin.
4. Peres, "Youth's Draft."
5. Interview with Amos Oz.

CHAPTER 34: PRESIDENT OF ISRAEL

1. Channel 10 News, 11/10/2005
2. The Man who would be president if not for these pesky elections, The New York Times, 4/17/2007
3. Zruya Shalev, The Number One feminist, Yedioth Aharonoth, 3/6/2013
4. Nahum Barnea, Peres, for good and bad, Yedioth Aharonoth, 9/16/2016
5. The President at the Presidents' Conference, The regime in Iran will be changed by the people, not by foreign intervention, Haaretz, 2/16/2011
6. Peres's speech at the UN General Assembly, Peres Archives
7. Peter Baker, Obama and Shimon Peresd: Fast friends who found peace out of reach, The Jerusalem Post, 9/28/2016
8. Read President Obama's Moving Eulogy for Shimon Peres, Time, Internet edition, 9/30/2016
9. Peter Baker, op.cit.

CHAPTER 35: A SKULLCAP IN THE REICHSTAG

1. Yoram Dori, Peres's close adviser remembers: three major moments with the President, Maariv, 7/23/2014
2. Interview with the author for the French television, President's residence,6/16/2009
3. At a meeting with students in Kfar Hayarok, President's Internet site, 9/24/2009

CHAPTER 36: ALONE

1. Amira Lam, Leaving Home, an interview with Shimon Peres, Yedioth Aharonoth 5/5/2014
2. Amira Lam, I'll live to see Peace, Yedioth Aharonoth, 7/30/2010
3. Sheri Makover Belikov, The Nation's Baby, Maariv, 5/9/2011
4. Amira Lam, A free heart, Yedioth Aharonoth, 7/8/2016

CHAPTER 37: GONE

1. Time, op.cit.
2. Shimon Peres, Prayer for the road, translated by this book's author

ABOUT THE AUTHOR

MICHAEL BAR -ZOHAR

Michael Bar-Zohar is the award-winning author of more than thirty fiction and nonfiction books. *Ben-Gurion,* his definitive portrait of Israel's founder, has been translated into fourteen languages. Bar-Zohar himself has been very active in Israel's political life and has served two terms in the Knesset, the Israeli Parliament. He has known Shimon Peres since 1961. In addition, Bar-Zohar was the Labor Party Campaign Chairman at the Knesset election in 1981. He also served as Moshe Dayan's media adviser. Professor Bar-Zohar has taught political science and history at Haifa University and at Emory University in Atlanta. He lives in Tel Aviv, Israel, and spends a few months a year speaking and lecturing in the US. His book *Mossad* (with Nissim Mishal) was a worldwide bestseller, published so far in 30 countries. Visit his website at www.barzohar.com

www.ingramcontent.com/pod-product-compliance
ghtning Source LLC
ambersburg PA
HW030634150426
11CB00048B/98